Cattle and Kinship among the Gogo

A Semi-pastoral Society of Central Tanzania

1   Youth

Cattle and Kinship among the Gogo

A Semi-pastoral Society of Central Tanzania

Peter Rigby

Cornell University Press

ITHACA AND LONDON

First published 1969

This book is based upon research sponsored by the East African Institute of Social Research, Makerere University College.

Standard Book Number 8014–0513–0

Library of Congress Catalog Card Number 69–18216

PRINTED IN THE UNITED STATES OF AMERICA
BY THE COLONIAL PRESS INC.

To the Wagogo People

Preface

The fieldwork on which this study is based was carried out from September, 1961, to September, 1963. During this period I spent nineteen months in Ugogo, the country of the Wagogo people, which lies in the Dodoma Region about 300 miles west of the Tanzanian capital at Dar es Salaam. The rest of the research period was spent at the stimulating conferences held by the East African Institute of Social Research, Makerere College, Kampala, Uganda. To my colleagues at the Institute I owe thanks for the benefit of discussion upon various papers I presented on aspects of Gogo social structure.

The first four months of fieldwork were spent on intensive study of the Gogo language, Cigogo, in which the whole of my fieldwork was carried out. I recorded about 60 percent of my field notes in Cigogo. I refrained from employing a fluent English-speaking interpreter. I learned enough Kiswahili to extract information from local court records, which are written in that language, and to appreciate the influence of Kiswahili upon modern Gogo linguistic usage. But the medium of communication in Ugogo is still predominantly Cigogo. The orthography used for the Gogo language in this book conforms basically to that currently employed in the few publications available in the language, except for word division in some contexts. (The system of word division used is essentially that recommended for the Bantu languages by Professor C. M. Doke.) Although this is far from an ideal orthography, it was thought best to conform as closely as possible to the attempt at standardization represented by it. But I have indicated long vowels by double vowels (thus, *uu* in *kutuula*) where they are significant; these are not used in the standard orthography. The velar nasal ŋ is represented by the symbol ng'.

Without the help of my assistant, close friend, and companion, Mr. Madinda ala Mutowinaga, much of the material presented here could not have been obtained. I am also indebted to Muwaha Mujilima ala Sandiya and Muwaha Mutimila ala Lehawo, who took me into their homesteads and families and made me as much of a Mugogo as I could be. To all other Gogo who taught me so much about their language and society, I express my sincerest gratitude.

I owe most to my teachers in social anthropology: to Professor Monica Wilson, who introduced me to it; to Dr. A. I. Richards, Professor M. Fortes, and Dr. E. R. Leach. In the field I received constant help and encouragement from the late Dr. D. J. Stenning and Professor A. W. Southall. The manuscript was read in whole or in part by Professors V. W. Turner and E. H. Winter, Dr. Richards, and Professor Fortes, whose comments were indeed valuable.

My fieldwork was financed by the then Colonial Social Science Research Council until December, 1961; I completed it as a Fellow of the East African Institute of Social Research. My thanks are due to both these organizations. Much of the time spent in writing was made possible by a Crawford Studentship at King's College, Cambridge, for which I am deeply grateful.

PETER RIGBY

New York
July 1968

Contents

I Introduction   1

II Ugogo: Cattle Values and Agricultural Subsistence   11

Famines, spatial mobility, and demography   20
Historical factors and available data   23
Cattle values and agricultural subsistence   24
The basis of subsistence   26
Rainfall, seasons, and activity   33
Cultivation and cooperation   38
The economic role of cattle, and livestock husbandry   43
Cattle exchange and property relations   47
Cattle trusteeship contracts (*kukoza*)   50
Cattle values and agricultural values   53
Cattle culture, terminology, and identification   56
Conclusion   60

III Clanship and the Ritual Areas   63

Clan histories and their significance   65
The concept of *mbeyu* (clan)   76
The concept of *mulongo* (sub-clan name)   81
Other institutionalized inter-clan relationships: joking-
  partners (*wutani*)   88
Clanship and ritual leadership (*wutemi*)   93
The functions of ritual leadership   97
Localities and ritual areas (*yisi*)   104
Conclusion   106

IV Kinship and Neighborhood   109

The neighborhood (*itumbi*)   110
Residential mobility   116

Temanghuku neighborhood and population mobility   119
The founding of a neighborhood   128
Neighborhood sub-divisions and clusters (*vitumbi*)   131
Neighborhood expansion   139
Kinship and neighborhood   142
Kinship and homestead clusters   147
Conclusion   150

V   **Homesteads, Domestic Groups, and Property**   154
Architecture and orientation   156
The protection of homesteads and its significance   161
Houses (*nyumba*), property, and production   169
Homestead heads and the composition of homesteads   175
Cycle and fission in domestic groups   187
Conclusion   200

VI   **Marriage, Bridewealth, and Kinship Network**   202
Preparation for marriage   205
Procedures and phases of the marriage contract
     (*wutole*)   211
The composition and distribution of bridewealth
     (*cigumo*)   225
Marriage, locality, and kinship network   235
Marriage stability and affinal relations   242
Conclusion   245

VII   **Kinship**   247
Ideology and terminology   251
Father/son relations and agnation   256
Husband and wife   271
Affines: *wakwe* and *walamu*   276
Mother's brother and sister's son   284
Cross-cousin relationships   286
Conclusion   291

VIII   **Conclusion**   295
Kinship and property relations   297
Structure, process, and the locality factor   304
Descent and affinal relationships   306

Contents

Appendixes

A. Provisional List of Gogo Clans, with Areas and Other
   Associations Where Known   309
B. Shortened Version of the History of the Pulu Clan   319
C. Clan Affiliation (*mbeyu*), Sub-clan Names (*mulongo*), and
   Avoidances (*muzilo*) of Homestead Heads, Temanghuku
   Neighborhood, 1961–62   325
D. Kinship Terminology: Reference and Address Systems   326
E. The Case of Lubeleje and Cedego: Father/Son Relations   329

Bibliography   337

Index   351

Illustrations

Plates

1	Youth		*frontispiece*
2	Dry-season landscape, southern Ugogo	*facing page*	14
3	A young man taking his herd out to graze		14
4	A mother about to pound grain		15
5	A ritual leader tending his rainstones		46
6	Looking out over the gate of a cattle byre		47
7	Mother and child		47
8	Part of a bridewealth herd leaving the groom's homestead		206
9	Young men cutting up a sacrificial ox		207
10	An elder admonishing the heir at an inheritance ceremony		238
11	The principal heir receiving the symbol of inheritance		239

(*Photographs by the author*)

Maps

1	Ugogo and its divisions	*page*	16
2	Distribution of homestead fields and garden plots		30
3	Temanghuku and adjacent neighborhoods showing clusters and homesteads		126

Figures

1	Gogo seasons, months, and associated cycle of agricultural activities and rituals	*page*	36
2	Diagrammatic representation of Pulu clan history and ritual areas		73

 3 Diagrammatic representation of Nyagatwa clan history
    in Cikombo and Ibwijili   74
 4 The case of Luzu   124
 5 Sandiya and the founding of Temanghuku neighborhood   129
 6 Some kinship and affinal links among homestead heads,
    "Kwilamba" cluster, Temanghuku neighborhood   132
 7 Majima's propitiation   166
 8 Plan of Mujilima's homestead, 1962–63   171
 9 Fission between "houses": sets of half siblings   188
10 Present composition of Mujilima's homestead   191
11 Domestic groups and houses of Balidi and his son Hata   196
12 Composition of houses in Kazimoto's homestead   198
13 The case of Nyawombo and Cidong'a   214
14 The composition of bridewealth, a case   231
15 The distribution of bridewealth, a case   231
16 The case of Madeje and Muguji   233
17 The joking context between male cross-cousins (*wahizi*) 291
18 "Conventional attitudes" in Gogo kinship relations   293
19 Genealogical relationships of those involved in Cedego's
    case with his son Lubeleje   331

Tables

1 Gogo chronology of famines, droughts, and heavy rains within Gogo memory   *page*   21
2 Average numbers of cattle and small stock in homestead herds, under ownership and trusteeship contracts: Temanghuku neighborhood and Cilungulu ritual area (1962)   51
3 Claimed cultural origins of Gogo clans   68
4 The sub-divisions of two clans and their ritual areas   87
5 Spatial mobility of homestead owners: place of birth and present residence, by age   120
6 Number and proportion of residence changes of (1) dependents, (2) homestead heads, (3) 44 homestead owners within their own neighborhood, Temanghuku   121
7 Frequency of links between homestead heads in Temanghuku neighborhood, by category of relationships   143
8 Age distribution of homestead heads, Temanghuku neighborhood and Cilungulu ritual area, 1962–63   177
9 Residence and age of homestead heads whose fathers are still alive, compared with those whose fathers are dead (Temanghuku, 1962–63)   179
10 Homestead heads and their married dependents, by distribution of wives living with them in 1962–63: Temanghuku and Cilungulu examples   181
11 Average size of bridewealth herds, by agreed number, those said to have been given by wife-receivers, and those claimed to have been obtained by wife-givers   229
12 Spatial range of marriage, by residence of spouses at

marriage, with reference to neighborhood and ritual
   area   240
13 Spatial range of marriage, by residence of spouses at marriage   240
14 Extant and recent marriages, divorces, and separations:
   Temanghuku (male and female informants)   243

Cattle and Kinship among the Gogo

A Semi-pastoral Society of Central Tanzania

I
Introduction

The Gogo live in what may be called a "marginal" economic environment. Other societies of eastern Africa with similar marginal economic conditions are the Jie and Karimojong of Uganda, the Turkana of Kenya, and the Nuer of Sudan (see Gulliver 1952, 1955; Dyson-Hudson 1966; Evans-Pritchard 1940). This marginality is manifested in erratic and unevenly distributed rainfall, periodic droughts, floods, and famines, and their consequent effects upon residence, spatial mobility, and social relationships in general. Hence, in societies which are adjusted to such conditions, the structural processes influenced by environmental factors are "recurrent processes" rather than "directional processes," although in the long run "directional processes" may be observed (cf. Vogt 1960). This means that units more comprehensive than the domestic group (but including it) have to be analyzed in terms of process rather than as "static-structure" units. The "time factor" must be taken into account before the structure of local communities and larger political groupings can be understood (cf. Fortes 1949b, 1958; Leach 1954, pp. 4–7; Harries-Jones and Chiwale 1963; Swartz, Turner, and Tuden 1966).

Environmental factors are linked with the kinship system primarily through the crucial role in kin relations of the "most valued productive property" (Fortes 1953), that is, through property relations. In the Gogo case, at least, *effective* kinship and affinal relations are primarily viewed in terms of the carrying out of certain jurally defined rights and obligations concern-

1

ing the most valued form of property, viz., livestock.[1] But the
maintenance of these effective kin/property relations *in action*
depends largely upon close residence; the factor of locality
becomes crucially important. Although Gogo walk (and now
take other means of transportation) many miles to press claims
to property (say, on the marriage of a kinswoman), prolonged
residential separation beyond the range of frequent contact leads
to the decay of active property (and therefore kinship) relations,
particularly when generation lines are crossed. Furthermore,
Gogo homestead groups (not so much individuals) are residentially mobile, sometimes moving considerable distances.
This residential mobility is partly a function of ecological conditions. But it results in the fact that the potential range of
kinship (property) relations in the network of kinship is wider
than the effective range. The limits pertaining to the latter are
"historical" and spatial ones. They lie primarily within the
local community where such relationships are continually created (through marriage), maintained, and activated by the
reciprocal exchange of goods and services, economic, political,
and ritual.

Thus, one of the central areas of interest in the present analysis concerns the following facts. The Gogo are sedentary but
mobile cultivators who subsist upon sorghum and millet grain
crops, but who also have considerable numbers of livestock. They
have a cultural bias almost inextricably bound up with the possession and exchange of livestock, particularly cattle. In order to
elucidate the structure of Gogo kinship relations, therefore, the
significance of property relations involving livestock must be
established.

To do so would lead the investigator to certain key factors
which influence Gogo social structure. The ambiguity implied by

[1] Cf. Leach (1961), p. 305: "What the social anthropologist calls
kinship structure is just another way of talking about property relations
which can also be talked about in other ways." See also Gulliver (1955)
and Gray and Gulliver (1964).

subsistence upon agriculture and a value system entirely oriented towards pastoralism should not be considered as a "paradox," nor as a kind of dichotomy between "norms" and "behavior," the resolution of which leads to explanation.[2] All important relationships in Gogo society are expressed in the idiom of kinship. The fact that Gogo view kin relationships primarily in terms of mutual rights and obligations over livestock must be taken as an aspect of the cultural facts. So too, their subsistence primarily upon an unreliable agricultural system embodies an aspect of their culture. But the distinctions which Gogo make between the values attaching to livestock and the necessity of reliance upon a precarious agricultural system is a part of our data, not of sociological explanation. Sociological explanation must be found for it. The ambiguity lies in the conscious, "homemade" model Gogo have of their own society, but as such it is a fact of extreme importance in the construction of our own structural explanation of their society.[3] The ambiguity thus evident in values and economic activity is an intrinsic part of Gogo society and is, at least in part, a function of its ecology.

A further aspect of the same general problem is that of the relation between economic systems and "types" of kinship structure. The economic preconditions of segmentary lineage systems with corporate unilineal descent groups have frequently been indicated and stated as crucial factors in the type of kinship structure characteristic of these societies. Fortes (1953, p. 24), in discussing corporate unilineal descent groups, states:

Where these groups are most in evidence is in the middle range of relatively homogeneous, pre-capitalist economies in which there is some degree of technological sophistication and value is attached to rights in durable property.[4]

[2] Cf. Fortes (1957) in Firth (1957), pp. 159–162; Leach (1961), pp. 297–298.

[3] See Lévi-Strauss (1958), p. 309; (transl.), p. 282.

[4] See also Worsley (1956), *passim;* Forde (1947); Sahlins (1961). Sahlins suggests an interesting correlation between the existence of

The absence of such conditions has also been cited to explain the absence of corporate unilineal descent groups (e.g. Richards 1950, p. 25 *et passim;* Fortes 1953, p. 35).

However, I would suggest that it is not simply the incidence of rights in heritable (durable) property which is the crucial point in the correlation between types of kinship structures and economic systems, but rather the economic conditions which allow a certain "degree of stability and density of settlement" (Forde 1947, p. 219). Thus, the *type* of property in which the rights are vested is also a factor. It would appear that corporate unilineal descent groups are often (but not always) associated with subsistence economies centered upon heritable land rights, which stabilize groups of kin in fixed localities (cf. Worsley 1956, p. 69). Such rights, as among the Tallensi (see Fortes 1945 and 1949a) are not divisible, and therefore must be held and transferred within a necessarily localized, exclusive, kin group. But of course, this does not mean that all societies with segmentary lineage systems have this type of economic system: for example, the transhumant Bedouin of North Africa, the nomadic Somali, and the Nuer (Peters 1960; Lewis 1961; Evans-Pritchard 1940). In this type of society, rights in property are primarily in livestock, but they have developed segmentary lineage systems. It would appear that in the case of more nomadic or semi-nomadic groups with livestock, in an environment with extremely scarce resources of grazing and water, the political functions of lineage organizations assume an importance in demarcating *areas* within which only members of particular agnatic groups may have rights, for example, in grazing and water (but cf. the important differences among such societies as pointed out by Lewis 1965). It will be seen that among the residentially mobile Gogo, rights in grazing and water are free everywhere, although relatively scarce. This is also the case among the Jie

---

"true" segmentary lineage structures and a situation in which one society is expanding at the expense of another, intruding into already occupied territory.

and Turkana, who do not have segmentary lineage systems
(Gulliver 1965, pp. 34–35, 255–256).

But the main point is a limiting one. Where rights in a fixed
land unit are heritable, in the context of a subsistence economy,
the localization of those with interests in that land is inevitable.[5]
When land is not heritable property, rights tied to local areas are
irrelevant in the formation of kin groups.[6] If cattle or other livestock constitute the primary form of property, the dispersal of
kin in each generation is not only a possibility but often a necessity. The Gogo provide a case where livestock form the most
important heritable property, and dispersal of agnatic kin in each
generation is the usual pattern. Although agriculture is the basis
of subsistence, usufructuary rights in land are not inherited, and
thus the localization of descent groups does not occur on the
basis of such rights. Although the central feature of Gogo kinship "ideology" is patrilineal descent, agnatic kin groups of any
depth are not corporate in terms of livestock possession. In such
a situation, agnatic descent ties beyond those of full and half
siblings (the children of one man) are of secondary significance;
locality (independent of agnation) and a network of interpersonal kinship and affinal ties assume primary importance. It is
in terms of the co-residence and cooperation of a wide variety of
kin and affines (within a generally fluid pattern of residential

[5] Cf. Worsley (1956), pp. 45, 62–63, 69; Fortes (1945), p. 180, says
of the Tallensi: ". . . every unit of farmland corresponds to a unit of
social structure . . ." For other examples of segmentary lineage systems
where corporate landholding virtually defines the primary functions of
lineage organization, see Southall (1952), pp. 25, 26; (1953), pp. 61–62:
"The Alur express in work and deed that the lineages which matter, and
those which conform to the idea of what a lineage should be, are those
which maintain their local corporate identity."

[6] Fortes (1953), states: "It is not surprising . . . to find that the
lineage in African societies is generally locally anchored; but it is not
necessarily territorially compact or exclusive. A compact nucleus may
be enough to act as the local center of a group that is widely dispersed
. . . As I interpret the evidence, local ties are of secondary significance.
. . . There must be common political or kinship or economic or ritual
interests for structural bonds to emerge . . ."

mobility) that "common political, kinship, economic, and ritual interests" are expressed and underlie the most important "structural bonds." This is in sharp contrast to the picture given of Nuer social structure by Evans-Pritchard's analysis (1940, but cf. 1953). The apparent differences between Gogo and Nuer kinship structures may lie partly in different analytical approaches, and not only in empirical fact. However, many similarities exist between the Gogo and Nuer kinship systems, and I make structural comparisons between them at several points in the present analysis.

The domestic group is the point of articulation between the sphere of cognatic, interpersonal kinship relations on the one hand and the external "politico-jural domain" on the other (Fortes, 1958). If the structure of the latter is not based upon corporate unilineal descent groups (as is the case in Ugogo), what *kind* of articulation is there between the structure of domestic groups and the type of structure that exists in the politico-jural domain? I consider this problem in depth in this study. It will be seen that the external domain in the Gogo case is composed of two aspects: (1) an ideology of kinship based upon clans, sub-clan names, and patrilineal descent, and (2) the system of ritual areas (bounded) and vaguely defined and fluid local communities (neighborhoods). I do not here present an analysis of the politico-ritual structure of Gogo society; this requires a separate volume. But I do examine the pattern of residence, kinship relationships, and cooperation in local communities at the neighborhood level; and I examine the influence upon this pattern of a patrilineal descent system that produces dispersed, broad descent categories, "corporate" only in the sense of being "exclusive name-owning" groups (Fortes 1959, p. 208).

The primary political, ritual, and property-holding unit is the homestead group, within which property rights are differentiated and livestock are inherited through a well-defined house-property system.[7] The head of a homestead has political,

[7] Gluckman (1950), pp. 193–198. The house property system in in-

jural, and ritual authority over the persons who reside in it, and he is *ipso facto* an elder in the community. Such homestead units are comparatively mobile, moving considerable distances some three to four times during the period from founding to fission and dissolution, depending upon ecological conditions and other factors (see Chapters IV and V). Even small-depth agnatic groups become rapidly dispersed, and cooperation over mutual rights in livestock becomes impossible within them. Hence, although the broader ties of agnatic descent embodied in clan, sub-clan, and "maximal lineage" membership are present and influence Gogo kinship structure, they are of limited importance in its actual operation and in the property relations in which kinship ties are expressed. They express rather a set of *categorical* relationships and are significant primarily on certain levels of ritual action (Chapter III; cf. Apthorpe 1967). A person relies instead upon a network of genealogically close agnatic, matrilateral, and affinal kin in all spheres of social activity: in residence, agriculture, and the exchange of livestock (for example, at marriage). Every person has a different set of such relationships, which constitute a series of overlapping, ego-oriented networks, although full brothers, the sons of one "house," would have very similar, if not identical, links of importance with other kin.[8] At no time do such kin constitute corporate groups; there are no corporate groups beyond stock-owning units.[9]

It is not my intention here to pursue explicitly the relevance of the present analysis either for "types" of general kinship theory,

---

heritance is the "key" to the Jie property system: see Gulliver (1955), Chapter III *et passim*. Various aspects of the Gogo house-property system are discussed in detail in Chapters V–VIII below; but I show that although the Gogo do have such a system, it differs in some respects from those already described.

[8] I am in a sense talking here about what could be termed a "kindred." However, I avoid this term as it has gained a specialized usage in the study of bilateral kinship systems (see Murdock, 1960; Freeman, 1961).

[9] This is almost identical to the situation among the Jie and Turkana; see Gulliver (1955), pp. 247, 248.

or for "types" of kinship system (cf. Schneider 1965). But the
material presented here bears directly upon these problems. The
emphasis in my analysis of the Gogo kinship system lies upon the
operation of "kinship network" in terms of locality and residential
mobility. The reason for the relative weight I assign to cognatic
and affinal ties in the context of locality and cooperation, over
those of descent embodied in clan, sub-clan, and patrilineal group
affiliation, will, I hope, seem clear. An analysis of this type necessarily involves considerable (but not entire) reliance upon
numerical data, upon the "statistical" facts of social action rather
than normative statements about it.[10] But naturally, both kinds
of data are relevant and significant for structural analysis, though
one must beware of assuming a *necessary* convergence (or di-
vergence) between them.[11] The "homogeneity" or "heterogeneity"
of Gogo social institutions may be judged from the data presented below.

The Gogo kinship system, therefore, cannot be understood
without isolating the various processes which occur within it,
both in the domestic domain and the politico-jural domain. Relevant to this point is the problem of combining into a coherent
analytical tool the two aspects of "social structure" and "social
process" (Vogt 1960). Or, putting it another way round. I am
concerned with the introduction of the "time (and space) factor"
into the concept of social structure.

In the field of kinship studies, one of the most fruitful advances
has been the introduction and application of the developmental
cycle concept in the study of domestic groups (Fortes 1949b;
Goody 1958; Gulliver 1955; Gray and Gulliver 1964; etc.).
This freed the study of "family" organization, or the domestic
domain of kinship relationships, from the limitations of typology-
making, and established the idea of "process," albeit cyclical.

Most of the studies which have resulted from this advance have
assumed that the "unit of social reproduction" is articulated with

[10] See Fortes (1949b), pp. 56–59; Leach (1961), pp. 8, 9, 300.
[11] Beattie (1959), pp. 46–47; Nadel (1951), pp. 107–114.

a broader social structure which could still essentially be described in formalized terms: usually a set of "perpetual" kinship
groupings (corporate lineages) which, even if segmentary, re-
tained over considerable periods of time their corporate identity.
Thus the "external domain" could be described in formal structural terms of, for example, the relation between corporate
groups, property (land), and the political relations which then
arise among them.

I show in this study of the Gogo kinship system that the
politico-jural domain cannot be described formally as a set of
patrilineal descent groups which provide the basis for corporate
political action and local organization. For Gogo society, local
organization in the neighborhood must be analyzed in developmental terms; no formal rules exist to relate descent groups to
local units, except at the widest ritual and symbolic level. The
pattern of residence in turn cannot be seen outside of a consideration of the cycle of development of domestic groups, the property
relations which provide its mainspring, the early fission of agnatic
groups, and the role of affinal relationships. The setting of these
processes in the general ecological context in which they occur
and the economic system that influences them are integral to the
analysis.

To achieve the type of analysis envisaged above, I have arranged my material as follows. Chapter II describes the geographical area and sets out the ecological and economic conditions of Gogo society: reliance upon agriculture and the economic
and symbolic roles of livestock. Chapter III discusses briefly
the wider aspects of Gogo kinship and politico-ritual organization: clan affiliation and its significance, ritual leadership, rain-
making and the ritual areas, and indicates the lack of well-defined
political and judicial roles. These aspects of Gogo social structure are obviously of fundamental importance and intrinsic
interest. As such, they provide the necessary background for
the rest of the work (Chapters IV–VIII), which is devoted to
a detailed analysis of kinship and marriage along the lines of the

problems noted above: in relation to locality, residential (home-stead) units, mobility, and the role of livestock property relations. Brief conclusions appear at each stage of the analysis and are summed up in a concluding chapter.

II
Ugogo: Cattle Values and Agricultural Subsistence

The area which is now known as Ugogo[1] is composed mainly of the thorn-scrub plain of central Tanzania, which is between 2,900 and 3,900 feet above sea level. Ugogo lies within the area where the eastern arm of the Rift Valley breaks up and becomes less marked. To the south, southeast, and east, mountainous or hilly country dips down to the Ruaha and Kizigo (Cizigo) valleys and the lower coastal plain respectively. In the east the mountains are the Kiboriani and Mlali ranges, which border Ugogo, and farther east the Itumba range in Ukaguru.[2] What remains of the western escarpment of the rift at this point runs through western Ugogo, though it is not much greater in altitude than the plain. The Gogo overflow onto the higher land to the west of it, and call the escarpment simply *lugongo* (ridge). There is a great mixture of population in this area, including Nyamwezi, Kimbu, Nyaturu, Taturu (Tatog), and so on. Gogo occupation of this area is probably comparatively recent.

To the north, the Sandawi hills[3] provide a boundary and

[1] The country of the Gogo people (Wagogo) is known generally as "Ugogo," the Kiswahili name for the area. I use this term throughout for simplicity. Gogo themselves, since recently accepting the term "Gogo" (see below), refer to the area as "Wugogo" or "Cigogo." The latter term refers primarily to a "way of living," a culture, and implies only a very general geographical area with no fixed boundaries.

[2] See Moffet (1958), pp. 1, 3, 151–153; Schaegelen (1938), pp. 196–198; and Claus (1911), pp. 1–2.

[3] The Gogo use the terms "Wasandawi" and "Wabulungi" for their northern neighbors. The more frequent spellings for these terms are "Sandawe" and "Burungi," but I use the Gogo versions throughout.

extend into northeastern Ugogo, cutting off from the main Gogo area the Gogo populations that live northeast of them, in the Itiso area (see Map 1, p. 16). The northeastern "boundary" of Ugogo, from Segala through Zoisa to Kongwa and Sagala, is really an extension of the southern Masai steppe, and relations between Gogo and Kisongo Masai in this area have fluctuated between cooperation that includes cultural interchange and hostility and conflict over livestock, grazing, and water. But in the east-northeast area, near Zoisa and Hogoro, Ugogo fades into the western part of Ukaguru. The matrilineal Kaguru are linguistically closely related to the Gogo, though sociologically they are very different.[4] The Gogo and Kaguru living in the Zoisa and Hogoro areas (see Map 1) display a very heterogeneous cultural and sociological picture, yet this is an overlapping typical of all the Gogo boundary areas. Although many people in the area speak the Cigogo language and now identify themselves as Gogo, matrilineal succession and inheritance are common, and bridewealth is a fraction of that normally given by Gogo in more central areas. The cultural and sociological overlapping in border areas is probably common to most of the peoples of central Tanzania, who have no centralized political systems and who inhabit fairly sparsely populated areas.[5] Though these boundaries are sociologically important, it is not possible to consider them in any detail here. The material presented in this

[4] See Tucker and Bryan (1957), pp. 40–43; also articles on the Kaguru by T. O. Beidelman, cited in the Bibliography. The Gogo are a "Bantu-speaking" people whose northern neighbors are mostly non-Bantu. In addition, the "Nilo-Hamitic" (now probably more correctly known as "Southern Nilotic") Baraguyu, who speak the same language as the Masai, have lived for a long period throughout the Gogo and neighboring Bantu areas (again see Beidelman). The influence of Sandawi, Baraguyu, and Kisongo Masai upon Gogo linguistic usage and other institutions will appear in subsequent analysis in this volume.

[5] In general this is probably true of all noncentralized systems, nonsegmentary or segmentary. For a discussion of cultural overlapping on the borders of a segmentary society, see Southall (1953), p. 21 n; see also Fortes (1953), p. 22.

book applies mainly to Gogo social institutions common to the
more central parts of their cultural area. My fieldwork was carried
out mainly in the Cilungulu area of north-central Ugogo (marked
usually on the map as Kilunguru, the Kiswahili version; see Map
1) and the Loje and Ciboli areas (marked often as Logi and
Chibole) in the extreme south of Ugogo. I visited briefly many
other parts of Ugogo.

The Gogo area is easily accessible from all directions. In fact,
all Gogo clans (*mbeyu*) claim to be descended from founders
who come from a great variety of surrounding peoples, in all
geographical directions. This is described briefly, with examples,
in Chapter III. Unattractive though the country is (the rainfall
averages about 20 inches a year, no rivers in the area run throughout the year, and droughts and famines are periodic), Ugogo
is, on the whole, a good area for livestock husbandry. It also
provides the possibility of quite extensive (though precarious)
agricultural activity. The fact that many Gogo have fairly large
herds of cattle and other livestock has caused them to be the
victims of cattle raiding at various times in the past, by the
Kisongo Masai in the north and the Hehe in the south. In such
situations the Gogo have fought as allies with the Baraguyu who
live in their area. The Gogo explicitly took from the Baraguyu
the incipient age-set organization that is still evident, although
its importance is diminishing now that fighting and raiding, its
primary functions, have been curtailed.[6]

Gogo point to the multiple origins of their clans, embodied
in the clan histories, to explain their lack of any broad political
cohesion. So strongly do they feel this and the lack of any well-
defined political roles that they say quite explicitly that they have
never been able to take concerted action against unwelcome

[6] Various aspects of Gogo age-organization, which is explicitly modeled
on the Baraguyu age-set system, will appear in the following discussion
of neighborhood and kinship structure. A fuller analysis of Gogo age-set
organization will appear elsewhere. For a brief description of the Baraguyu
system, see Beidelman (1960).

administrative measures because of it. Elders explain, *"Ase Wagogo hamba ikatali cali cisina cihuliko"* ("Even from long ago we Gogo have had no cohesion"). And while no centralized political system or systems exists, no segmentary lineage system provides the basis for the political structure.[7] Instead, the pattern is one of tiny ritual areas or "countries" (*yisi*) with geographical boundaries within which certain clans have ritual authority. These ritual areas are populated by homestead groups, which move fairly freely through them and whose members belong to a wide variety of clan affiliations. But among the members of homesteads in neighborhoods and neighborhood-clusters there exists a complex network of inter-personal kin and affinal relationships, and it is the structural principles underlying these relationships which is the central topic in this analysis.

Because of the general pattern described above, Gogo have a relative idea of the boundaries of the area they inhabit as a "cultural group" and of the identity of their neighbors, both Gogo and non-Gogo. Although they move residentially over quite extensive distances, and individual men move even greater distances with their herds in the quest for grazing and water, the identity of Gogo living at any distance from a fixed point is usually expressed in an extremely broad (and relative) classification or in terms of their non-Gogo neighbors (see Map 1). For instance, the "Nyambwa" who inhabit the Cinyambwa area of westcentral Ugogo, refer to their *immediate* neighbors to the east as "Nyawugogo," "The owners of Wugogo," and to the Gogo who live in central and eastern Ugogo as "Itumba." [8] The inhabitants of

[7] Several typological subdivisions of noncentralized societies have been made, but most detailed discussion along these lines has been confined to true segmentary systems: see Middleton and Tait (1958), p. 3 *et passim*. Of course, many noncentralized societies without segmentary lineage systems have been the subject of detailed sociological analyses: cf. Colson's work on the Tonga of Zambia.

[8] The Cigogo versions of all these terms are prefixed by the plural prefix *wa-*: thus, Wetumba. I have omitted these in accordance with

2 Dry-season landscape, southern Ugogo

3 A young man taking
his herd out to graze

4   A mother about to pound grain in the traditional mortar (*ituli*)

central Ugogo, on the other hand, although they refer to themselves as "Nyawugogo," refer to all those to the west of them
(including groups called "Nyawugogo" by the Nyambwa) as
"Nyambwa." All to the east are "Itumba." Those who live in
eastern Ugogo may refer to themselves as "Nyawugogo" and
those to the west as "Nyambwa" (including those who live in
central Ugogo); all those further west are dismissed as "Kimbu,"
the neighbors of the Gogo on the west-southwest.

The same relativity of broad classification is seen on the north/
south axis. Gogo in the north label all Gogo at any distance to
the south as "Hehe," who are the neighboring people on the
south, beyond the Ruaha river. Although many clans in this area
claim descent from the Hehe (see Chapter III), the classification
is used broadly, and in the relative sense described for the east/
west directional classifications. People in central Ugogo, however, call those in the north "Sandawi" (if they live in the northwest) and "Humha" (the Gogo word for "Masai") if they live
in the northeast. Those closer at hand are called "Nyamaseya."
To the central Gogo, only those in the extreme south are "Hehe,"
or "Kozisamba," a small pocket of people in the Ilangali area
who are strongly influenced culturally by the Hehe and Kimbu.
Gogo in the south call most of those to the north of Dodoma
"Nyamaseya" and "Sandawi," and so on.[9] However, these terms
are only collective ones used in reference to people living at
some distance by lumping them together. Actual identification in
more specific circumstances is always by clan and sub-clan name,
and the ritual area and neighborhood of present residence. But
I have marked the broad classifications on Map 1, in the various
"directional" areas to which they apply. The terms must be seen

---

current ethnographic usage. The term "Itumba" is derived from the
Itumba mountains of Ukaguru and is used by Gogo to refer to all
Kaguru and Sagara, who live to the east of them. It is also the name of a
Gogo clan (*mbeyu*) whose founder came from the east.

[9] Cf. Mnyampala (1954), pp. 16–18.

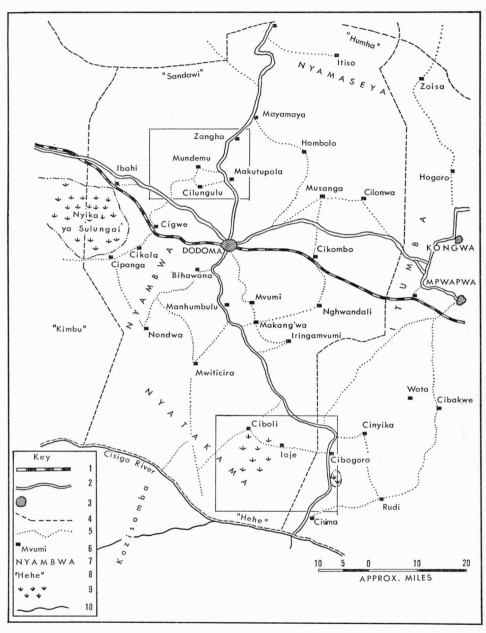

"Humha"

Itiso

Zoisa

"Sandawi"

N Y A M A S E Y A

Mayamaya

Zangha

Hombolo

Mundemu

Hogoro

Ibahi

Makutupola

Cilungulu

Musanga

Cilonwa

Nyika

Cigwe

ya Sulungai'

DODOMA

Cikombo

K O N G W A

Cikola

Cipanga

Bihawana

MPWAPWA

N Y A M B W A

I T U M B A

Mvumi

"Kimbu"

Manhumbulu

Nghwandali

Makang'wa

Nondwa

Iringamvumi

Mwiticira

N Y A T A K A M A

Wota

Cibakwe

Ciboli

Cinyika

Cisigo River

loje

Cibogoro

Key

Rudi

K o z i s a m b a

"Hehe"

Cisima

▬▬▬▬▬	1
∿∿∿	2
◍	3
– – –	4
··········	5
■ Mvumi	6
NYAMBWA	7
"Hehe"	8
↓ ↓ ↓	9
∿∿	10

10   5   0   10   20

APPROX. MILES

Map 1. Ugogo and its divisions

1: Railway. 2: Main roads. 3: Townships. 4: District boundaries.
5: Tracks. 6: Some modern divisional centers and traditional ritual
area and neighborhood centers mentioned in text. 7: Broad, "directional" divisions of the Gogo people mentioned in text. 8: Terms
associating Gogo with neighboring peoples. 9: "Swampy" areas
(*nyika*), excellent for grazing at certain times of the year. 10: Rivers.

to be totally relative to the spatial position of the speaker, as outlined above. It is not possible to record the very numerous clan ritual areas, but a full list is given in Appendix A.

I have noted that residentially Gogo homesteads are extremely mobile, and I will substantiate this in Chapter IV. Differences in dialect are, however, quite evident throughout Ugogo, in areas of language including consonant pronunciation, tone structure, vocabulary, and grammatical variation. The most marked are seen in a dialect gradation from northeast (near Ukaguru) to southwest (near Ukimbu). The inhabitants of central Ugogo and those of Cinyambwa, joke with each other over linguistic peculiarities. The adult Gogo who move from one area to another may retain many of their former local usages, and these are remarked upon in conversation. Youngsters, however, soon adopt local usages and pronunciation. Certain economic and sociological differences, particularly between the Cinyambwa area near the Sulungai grass pan (see Map 1) and the rest of Ugogo, will be noted in context in the following analysis.

Despite internal distinctions, there is a relative cultural homogeneity among most of Ugogo, including some even in peripheral areas; this is accompanied by considerable sociological homogeneity as well. Any homogeneity is quite remarkable, in view of the impact (both contemporary and historical) of neighboring peoples and the lack of any centralized political organization. All Gogo dialects are almost fully mutually intelligible, and Gogo are generally so mobile that most of them know, or have heard about, the more obvious dialectal variations in different areas. Apart from the far-reaching implications of common language,[10] most Gogo have basically similar features of material and other cultural elements which identify them to each other and separate them from other peoples. These rather superficial cultural elements are distinctive only when taken together; several of them may be common to neighboring peoples as well. The most obvious and apparent of these are: male circumcision

[10] Cf. Southall (1953), p. 21.

and female clitoridectomy (*kulawa, kugotola* or *sona zacigeto-goto*);[11] the piercing of ears (*kutobola makutu*) and insertion of ornaments (men and women); the plaiting and ochre-dyeing of the hair by men (*kubota lusiga* or *ludayiga*); and the removal of the two lower incisors (*kutowa nyhende*) by both boys and girls. Although the architectural style of low, flat-roofed mud home-steads is common in central and northern Tanzania, Gogo home-steads do have distinctive architectural features. There is some variation in building styles (*cizenjere*) within the Gogo area as well.

The Gogo share many of these material culture features with the Baraguyu and Masai[12] (indeed the Gogo have often been confused with the Baraguyu by outsiders or denigrated by Euro-peans for "imitating" the Masai), but the distinctive features of Gogo material culture soon become apparent to the observer. Among these are distinctive smithing and metalwork (*wutyani*), beadwork (*kuhona zisanga*), a variety of musical instruments, songs, dance styles and so forth. Another distinctive physical feature that contributes to the "social visibility" of Gogo and marks them off from their neighbors is the circular burn on the forehead (*cinindi*) which is given to very young children as a part of protective or curative medicine for eye diseases.

But I noted that, until recently, Gogo did not refer to them-selves by that term collectively. To establish general identity the only question one can ask is, "To which clan do you belong?" (*"Uli wambeyu ci?"*). The response that this question still most frequently receives is the name of a particular clan (*mbeyu*). But the people of this cultural area have long been known by

[11] A brief discussion of these terms is given in Rigby (1967d); a fuller analysis of Gogo circumcision and initiation ceremonies is in preparation.

[12] The Baraguyu who live in Ugogo tend to be much more assimilated to Gogo cultural elements than Baraguyu who live in other Bantu areas are to the culture of their Bantu neighbors. This may be an indication of the closer cultural compatibility between Baraguyu and Gogo: cf. Beidel-man (1960), (1961a), (1961b) and (1964).

outsiders as "Gogo." It is probable that they were given the name long before colonial penetration in the area, by Nyamwezi from the west who traveled through Ugogo on their way to the coast. It is certain that they were given the name by outsiders and not by themselves. Gogo have a legend that the Nyamwezi caravans on their journeys to the coast had a stopping-place at Cigwe in west-central Ugogo. A number of large logs (*matindi*) were lying about near the camp; so the Nyamwezi called the local people "Gogo," because a "log" in Swahili is *gogo* (pl., *magogo*).

FAMINES, SPATIAL MOBILITY, AND DEMOGRAPHY

The residential mobility of homestead groups is frequent and extensive throughout Ugogo and is of fundamental sociological importance. A major cause of this movement is the frequency of drought and famine conditions which beset the area.[13] This is an intrinsic aspect of Gogo ecological adjustment and economy. Gogo move primarily in search of grazing and water for their livestock, but they also move to find food for themselves. Droughts, however, are often minor and localized, causing residential mobility only in limited areas; but the cumulative result is extensive. Some droughts are extensive and affect the whole Gogo area and, in many cases, neighboring areas as well.

Gogo date the past in terms of droughts (*ncilu yamalenga*) and famines (*nzala* or *malogo*), or in terms of exceptionally heavy rain or good crops (*igombo*), as the case may be. Most, but not all, famines are caused by drought. In view of the significance of these factors for residential mobility, and the latter in an analysis of Gogo social structure, a list of remembered famines which were fairly extensive are given in Table 1. These include famines from the late nineteenth century until my fieldwork in 1961–63, both of which were famine years for some parts of Ugogo. The frequency of famines provides the Gogo with a highly

---

[13] Other causes of residential mobility are witchcraft and sorcery accusation, and the exhaustion of local resources of cultivable land and grazing (see below).

adequate basis for a historical chronology and accounts for the endemic nature of drought and famine conditions in Gogo economy and ecology (cf. Brooke 1967, which gives different dates and names for some famines).

Table 1. Gogo chronology of famines, droughts, and heavy rains within Gogo memory

Gogo name of famine (*nzala*)[14] or heavy rain (*igombo*), so marked	Meaning	Approximate year
Conyamagulu	From *konya magulu*, "to tie legs together so you cannot walk"	1860
Mudemu	—	1870
Magubika	"You have covered up [the pot]"	1888/89
Nzije	"Locusts"	1894/95
Sabatele[15]	"The dry-measure for grain"	1913/14
Mutunya	"Scramble for food"	1918/19
Wanyambwa	"The Nyambwa people"	1919/20
Nzala-ndodo/nzala-ndele	"Little famine"	1924/25
Mabilazi	"Of things given gratuitously"	1928/29
Nghumhula (heavy rain)	"Thumping down" (?)	1930/31
— (localized, slight)	—	1933/34
Joni[16] (also Masaje, Manghalanga, Mucele, or Makambi)	"John's famine" (also, "flour," "groundnuts," "rice," or "famine relief camps")	1939/44
Hambaya	—	1946/47
Muvuje	From *muvuje lulu, zemitonde sicizimanyire,* "You cook today, tomorrow is an unknown quantity"	1949/50
Maumau	(The time of trouble in Kenya)	1953/54
Mang'ung'u	(Type of beetle)	1954/55
Matama (or yaAmerika)	"Of the (American) maize" (given as famine relief)	1961/62
Makombelele	"Of the green-beetle pest"	1962/63

[14] Several famines have different names in different areas; and, of course, some famines have affected only some areas. More than one name indicates an extensive famine known by different local names.

[15] "Sabatele": from the Swahili, probably *"Kibaba cha tele,"* "a full, heaped measure."

[16] After John Mbogoni, treasurer of local authority at the time.

Such conditions do not permit a high density of population in Ugogo, although there have been considerable increases in the Gogo population over the past fifty years or so, especially after the terrible depredations of the Anglo-German war which led up to the drought and famine of 1918/1919 (Mutunya).[17] It is likely, however, that more recent figures are accurate and the earlier ones underestimates. The 1957 census showed that of a total Gogo population of 299,417 persons, about 270,000 were resident in Ugogo.[18] The area now inhabited by Gogo is very roughly 15,000 square miles (120 by 128 miles), which give an overall density of population of about eighteen persons per square mile.[19] Of course, these overall figures indicate little as there is a great variation in local densities.[20] However, the similarity of population density in Ugogo to other semi-pastoral areas such as that of the Jie of Uganda is indicated. Grazing and land for cultivation are not yet scarce except in a few areas of concentrated population near administrative centers. Residential mobility is further facilitated by the fact that rights in land are never inherited and there is complete freedom of pasturage and water resources for all Gogo, throughout the area.[21]

[17] In 1925 an administrator in Dodoma estimated that, apart from those who had died during the Anglo-German war, 30,000 Gogo died of the famine and influenza epidemic of 1918/19 (*Dodoma District Book*).

[18] *Tanganyika Census (1957)*, East African Statistical Office. Although many young men go away as migrant laborers for short periods of up to two years, they seldom make a second trip. The 1957 census indicated that only about 13,000 of 143,000 Gogo men (i.e. 9%) were away as migrants at that time (the figures include children). The low numbers are confirmed by my own observations for local areas. Migrant labor has had little impact on Gogo economy or society.

[19] Cf. Jieland, which has an overall density of some 14.0 persons per square mile, although in this case most are concentrated in the central residential area of the country: see Gulliver (1955), p. 42.

[20] Populations of Gogo ritual areas are noted in Chapter III.

[21] This is so in many East African societies oriented towards pastoralism: cf. the Jie and Turkana, Gulliver (1955), pp. 34, 35. Other more nomadic pastoralists, however, have grazing and water rights regulated by lineage and clan segments: cf. Lewis (1961), pp. 50, 51 for Somali.

HISTORICAL FACTORS AND AVAILABLE DATA

Gogo ideas of their own history are embodied in their clan legends and knowledge of historical events. It is most probable that the Gogo have lived in their present area for several hundred years, but many who have written about them have suggested that they are a recent amalgam of other peoples. This conclusion is based upon a mistaken interpretation of Gogo clan histories, which have a shallow time-depth. It ignores genealogical telescoping, which is their most common feature.[22]

In the following analysis I will deal mainly with the Gogo social institutions which in a sense may be said to be "traditional": that is, aspects of Gogo society which have not been deeply affected by the wider money economy and political units of Tanzania and East Africa. The Gogo have been the subject of numerous administrative and development plans and operations since colonial penetration in the area in the 1890s. Since Tanzania's independence in December, 1961, the Tanzania African National Union (TANU) government has introduced far-reaching administrative and political changes. For example, before its withdrawal, the British colonial administration had applied the policy of "indirect rule" from 1926 onwards. It created government "chiefships" and an administrative hierarchy based upon them. All this has been radically changed since independence. I discuss these developments and their relation to Gogo society elsewhere (see Rigby 1967b, in press; also Bates 1962). Yet in spite of all these changes, the main Gogo social institutions remain intact. Ritual leaders still perform their functions, though they are now limited. The "traditional" Gogo social system has been, and still is in many ways (my last visit there was in August, 1967), present "below the surface" of the

[22] Estimates based upon the clan histories recorded in the *District Books* of Dodoma, Manyoni, and Mpwapwa would lead to this erroneous conclusion of recent amalgamation: cf. Oliver and Mathew (1963), pp. 197, 202 *et passim*. Other writers have also stressed recent amalgamation: e.g. Claus (1911) and Schaegelen (1938).

broader changes and political institutions of modern Gogo society. In any case the latter are of concern particularly on the level of the formal political and legal systems of Gogo society, which do not fall within the purview of the present analysis.

One reason for the tenacity of Gogo social institutions arises out of the fact that the cohesion and continuity of Gogo society is at the "low level" of locality and kinship organization. The Gogo, in keeping with other East African pastoralists, are considered a conservative people, and the wider political changes have left many of their institutions intact. For example, Gogo society is now a part of a money economy and Gogo sell their livestock and produce to traders in order to pay their taxes and meet other minor cash needs. Yet they distinguish the value of livestock in cash terms from their value in more traditional transactions, such as the transfer of bridewealth. Missionary teaching and proselytizing for many years had limited success in Ugogo, though their impact has been rapidly strengthening in the past ten to twelve years.

Thus, the present study is in no sense a hypothetical reconstruction of a past social system which no longer exists. It is an analysis of certain aspects of contemporary Gogo social structure, of a kinship system that still functions. As such it is an analysis of a continuing system, though one undergoing change as all such systems. How long the system will remain so is a question beyond the scope of this book.

CATTLE VALUES AND AGRICULTURAL SUBSISTENCE

Rights and obligations over livestock and their exchange provide the most important indexes of effective kinship relationships in Gogo society. It is also true, however, that the basis of subsistence in Ugogo is primarily agriculture.[23] It is desirable to view cattle husbandry and agricultural activity in contradis-

[23] For present purposes I term "agricultural" only those activities concerned with crop production and cultivation, and thereby distinguish them from herding and other activities concerned with livestock.

tinction and, in a sense, as complementary to each other. This is so first because Gogo themselves view them as such, and second because the varying emphases placed upon each are of fundamental structural importance in Gogo society. The latter point will emerge in the main body of the analysis presented in subsequent chapters. Here I wish to show how Gogo themselves express a distinction between the two spheres of activity. The "cultural background" must be set by an examination of cattle husbandry and agricultural economy, and some of the attitudes attached to them. At various points I relate this description briefly to economic cooperation and settlement patterns, although the latter are presented in much greater detail in later chapters.

It may be said, as with other pastoral and semi-pastoral peoples, that the primary significance of livestock for the Gogo lies in rights and obligations in them as property. It is in property relations that some of the fundamental variables in kinship and affinal relationships lie.[24] Therefore, I have chosen to make a discussion of property relations concerning livestock central to the main analysis. But it is also of considerable importance to examine the cultural setting within which such relationships operate.[25]

I have already indicated that, because the Gogo economy relies so heavily upon the production of food crops, it may not properly

[24] What I mean by "property" and "property rights" here will emerge as the analysis proceeds, and I therefore do not discuss the theoretical implications of these concepts at this stage. However, I do frequently refer to the use of these concepts in Leach's analyses of Ceylonese and Kachin social systems (Leach, 1954, 1961a).

[25] "Culture" here is used in the sense of ". . . accumulated resources, immaterial as well as material, which the people inherit, employ, transmute, add to, and transmit" (Firth 1951, p. 27); but also with the implication that it is in "culture" that structural relations "find expression." Cf. Leach (1954), pp. 16–17: "Culture provides the form, the 'dress' of the social situation . . . the structure of the situation is largely independent of its cultural form . . . [But] Differences in culture are . . . structurally significant." Cf. also Fortes (1949b), p. 57; Beattie (1964), pp. 21–22.

be termed "pastoral." This is, of course, a mere matter of definition and need not detain us.[26] But livestock are also of considerable economic importance, even from the point of view of subsistence; and on the level of kinship relationships and ideology Gogo society may easily be said to be a pastoral one. Hence, Gogo are not simply cultivators who happen to keep cattle. If the "total" cultural situation is taken into account and the structural emphasis (necessarily) laid upon the network of kin relationships, the correct description for the Gogo might be "cultivating pastoralists."

THE BASIS OF SUBSISTENCE

Gogo hoe-cultivate several varieties of sorghum and bulrush millet (*Pennisetum*). All of these together are termed *wuhemba* (grain), but are distinguished by separate names for each variety. Different grains are known by Gogo to be suited to distinct soil types, and also to be resistant in varying degrees to crop pests. Among the latter are a green beetle called *nghombelele* (*Pentatomid nezara*) and a large variety of birds and other pests. Gogo classify soils by the vegetation on them and the color and texture of the soil itself. Since there is no control over the distribution of land for cultivation (other than current use and a subsequent two-year fallow period), different crops are planted in different soils according to the "culturally-agreed" knowledge concerning soil utilization. The general pattern is also influenced by varying ecological conditions in different parts of Ugogo.

Bulrush millet (*wuwele*) is known to do well in light soils (*mahangha*) or red soils (*nghuluhi*) and to be more resistant to drought conditions than sorghum. Most of the sorghums, including *lugugu,* the commonest, and *hembahemba,* are planted in the heavier soils which are said to need more rain to produce a successful crop. These include the very heavy black-cotton soil

[26] In the relative emphases laid upon livestock and agriculture, the Gogo are similar in many respects to the Jie of Uganda. See Gulliver (1955), *passim.*

(*matinhi*) found near swamps (although these are usually used for crops other than grain) and *ngogomba*, a dark-gray heavy soil. Although all these grain crops are grown in most localities, the varying soil, water, and pest conditions cause different types to be typical in different areas.[27]

A great variety of subsidiary food crops (and these days cash crops as well) are cultivated by Gogo. Some of these are inter-planted with the grain crops in the main fields; others are planted in small garden plots (*vigundu*) in which the soil is turned before sowing. These subsidiary crops include sweet potatoes (*mandolo*), cassava (*muhogo*), several varieties of groundnuts (*nghalanga*), Bambarra groundnuts (*nzugu*), cowpeas (*nandala*), pigeon peas (*mhanje*, uncommon), gram (*mhozo*), and so on. Other crops which are grown purely for cash returns are sesame (*mheza*) and castor (*nyemba*). Tobacco (*itumbako*)[28] is cultivated mainly in old homestead sites (*matongo*), rich in manure, for local consumption or sale in round, compressed, and dried cakes (*mawande*).

More traditional crops grown exclusively for household con-sumption include marrows (*mayungu* and *mahikwi*), water-melons (*matigiti*), cucumbers (*matanga*, or *magogo* for the small, round, sweet ones), pumpkins (*majenje*) and so on.[29] Gourds (*mheyu*) and calabashes (*nhungu*) of several varieties are grown, scraped out, filled with mud and dried to make con-tainers and drinking utensils. In addition to these, many un-

[27] In recent years, Gogo have begun to grow considerable quantities of maize, sometimes in response to famine relief measures. However, they still prefer sorghum and in parts of Ugogo eat maize mainly on the cob.

[28] Among the linguistically closely-related Kaguru northeast of Ugogo, tobacco is called *nghonde*. This term is used by Gogo to refer exclusively to Indian hemp (*Cannabis sativa*), called *bangi* or *bhang* in Swahili (from Persian-Arabic).

[29] Plants whose seeds form the edible part are distinguished from those whose flesh or fruit is edible, by reference to the seeds themselves. The seeds of all grains and pulses are thus *mbeyu* (the same term used for "clan" or "type"—see Chapter III). The seeds of marrows, etc. are called *nhetele*.

cultivated plants grow up with the crops in Gogo fields and are left standing during cultivation, to be picked and utilized later. The most common of these is *ilende,* a small, ubiquitous, green plant related to okra and eaten with meals when milk is scarce.

The food-producing, storing, cooking, and consuming unit in Gogo homesteads is the house (*nyumba*), the matricentral unit of one wife and her children (see Chapter V). Each married woman plants her various crops in her own set of several different categories of fields and garden plots, to which she has usufructuary rights at any particular time.[30] Neither the ritual leaders, the founders of neighborhoods, nor any homestead head have control over the distribution of usufructuary rights in arable land. The definitive factor in establishing these rights of cultivation is residence in a homestead near the fields. Naturally, no one will go an uncomfortable distance, farther than one's kin and neighbors would come for a communal work party, to establish fields; but the fields of persons of adjacent homesteads and neighborhoods are usually mixed up and scattered through suitable arable areas in the vicinity.[31]

As it is men's work to clear new fields (*kutemenga mbago*), it lies with a husband to establish usufructuary rights in various fields for his wives. A married woman's parents or other close kin often live close by and might give rights to her in some fields. Usufructuary rights are established and maintained by clearing and actual cultivation of arable land, or up to two years of fallow after the last crop has been harvested. After this, anyone can establish his rights of usufruct by cultivating the field himself. If the previous cultivator is still in the same neighborhood he should be asked for permission.[32] Such rights are

[30] Unmarried girls may also have fields, and the owner of a homestead may have his own apart from his wives. But this is unusual, and all the grain from an unmarried girl's field would belong to her mother's *nyumba* (house) in terms of rights in the crop.

[31] See also Chapter IV and Map 2.

[32] This is not a legal necessity but a moral obligation, to prevent any possibility of conflict. In some areas, due to the heavy concentration of

never inherited. Arable land is usually plentiful in Ugogo, and if it is not in any area, the population simply moves away to new and less congested areas. In fact, the non-attachment of Gogo to any type of land, arable or grazing, is an essential part of their ecological adjustment and a condition of the continued functioning of the economic system.

Fields (*migunda*) to be planted with grain crops are usually divided into two categories: (a) *migunda yakukaya*, the fields near the homestead which can be manured from the existing byre or old homestead site byres when yields fall, and (b) *migunda yakumbago*, "bush fields," which are used for two or three years and then left to fallow. The homestead fields are usually in the cleared, open land (*ihala*) around the homestead clusters (*vitumbi*, see hapter IV), and are often quite tightly packed together (see Map 2). The boundaries are marked by thorn bush fences (*milulu*) or simply small ridges of soil built up between two adjacent fields. Cattle tracks (*mapalilo*) must be left between them and also fenced with thorn bushes.

Bush fields, on the other hand, are usually separated from each other by considerable distances. Some are also fenced with *milulu* to prevent damage by livestock. When a bush field is cleared (*wusala*) the cut undergrowth on it is raked and piled together and burnt to provide ash. This field in its first season (*nghangale*) is popular with the Gogo for two important reasons. First, it provides a good yield if other conditions have

---

population around administrative centers (the division headquarters) in Ugogo, people now sell (*kuguza*) for money, grain or livestock, usufructuary rights in fields. This is a direct result of the increasing scarcity of cultivable land in these limited areas. Traditionally, it was impossible to obtain a return for rights in fallow fields and the idea would appear ridiculous to Gogo. The closest parallel was the transfer of usufructuary rights in a newly-cleared bush field which had not yet been burnt (*wusala*). If a man abandons such a clearing before burning (whence it would become *nghangale*) and cultivating, he could transfer the usufruct *in that year* to another man for payment, usually in livestock. In subsequent years it would need recleaning in any case and could not be transferred for payment.

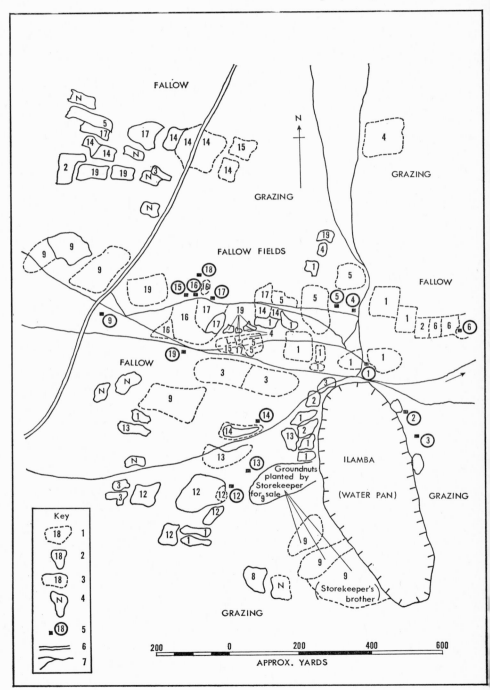

FALLOW

N

GRAZING

GRAZING

FALLOW FIELDS

FALLOW

FALLOW

Groundnuts
planted by
Storekeeper
for sale

ILAMBA

(WATER PAN)

GRAZING

Storekeeper's
brother

GRAZING

Key

1
2
3
4
5
6
7

| 200 | 0 | 200 | 400 | 600 |

APPROX. YARDS

Map 2. Distribution of homestead fields (*migunda*) and garden plots (*vigundu*) of homesteads in "Kwilamba" cluster (I), Temanghuku neighborhood, 1962

1: Grain crops (sorghum, millet, and maize) interplanted with marrows, gourds, etc., in homestead fields (*migunda yakukaya*). 2: Small crops (groundnuts, tobacco, cow-peas, etc.) planted in small plots, some of which are old homestead sites (*matongo*). 3: Mixed crops of several kinds, particularly maize and small crops (numbers refer to homestead in which holder of present usufruct of field resides, but houses within homestead, i.e. those of married women to whom usufruct is allocated, are not distinguished for purposes of identification). 4: Fields or plots worked by persons from another cluster or neighborhood. 5: Homesteads of "Kwilamba" cluster (numbers refer to text and genealogies; see Chapters IV and V and Map 3). 6: Track. 7: Paths and cattle tracks

been favorable; and second, it requires no weeding (*kulima*) as the crop is ripening. The more frequently cultivated homestead fields get a thick covering of secondary grass weed (*musote*) and must be weeded at least twice during the maturing period of the crop. This requires considerable labor and outlay of beer for work parties.

A rough indication of the distribution of fields and garden plots cultivated in 1961–62 by members of the "Kwilamba" cluster of homesteads in Temanghuku neighborhood is shown on Map 2.[33] The numbers refer to the homesteads in which the persons with usufructuary rights in that year reside, and who had actually cultivated them in that season. It must be remembered that rights in the various fields and plots are held by different married women in each homestead; that is, each "house" (*nyumba*) in that homestead. The produce of their fields belongs exclusively to their houses. Such house rights are not distinguished on the map. Bush fields cultivated by members of these homesteads are also not shown; hence the map does not cover all of the plots cultivated by them. Nevertheless, the fragmentary and uncontrolled distribution is apparent; the only factor which influences to some extent the siting of homestead fields is vague proximity to the homestead. The fluidity in the pattern of rights in cultivated land is further emphasized by the changes occurring in each season, so that after a period of two or three years the whole pattern of distribution will have changed. New fields will have been cultivated and old ones left fallow. Some homestead groups will have moved away and others come in, and the usufruct of fields transferred to other persons.

When yields from the homestead fields diminish, manure is spread by a work party that carries dung in baskets from one of the byres (old or in current use) associated with that homestead

[33] The homestead groups of this neighborhood and its clusters are the subject of the detailed analysis presented in Chapters IV and V below. See also Map 3.

and throws it in piles on the field (*kukupa suji*). The cluster of tiny plots (*vigundu*) in the center of the area shown, concentrate about old homestead sites (*matongo*) which are still rich in manure.[34] The distance between homesteads is maintained not only by the arrangement of homestead fields, but also by the necessity of keeping cattle tracks (*mapalilo*) and livestock resting areas open (*milaga*, and near the homestead, *milazo*).

RAINFALL, SEASONS, AND ACTIVITY

The problem of obtaining sufficient water for humans and livestock and sufficient rain for the crops (rainmaking is the chief function of Gogo ritual leaders; see Chapter III) is a constant one in Ugogo.[35] The short and erratic, single rainy season each year has a profound effect upon the ecology of the

[34] In surveys carried out by the Agricultural Department in 1944–46 (see Rounce, 1949; and *Dodoma District Book*) it was calculated that, in central Ugogo (in an area very similar to the one described here), an average of about 1.34 acres was cultivated per adult each season. Of this, 38% was manured in one way or another; 65% was planted with pennisetum (*wuwele*) and 18% with sorghum; 12.6% consisted of small plots (*vigundu*) under pulses and roots. In southwestern Ugogo near the nyika yaSulungai ("Bahi swamp") (where the cattle-human ratio is much higher, as will be shown later), 0.94 acres per adult (male and female) were cultivated, 19% manured; 4% was pennisetum and 94% sorghum. The area of land cultivated per adult appears to vary inversely with the availability of livestock and reliance upon its products, primarily milk (see below).

[35] The average rainfall is just over 20 inches. Over a period of 29 years, the average recorded at Dodoma (central Ugogo) was 22.24 inches; 26.25 inches at Mhamvwa (the best-watered part of the southeastern boundary of Ugogo); and 25.15 inches in Manyoni, the western boundary of Gogo country. Droughts, however, are so frequent that the 80% expectancy is about 15 inches. See Moffet (1958), p. 155. In the 1960–61 season, the rainfall in eastern Ugogo (Kongwa) totaled only 8.08 inches and was much the same for most of Ugogo. Severe drought was experienced and crops failed over most of the area. This average rainfall and expectancy is somewhat less than that for Jieland (where a similar economic and ecological pattern obtains) but much more than in Turkanaland: see Gulliver (1955), pp. 17, 22 n.

area, and thence is an important factor in social organization. Droughts are frequent and constitute one of the primary factors influencing residential mobility, which is of fundamental importance in social relationships. The rains seldom last more than five months. Light, unexpected showers may occur as early as October or November, but this is considered much too early; the rains usually last the four or five months from December until March or April. They come in heavy, erratically distributed showers with consequent rapid run-off which is only partially alleviated by the general flatness of the terrain. The fact that most of the rainfall of the season comes in three or four heavy downpours, each of which may last one or more days, is recognized in Gogo rain-making ritual. A diviner often informs the ritual leader to expect, say, "four downpours" (*mavunde mane;* lit., "four clouds") during the season. Rainfall and rain-making also constitute one of the chief factors in distinguishing between ritual areas and in the significance of ritual boundaries.

Gogo divide the year broadly into two seasons: *cifuku* (the rains) and *cibahu* (the dry season). With the onset of the first rains at the end of the dry season, the change of scrub from gray-brown to brilliant green (Gogo say, "*mbago yadedewala*") with the new young grass is very marked. The transformation appears to occur almost overnight. Similarly, at the end of the rainy season the bush rapidly dries, and Gogo say, "*mbago yabahuka*" ("the year has burst"). The ratio of *cifuku* to *cibahu* is roughly five months to seven months, though there is some variation each year.

Gogo divide the two seasons into phases named primarily after the activities associated with them, as well as by lunar months. There are thirteen lunar months (*myezi;* sing., *mwezi*)[36]

[36] The term *mwezi* means "moon." It is not possible here to enter into details of Gogo time reckoning but I hope to publish a paper on this topic elsewhere. A somewhat similar (though far from identical) system of time reckoning is used by the linguistically related Kaguru, neighbors of the Gogo to the northeast. See Beidelman (1963e), particularly pp. 14–18.

in the Gogo year (*mwaka*).[37] The exact number of days in each lunar month is of no particluar concern to them. The beginning of a new year is not determined by the months, so the discrepancy between the cycle of lunar months and the start of each year is readily adjusted at the appropriate time. Gogo lunar months, their approximate Gregorian calendrical equivalents, and the named phases and associated activities of the year are summarized in Figure 1.

Although it is the commencement of the rains (*mvula*) that properly marks the beginning of the new year (*mwakafiko*) and the end of the old (*mwaka wafwa,* the year is dead), Gogo begin planting before the first rains. The time for planting is judged by the appearance of the constellation Pleiades (*Cilimila*) on the southern horizon in the early evening; this indicates that the rains (if they come at all) are about to commence. Most of the other phases of the year and their associated activities are adjusted to the rainy season, the maturing of the crops, and the harvest. Bulrush millet, which is the most drought resistant grain, matures in about four and one-half to five months. Sorghum matures in from three to six months, depending upon the variety and rainfall conditions. Other crops such as squash, cucumbers, and watermelons usually ripen earlier and are picked before the main harvest (*kududula*) in the period called *itika*. Herding activities are, of course, continuous throughout the year, but assume particular prominence in terms of time and decisions during the dry season, particularly the last few months (see below).

[37] The word *mwaka* (pl., *myaka*), year, is a common Bantu root. Gogo also, however, use the term *isili* (lit., "hoe"; pl., *masili*) to denote "year," i.e. one hoeing season. Length of residence in a neighborhood is often referred to as in this example: "We hoed three hoeing seasons" (*Calima masili madatu*), i.e. we stayed three years. Cf. Beidelman (*ibid.*), p. 15. It is not possible here to discuss whether in fact the Gogo lunar calendar is "traditional" or modeled on the Swahili/Arabic calendar and adopted since Islamic contact. The seasons, phases of the year, and astronomical knowledge would actually provide a sufficiently accurate calendar on their own (see Figure 1).

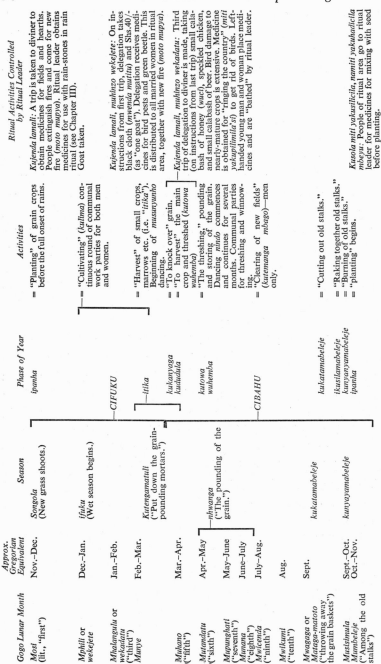

Gogo Lunar Month	Approx. Gregorian Equivalent	Season	Phase of Year	Activities	Ritual Activities Controlled by Ritual Leader
Mosi (lit., "first")	Nov.–Dec.	Songola (New grass shoots.)	ipanha	= "Planting" of grain crops before the full onset of rains.	Kujenda lamali: A trip is taken to diviner to obtain medicines for fields and hearths. People extinguish fires and come for new fire (moto mupya). Ritual leader obtains medicines for use with rain-stones in rain ritual (see Chapter III). Goat taken.
Mphili or wekejete	Dec.–Jan.	ifuku (Wet season begins.)	CIFUKU	= "Cultivating" (kulima) continuous round of communal work parties for both men and women.	
Mhalangulu or wekedatu ("third") Munye	Jan.–Feb. Feb.–Mar.		itika	= "Harvest" of small crops, marrows etc. (i.e. "itika"). Beginning of musunyunho dancing.	Kujenda lamali, muhinzo wekejete: On instructions from first trip, delegation takes black cloth (mwenda mititu) and Shs.40/- (as "one goat"). Delegation receives medicines for bird pests and green beetle. This is distributed to all married women in ritual area, together with new fire (moto mupya).
		Katengamatuli ("Put down the grain-pounding mortars.")		= "To knock over" grain.	
Muhano ("fifth")	Mar.–Apr.		kukanyaga kududula	= "To harvest" the main crop and threshed (kutowa wuhemba)	Kujenda lamali, muhinzo wekedatu: Third trip of delegation to diviner is made, taking (on instructions from last trip) small calabash of honey (wuci), speckled chicken, and small calabash of beer. Bird damage to nearly-mature crops is extensive. Medicine is obtained for "ringing the country" (miti yakuplimilia'si) to get rid of birds. Left-handed young man and woman place medicines and are "bathed" by ritual leader.
Mutandatu ("sixth")	Apr.–May	nhwanga ("The pounding of the grain.")	kutowa wuhemba	= "The threshing," pounding and storing of the grain. Dancing nindo commences and continues for several months. Communal parties for threshing and winnowing.	
Mupunghati ("seventh") Munana ("eighth") Mwicenda ("ninth")	May–June June–July July–Aug.		CIBAHU	= "Clearing of new fields" (kutemanga mbago)—men only.	
Mwikumi ("tenth")	Aug.				
Mwagaga or Mataga-matoto ("throwing away the grain baskets")	Sept.	kukatamabeleje	kukatamabeleje	= "Cutting out old stalks."	
Mutsimula Mumbeleje ("Among the old stalks")	Sept.–Oct. Oct.–Nov.	kunyayamabeleje	ikusilamabeleje kunyonyamabeleje ipanha	= "Raking together old stalks." = "Burning of old stalks." = "planting" begins.	Kusola miti yakusilicila, namiti yakuhadicila mbeyu: People of ritual area go to ritual leader for medicines for mixing with seed before planting.

Figure 1. Gogo seasons, months, and associated cycle of agricultural activities and rituals

The need for intensive and heavy agricultural activity during the four or five months of the rainy season, from planting to harvesting, severely restricts other activities for both men and women in Ugogo. Husband and wife share the work on the small plots (*vigundu*), and most of the heavy cultivation in the grain fields is carried out by communal work/beer parties (*wujimbi welima*) which both men and women attend. The only agricultural activities which are completely separated (by cultural norms) between the sexes are bush-clearing (*kutemenga mbago*) and threshing (*kutowa uwuhemba*), carried out exclusively by men, and seed-planting (*kuhadika mbeyu*) and winnowing (*kukwera mawaje*) by women. Bird damage to maturing grain crops is extensive in Ugogo, as is damage to crops in bush fields by wild animals (*nimu*) such as boars (*ngubi*), wart hogs (*njili*) and baboons (*mhuma*). It is up to men and adolescent boys to protect the bush fields, even during the night. Shelters (*vilingo*) are constructed in these fields so that someone can be there all of the time. Men, women and children are expected to help protect the homestead fields from bird damage (*kwamira ndeje*), particularly in the evenings at dusk when birds are most likely to attack. This is accomplished by much banging of tins and rattles, and shouting. Homestead heads who have few children to help in this task must assist their wives by constructing a system of rattles (*makoyogo*) on poles about fifteen to eighteen feet high through the fields, connected to a *cilingo* platform by bark string, so that the whole set may be kept rattling by one person.

Apart from the physical measures taken to ensure a crop against a great variety of destructive agents, several medicinal and "supernatural" techniques are used to protect crops from physical attack by birds and other pests, as well as from the evil influence of men. The ritual leader (*mutemi*) obtains medicines from a diviner and distributes them to the members of all the homesteads within his "country" or ritual area (*yisi*).[38] The

[38] It is not possible in this book to describe in any detail the extensive

medicines are for mixing with the seed before planting (*miti yakuhadicila mbeyu*), for "sprinkling" in the fields (*miti yakuminza*), "surrounding the fields" (*yakupilimila migunda*), and so on. Crop medicines are not, however, distributed by the ritual leaders to homestead heads, to distribute in turn to their wives. Each married woman must go herself, or send a member of her "house," to the ritual leader's homestead (*ikulu*) to obtain the medicine for her own fields. This further emphasizes the legal and ritual separation of the houses (*nyumba*) within each homestead group (*kaya*) in terms of crop production and consumption, a point to which I return in other contexts.[39] Individuals may also obtain their own medicines from diviners for the protection of fields and crops.

CULTIVATION AND COOPERATION

After a fair or good harvest in the previous season, women normally have enough grain left over in their granaries (*madong'a*) to prepare beer for communal work parties in the next cultivation season.[40] If they do not have the resources, they may invite kin and neighbors to a work party on the promise of a beer party when the present crop is harvested. This is called *kugubika cipeyu* (to turn the drinking gourd upside down). Beer for agricultural work parties is brewed by a married woman, using only the grain belonging to her own house, for the cultivation of her own fields. Co-wives should attend each others' work

and complex set of activities associated with ritual protection of people, livestock, and crops, and the ensuring of rain, carried out by the ritual leaders in conjunction with diviners. Some aspects are discussed in Chapters III, IV and V below.

[39] The symbolic opposition between men and women in relation to other symbolic oppositions, and in relation to ritual, is explored in Rigby (1966a) and (1967a).

[40] Beer (*wujimbi*) should be made from whole grain, although husks (*mhumba*) are used as the fermenting principle. These days it is possible for Gogo women to use husks as the fermenting principle and then add sugar (brown or white), bought in the shops, to give the beer body. This is called *"malanji-tatu,"* a corruption from the Swahili.

parties, but there is no legal obligation to do so.[41] Co-wives who get on well together often brew beer together for a communal work party on both of their fields at the same time, but this is most common if they have both had *kugibika cipeyu* before. When the crop is in, they jointly brew enough beer to throw a party for all those who attended the work party of each.

People are "invited" (*kulalikwa*) to attend work parties, usually the evening before, by young boys or men of the homestead who go around and inform them of the field at which it is to be held. Thus, the cooperating group is restricted to those who reside a fairly short distance from each other: neighbors, kin, and affines. Uninvited persons in these categories also attend if they wish. There is no offence if one does not attend for good reason, but a man or woman who consistently refuses to help will soon lose reciprocal services, even if they provide large quantities of good beer. Work begins soon after dawn and goes on until the field is finished. This may be very late in the evening, if the field is large and the soil heavy-going. Individuals join in during the course of the day and others leave to attend to other activities. All who have worked come in the evening to the homestead for the main beer (*wujimbi wesima*) party.

An average of about twenty people, men and women, attend a work party during the height of the cultivating season (about January to March).[42] People may walk up to five or six miles

[41] Persons, men or women, who make an agreement of reciprocity to help each other in agricultural work (with no additional rewards) are said to *kulima cisanji* (to hoe *cisanji*). This contains the root of the word used for "co-wife" (*musanji muyagwe*). Thus co-wives are expected to cooperate in cultivation simply on the basis of reciprocity and fellow-feeling, with no added inducements. This certainly is consistent with Gogo norms about behavior between co-wives (see Chapters V and VII).

[42] Of 21 of the work parties I attended and took detailed notes on, from 6 (3 men and 3 women) to 33 (16 men and 17 women) persons attended, giving an average of 21 persons (12 men and 9 women). Since the average number of adults in a homestead is about 6 (see Chapter V), each party involves at least three or four homesteads; usually there are individuals from many more. On the whole, slightly more men attend

for such a party, though usually they are confined to much closer neighbors. The whole party usually forms a single line, shoulder to shoulder, as it works across the field, unless a "son-in-law" party (*wakwemulima*) is present. They will be given a separate section of the field to cultivate. At a good hoeing party, the line is kept correctly, songs are sung, and the hoes strike the ground in unison. The work seems to be lightened in an atmosphere of conviviality and conversation, and the whole job is completed in one day or less. People look forward to the next day's party on someone else's field. Indeed, during this period, there is almost always a hoeing party going on somewhere in the neighborhood.

It is not through mere pedantry that I emphasize the details of this procedure; many cultural values of importance attach to it, and I am trying to establish the extent of commitment, economic and cultural, that Gogo have to a system of cultivation, which is inherently precarious. This is necessary before a fruitful comparison can be made with the role of livestock (and associated values) in Gogo social organization. Within the present limits of space, it is difficult to describe in detail the agricultural basis of Gogo economy. But lest I give, in the following analysis of the role of livestock in Gogo kinship, the impression that the Gogo are only interested in cattle, I describe here very briefly a set of ideas concerning agricultural activity that are fundamental to Gogo cosmology.

If a field is flat, the line of men and women who hoe it in unison during a work party begins at the western boundary and moves across the field from west to east.[43] They also first traverse the field at its north end, so that each successive row of hoed land (the width covered by the line) is on the south of the pre-

---

than women, who may be doing homestead chores or working on their own garden patches. Most were from the same or adjacent neighborhoods, including "sons-in-law" parties (see below and Chapter VII).

[43] If the field is on a slope, it will always be hoed uphill, and geographical orientation becomes irrelevant.

vious one. They thus cover the field from north to south in rows running west to east. The men form the southern part of the line (i.e. on the right when facing east) and the women the northern (the left), unless special circumstances intervene.[44] If this pattern is adhered to, it may be seen that the women are always on the end of the line abutting the "cultivated part" (*wulime*) of the field, the men on the "uncultivated," "wild" part (*ilale*).

The reasons given by Gogo for this procedure fall into two categories. (a) Men are supposed to go first over the thick weeds (*musote*) that surround the crop and cut the first "swath" (*muvizi* or *nghuwo*).[45] At the next traverse, the women go over again what the men have already covered (now called *nheje*), while the men open a new swath from the uncultivated part of the field. This, Gogo say, is because men have more "strength" (*vilungo*) and therefore must do the heavier task of clearing the new strip. These reasons alone would not, of course, necessitate the total hoeing pattern described and its geographical orientation. (b) The second set of reasons, however, taken with the first, necessitate the pattern. First, men should always be on the right of women (the right hand is literally "male hand," *muwoko wokulume*) and women always on the left of men (the left hand is "woman hand," *muwoko wokucekulu*). Then, the wind blows from the east and the east is associated with fertility: thus the line moves from west to east when hoeing. Also, a field should not be "split" (*kudumulwa*) from north to south. It would immediately be so divided into "cultivated" (*wulime*) and "uncultivated" (*ilale*) were the hoeing party to move from

[44] The special circumstances are as follows: if the field adjoins another immediately to the south and there is open bush on the north, the line will begin its traverse along this southern boundary (*mimbi yatakama*) and the whole pattern is reversed.

[45] The noun *nghuwo* for the new swath is derived from the verb *kukuwa* (to wear a new path, bring into common use, or domesticate). I found no other association for the term *muvizi*, except that the verb *kuviza* means "to spoil."

north to south. This, to Gogo, is "wrong," just as building a house with the wrong orientation is "wrong" because one "cuts the country" (*kudumula yisi*) by so doing.

Many Gogo are now unaware of this second set of reasons, and in fact may deny altogether that they usually hoe fields in this manner.[46] The denial is given support by the fact that it is not obligatory to hoe in this way, and many work parties do not, even when the field is flat. But the majority do adhere to this pattern; and a perceptive elder, when discussing hoeing techniques in company with others, explicitly related them to other general concepts of space held by Gogo:

> We should not hoe a field from north to south, because we cannot cut up a field into sections along a north-south line (. . . *sicidahile dumula mugunda cipinga, itakama nesukuma*). Do we not also, in our Gogo custom (*cigogo cetu*), begin building a house at the east? . . . Also, it is on the left hand that women should stand. Now, if they were on the south, would they not be on the right hand? And would they then cut first swath (*muvizi wenenco*)? It is the "bulls" (*zinghambaku*, i.e. young men) who cut the *muvizi*. . . .

I refer again to some of these concepts of space in other contexts below.

A further exploration of these areas of Gogo thought and cosmology would lead us far afield, and I have analyzed them in detail elsewhere (Rigby, 1966a). I have recorded these few facts in order to emphasize the importance of cultivation in the Gogo economy, and to illustrate the extent and elaboration of Gogo culture in the sphere of agricultural activity, however insecure the results of such activity may be. Nevertheless, in the

---

[46] It was not, in fact, through any informant's theorizing or elder's whim that I noted this pattern, but from the fact that, of 21 workparties that I observed in detail, 13 (62%) were carried out in this way. This fact, together with a new informants' (unsolicited) knowledgeable discourse, provided an insight into the way in which cultivation patterns were (almost "unconsciously") related to cosmological ideas which pervade Gogo thought. (See Rigby, 1966a for a detailed analysis.)

Gogo system of values and in the all important sphere of kinship, cultivation plays a secondary part to livestock, their husbandry, and the values attaching to them, particularly cattle.
Some types of land are prized for their qualities in good crop
yields, but no ties of any duration are set up between such land
and the persons who cultivate it. Survival depends upon the
land, yet decisions about livestock (particularly their movement
to new areas) always take precedence.

THE ECONOMIC ROLE OF CATTLE,
  AND LIVESTOCK HUSBANDRY

The "livestock cycle" is essentially separate from the "agricultural cycle" in Gogo thought, economy, and social organization, and often conflicting decisions have to be taken between
them. But livestock impinge upon the agricultural cycle at several
important points: (a) the use of manure, (b) the exchange of
livestock intermittently for grain (*kuhemela*) in normal years,
and (c) the use of livestock as an insurance against famine in
bad years, enabling Gogo to obtain food enough to have the
strength to carry out cultivation for the following season.

There are basically two important ways in which Gogo traditionally use cattle manure (*suji*) to increase crop yields, as
we have seen above. The contention that they are traditional
methods is supported by most of the evidence, including even
the terms used for the manure and the operations involved. The
fact that, in this largely cattle-keeping society, dung is not
normally used for building also supports the contention. The
dung of the cattle byre, which forms a very thick deposit
(liberally laced with urine) in most cattle-owning homesteads,
is called *suji*. Cattle dung outside the byre (often kept smoulder-
ing and used for lighting pipes by men as they sit under the
shade tree outside the homestead) is called *wutope*. The two
manuring methods already described—of planting into old de-
posits of dung (*matongo*) and manuring homestead fields
(*kukupa suji;* lit., to throw down the manure)—show a visible

increase in the size of the plants and the yield. A third and minor way in which dung is utilized is by grazing cattle over the stalks (*mabeleje*) in the fields after the harvest; this is a right which is open to all, irrespective of who cultivated the field in that season and who holds the agricultural usufruct. The institution of cattle-trusteeship (see below) ensures the distribution of manure to non-cattle-owning homesteads and also widens the distribution of milk, fat, and meat.

The most obvious direct economic use of cattle is in the consumption of milk. Milk is a highly valued food and one to which the prestige of wealth attaches. The staple thick porridge (*uwugali*) made from sorghum or millet flour, is always served with a side dish of some kind. When milk is scarce, these are usually made from green vegetables.[47] But if a man has a herd large enough to give milk to drink to his visitors and friends, along with a meal of *uwugali,* he will be known to be wealthy in cattle. In fact, it is preferable to offer a visitor *uwugali* with milk than to offer it with a meat dish, though the gift of an animal (which is usually slaughtered) is preferable to both. But milk is only plentiful during certain times of the year, even for comparatively rich homesteads. Particularly towards the end of the dry season and the early part of the wet season, the yield of milk from Gogo cattle is very small and may all be consumed by children. Gogo do not even pretend that they could subsist entirely upon the products of their cattle and small stock, though there is some evidence that the higher the number of cattle per person in any part of Ugogo, the lower the corresponding average acreage planted. Gogo look upon milk as an important, though subsidiary, part of their diet. The high prestige value which attaches to hospitality in which milk plays a major part is in itself an

---

[47] Whatever the side dish is, it is called *mboga*. Apart from *ilende,* which I have noted is the most common green vegetable, other uncultivated green-vegetable side dishes are made from the leaves of cowpeas (*nandala*), the *musima* shrub (*Gynandropsis gynandra*), the *ngazi* shrub (*Crotalaria*), the flowers of the *musanghala* bush (*Fockea schinzii*), and a great variety of other plants.

indication of its relative scarcity. This could not be otherwise, when the relatively low proportion of livestock to human population in Ugogo is compared with those among peoples who rely more heavily upon cattle for subsistence (see Table 2).

Milk (*mele*) is consumed in a variety of ways. It is drunk fresh (*mele masusu*), but mostly by children. It is allowed to thicken without the removal of fat by churning, when it becomes *mhopota*. This is considered the most delicious form and *mhopota* is most commonly served with a meal of *uwugali*. Also, after churning and the removal of fat (which is itself further prepared by boiling, to be used as a sauce), the reduced sour milk (*masuce*) may be drunk or served with *uwugali*. Again, in all of these forms, the milk may be flavored in a variety of ways by smoking, with burning tapers (*mizinga yakufusisa mele*), the containers in which it is kept.[48] Butter fat (*mafuta*) is also used to anoint the body by both men and women.

Cattle are milked by married women who are the heads of the houses to which they are allocated, or their daughters or other dependents. All of the milch cows in a homestead herd are usually allocated to one or other of the "houses" (*nyumba*) of which it is made up. If a house has cattle which are not producing while others are, milk may be given to the wife of that house for her use and for her children: but only with the permission and knowledge of the wife who is head of the house to which the beast belongs. Men and boys only milk cattle when there is no woman available to do so, though at other times they may assist in the milking of a difficult cow. The rights of women in milch cows (*nghamwa*) is yet another aspect of the rigid division of property rights between the houses of the home-

---

[48] The extent of Gogo interest in matters pertaining to milk and its consumption can be seen from the fact that I counted at least seven varieties of trees and bushes from which tapers may be prepared for smoking milk containers; there are undoubtedly several more. Among these are the *musinjisa* tree (*Maerua parvifolia*), the *mutumba* tree (*Boschia mossambicensis*), the *mubukwe* bush (*Terminalia stuhlmanii*), and the *mutanasanje* shrub (*Capparis fascicularis*).

stead group (see Chapter V). The milk of small stock is not utilized by Gogo.

Livestock are never slaughtered solely for meat. When an animal is too old and weak to go out to pasture, Gogo kill it off (*kumalilila*) and distribute the meat. Livestock are also slaughtered in considerable numbers for medicinal and ritual purposes.[49] They are killed at propitiation ceremonies to the spirits of the dead (see below), at funerals, marriages, and initiation ceremonies. Such occasions are quite numerous in any neighborhood and must be considered important as a source of meat in terms of subsistence. Each animal which is slaughtered on such occasions involves the obligations of kin and affines of various categories, some of which will be described in their contexts below.

But apart from their secondary use (though perhaps of primary importance in terms of subsistence) as a source of meat and milk, livestock in Ugogo serve as the main medium for the accumulation and exchange of "wealth" (*sawo*). It is still true to say that, except for the minority of young men who have been to school for over two or three years, most Gogo men have as a primary aim the accumulation and control of a large number of livestock in general (*mitugo*) and cattle (*ng'ombe*) in particular. Apart from their exchange in bridewealth, which is the single largest transaction in the Gogo exchange system, livestock also change hands in several other contexts. Although they are not

[49] Most livestock killed on ritual occasions, apart from sheep and goats, are young oxen (*nzeku*). Analysis of the composition of the average herd gives some idea of the rate at which animals are slaughtered. A survey carried out by the veterinary department in Ugogo in 1946 gave the following figures:

Adult Males uncastrated	:	7.5%
Males castrated	:	4.0%
Females	:	54.6%
Calves (under 2 years)	:	33.9%

The low proportion of adult oxen in the herd is indication of the rate at which they are reduced by killing: cf. Schneider (1957), pp. 287–288.

5 A ritual leader tends his rainstones (*mabwe gemvula*). The pestle (*mutwango*) is also part of the ritual regalia and has medicines embedded in hole in the tip.

6   Looking out over the gate of a cattle byre

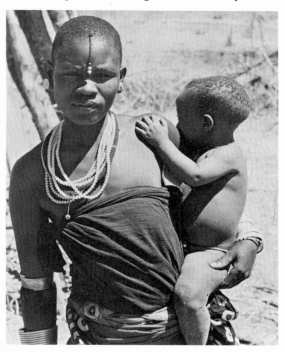

7   Mother and child

themselves considered as consumption goods (they supply these only incidentally, in Gogo values), they can be converted into agricultural produce for consumption in times of famine. The idea that livestock, especially cattle, are never slaughtered for food only, even during famines, is very strong.[50] It provides the basis for many stories and anecdotes on the subject of what others say about the (comparatively) stock-rich Gogo when they are dying of hunger during a famine.[51] This is consistent with Gogo values about livestock and their primary function in Gogo social organization.

CATTLE EXCHANGE AND PROPERTY RELATIONS

Cattle serve as the basic "value units" in Gogo social values. They can be used to evaluate anything from wives and children (e.g. two head of cattle for the custody of the child of an un-married girl, apart from the fine for fornication. See below) to the seriousness of an offence, and the number of bags of grain borrowed in a famine year. Their value in terms of modern external market (*minadi*) prices, or in grain trading, is con-stantly changing. But this bears no relation to the values at-

[50] Gogo practice bloodletting (*kuguma daho*) on cattle during famines when all other sources of food have failed. Also, when an animal is slaughtered for ritual purposes, Gogo sometimes drink the blood which is carefully collected in a fold of skin to prevent it from spilling. When they practice bloodletting during famines, Gogo drink some of the blood (*sakami*), but most of it is usually whisked (*kupuga*), cooked and consumed mixed with milk. The Baraguyu, many of whom live in Ugogo (see Beidelman, 1960 and 1962), practice this more frequently and consume more of the blood (*osarge*) raw, as do the Kisongo Masai.

[51] For example, on one occasion an elder recounted how he and two companions had nearly died of hunger on a journey to Cigaji (Chakwale, in Ukaguru) to trade small stock for tobacco. (Such an enterprise is called *kukwawa*.) When he had completed his story of severe hardship and near death, another elder laughingly said, "Now see, that is why the foreigners (*makonongo*) laugh at us and say: 'A Gogo can die of hunger even while he still has food.' Now you had goats with you. What if you had eaten them?" To which the other replied, "Who (of the three) would have agreed to kill his goats?"

tached to livestock in the contexts of bridewealth exchanges, compensation, and trusteeship contracts.

A single herd (*itewa limonga*) is said to belong to the homestead head in whose byre the livestock are kept. He is responsible for their physical and ritual welfare and has the major authority in their control and distribution, unless they are trusteeship cattle (*nghozwa*). The herd is said to be "his herd" (*itewa lyakwe*), but seldom does an individual have exclusive ownership of a herd in the sense that he has sole rights over its use and disposal.[52] The kinds of rights over particular cattle and small stock are constantly changing in any herd, as are the persons exercising those rights. A man seldom "owns" many head before he is married; and as soon as he has children, particularly sons, his rights over the herd he does "own" are curtailed and modified. He has constant obligations to fulfill in respect of his herd, not only to agnatic kin and affines, but to uterine and matrilateral kin as well. Thus, the rights a man may expect to have over livestock during his lifetime must be viewed within a cyclical pattern, and he seldom has sole rights over any large number. The crucial unit in the ownership of the herd is the domestic group; I discuss this fully in Chapters V and VII. Rights within this group are distinguished by houses, and the house-property system concerning livestock is described as an integral part of the following analysis of kinship relations.

Bridewealth transactions involve comparatively large num-

[52] The matrilineal Plateau Tonga of Northern Rhodesia had a rather similar cattle-to-human population and were one of the main cattle-keeping societies in that area. In many other ways (as it will appear), Tonga society shows similarities to Gogo: in the dispersed clanship ties, the manipulation of a network of wide-ranging kinship ties, residential mobility through areas defined only in ritual terms, and so on. Colson (1962) says of livestock ownership: ". . . cattle can be said to be owned by individuals rather than local or kinship groups. . . . Nevertheless, ownership does not have the same connotations of rights to independent action with respect to the property that it has to the European" (p. 125).

bers of livestock. Mutual obligations and rights over bridewealth herds (*cigumo*) involve, in a single transaction, a wide range of kin, both agnatic and matrilateral; and this is so among both givers and receivers. Bridewealth herds are thus composed of animals which come from several different individual (homestead) herds. They are also divided up in a similar manner amongst the several herds of the receivers. It will be seen that such large transfers of livestock can, in fact, only be accomplished with any frequency with the cooperation of several categories of kin.[53]

The average Gogo homestead head does not possess a very large herd, although I know two or three individuals with 800 to over 1,000 head of cattle and more small stock.[54] This, however, is exceptional; a homestead head with anything over 100 head of cattle is considered a rich man (*mugoli wang'ombe*). The size of the average herd varies over time as well as locality. Droughts and famines, particularly those of 1918–19 and 1953–54, reduced Gogo herds to what is probably a smaller average than that which obtained before colonial penetration in the area.[55] At any rate, the general pattern is one of fluctuation in wealth in livestock. Figures for homestead herds in an area in north-central Ugogo are given in Table 2.[56] These figures are probably fairly typical of the more densely populated parts of most of north, central, and eastern Ugogo. In the Sulungai grasspan area (see Map 1) of western Ugogo, in northeastern Ugogo

[53] A detailed analysis of bridewealth transactions, ideal and actual, is given in Chapter VI. Here I wish merely to examine the implications of such transactions in terms of the general pattern of Gogo wealth in livestock.

[54] I use "possess" here in the sense of "ownership" as described above: a homestead head's rights over his own herd.

[55] The rinderpest epidemic which swept large areas of Africa, East, Central, and South, toward the end of the last century, also reduced Gogo herds in the 1890s. Gogo refer to it by the Swahili term *Sotoka*.

[56] These figures concern the homesteads and area which provide most of the material presented in the following analysis.

(Itiso), and in parts of southern Ugogo, the average herds are probably larger; in some areas, they are nearly twice as large.[57]

From the point of view of the crucial importance of kinship rights and obligations in bridewealth transactions it should be noted that the average bridewealth herd is considerably larger than the average homestead herd. A glance at Table 11 shows that the average bridewealth is fifteen head of cattle and eleven small stock (the ideal is over twenty head of cattle and sixteen to twenty small stock). Further, considering that the rights in the average homestead herd of twelve head of cattle and twelve small stock are usually further subdivided among the members of more than one matricentral house unit, the major problem facing a man who wishes to marry becomes immediately apparent. It is in this circumstance that he must, through the rules governing the mutual obligations of a wide range of kin in livestock, manipulate his relationships within the network of kinship. In the following analysis it will be seen that these relationships are often defined, and "activated," in relation to these rights in livestock.

CATTLE TRUSTEESHIP CONTRACTS (*KUKOZA*)

A further contract of considerable importance involving livestock is that of cattle trusteeship (*kukoza*). A homestead head

[57] In surveys carried out by the veterinary department in 1944–46 (see *Dodoma District Book*), the following figures were given for Ugogo. In Mulebe neighborhood (an area very similar to that discussed in the present analysis) there was an average of 15 stock-units per homestead. This gave an average of 1.55 stock-units *per capita* (9.65 persons, adults and children, in each homestead); figures which compare favorably with those I obtained (Table 2). In Nagulo neighborhood, just near the Sulungai area, the corresponding figures were 24 stock-units per homestead, giving an average of 2.52 stock-units *per capita* (9.51 persons per homestead). Rounce (1949) gives the figures of 20.10 stock-units per homestead as an average for "Ugogo." This gives, in Rounce's figures, 2.10 stock-units *per capita,* at 9.57 persons per homestead. (It might be noted that this makes the Gogo "more pastoral" than the Nuer in terms of livestock-human population ratios, particularly if only bovines are reckoned; cf. Evans-Pritchard, 1940, *passim.*)

(*nghozwa*) contracts: Temanghuku neighborhood and Cilungulu ritual area (1962)

Area (sample)	Livestock "owned" by members of homestead in homestead herd		Stock units[58] "owned" per homestead	Total livestock in homestead herds, "owned" + trustee[59]		Total stock unit per homestead
	Cattle	small stock		Cattle	small stock	
Temanghuku neighborhood (own figures) N = 44	11.7	11.6	14.0	13.9	13.9	16.8
Cilungulu ritual area (tax figures) N = 340	—	—	—	11.2	16.0	14.4

	Livestock "owned" per capita in homestead herd		Stock units "owned" per capita	Total livestock in home herds per capita		Total stock unit per capita
	Cattle	small stock		Cattle	small stock	
Temanghuku (as above)	1.25	1.23	1.50	1.49	1.48	1.79
Cilungulu (as above)	—	—	—	1.23	1.87	1.68

Percentage of homesteads with livestock of any kind:

Temanghuku (own figures): 85.0%
Cilungulu (tax figures): 85.6%

Average number of persons in each homestead (children + adults):

Temanghuku (own figures): 9.4
Cilungulu (tax figures): 8.6 –

[58] One "stock-unit" equals 1 head of cattle, which is (arbitrarily) taken by the government veterinary department to be equivalent to 5 small stock. This has, of course, no relation to Gogo values and is quite unacceptable for any evaluation of stock in traditional terms. I use it here for convenience of comparison.

[59] Government figures make no distinction between livestock owned and those held under trusteeship contracts.

with more than thirty or forty head seldom keeps the whole herd in his homestead, although those with larger herds often keep many more than this number with them. It is not desirable, say Gogo, for people to know the number of cattle in one's control, and the problems of herding are much greater.[60] The owner thus gives out a fair proportion of his herd to trustees (*wakozigwa*). He hands over in front of witnesses not more than three or four head to each stock trustee, unless the herd is very large, when he may hand over twenty or thirty animals. This gives the latter the exclusive use of the milk and milk fat produced and a share of the meat on the death of an animal; or all of it if he lives a considerable distance away.[61] The hide (*nhyingo*) is always the property of the owner and must be taken to him as soon as is reasonably possible. The cattle and all offspring (collectively termed *nghozwa*) are also the property of the owner (*mugoli* or *munyang'ombe*) and the trustee is not entitled to any further rights over the livestock. If he fulfills his part of the contract satisfactorily, he may be given one or two beasts, but these are gifts (*ilumbo*) and do not accrue to him as a result of the contract.

The contract may be terminated by either party whenever they wish, without notice (but again before witnesses, *wahomelezi*). I have called this a trusteeship relationship because it implies no social or political inequality, apart from that simply of wealth differential in livestock. The contracts may be made with any-

[60] The cattle of one homestead always herd together. Homesteads with average herds join together (*kuhanza*) in neighborhood clusters to form herding groups. Herding groups are normally composed of closely related kin and affines in neighborhood clusters, analyzed in Chapter IV. The members of the various homesteads involved herd on a roster basis (*kuhanza ndimo*). Herding is carried out by young men and boys (*wazelelo*), although I have seen women herding in exceptional circumstances. A very rich man with a large herd at his homestead cannot usually join a group, and it is hard for him to find sufficient help in herding.

[61] Trusteeship cattle (*nghozwa*) are also allocated to the various houses (*nyumba*) of the trustee's wives.

body, but never include close, or even distant, agnates. Agnates, Gogo say, may not honor the contract when the owner goes to collect (*kudaya*) his livestock. A *nghozwa* contract with non-kin often entails (or at least did in the past) a blood covenant relationship (*ndugu yalusale*), a compact much closer in affection and cooperation than most agnatic ties.[62] But most *nghozwa* relationships are created between affinal kin of the same or different generation. They form an aspect of the close ties of cooperation and interdependence between affines which are analyzed in detail below. They also form but one part of a complex of relationships involving livestock exchange, rights, and obligations.

CATTLE VALUES AND AGRICULTURAL VALUES

I have outlined very briefly the economic role of cattle; the role of livestock in property and exchange relationships has been noted and will appear as an integral part of the following analysis of kinship. But what of Gogo values concerning cattle husbandry? It has been demonstrated for several East African peoples, who exhibit the "cattle-complex," that livestock do not only serve economic functions, nor are they just units of value in exchange transactions. There is also an emotional identification and proliferation of cultural attitudes, norms, and values concerning livestock. Cattle come to be used as symbols in a great variety of social contexts. Social relations are expressed in the "idiom" of cattle-culture. A multiplicity of terms and linguistic usages relating to cattle also serve as an index of their social significance.[63] Gogo culture includes all of these associations to some extent. But there is the further question in Gogo society as to how Gogo relate their values about cattle with the fact that they subsist primarily upon an agricultural economy, however precarious.

[62] I hope to publish material on the blood covenant relationship in Ugogo, which is still remembered but no longer practiced. It is referred to again in one or two contexts below. Cf. Beidelman (1963c).

[63] Cf. Evans-Pritchard (1940), pp. 41–48 *et passim;* (1953). This is also true of such non-Bantu groups in East Africa as the Masai, Baraguyu, etc., and several of the southern Bantu peoples.

In view of the importance of livestock as property in Gogo kinship relationships, I conclude this chapter with a brief comparison of Gogo cattle and agricultural values.

At the most material level, Gogo are aware that the ideological involvement they have with cattle and cattle husbandry is at variance with the facts of subsistence.[64] Nevertheless, they are also aware that, without livestock, the pattern of residential mobility and the creation and manipulation of a wide variety of kinship and affinal ties which is characteristic of their social system would not be possible. Wealth in livestock means gathering dependents about one within the homestead group, which is of fundamental importance in all spheres: economic, political, and ritual. This is achieved through not only the acquisition of wives and children but also the accretion of dependent kin, affines, and even non-relatives (*wewisa*).[65] Livestock really is the only medium in which wealth can be accumulated over a considerable length of time. With the storage methods available, grain can only be stored at the most for three years. After a series of good crops, wealth in grain is converted immediately to livestock by trading. Wealth in grain also lays one open more easily to accusations of sorcery and witchcraft than wealth in cattle, though both may result in this.

Thus, Gogo distinguish between wealth in livestock and

[64] The Bemba value hunting more than agriculture, as do the Ndembu of Zambia; in neither case is hunting the basis of the economy: see Richards (1939) and Turner (1957). But in the Gogo case, livestock is *property* and of basic importance in kinship relationships.

[65] Young Gogo men who are too poor to marry, or strangers from other Gogo areas or neighboring peoples who have suffered famines or other setbacks, often attach themselves permanently to the homesteads of rich men. The homestead head provides them with bridewealth to marry (*yakuwatoza*) and in return receives their services and increased prestige by their enforced residence in his homestead. The size of one's homestead (i.e. the number of one's dependents) is one of the few criteria of prestige in this egalitarian society. In homesteads of almost every man rich in livestock (200 or 300 head), one may find such young men who have "asked for a living" (*kulomba wikalo*).

"humans" (i.e. dependents), *sawo,* on the one hand, and wealth in grain (*uwuhemba*) and agricultural produce on the other. A man wealthy in grain which can continually be traded for live-stock is called *mupula,* or *mutwanga-wuhemba* (lit., the one who pounds grain); a man who devotes himself to the accumulation of livestock only through trade of other livestock and natural in-crease assisted by fertility medicines (*nghome yang'ombe*), is called *mugoli* or *"musawa-ng'ombe."* The latter is by far the more prestigious.

Yet Gogo values in other contexts must emphasize the necessity of diligence in cultivation and the correct use of crop-fertility medicines. Many successful and wealthy men in middle age re-late how, through the warnings of their parents, they turned to serious cultivation and accumulated livestock through trading in grain, rather than "following [the business of] cattle" (*kutyatya zing'ombe du*). Agricultural activity in Ugogo is heavy and often heartbreaking work; yet it is essential for existence. This am-biguity in values is illustrated by a song, common in most of central Ugogo, which is sung at agricultural work parties, with the hoes biting into the soil in rhythm:

Musawa-ng'ombe, nomutwanga-wuhemba,
The rich man in cattle, and the rich man in grain (lit., "the pounder of grain"),

Ciswanu cici?
Which thing is the better?

Wuhemba, gwe, woyi woyi. . . .
It is the sorghum, you see, *woyi woyi.* . . .

Cattle also serve to define the strongest distinctions between the sexes in symbolic terms. Although women play a prominent part in the distribution and use of livestock and have clearly defined rights in them, they do not "own" them as men do, ex-cept in some unusual circumstances. Cattle are men's business and consequently so also is "wealth" (*sawo*).[66] Women are

[66] See Rigby (1966a), (1967a).

thought to feel deprived of this legal right to the acquisition and accumulation of property in these terms, though they make up for this in active control and influence over the distribution of livestock. On the other hand, married women are almost in sole control of the production, storing, and consumption of grain. This dichotomy is also illustrated in a song sung at hoeing parties by both men and women, but composed by a woman as a drumming song (*lwimbo lwang'oma*):[67]

Mugoli wezing'ombe,
The person rich in cattle,

Ukwiwona kuko nemagombe gako,
There you are priding yourself with your cattle,

Waza longa cigoli-goli,
You have begun boasting of wealth.

Konghomaza gwe, nemagombe sina.
You will anger me, you; and cattle I have none.

Muzelelo mono yazize hamisia yaze,
The youth who comes at midday, let him come,

Kolanga cisomeko cemanjeci,
He will gaze at the wall-peg with the woman's bead waist-rings,

Nasemwa.
I forgot.[68]

CATTLE CULTURE, TERMINOLOGY, AND IDENTIFICATION

Gogo have considerable knowledge of good herding and husbandry. They know the good grasses for livestock and where they

[67] Drumming, and singing and dancing to drums, are exclusively feminine activities in Ugogo (see Chapter VI).

[68] That is: "The youth who came to see me (a woman) at home, at midday, will find only the waist-ring of beads (*injeci*) hung on a peg," for she is hoeing at the fields for her grain and livelihood. Thus, in her need to cultivate, she has forgotten his coming. It is expressed in this manner in spite of the fact that the activities of cultivation are almost equally divided between men and women.

may be found in abundance at certain times, particularly during the dry season when cattle may have to be moved many miles in search of grazing and water (*kuwudimizi*).[69] Penalties for burning grazing (*kupembela mahanze*) at any time of the year (but particularly during the dry season) are comparatively severe. They range from one goat to one or two head of cattle, depending upon the extent of the damage and negligence. The fine is eaten by the elders present at the spot of the burning.

Another fact also indicates the relation between the possession of livestock and the pattern of residential mobility. Water resources in all areas of Ugogo are open to anyone who may wish to use them, for themselves and their livestock, as long as reasonable care is taken in their preservation. This applies to streams (*makolongo*), water-pans (*malamba*), natural ponds, and *mapondelwa;*[70] and also (with some reservations) to wells (*masima*) sunk by men.

Although Gogo probably do not have as many cattle and small stock terms as some pastoral people of East Africa, their classification of livestock is quite elaborate and the permutations and combinations of the terms quite prolific. It is not possible to list these in detail here, but some examples are given to illustrate Gogo interest in, and attitudes toward, cattle.

Gogo call all livestock (cattle and small stock, but not donkeys) *mitugo;* sing., *mutugo*.[71] Cattle in general are *ng'ombe,*

[69] A grass which is particularly sought during the dry season is called *masupa*. Baraguyu, who are known for their knowledge of herding and livestock and who are culturally linked with the Kisongo Masai (see Beidelman, 1960), also move their herds and residence in search of this grass.

[70] *Mapondelwa* (sing., *ipondelwa* or *mhondelwa*) are artificial ponds formed by earth dams placed at strategic points in the very slightly undulating plain drainage areas of Ugogo. They catch and hold considerable quantities of rain water. Clearly they were constructed some time ago; but Gogo have no traditions of digging or planning them.

[71] Donkeys (*ndogowe*) are numerous in Gogo herds but tend to run rather wild. No one seriously cares for them or accumulates them. They are used as pack animals in grain trading (Gogo would never dream of

goats *mhene* and sheep *ngholo*. Within each of these categories, animals are classified according to color, age, sex, size, reproductive state, completeness, time of castration, individual peculiarities, and other characteristics of temper and affection. For example, very small calves, both male (*nhume*) and female (*nhyekulu*) are called *nyehe* (while it is suckling it may be called *nyonci* also). A female calf of about six months is called *nyehe wugwada,* and a heifer is called *ndama*. When a cow has calved once or twice it is *ngadada*. If it calves three times it becomes *mbuguma*. If it has calved twice and ceased to bear (*yitasale*) it becomes *nhasa*. A cow which reaches maturity without having calved is called *same*.

Similarly, there are a variety of terms used to describe males, by age, completeness, and time of castration. Young steers are *nzeku,* mature oxen *nghongolo*. A bull which is castrated fairly late is *nghalama* (which later may also become *nghongolo*) and a complete bull is *nghambaku*. There are many more terms. With the exception of one or two common terms, the words used to describe goats are quite distinct, and further terms are used to describe sheep at various sizes, ages, and reproductive states. Again, although there are one or two terms which describe some color configurations common to cattle and small stock, most of the color terms used for each are different.

Gogo color terminology (*mawala*) for animals is based not only on the colors involved but also their configuration. The system is very elaborate and only a few examples are given. A beast which is black or brown with a white head is *yina imala*. Thus such a cow, which has calved twice, is *ngadada yina imala*. A completely dark-brown beast (a dull brown with no red in it) is *yili imuli*. A goat of similar color is *yili wuswala*. A white beast with black on or around the neck is *yili wucinyinha*.[72] Men,

---

using cattle as pack or draught animals); they are not eaten, while all other domestic animals except dogs are.

[72] Some color terms are derived from other objects, animals or birds, which have the same color configurations. Thus *wucinyinha* is named after a large black and white heron called *ncinyinha*. Through this

even those with comparatively large herds, can remember the exact markings and descriptions of most of their animals. They also remember those given or received in bridewealth transactions and other exchanges, or in trusteeship contracts. Married women also have this knowledge of the animals in which they have rights, or even those given for them in bridewealth. This knowledge is invaluable in cases of theft or breach of contract in various transactions.

Gogo also mark their livestock with clan ear marks (*kutema mitozo*). Several clans may, however, have the same ear mark and the system is not as elaborate as that found among the "Nilo-Hamitic" Baraguyu or Kisongo Masai.[73] This does not mean that all the animals in a man's herd have his clan's ear mark, for cattle are constantly circulating between herds and their owners. But it is a further aid to identification.

Gogo do not have songs associated with clan markings or in praise of individual beasts, as do the Masai and Baraguyu. But men often have individual beasts in their herds for which they have special affection and which they discuss lovingly with their friends and contemporaries.

In certain contexts Gogo use cattle terms to refer to people. The implications of such usage in kinship terminology are examined in detail in Chapter VII.[74] Apart from this, in general usage, women may affectionately be referred to as "cows"; and even their reproductive state may jokingly be referred to by the cattle terms noted above. Men who have distinguished themselves in any way are often referred to as "bulls" (*nghambaku*), or the term may be used simply in distinguishing men from women (see above, p. 42). Such usages are not surprising in a society in

---

association, livestock of some colors become avoidance objects (*mizilo*, see Chapter III) of some sub-clans.

[73] Cf. Beidelman (1960), p. 260. Baraguyu cattle ear marks (*olponoto;* pl., *ilponot*) are very much elaborated and associated with clans; praise songs (*osingolio*) concerning cattle are an important part of Baraguyu cultural attitudes toward livestock (Beidelman, 1965).

[74] See pp. 253–254.

which relationships of the greatest importance (affinal relation-ships) are created by the passage of women and livestock (in opposite directions) between groups of kin. But it is in the sphere of ritual that the strongest (if only implicit) identifications of human beings (or spirits) with livestock are made.

When a propitiation with beer (*wujimbi wemisambwa*) for the spirits of the dead (*milungu*) is being performed, a trough of beer lees (*manhindya*) or mud is made around a certain pole in the front room (*ikumbo*) of the homestead. This trough is called *mulambo* (pl., *milambo*), the term used for the clay troughs made near wells to water livestock. Beer is poured into this trough while the spirits are called, and they are said to "drink" from it. When the propitiation is over, a breach is made in the wall of the trough in the direction from which the clan founders came, so that the beer flows out in that direction. This breach is called *ideha,* the "gate of the cattle byre." Further, the propitia-tion must be held early in the morning, before the cattle go out of the byre to pasture:

We propitiate in the early morning because, we say, the spirits of the dead are still asleep (*milungu yikali yigonile*). If we let them disperse, when the sun has risen some distance in the sky (*izuwa liwalice*), the spirits are gone. If one delays in the morning, one must wait until the evening (when the cattle return to the byre), when the spirits have returned to the gravestones. When the cattle have gone out in the morning, the spirits have dispersed (*milungu yeyagala*); they will not hear your words.

It may also be noted that the best way to propitiate the spirits is by the sacrifice of cattle or other livestock, although only beer is used in minor propitiations (which are very frequent).[75]

CONCLUSION

In this chapter I have attempted to sketch in the cultural back-ground of Gogo economy and values against which the following

[75] Some aspects of Gogo religion and cosmology are discussed in Rigby (1966a), (1966b), (1967a), (1967d), (1968a).

analysis of kinship will be set. I have indicated Gogo dependence upon agriculture and provided a glimpse of the necessary diversification of interests and activities in that field. But in contradistinction to cultivation is cattle husbandry, and the attitudes and values concerning livestock predominate over those attaching to agriculture. All of these values influence Gogo cosmology, but cattle are much more closely associated symbolically with kinship and the sphere of men. Yet women play a major part in the distribution and control of livestock. Women are also not excluded by any strong prohibitions against physical contact with livestock, and they may even herd them.[76] Within the cattle-owning unit of the homestead group, livestock are divided up among the various matricentral houses, the members of which have exclusive use of them. Thus women intrude directly into the "world of cattle," both in respect of distribution and husbandry. Because of this women are thought to feel more acutely their legal inability to "own" livestock and thus to have wealth. In the final analysis it is men who exchange cattle for women.

In a sense, Gogo ownership of their herds both necessitates as well as facilitates the pattern of residential mobility which is essential and characteristic of their society. Livestock provide the means whereby new relationships of cooperation and interdependence are set up by homestead groups when they change residence. Yet one of the primary "immediate" causes of residential mobility is the quest for grazing and water for livestock. But in the long run, livestock are essential in a situation of dependence upon precarious agriculture; and also, Gogo cannot even pretend to subsist only upon the products of their livestock.

Thus, ecological adjustment is more than a mere "limiting factor" in Gogo social structure; the residential mobility and the independence of homestead groups which result from this ecologi-

[76] Women not only herd cattle when men are not available, as I have noted, but are obliged to on certain occasions. One such occasion is when cattle disease affects the herds; women ceremonially herd the cattle for two days, dressed as men (*kudima cahola*) to effect a cure (see Rigby, 1967a).

cal adjustment are of fundamental structural importance. But before we proceed to this analysis, the wider outlines of Gogo kinship and politico-ritual systems (clans, ritual leadership, and ritual areas) must be drawn.

III
Clanship and the
Ritual Areas

All Gogo clans have histories which link them, through their
founders, with one of many neighboring peoples. These histories
are narrated by elders on occasions when clan affiliation is important, such as funerals and weddings. The elders record the
origin, migrations, and activities of the clan founders and also
provide explanations of particular clan names, sub-clan names,
and avoidances, or prohibitions, linked with the sub-clan names.
Most "complete" clan histories also provide a rationale for activities common to all Gogo, such as circumcision, inter-clan joking-partnerships, and "perpetual kinship" links between members
of particular clans in particular areas. They are primarily concerned, however, with recounting how each clan initially established (or took over from another) ritual leadership (*wutemi*)
in the ritual areas or "countries" (*yisi*) in which they have it.

Although this study is not primarily concerned with political
relations and the political community, it is necessary to sketch
some aspects of clan affiliation and its features. The members of
Gogo clans are residentially mobile and do not necessarily reside in the areas in which their clans have ritual precedence.
Thus, ritual areas and clan affiliation in Ugogo are two cross-
cutting principles which furnish some "anchor-points" of identification in a society with no political centralization. In order to
appreciate this fully, some analysis of aspects of clan history is
necessary.[1] Gogo clans are not localized corporate groups, never

[1] The Mandari of the Sudan are another "multi-origin" group, although

Cattle and Kinship among the Gogo

act as total groups in any situation, and are not even completely exogamous. Neither are there any *corporate* unilineal descent groups on a lower level of comprehensiveness. However, they provide Gogo with the primary categories into which all members of the society are classified and also form the basis for a substantial variety of relationships between individual persons and groups. Much of the Gogo conceptualization of these relationships is embodied in the clan myths and histories.

Clan affiliation also forms the major aspect of the ideology of patrilineal descent and influences the kinship system through such factors as choice of marriage partner, the operation of kin and affinal roles and property relations, apart from being the foundation upon which most communal ritual activity is organized. Clan affiliation is the most permanent identification available to members of widely scattered residential groups, within the continually changing pattern of neighborhood populations. But the territorial dimension of clanship is shown primarily in the "bounded" ritual areas, which are of an importance in the Gogo social system equal to that of the broader descent categories. The description of these ritual areas is not a matter of historical reconstruction. They exist as functioning units today as they did before external contact, colonial penetration and, recently, administration by local government bodies under an independent Tanzanian government.[2] But the powers and functions of ritual leaders have naturally been considerably diminished and altered. Some of the analysis presented in this chapter is thus necessarily

---

their political organization in relation to territorial units is entirely different from that of the Gogo. Buxton (1963, p. 18) records the histories of the main Mandari groups and says: "This history is very important for a study of present-day political relations, because it in fact records the way certain groups of people moved around in the past, who these migrating people were, how they regarded one another, and the relationships between them which eventually emerged."

[2] The local government bodies have overlaid the traditional Gogo ritual areas at successive historical phases with different types of administrative hierarchy, political units, roles, and processes. I discuss these processes of change in Rigby (in press).

based upon what elders remember and upon the little written historical evidence available. Most of the analysis, however, describes the contemporary situation.

CLAN HISTORIES AND THEIR SIGNIFICANCE

Several previous writers on Gogo ethnography have discussed Gogo clans and their histories, but few have done so in a systematically comprehensive manner.[3] There has been a great deal of conjectural history written on the "recent" origins and mixed "ethnic composition" of the Gogo people, because most Gogo genealogies are "telescoped" and of very limited time-depth. Furthermore, all of these observers have recorded the names of only the numerically larger clans, in or near the areas in which they themselves were working.[4] It would be tedious and

[3] For example: Paulssen (1922); Claus (1911), pp. 61–64; Hartnoll (1942) and (1932); Culwick (1931); Carnell (1955a); Cory (1951), pp. 1–2; Schaegelen (1938), pp. 198–203; Mnyampala (1954), pp. 3–55. The last two writers offer the most knowledgeable and valuable descriptions.

[4] Thus Cole, who lived at Mpwapwa (Mhamvwa) on the southeastern border of Ugogo, lists thirty three Gogo ". . . clans, with corresponding Muziro (things forbidden to be eaten or used)." See Cole (1902), pp. 305–306. But on the list are represented clans (*mbeyu*) and sub-clans names (*milongo*), and no distinction is made between them. Consequently, descent categories of different order are juxtaposed. Schaegelen lists 27 "chiefdoms" (*chefferies*), the names of the 17 associated "chiefly families," and the areas and directions from which they came to Ugogo. See Schaegelen (1938), p. 203. Those listed by him are confined mainly to western and west-central Ugogo, and most of the ritual areas of north and northeastern Ugogo are omitted. He also refers to the totally different list and distribution given by Claus (1911), pp. 61–64. Mnyampala, on the other hand, deals only with those clans which successfully maintained government chiefships during the period of British colonial administration. He explicitly discusses only these clans, and again only those in what are now Manyoni and Dodoma districts. He lists 25 Gogo "chiefdoms" and their 18 "ruling clans" (some of the chiefdoms have subdivisions of a common clan as ruling group), and gives an outline of these "clans'" histories. See Mnyampala (1954), pp. 18–75. All of these authors overlook the real significance of Gogo clanship and the considerably greater number of ritual areas associated with Gogo clans.

irrelevant here to compare in detail these previous writings with
my own material. I thus present my own findings and note differences and additions from the sources cited in the form of foot-
notes.

I have recorded, in varying degrees of detail, information on
eighty-five patrilineal clans in Ugogo; that is, clans whose members reside in what is now generally accepted by the people themselves to be "Ugogo," and who share the culture of "Cigogo."
Many of these clans are also represented among neighboring cultures and peoples, and I have indicated that the "cultural" boundaries of Ugogo are by no means marked.

Gogo elders realize that they can enumerate only a fraction of
the number of clans represented in the area. Apart from those
which are represented in their own areas and areas in which they
have at some time resided, they can usually name only the numerically more predominant clans or those whose members are
renowned for some peculiar qualities, traditional and modern.[5]
But because of their residential mobility (and Gogo are also good
travelers), the average person's knowledge of the physical and
"ritual" topography of large areas of a relatively large country is
good, particularly in the case of men. I was unable to reside in,
or even to visit, a number of the ritual areas; but most of the
eighty-five clans listed and the histories obtained were from personal contact with members of the particular clans living in other
areas, or other reliable informants. There are probably a larger
number of clans than this figure suggests, and ritual areas are
probably even more numerous. Most, but not all, clans have, or
claim, ritual leadership in some area within Ugogo. Some clans
have several ritual areas associated with their sub-divisions, along

[5] Among these are such qualities as honey-gathering (*kubakula uwuci*),
knowledge of medicines for stock fertility (*nghome yang'ombe*), metal-
working (*wutyani*), and witchcraft power (*wuhawi*); and more recently,
success in government chiefships and politics. For example, the Nyamzura
clan has ritual control in a small area of what later became Mvumi
chiefdom, and during the British administration had government chiefship over the whole area. The members of this clan are notorious for
their alleged rain-stopping capabilities (*wukoma-mvula*).

the lines either of different sub-clan names (*milongo*) or smaller patrilineal descent groups which may be called "maximal lineages" (*milango:* see below).

Through the eighty-five clans are distributed unevenly a total of fifty-three sub-clan names, to which are linked thirty-one prohibitions or avoidances (*mizilo*). So it is evident that the names of the sub-clans of some clans are common to other clans, and that some sub-clans share common avoidances. However, individuals with the same sub-clan name (*mulongo*) and avoidance object, but who belong to different clans (*mbeyu*), will not consider each other kin, nor use kin terms of address to each other. Nor do they act together in any context if this is the only link between them. The difficulties presented by the concept of *mulongo* will be better appreciated after a description of the content and significance of clan histories. It is in the histories that Gogo ideas of the historical acquisition of these various category designations may be seen.

It has been suggested by several writers that most Gogo "ruling clans" are descendants of Hehe founders.[6] In a recent discussion of the movements of peoples and the "spread" of territorial/political chiefship ("ntemiship") in Tanganyika, Roland Oliver states (primarily on the basis of clan traditions collected by administrative officers from members of "ruling families" and recorded in district notebooks): "Half the ruling class [*sic*] of Ugogo came from Uhehe during the second half of the eighteenth century." [7] While I do not here dispute the dating of these move-

[6] Writing of the clan traditions of "ruling families" in the Dodoma District Book, an administrator states: "Over central Ugogo the people are mainly descended from the Wahehe and other tribal fragments, pushing up from the south, possibly as a result of the Angoni invasions." Of the seventeen "ruling clans" (*familles régnantes*) given by Schaegelen (1938), p. 203, he states that 7 come from Hehe ("south"), 4 from "Ituru" (i.e. Nyaturu, "west"), three from Itumba ("east") and one from Burungi ("north"). The 18 clans whose histories are recorded by Mnyampala (1954) are derived as follows: 7 from Hehe, 3 from Kimbu, 2 from Nyaturu and Ng'omvia, and 1 each from Sukuma, Ngulu, and Sangu.

[7] Roland Oliver, in Oliver and Mathew (1963), p. 197.

Table 3. Claimed cultural origins of Gogo clans

Total clans: 85 Area of origin	Total origins recorded: 67 No. of clans from each area and people
Hehe (south)	21
Ng'omvia (north and Ugogo)[8]	8
Bulungi (Burungi) (north)	4
Cimbu (Kimbu) (southwest)	4
Itumba (east)[9]	3
Nyaturu (west-northwest)	2
Taturu (Tatog) (northwest)	2
Kamba (north)	2
Sandawi (north)	2
Ngulu (Nguu) (northeast)	2
Sagala (southeast)	2
Itiliko ("Hehe") (south)	2
Fyomi (Gorowa) (north)	2
Mbugwe (north)	1
Masai (Humha) (northeast)	1
Ilanji (north)	1
Zigula (east)	1
Bena (south)	1
Nyamwezi (west)	1
Sukuma (northwest)	1
Itusi (west)	1
Icinga (south?)	1
Sangu (south)	1
Manghala (north-northwest and Ugogo)[10]	1
Total areas of origin: 24 Total origins recorded: 67 Total clans: 85	67

[8] Several clans in north-central Ugogo claim to be Ng'omvia. There is no other cultural group or people in Tanzania with this name. Remnants of Ng'omvia clans still speak their own non-Bantu language and try to maintain some non-Gogo cultural identity. Such is Fweda, the ritual leader of Wuselya in north-central Ugogo. Most Ng'omvia, however, have been completely Gogo-ized. But Fweda spoke Cigogo "like a foreigner" and claimed that his clan's founders came originally through Bulungi,

ments, it should be noted that the "ruling power" of these clans has been overstated in the case of Ugogo. This is a direct result of the recent creation, by the colonial administration, of government chiefships with considerable political power. With this has gone an association with Uhehe, whose spectacular and recently evolved centralized political organization served as a model for the application of the policy of indirect rule in colonial Tanzania. Nevertheless, the single most common derivation given by Gogo clans is Uhehe, although it is by no means the origin of the majority. Of the eighty-five clans I listed, I have sufficient information on the traditions of sixty-seven, and the distribution of their origins is set out in Table 3.

Gogo clan histories are long and involved and contain many dramatic incidents (some of them obviously mythical) which are given full play in their presentation. Particularly at large funerals and inheritance ceremonies where elders represent the various clan connections of the deceased, they vie with each other to produce the better and more effective historical account and so "claim" the inheritance (see Chapter VII). Gogo distinguish between the retelling of historical events, which is *kusimula,* and the telling of folktales and stories for pleasure, which is *kusima.* In central Ugogo, however, the narration of clan histories at in-

---

Sandawi, and Zigula, but were of "Arabic" origin (*cili Waalabu*). The Ng'omvia language appears to have affinities with Burungi/Iraqw, and has recently been classified as "Southern Cushitic," mainly on the basis of research carried out by Dr. Chris Ehret. Some Ng'omvia groups reside in Sandawi, as I learned in a personal communication from Mr. E. Tenraa. See also Claus (1910).

[9] The term "Itumba" is used by Gogo to denote anyone coming from the neighboring peoples to the east. This means that "Itumba" clans claim to have founders who came from Kaguru or Sagara. But there are also clans *called* Itumba in Cigogo, and their differentiation is given in Appendix A. A substantial number of Kaguru and Sagara clans claim origin in Uhehe also: see Oliver, in Oliver and Mathew (1963), p. 197.

[10] The Manghala are said to be the first Gogo clan and to have been hunters in the area before the present clans arrived: see Mnyampala (1954), pp. 3–5.

heritance ceremonies is often called *kukomanghoma*. This literally denotes a way of walking, when one approaches something reluctantly and hesitatingly, and refers to the extremely lengthy and elaborate way in which the elders recount clan histories at such ceremonies. The whole night before the actual installation of the heir is taken up with the public narration of clan histories. The corresponding nouns are *nghomo*, which only in this context may be translated as "verbal histories," elaborately related in public, and *simo* (sing., *lusimo*), folktales or stories. This distinction is not always explicit, but it is generally accepted that *nghomo* are about the "real" past, are of interest to adults, and are told at funerals, marriages, or other gatherings; *simo* are tales told to children in specific story-telling situations. Both are said to require the powers of good narrative, but invention and its accompanying reputation in story-telling is usually reserved for *simo*.

The several versions of a clan's historical traditions given by different elders at different times vary considerably in detail. This is especially so because the members of Gogo clans are so dispersed and do not gather as a group at any time. But the over-all outline is the same in each, if the speaker knows the correct form.[11] The places where certain events take place vary, and sometimes even the actors involved; but the same events are always present and carry more or less the same significance in each version.[12] One elder's version of Pulu clan history is given in Appendix B. It is a shortened account of one among many lengthy and detailed narratives I collected, either with the specific purpose of writing them down, or those spoken at funerals by elders when they were unaware that I was doing so. Thus, the

[11] Richards (1960), p. 178, says of clan histories and myths in general in pre-literate societies: ". . . a myth which validates a political claim must be preserved in its authentic form if it is to act as a charter; it may in fact have to be preserved in a particular form of words and some of the myths told are long and elaborate."

[12] For an interesting exposition of varying versions of clan histories and traditions and their significance, see Buxton (1963), pp. 18–33.

versions I collected of this and other clan histories were given
in widely varying places, times, and contexts. They all exhibit
a remarkable consistency of outline.[13]

Owing to their theory of the diverse origins of clans, Gogo do
not have a generally known myth explaining the origins of the
first human beings. But in contradiction of the diverse origin
theory, there are one or two myths of human genesis which are
current in Ugogo. The "traditional" myths put forward the idea
that two individuals, male and female, came out of the earth
where a great rock split in two at a place called Cibwepanduka,
and then populated the earth. Another myth is a Gogo-ized version of the Biblical story of Genesis and was given to me by a
diviner whose sons were Catholic converts. The Gogo seldom
find it necessary to go so far in historical explanation. The
"ultimate" explanation of the founding of Gogo clans is assumed
simply to be that for a certain reason the clan founder left the
area and people of his birth and came to Ugogo.

Gogo clan histories are concerned with the explanation of
other kinds of problems. It may be seen from the typical history
given in Appendix B that it establishes the following: the identity
of the clan founder and the people he came from; the justification
for his leaving there (in moral terms) and coming to Ugogo; the
intelligence and quickness of the founder and his fellows in surviving the hazards of the migrations; the shedding of all kin and
other ties with the group of origin; the supernatural powers and
insight possessed by the founder, and his constant association with
ritual leaders and their homesteads throughout the migration. The
clan history also justifies the transference of political and ritual
rights in a particular area to the founder, either through adopted
kin links or newly established affinal links.[14] It also establishes

[13] I have noted that Gogo homestead heads are *ipso facto* "elders." The
repositories of clan history are usually senior elders, and young men come
to funerals to learn.

[14] The importance of establishing new ties in new areas (through
fictitious kin links or the creation of affinal ties) for Gogo social structure in general will emerge clearly in later chapters.

joking-partnership links with some clans (usually those with ritual leadership in neighboring areas) and "perpetual kinship" with others.[15] The "supernatural" characteristic of clan founders is emphasized in some clan histories: they do not die but simply disappear.[16] Clan founders' names are seldom called in propitiation ceremonies, and then only in those held by the possessors of the ritual leadership and in situations concerning the welfare of the whole ritual area.

In spite of individual variations, Gogo clan histories do fall broadly into the three-phase division suggested by Richards as characteristic of such histories:[17] a first phase of not very detailed but stylized origins and journeys; a second phase of lineage differentiation and telescoping of genealogies; and a third of "remembered" genealogical history. The general form of Pulu clan history is diagrammatically represented in Figure 2, and that of another clan in Figure 3.[18] The three-phase division is clear. Gogo laymen not concerned directly with the small-depth agnatic group in each clan which holds the ritual leadership (see below), usually omit altogether the middle phase of lineage differentiation. They count two or three generations from the eldest living member and then add on the name of the clan founder. The exact relationship between the earliest remembered lineal ancestor and the clan founder is thought unimportant. Gogo either profess to be ignorant of it or simply say, "He was a grandson" (*yali mwizukulu*), which implies descent from two to any number of generations in depth.[19] The spirits of the dead

[15] See pp. 88–93 below, and Rigby (1968a).

[16] This disappearance is a common feature of clan-founding myths in many areas, including the interlacustrine kingdoms of East Africa. Ruling dynasties at certain phases of history simply disappear; for example, the Cwezi dynasty among the Nyoro of Uganda (Beattie 1960).

[17] Richards (1960), p. 178.

[18] See the representation of Nyagatwa clan history, pp. 74, 95 below.

[19] Gogo do not differentiate kinsmen terminologically beyond the second ascending generation. The terms for "grandfather" and "grandmother" are used generally for "our ascendants" to any number of generations (see Chapter VII and Appendix D).

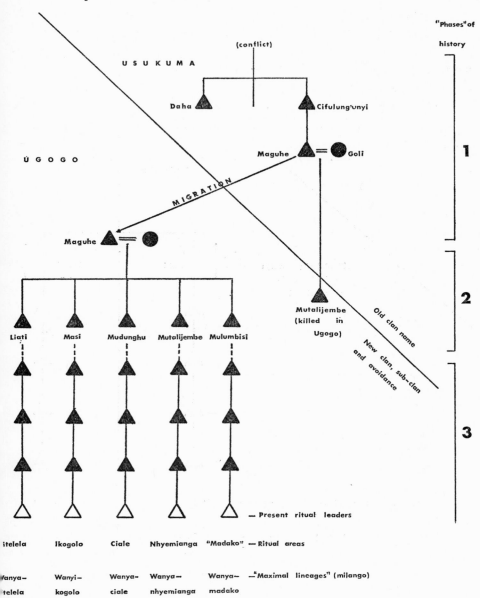

Figure 2. Diagrammatic representation of Pulu clan history and ritual areas

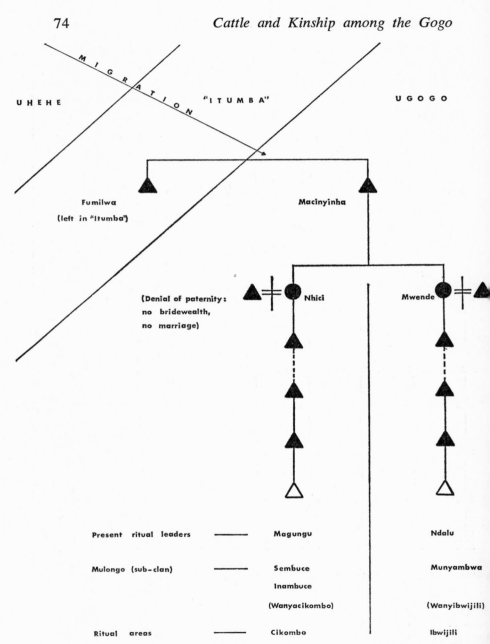

Figure 3. Diagrammatic representation of Nyagatwa clan history in Cikombo an
Ibwijili

(*milungu*) called by Gogo during propitiation rituals are those of a great variety of kin, including ancestors of affines of the present living generations. Thus, the spirits of *lineal* ancestors called seldom go back further than three or four generations (see below).

It is also clear that clan history emphasizes the severance of all previous links the clan founder may have had. He acquires new clan names and affiliations and avoidances; he becomes Gogo and different to what he was before (see Appendix B). The almost exclusively ritual functions of Gogo ritual leaders, such as in rain-making, appear rare in neighboring cultural areas where political chiefship is more common, though these chiefs do have ritual functions. But the character of Gogo ritual leadership is acquired, according to the histories, on coming into the Gogo cultural milieu. The clan histories serve to establish claims to ritual precedence in the territorial and political sphere. This is of fundamental importance in a discussion of the only politico-ritual office (above that of homestead head) available in the Gogo social system: that of ritual leader (*mutemi*).

In concluding this section it might be noted that Gogo clan histories should not be treated *merely* as mythical charters. There is a good deal of mutually corroborative detail about *some* events in Gogo history as recorded in different clan histories. This is not the place to go into this problem in detail. But, in spite of their mythical and stylized elements, these legends are of definite historical value in the study of political relations among the ritual areas of Ugogo.[20] However, these questions concern primarily

[20] Since Malinowski's formulation of the concept of "mythical charter" and the later development of functional analysis, many anthropological monographs have provided functional interpretations of myths and historical traditions in pre-literate societies. But the functional interpretation of myths and legends can seriously be objected to on epistemological grounds. The structural study of myth is yet in its infancy (cf. Lévi-Strauss (1958), pp. 227–255). But this does not imply that all pre-literate "history" must simply be assumed to be myth as far as sociological analysis is concerned and that the interpretation of clan history on another

the agnatic groups within each clan holding ritual precedence within each ritual area. Some clans do not have ritual control anywhere, and in any case the average homestead owner is not of the same clan and agnatically related to the ritual leader of the area in which he resides. But clan affiliation in Gogo has aspects other than those of ritual and very limited political authority in territorial areas. It is to these other aspects that I now turn.

THE CONCEPT OF *MBEYU* (CLAN)

I have already noted that Gogo did not until very recently refer to themselves as such. There is no indigenous concept of "tribe" or "people," other than a vague one of basically common language and culture (Cigogo). The immediate question a person will ask of a stranger is, "Of what clan are you?" [21] The word I translate here as "clan" is *mbeyu,* which means literally, "seed," "kind," or "type." [22] The term denotes a classification into the most fundamental categories possible, and the clan histories of diverse origins already discussed emphasize this.[23] In some contexts, the category of persons denoted as being of "one clan"

---

level is irrelevant. Evans-Pritchard (1962), p. 53, distinguishes between myth and history: ". . . myth and history are in important respects different in character, not just in the degree to which they can be substantiated by appeal to evidence or the laws of natural science. Hence a story may be true yet mythical in character, and a story may be false and yet historical in character." He suggests (p. 50): "We have not yet learnt . . . how to treat historical material sociologically." See also Vansina (1965).

[21] It is usually phrased in the plural, *"Muli wambeyu ci?"* ("Of what clan are you people?"). The relative emphasis given to clan and sub-clan names in different parts of Ugogo varies considerably. I will refer to this again.

[22] Gogo nowadays freely equate the word *mbeyu* with the Swahili *kabila,* "tribe": a smaller group than "a people" or "nation" (*taifa*), and of a different category from "community" (*jamaa*). The word *"kabila"* is also commonly used for "kind" or "type."

[23] It should be noted that different clans which claim origin from the same area outside Ugogo are not necessarily considered related in any way. They have distinct founders in Ugogo.

(*mbeyu imonga*) may be said to have "one trunk" or "stem" (*isina limonga*).[24] The relationship between these two terms and their difference from that of sub-clan name (to which I devote a section below) is illustrated by the following. The ritual leader of the Loje ritual area, who belongs to the Nyagatwa clan, told me that there are other Nyagatwa with their own ritual areas elsewhere in Ugogo (actually in several places: see Appendix A). But although the latter may have different sub-clan names, they were all of one clan or "trunk." He said:

The family [*ikungugo:* i.e. the actual ancestors of all the Nyagatwa groups] from which our earliest ancestors came, all of us, I am not sure of, because we Nyagatwa are so many. Some are over there at Ludi, some elsewhere. With some we share a sub-clan name, with others we are joking partners.[25] But in their original stem (*isina lyawo*), whence all our founding ancestors came, they are all one (*ndugu yawo imonga*).

The categorization of all persons into clans is so fundamental to Gogo thought that it is inconceivable that anyone should not have some clan affiliation, sub-clan name, and avoidance.[26] Ideally, this affiliation is determined by patrilineal descent. It may be noted that Gogo have no jural concept of illegitimacy.[27] A child in whatever circumstances has a legal *pater* and therefore a clan affiliation and its linked elements.[28] The possibility of clan

[24] The term *isina* (pl., *masina*) means the trunk or the base of a tree, or the stem of a plant. It also denotes the clump of grain stalks which result from the Gogo technique of planting several seeds together in the shallow hole made by one stroke of the hoe.

[25] Joking partnerships usually exist between different *clans,* but if one clan is sufficiently dispersed and differentiated by sub-clan and avoidances, joking partnerships may occur within it, as in this case. See Rigby (1968a).

[26] This, of course, is true of all clan systems, which constitute what may be termed "kinship by assimilation." For a very similar concept, in this case of matrilineal clanship among the Tonga of Northern Rhodesia, see Colson (1962), p. 69.

[27] Cf. Cory (1951), ¶192.

[28] This is fully described in Chapter VII. See also Chapter VI.

affiliation through uterine descent, in spite of the ideology of patrilineal descent, is illustrated in a historical case later in this chapter and an observed case in Chapter VII.

Slaves or captives taken in war (*wawanda*) invariably adopted their masters' clans. Men, either Gogo or "foreigners" (*wako-nongo*), who have no property or relatives to help them after a disaster (such as a famine), adopt the clan of those to whom they go to "ask for a living" (*kulomba wikalo*). This is symbolized by their adoption, after a time, of the spirits of the dead (*milungu*) of their master or mentor, with the rejection of their own. In the next generation (their children) the assimilation is complete. The following case illustrates this:

During a recent bad famine [sixteen years ago] which affected most of Ugogo and Usandawi to the north, many Sandawi came into Ugogo in an attempt to live by hunting and selling the meat to more fortunate Gogo. [The Sandawi are renowned hunters.] Tamba, a young Sandawi man of about 23 at the time, became friendly with a Gogo age-mate in Mugu neighborhood and asked him to find a homestead head who would take him in. The Gogo youth took him to his own mother's brother, a fairly rich man with a large homestead, and the adoption was arranged. Tamba worked at herding for several years. The homestead head arranged a marriage and paid bridewealth for his adopted "son" [*yakamutoza*]. The young couple had several children. Despite the short period involved and certain disagreements between the two men, the assimilation is considered complete. An elder remarking on the case told me: "If Tamba were to fall sick, he *might* call upon the spirits of his fathers who bore him [i.e. his Sandawi progenitors], but also the spirits of that person who has "saved" him [*mono amuwika mwigoda;* lit., "who placed him upon a stool"].

The importance of acceptance within a homestead/domestic unit in effecting this assimilation is discussed in Chapter V. There are a number of recognized techniques through which a youth may "ask for a living" without running the risk of verbal refusal by the homestead head concerned.

If two persons living in the same neighborhood and in daily

contact with each other have no traceable kin or affinal connections between them, common clan membership will be recognized as "relating" them. If they are men of approximately the same age, they will address each other as *"alaba,"* the term of address commonly used between paternal parallel cousins. But they would not usually be referred to as "being parallel cousins" (*wali cana cawasewo*) but rather as "being relatives" (*wali ndugu*) or as "sharing one clan" (*wahanjire mbeyu*).

Similarly, unrelated persons who belong to clans between which there are special "perpetual kinship" links recognized in one neighborhood or more, will address each other by the appropriate kinship terms.[29] For example, Mukunya belongs to a clan (Hehe, Kami) who are in the category "sister's sons"

[29] I use with reservations the term "perpetual kinship" for these inter-clan links. But they are permanent in the sense that they are enshrined in the past history of each clan and provide a basis for relationships between individual members of each clan who are not related in any other way. In Gogo these links do not depend upon "positional succession" to political roles (such as lineage heads), as is the case among some Central and East African peoples: cf. Richards (1950); Gray (1953); Cunnison (1956). There are no such lineage leadership roles in the Gogo political system. However, Gogo inter-clan kinship links do persist beyond those of the type specifically excluded from the category "perpetual kinship" by Cunnison (*ibid.*, p. 30). "Perpetual kinship" relationships in Ugogo *are* between clans, not between local groups like "villages." And they are carried on beyond one generation, although any particular relationship between two clans may have currency only in certain localized areas. Hence, although it excludes "positional succession" to leadership roles, the Gogo concept closely approximates in other respects the kind of relationship called "perpetual kinship" among the Luapula peoples. Cunnison's statement (*ibid.*, p. 44) could equally well apply to the Gogo relationship: "It appears to function . . . mainly in maintaining direct relationships between the groups . . . [which are not corporate: p. 47] . . . and allowing members to place themselves readily in kinship relationships to each other." Further, links between ritual areas and ritual leaders are expressed in these terms in Luapula (*ibid.*, p. 45) as they are in Gogo (see below). Clan joking-partnerships also fall into the same category (Cunnison, *ibid.*, p. 48; and below for Gogo). I discuss this problem in greater detail in a forthcoming volume on Gogo-politico-religious structure; but cf. Rigby (1968a).

(*wehwa*) to the Itumba (Munongwa) clan to which Masenha belongs. These two elders are rich homestead heads in the same neighborhood and ritual area. Mukunya refers to Masenha as his "mother's brother" (*kuku'ye*) and Masenha refers to him as his "sister's son" (*mwihwa'we*); they address each other as *"bulayi,"* the reciprocal term of address between these categories of kin.

Ideally, Gogo clans are exogamous, and Gogo say it is "bad" (*vibi*) to marry someone of the same clan. It is probable that the numerically smaller clans with few sub-divisions conform to this norm. I was unable to confirm this statistically as the neighborhoods I worked in were populated mainly by members of several numerically predominant clans. However, I recorded a significant number of intraclan marriages in all of the areas I visited and lived in (see Chapter VI). When faced with this fact, Gogo say that it is possible to marry someone of the same clan, but definitely not if they have the same sub-clan name as well, or if they belong to the same "maximal lineage" (*mulango:* see below). But again these marriages occur, although in most of these cases the existing relationship must be ritually severed (*kuwulaga ndugu;* lit., "to kill the relationship"). This ceremony is called *cifuta*. But *cifuta* is also performed for marriages between cross-cousins, although it is more frequent in marriages between agnates. In the final analysis, even Gogo define the rules of exogamy basically in terms of the mutual obligations involved over rights in cattle paid in bridewealth, and not in terms of clanship or smaller unilineal descent groups. Nevertheless, the norm of clan exogamy is an immediate subjective response expressed by Gogo, and is seen to be not universally adhered to only on deeper consideration.

I have noted that there is variation in the emphasis laid upon clan and sub-clan affiliation in different parts of Ugogo. In south and east-central Ugogo the most common categorization of persons is on the basis of their *mulongo,* or sub-clan name, rather than their clan, although both concepts are present throughout the area. The concept of *mulongo* requires deeper examination.

THE CONCEPT OF *MULONGO* (SUB-CLAN NAME)

I have translated the Gogo word *mulongo* (pl., *milongo*) as "sub-clan name" because most clans are sub-divided into further categories, each of which is referred to as a *mulongo* and has a distinct name.[30] But I have noted that some *mulongo* names are very common and occur in several different clans (see Appendix A). Equally, a good proportion of clans have only one *mulongo*. In some senses, *mulongo* affiliation may be said to cut across clan affiliation, as is the case with the associated avoidances. But this would not be the Gogo view. The same *mulongo* in different clans is usually associated with the same avoidance; Gogo who have the same avoidance and *mulongo* name would feel they had some kind of common origin, as do people with the same personal name (who address each other as *walina*). But they would not consider each other kin and would not normally use terms of address or reference to each other purely on the basis of this link. They have also to be of the same clan (*mbeyu*) before "kinship" by "assimilation" is established.

I have shown that the concept of *mbeyu* (clan) is easily (and explicitly) associated with the ideas of "seed," "kind," or "type." The other referents of *mulongo* are more obscure. Conceptually, it is closely associated with both the ideas of avoidance (*muzilo*) and "clan oath" (*cilahilo*), which I describe below. An informant, speculating on the term, said:

[30] The position is roughly as follows: of the 85 clans listed, 25 have two or more sub-divisions with different *mulongo* names; 37 have only one *mulongo* and are thus not sub-divided on this basis; on 23 I have insufficient information to judge one way or the other. These figures should be taken as of extremely limited accuracy. Although I have always enquired of my informants about *milongo,* I may not have been informed of all the *milongo* of some clans recorded here as having only one.

I think *mulongo,* the word, comes from *kulonga* [to speak]. Because when there is something you love very much [*cinhu cono wendile hawaha*], you use it as an oath [*ukwilaha cinhu cico;* that is, you speak it out in difficult situations]. So that object comes to be like a relative [*ndugu*] and so you may then "avoid it" in certain ways [*udahile kuzila cico*]. Let me give you an example: it is as if you swore by your "sister" or your "mother"; that you would call an avoidance [*muzilo*].[31] You may not do anything to your "mother" whom you swear by, or your "sister," even if she is very beautiful. You cannot say, "Let this girl be my lover!" It is forbidden! That is an avoidance. And so it is with avoidances concerning food, perhaps a kind of meat, or whatever it is.

Some *mulongo* names are based upon the avoidance themselves. An example of this: a common *mulongo* name is Munyanzoka, associated with the avoidance *nzoka* (lit., "snake," usually a head of cattle which dies as a result of snakebite). Gogo explicitly link the acquisition, both historically and in terms of descent, of the two characteristics. Thus, it is said:

The avoidance object is the *mulongo* . . . if you avoid something, all the members of your clan will not eat it until death; that is the avoidance object . . . The *mulongo* comes from the avoidance in the sense that, when a person has an avoidance, he also has the *mulongo* linked with it.

In south, central, and eastern Ugogo, the *mulongo* name is used as a form of address in everyday conversation; but in northwestern, western, and southwestern Ugogo, it is used as a collective term of address between groups only on formal occasions such as funerals and weddings.[32] Gogo themselves are at times un-

[31] I use kinship terms in quotation marks to indicate that Gogo generally mean classificatory kin in such usages. In this case, the persons referred to may not be one's "own" mother or sister. See Chapter VII and Appendix D for fuller discussion of terminology problems.

[32] In this sense the *mulongo* name is somewhat similar to the praise-names (*isibongo*) attached to patrilineal clans among the southern Bantu peoples: cf. Kuper (1954), p. 20; (1947), p. 110; (1950), pp. 86–87, 91; Gluckman (1950), p. 169.

clear as to whether they are giving a *mulongo* or a clan (*mbeyu*) name, although the names are usually presented in distinct grammatical forms, and the Gogo correct themselves on further thought. They also remark upon the varying emphasis given to these affiliations and their significance and do not formulate rigid rules about their operation, just as clans are theoretically exogamous but are not always so in practice. Thus, one informant said:

Many of us have the *mulongo* Munyambwa. The Nyambwa [now referring to the *clan*] came from the south, from Uhehe. They used to eat dogs [*walyaga mbwa*], and so others gave them the clan name "Walyambwa" ["the dog-eaters"] of the *mulongo* Munyatoma. But they changed the name and said "Wanyambwa."

Further, the word *mulongo* and its variants occur among neighboring peoples in Tanzania. The matrilineal Kaguru, with whom the Gogo share many linguistic features, a blurred northeastern boundary, and some clan names, use the word *mlongo* to denote a patrilineal group with which are associated forbidden objects. Its ". . . only function . . . is to prescribe some food or other items from its members during a certain period of their lives."[33] Thus it is not surprising that previous writers have confused clan and *mulongo* names, and even *mulongo* names with avoidances.[34]

Some avoidances (*mizilo;* sing., *muzilo*) are animals. They may also be trees, plants, or even actions rather than objects. They include field rats, birds, goat's pancreas, calabashes of particular types, animals to which peculiar things occurred at birth, and so on. One particular clan has two avoidances: the hoof of the warthog and "sharing an initiation camp with others at

[33] Beidelman (1963c), p. 326 n.

[34] Thus Cole (1902) lists both clan and *mulongo* names on the same list as the same category of classification (pp. 305–306), and later (p. 317) says, "Each *family* [sic] has its *mulongo* (forbidden thing) which is transmitted from the father to his children"; then again, "All members of a *clan* have the same *muziro* (forbidden thing)" (Cole's italics). *Muziro* is an alternative form to *muzilo*.

circumcision." It is clear that most avoidances are neither economically important nor a source of food, though some are (for
example, *nhongolo,* eland). Gogo avoidances are certainly not
"totems" and there is no identification of persons with them in
any sense, although there is an association between them and
"kinship" (see above, p. 82). They may, however, be said to
be "totemic." [35] Historically, they are acquired either by "accident," as already recounted (see also Appendix B), or simply
from a diviner to whom the clan founder or other ancestor went
when ill. But if one eats, kills or acts out an avoidance, the result
is sickness and the peeling off of the skin and hair from the body
(*kukubuka* or *kukoboka*). Breaking an avoidance never results
in death, which is always caused by witchcraft.[36] Some avoidances
are so obscure that Gogo admit there is little or no chance of
offending against them. The same term (*muzilo*) can be used
of any action or food prohibited by a diviner on an individual
basis during the course of a cure.

Another element linked with clan affiliation and its subsidiary
affiliations is the clan oath (*cilahilo*). A clan oath is commonly
spoken out when one stubs a toe on a journey or sneezes (*kutya-*

[35] Cf. Radcliffe-Brown (1952), p. 117 *et passim;* Fortes (1945), pp.
141–142. Gogo avoidances are not economically significant and there
are no "rites ensuring the multiplication of the totemic species." But in
some respects they do conform to the associations which have been
termed "totemic": cf. Fortes (*ibid.*); Lévi-Strauss (1962a), pp. 60, 104,
123 *et passim.* A discussion of this problem is not relevant here. But cf.
Radcliffe-Brown (1952), p. 122, on Australian institutions: "The only
thing that . . . totemic systems have in common is the general tendency
to characterize the segments into which society is divided by an association between each segment and some natural species or some portion of
nature. This association may take any one of a number of forms." But
see also, Lévi-Strauss (1962b) and Fortes (1966).

[36] But there is an association in thought between the violation of an
avoidance and witchcraft (*wuhawi*). A person who goes through the
boiling-water ordeal (*mhugu*) for witchcraft accusation is shown to be
guilty by his skin peeling off (*kukoboka*). It should be noted that sexual
prohibitions (*miiko;* sing., *mwiko*) are not usually thought of as *mizilo,*
in spite of the association made by the informant quoted on p. 82.

mula). It is designed, Gogo say, to remind one in such situations of his origins and ancestors and serves to ward off any supernatural dangers which may occur. Again, there is a good deal of local variation. Clans with ritual areas in central, northern and western Ugogo generally use as an oath the name of a hill, tree or well where the ritual precedence and control of the clan was first established (*matamelo*). Thus the oath of the Pulu clan is *"kuMbuli nghasuka"* ("At the hill of Mbuli I went bad": *kusuka*, to go bad, usually referring to beer). Mbuli is the hill where, according to clan history, Pulu ritual control was first established. Similarly, the oath of the Ng'omvia of Wuselya is *"Cibuga,"* the name of a conical hill in their ritual area where their religious control (*matemelo*) was first established. But in south and southeastern Ugogo some clans use their *mulongo* names as an oath; others use their own avoidances.

Some clans or sub-clans are further sub-divided into "maximal lineages" which are called *milango* (sing., *mulango;* lit., doorway). They may also be called *ikungugo* (pl., *makungugo*).[37] In spite of the fact that, in Ugogo, these *milango* are not corporate groups, nor are they made up of smaller segments which could be termed "minimal lineages," "maximal lineages" is perhaps the most useful term. The reasons for this are made clear by the following example.

A glance at Pulu clan history, as represented in Figure 2 and also in Appendix B, will show that the male founders of *milango* groups are "fixed" genealogically, in the second phase of "history." The genealogical segments which they founded cannot proliferate any more. Genealogical "telescoping" takes place "beneath" them. Basing our definition on morphological rather

---

[37] The term *ikungugo* is used in Cigogo to refer to any category of people who claim agnatic descent at any level, traceable or not, depending upon the context. Thus it denotes any patrilineal kin group from clan to the smallest group of genealogically related kin. By giving it a rigid definition, Schaegelen (1938), pp. 204–205, mistakes its real significance. *Ikungugo* is one of the terms used by the Kaguru to denote exogamous matrilineal clans: see Beidelman (1961d); and (1963b), p. 54.

than functional criteria, it appears to be legitimate to use this term,[38] in spite of the fact that it is desirable to limit the term "lineage" to corporate unilineal descent groups. Gogo less conscious of the ritual associations and areas of their clan and *milango* (see below) may leave the latter out altogether. But members of one *mulango* can *theoretically* trace genealogical descent from its founder.

Such sub-divisions only occur when a clan is numerically strong and has ritual control in more than one area and thus has more than one stool-holding agnatic group (see p. 87). In fact, most *milango* names refer specifically to the ritual area in which the group has ritual authority. Each maximal lineage is then described by a name meaning "the owners of such-and-such an area." But members of maximal lineages form neither corporate nor localized descent groups, and the term is primarily of importance when referring to the stool-holding group (*wanyaligoda*). The Pulu clan, all of whose members share the same subclan (*mulongo*) name (Munyambwa) and are therefore not divided in terms of sub-clan and avoidances, have several maximal lineages (*milango*), each linked with its own stool and ritual area. The pattern is set out in Table 4, where the Pulu organization is contrasted with that of the Nyagatwa clan in one locality where it has two ritual areas. But the Nyagatwa are divided into two sub-clan groups which are not again sub-divided into maximal lineages; or, alternatively, each maximal lineage may be said to have separate sub-clan names. The historical justification for this division is described in another context later in this chapter. These two examples illustrate the variety of internal structure in Gogo clans and their relationship to territorial areas.

What emerges from this rather complex set of affiliations and their local variations is that: although a person's clan (*mbeyu*)

---

[38] Cf. Fortes (1945), p. 33; M. G. Smith (1956), p. 40 *et passim*. It must be emphasized, however, that we are not dealing with a segmentary lineage system in which lineages have corporate political functions at different levels in the external domain.

Table 4. The sub-divisions of two clans and their ritual areas

Clan	Founder	Sub-clan name (*mulongo*)	Avoidance (*muzilo*)	Maximal lineages (*milango*)	Ritual areas (*yisi*)
Pulu	Maguhe	Munyambwa	Ndunghu	Wanya-Madako	Nhyemianga
				Wanya-Madako	Makutupola (two stools)
				Wany-Igoji	Igoji
				Wany-Ikogolo	Ikogolo
				Wanya-Citelela	Citelela
				Wanya-Ciale	Ciale
Nyagatwa[39]	Macinyinha	Sembuce	Mbofu	(Wanya-Cikombo)	Cikombo
		Munyambwa	?	(Wany-Ibwijili)	Ibwijili

places him in the most general and fundamental category of descent recognized by Gogo, his proper place vis-à-vis his ancestors, their activities, and the areas with which they are associated can only be established when his clan, sub-clan name, avoidance object, and clan oath are taken together. Each person acquires his set of sometimes cross-cutting affiliations normally through patrilineal descent. These place him in particular relationships with members of other clans linked in various ways and scattered in family groups (see below) through large areas of Ugogo. Hence, when I refer to clan affiliation in the subsequent analysis, I mean an identification based upon a conjunction of several of these factors, although membership in a clan (*mbeyu*) may be said to be the most fundamental.

[39] There are other Nyagatwa groups in other parts of Ugogo who trace descent from different founders and have other sub-clan names. They would all, however, consider themselves to be of "one trunk" (*isina limonga*).

OTHER INSTITUTIONALIZED INTER-CLAN RELATIONSHIPS:
JOKING-PARTNERS (*WUTANI*)

Gogo clan histories and myths, including the one I have quoted, record that several clans were given their names by others during the period of migration and settlement in Ugogo. These historical contacts between clans also serve to provide one explanation of the origin of clan joking-partnerships (*wutani*).[40] In some cases joking-partnerships occur between sub-clans of the same clan name (*mbeyu*) which are widely separated both physically and historically, as in the case of the Nyagatwa clan noted above.[41] Joking-partnerships also occur, however, between members of broader divisions in Gogo society than those of clanship. When people from Cinyambwa (in southwestern Ugogo), who are often equated by outsiders with the Nyambwa clan, though they in fact belong to a wide variety of clans (see Chapter II), meet people from central Ugogo (Wanyawugogo, also of diverse clan membership), they can "joke" like *watani* (sing., *mutani*: jok-

[40] Related words such as *utani* (in Swahili) are commonly used in many parts of East Africa to denote joking-partnerships between groups and categories of persons of many types and levels of comprehensiveness. These vary from localities to "tribes" and "peoples." The Swahili verb *kutania* means to behave in an over familiar manner, or jokingly, in a variety of contexts. Cf. Beidelman (1966); Moreau (1944); Christiansen (1963); Southall (1961), pp. 38–39. The institution extends to central Africa in both traditional and modern contexts, between tribal groups as well as between clans; see Richards (1937); Mitchell (1956), pp. 35–42. I deal with joking relationships in Gogo society in much more detail in Rigby (1968a).

[41] See note 25, above. If a functional definition of "clan" were to be taken (instead of the morphological criteria linked with the Gogo concept), it would be better to treat such separate *mulongo* groups as separate "clans," even though they have the same *mbeyu* name. But I think the evidence presented shows that this would not be a wise course to follow. I have adhered to more formal definitions derived directly from the Gogo concepts themselves, for "clanship" and "sub-clan names" are primarily "conceptual" phenomena in the Gogo case. They do not delimit corporate kin groups so much as provide a "theory of descent." I return to this point later.

ing-partner). A member of the Ikando clan who had lived most
of his life in Cinyambwa told me:

The Wanyawugogo and the Wanyambwa, you might say, joke with
one another. The Wanyambwa think of "These ghastly central Ugogo
people!" They can swear at each other (*wakwiliga*) but do not become
angry. A long time ago the Wanyawugogo used to get angry, but they
have become used to it now and are tired of losing their tempers.
They have begun to joke. If a Munyambwa comes across a Munyawugogo eating, he can just sit down and eat (without being invited).[42]
The Munyawugogo simply says, "Oh goodness, this lout of a
Munyambwa!" and the latter replies in like manner. And that is all
it comes to.

In the case of inter-clan joking-partnerships, it is usual for
a clan to have several others as joking-partners. Thus, the Pulu
have *wutani* links with the Ibago, Mhalala, and Donghwe clans.
The complex network of *wutani* links that results from this is
further complicated for the individual by the fact that a person
may consider the *wutani* partners of his mother's clan as his
joking-partners also. This is consistent with the importance of
matrilateral kin, which will be analyzed in detail in later chapters.
But such *wutani* links are not always remembered. Nevertheless,
it is said:

In the case of a mother's clan (*mbeyu yayaya*), if they are joking-
partners with others, when that woman has children those children
will also take those joking-partners. They are said to have taken over
the joking-partnerships of their mother.

Apart from the theory that joking-partnerships arose out of
historical events in which the founders of clans were involved,
by far the most common explanation given by Gogo for the origin
of *wutani* partnership is that they arose out of marriage between
the two clans. This leads to kinship of the category "cross-cousins"
(*wuhizi*), which in turn results in *wutani* partnerships. Joking

[42] A serious breach of manners in any other context.

relationships exist between several categories of kin in Ugogo, including cross-cousins. Although it is desirable to keep distinct clan joking-partnerships from interpersonal kin joking relationships (and Gogo make a distinction in the type of joking permitted in each case), the Gogo theory that clan joking arises directly out of the kinship category "cross-cousin" relates the two.[43] A third type of joking occurs between age-mates and is significant in several contexts, including the establishing of marriage and affinal links.

So an informant explained *wutani* to me: *"Wutani* arises out of us giving each other our clan (*mbeyu*) names." But then he went on to explain the basis of one specific *wutani* link by the fact that the clan founder's wife had been of the Nyagatwa clan (my informant was Igongo), "and from that came our joking relationship with the Nyagatwa." Another elder said:

Joking-partnerships long ago were kinship (*yali ndugu*). Children were born [of marriage between the clans concerned] and between them there existed a cross-cousin relationship (*wuhizi*) . . . Then, as the relationship grew further apart, it became (*yikenjila;* lit., it entered into) *wutani*. But it comes from kinship in the remote past.

Again, a ritual leader describing the history of his clan, said:

We have a joking-partnership with the people of Cisima, the Sagala,[44] and the people of Ludi (Rudi) who are also our joking-partners, are also Sagala. When we ask each other about these things, they say, "That joking comes from kinship: one 'grandfather' and one 'grandmother,' that is where it comes from." One person goes and marries there, from the other clan . . . Then after a considerable time has elapsed, when you have children through perhaps seven successive generations, then you begin to swear at each other (*kwilijila*). Joking-partnerships come from marriage.

[43] For a discussion of the relationships between cross-cousins and other categories of kin between whom joking relationships occur, see Chapter VII. Also cf. Goody (1956), pp. 79–80.

[44] Sagala is a Gogo clan in this area, which claims to have originated among the Sagara peoples in the east.

Contrary to the evidence from many other societies in Africa, joking-partners have few specific functions in Gogo ritual *as* joking-partners.[45] Only in one case was I told (in response to my persistent inquiries) that the person clearing the bush away from a gravestone before a propitiation ceremony was a *mutani*. Even then I was assured that anyone but a fellow clan member could have performed the task. In Gogo rituals, more specific categories of kin with whom genealogical links can be traced, such as "sister's sons" or "cross-cousins," perform these tasks. But an important role in burial and inheritance ceremonies is taken by a person in the category *lizenjere* ("those whom we marry"), and in some contexts those of the category *lizenjere* may be referred to as *watani*. An elder told me that the founder of his clan, Madeha, married Isuule, from another clan. He went on:

Now when we came to marry Isuule, we added on to our joking-partnerships a second time. Surely those whom we marry (*welizenjere*) are also *watani?* Yes, that is, also *wutani*.

However, it is on the basis of an actual affinal link (for example, a deceased brother's wife) that a person occupies a specific role in Gogo rituals, rather than on the basis of simply being *wutani*.

In terms of everyday actions and jural norms, Gogo do not place much emphasis upon joking-partnerships. They say that they serve primarily to ease the establishing of new relationships in areas where people have few kin and other ties, and to which they have moved in one of the several changes of residence most Gogo make during their lifetime.[46] But the theory that clan jok-

[45] Neither do Gogo *emphasize* that joking-partnerships have arisen from inter-clan relationships of hostility, although there is some element of hostility involved. *Wutani* in Ugogo does not arise from a theory of "totemic opposites" as in the case of some central African peoples, where this theory is used to explain institutionalized reciprocal relationships between clans: cf. Richards (1937); Mitchell (1956), pp. 37–38.

[46] *Wutani* links also ease the strain on meeting strangers while traveling or going in search of grazing. On one occasion I visited an area I had not been in before. My host told me that we should go over to a nearby homestead where beer for a communal work-party had been brewed.

ing-partnerships arose out of marriage, through cross-cousinship, has a corollary. All informants agreed that it is desirable for marriages to take place between members of clans linked as joking-partners. In Gogo theory, this eases the strain, both in the negotiation and setting-up of the marriage and in the affinal ties, which then take precedence over any previous, remoter relationships:

Joking-partners we can marry, we do marry. One could say, if you are joking-partners, it is preferable to marry; because you think, "These joking-partners, long ago they were our kin." Now you marry and you say, "We are strengthening the clan relationships (*cikugomola mbeyu;* lit., we are returning the clan)."

In such a situation, marriages can take place in both directions; one clan is not considered as "wife givers" to the other. Statistically, however, *wutani* links are not important in choosing a marriage partner; other factors are much more significant.[47] The link is usually emphasized *ex post facto,* to suggest that the marriage will be a good one because of it. The most common reference to such marriages is in historical traditions of clan relationships.

In many ways, then, *wutani* links between clans may be viewed in much the same light, and as having the same results, as the "perpetual kinship" links described in a previous section. They establish a network of historically justified connections between

When we arrived, all the people of the homestead were away at the fields, except the old lady to whom the fields belonged and who had brewed. At first she appeared very worried at my presence, but when we had talked a little I happened to mention that I was of the Pulu clan, by adoption. She immediately cheered up on hearing this and said, "Oh, then I can swear at you, for you are our *mutani.* We are Mhalala, Himbila (her own clan) and was fought with the Pulu. Our *wutani* with the Pulu is of the spear only. We fought with them; it is not as if they gave us our *mbeyu* name. Oh no!" Pulu clan history as recorded in Appendix B also illustrates this precise relationship, in terms (in this case) of hostility in the past.

[47] The frequency of *wutani* marriages and kin marriages is discussed in Chapter VI. The factors influencing choice of spouse are also fully analyzed in Chapter VI.

the members of very dispersed clans and ease the creation of new interpersonal kin and affinal ties in the network of kinship within neighborhoods. The importance of this for the mobile homestead groups which comprise the basic residential units of Gogo society will emerge in the following analysis.

CLANSHIP AND RITUAL LEADERSHIP (*WUTEMI*)

Gogo thus associate a number of different qualities with clanship. The most significant and institutionalized of these qualities is that of ritual leadership (*wutemi*).

Clans claim and maintain ritual precedence in their ritual areas by possession and reiteration of a clan history and myth of origin. Most elders know, or should know, these myths and histories of their own clans, since they are important at all ceremonies where clanship is significant. But the justification of clan ritual authority primarily concerns only the members of the stool-holding group and the ritual leader himself, who must possess the insignia of office. The stool-holding group comprises an agnatic group seldom more than two or three generations in genealogical depth—usually only the "sons of one man," the previous ritual leader. Agnatic groups of greater depth seldom have corporate functions, even among those closely concerned with ritual leadership.[48] The most important objects in the insignia of ritual office are the rain-stones (*mabwe gemvula* or *zimvula;* lit., rains) and the stool (*igoda*) upon which they are kept.[49] A black cloth (*mwenda mutitu*), in the past the skin of a black ox, is also important in ritual activities.[50]

[48] Among Gogo not closely concerned with the ritual leadership of their clan, as associated with its ritual area or areas, agnatic groups of greater depth than the "sons of one man" (*wana wamunhu umonga*) are never corporate in important property and other relations.

[49] Cf. Carnell (1955a); Hartnoll (1932) and (1942); Culwick (1931).

[50] Black is the ritually suspicious color in all Gogo rituals, including those for rain. It is explicitly associated with rainclouds (see Carnell, *op. cit.*; Rigby 1966a, pp. 9–10). It is not possible here to analyze in any detail the rich symbolism in Gogo rain-making rituals. But here is

The ritual leader himself is generally referred to as *mutemi*
(pl., *watemi*), but may also be referred to as *munyaligoda,* the
possessor of the stool. In some contexts he is also *munyawusi,*
the owner of the essence of the land; but this term is more commonly used in the plural (*wanyawusi*) to designate: (a) in particular, all the members of the clan with ritual precedence in
that area and (b) in general, all the residents of the ritual area
who cultivate in it, graze their cattle in it, and use its resources
in other ways. The latter belong to a great diversity of clans.

Succession to the office of *mutemi* is theoretically by the rule
of patrilineal primogeniture. The first son of the senior wife
(*mucekulu wanyumba imbaha*) is normally the heir.[51] In the
event of his physical disability, for example blindness (*cibofu*),
the next son of the senior house succeeds.[52] An heir to the ritual
leadership cannot be installed until he has a child by his first
wife.

---

an example of the ritual associations of black. The members of the delegation having gone from a ritual area to a diviner for rain and fertility
medicines (see below) sit on the skin of a black ox upon returning to
the ritual leader's homestead (*ikulu*). The ritual leader's mother or senior
wife (*munyakaya:* see Chapter V) sprinkles them with water to "cool"
them of the dangers of the journey. The skin in this ceremony is called
ivunde (cloud). Schaegelen (1938), p. 208, lists the insignia of the
mutemi as: the ritual stool and stones, a sceptre (*nghome ya mutemi*),
and leopard skin cloak and cap. I have never seen the latter, and elders
could not inform me about them. A pestle (*mutwango*) may take the
place of thet sceptre (see illustrations). I did not witness the installation
of a ritual leader. The adoption by ritual leaders today of a simple black
cloth as their main dress (very common throughout Ugogo) may stem
from their desire to remain inconspicuous to outsiders. I explain the
reasons for this elsewhere: Rigby (in press).

[51] That brothers never succeed to ritual leadership is also indicative
of the lack of corporate functions in agnatic groups of any depth.

[52] In such a case, the eldest son would marry and live a normal life
(blindness is not a serious impediment to marriage in a family rich in
cattle). But he would be required to live away from the *ikulu*, and
perhaps even from the ritual area. His name would not be mentioned in
the genealogies of the stool-holding group, but would be relegated to a
"junior" genealogical position.

But Gogo recount many historical cases in which, through an unfortunate incident or the fault of the heir, the "sister's sons" (*wehwa*) or just the clan linked to the stool-holding one as "sister's sons," usurp the ritual stool and keep it. Such an event is usually incorporated in a stylized part of the clan histories. The following case concerns the Nyagatwa clan who, in the area concerned, are divided into two sub-groups with different *milongo* and who have ritual control in the two adjacent areas of Cikombo and Ibwijili.[53] In this case not only is the ritual leadership transferred at one point through uterine descent, but clanship also (see Figure 3).

Ndalu, the ritual leader of Ibwijili, is a member of the Nyagatwa clan with the *mulongo* Munyambwa. Magungu is the ritual leader of Cikombo and is a close paternal parallel cousin of the government ex-chief Meshak. However, Magungu and Ndalu are described as "maternal parallel cousins" (*wali cana canyina*), because ". . . when their 'mothers' were born, they were the only children and had no brothers. When only these girls were born the country had no *mutemi* to succeed. So when these women themselves bore sons, they were made pregnant only by lovers [i.e. no bridewealth was given, and they were thus not married]. Then the mothers refused to state the names of their sons' fathers and said, 'Let these children we have borne take *our* clan (*mbeyu*), that of their maternal grandfather,[54] and so let them take the ritual leadership; because we do not have any brothers who can rule the country. So we shall not take these children of ours to the clans of their fathers.' Thus they became Nyagatwa and took the clan of their grandfather who had begotten their mothers and who was also the 'owner' of Cikombo and Ibwijili. That is how they came to have ritual precedence".[55]

[53] See Table 4.
[54] I translate the term *kuku* here as "maternal grandfather" because it is specified in the context. The same term is used for mother's brother and all males of two or more ascending generations in any line (see Chapter VII and Appendix D).
[55] This account was given to me by an elder at Mutumba, near Cikombo. It corresponds closely in form to that recorded by Mnyampala (1954),

In another case, that of the Nyalindi clan, the clan linked to them in "perpetual kinship" as "sister's sons" took the stool, and thus the ritual leadership was transferred to the latter. The relevant extract from the clan history of the Nyalindi of Lindi (*mulongo* Munyambwa) states:

We established our ritual leadership at the hill of Nghonghobila, the neighborhood of Bambala, and that was our center of ritual authority (*matemelo getu*). But from there we came here to Lindi, because our "mother's brothers," the people of the Igoso clan, called us since their country had no competent ritual leader. The Igoso had male heirs; but Lola, the ritual leader, said to his "son" and his "sister's son," "Come early tomorrow and I shall tell you something." At dawn the next day the "sister's son" got up very early and went to Lola, but the son was late, and when he arrived there the "sister's son" had taken the stool. They said to the son, "You were late and your companion has ruled." And that is how the Nyalindi came to have ritual authority in Lindi.

It is through this kind of historical incident that the "perpetual kinship" relationships between clans are thought by Gogo to be established.

These two instances of uterine succession to ritual office raise some interesting questions as to not only the normative functions of descent and succession principles but also the historical content of Gogo clan traditions. If these traditions were simply "mythical charters," it would have been a simple matter for the narrators of Nyagatwa clan history to change the sex of the founder's children in the story, bringing the succession into line with the jural norms of succession. The distinct *milongo* could be explained in any number of other ways by convenient "fictions." I am not concerned here with the historical validity of Gogo clan histories. The stories, however, can be given an explanation in structural terms when they are related to the ritual roles of "sister's sons" and cross-cousins in inheritance and suc-

pp. 42–44, for this same area. But the individual names of the ancestors involved and some details vary in the two versions.

cession.[56] The instances constitute part of the "home-made model" Gogo have of the relations of interdependence between certain roles in the kinship system. But it may also be said that such instances provide a body of "social knowledge" that serves to explain to Gogo the discrepancies between the processes and norms of succession and provides a "theory" for these discrepancies. I have recorded a case where ritual authority was usurped in part of a ritual area by a person who had no rain-stones or other ritual insignia. He took trips to a diviner for rain and fertility medicines for the area in which he had influence as a government "village headman." In some situations, his homestead is referred to as *ikulu* (ritual leader's homestead); but in all cases when the medicines are distributed, an elder member of the clan with historically justified ritual control in the area must be present and participate.

This pattern of the sub-division, or the extension, of ritual control is true of both the present and the past in Ugogo. However this does *not* mean, as has been suggested by some writers, that due to war, famine and other factors, Gogo ritual areas have little continuity in time. Both on the evidence of Gogo elders and the little historical material available, they appear to have been remarkably stable. This stability applies primarily to the association of a particular clan with a particular area, while the population of individual homestead groups is highly mobile.

THE FUNCTIONS OF RITUAL LEADERSHIP

Most of the early writers on Ugogo stressed the political importance of Gogo "chiefs," whom they called "sultans," following the practice nearer the coast. But these writers also stressed the smallness of the "chiefly" domains. This impression of political chiefly functions was gained from the fact that some Gogo out of necessity had to impose food and water taxes on passing caravans in a country where food and water are extremely scarce,

[56] See Chapter VII; also Rigby (1968a).

especially toward the end of the dry season when many travelers used to come through. No doubt the taxation was also profitable for the Gogo and worth the effort in organizing. In any case, the actual organization of tax-collection and the contact with the travelers seem to have been through the ritual leaders' assistants (*wandewa*) and other elders, not the *watemi* themselves. Physical contact with hostile strangers is thought to endanger the ritual leader, both physically and ritually, and thus affect the whole country.

The impression of the secular political authority of Gogo chiefs was developed and strengthened when the British administration took over and implemented the policy of "indirect rule." The British created government chiefships with considerable judicial and political authority over "chiefdoms" much larger than the Gogo ritual areas.[57]

A Gogo ritual leader, on the contrary, has few secular functions, and he did not have them in the past. His influence and functions may usefully be summarized as follows:

A Gogo *mutemi* has ritual authority over a small area with fixed boundaries.[58] Persons residing within these boundaries

[57] The relation between government chiefship and ritual leadership and between government chiefdoms and ritual areas is discussed in Rigby (in press).

[58] It is impossible to estimate the population of ritual areas in the past, and in the 1948 and 1957 censuses ritual areas were not, of course, taken into account. However, many of the areas designated "sub-chiefdoms" by the British administration coincided, for various reasons, with traditional Gogo ritual areas. (The main reason was that the ritual areas were not too small for sub-chiefdoms, and the boundaries between the latter were often drawn on the advice of local elders.) There is of course much variation in the population of ritual areas in different parts of Ugogo. A community development census in one chiefdom (where I was very familiar with all of the ritual areas) in 1962, showed that the population of sub-chiefdoms (ritual areas) ranged from 751 to 6,055 persons of all ages, with an average of 2,721. This included seven ritual areas. The 1957 census showed a total Gogo population of just under 300,000 persons, of which about 90% were residing in Ugogo. If we assume that there are about 85 ritual areas in Ugogo, this gives an average

must acknowledge the ritual precedence of the *mutemi* and some members of his clan. They must also carry out his ritual instructions on threat of expulsion, even today. The ritual leader controls the yearly cycle of rituals for rain-making and fertility within his country (*yisi*). In some years he also provides new and ritually purified fire for all the hearths in his country. He is expected to have medicines to protect the country from natural disasters and hazards, such as locusts and bird damage. He may prevent certain resources from being used for certain periods and close off areas within his country from exploitation of various types.[59] But he may do all this only for religious reasons. He carries out all of these activities only after consultation with a diviner (*muganga*). The latter is most often resident in another ritual area some distance away, and his services may be dispensed with and another substituted if he is shown to be inefficient.

In the past a *mutemi* himself never went on delegations (*wanyakujenda gandawega* or *wanyalamali*)[60] to consult a diviner for the ritual area, although he might consult a local diviner on family or personal matters. These days ritual leaders sometimes do go themselves. The delegation is chosen on the grounds of clan membership or simply a reputation for wisdom and knowledge of medicines; minor diviners living within the same area can also be chosen. Theoretically, a ritual leader should not leave the boundaries (*mimbi*) of his country, and seldom even his *ikulu*. But a ritual leader is indistinguishable from other

---

population of 3,176 persons in each ritual area; quite close to the above figure. It is probable that in the past there were stretches of unoccupied bush between ritual areas, more so than now: for impressions of Gogo neighborhoods and populations, see e.g. Southon (1881); Burton (1860); Stanley (1890); Speke (1863).

[59] Such areas are termed *luwindo*.

[60] The word *lamali* is derived from the Baraguyu/Masai term *olamal*, which means any group or delegation which goes to consult a diviner, usually on behalf of an age-set. Many rain diviners in Ugogo are Baraguyu, but the majority are Gogo. Cf. Beidelman (1960); Fosbrooke (1948), p. 18; Gulliver (1963), p. 27.

elders in everyday activities, and so is his homestead. He should
be rich in cattle (which symbolize his success in the control
of fertility and prosperity). He usually has a large homestead
and many dependents, but he wields little more influence in
secular activities than other homestead heads of comparable
wealth. In fact, ritual leaders are of all levels of wealth and
prestige.

The *mutemi* gives permission (after divination) for circumcision and initiation ceremonies (*sona zacigotogoto*), though
he is seldom their promoter, unless involved as a father of one
of the initiates.[61] The ceremonies, for both male and female, are
held on a locality basis at irregular intervals after a good harvest, and when there are enough young boys and girls to participate. The ceremonies are usually initiated in a ritual area by
a father and homestead head who has several young children of
the correct age. The necessity of the ritual leader's permission
(unless he is a close, involved kinsman of the initiates) is a
result of the religious significance attaching to all human blood
spilled in his ritual area. The spilling of human blood causes
ritual pollution. It is one of the most serious offences and cannot be settled without the intervention of the ritual leader.[62] This
applies equally to the "legitimate" spilling of blood at circumcision as to homicide or serious assault. It is for this that the
ritual leader receives certain symbolic payments after circumcision ceremonies have been performed in his area, but no trib-
ute. A ritual leader told me:

There are no livestock payments for permission to hold circumcision
ceremonies. But in proper Gogo custom, when they have finished the
cutting [operations], there is *sinyini*. They should present a goat, or
if there is no goat they bring money, here to the *ikulu*. This goat is
called *sinyini,* because they have spilled the children's blood in my

[61] But cf. Schaegelen (1938), p. 532.

[62] The relation between ritual influence, the spilling of blood, and the
delimitation of local and political units for many societies has often been
described: e.g. see Goody (1956), p. 93.

country (*wamwaga sakami yewana musi yangu*). And so they present *sinyini*. *Sinyini* is also called "the basket of grain flour" (*nhoto ya uwusaje*).

Nevertheless, the ritual leader affords supernatural protection for all undertakings. If no circumcision ceremonies are being held in his area in a particular year, but a boy feels he is too old to wait, he may run off to a neighboring ritual area where such ceremonies are about to take place. This is considered dangerous and must be carried out "secretly." The boy is said to "throw himself away" (*kwigumila*) at such an external ceremony, because he forfeits the ritual protection he would receive in his own ritual area during a physically and spiritually very dangerous period.

Hence, a ritual leader is also arbitrator in cases of homicide, witchcraft accusation, and serious assault. All of these acts "destroy the country" (*kuwulaga yisi*). The person accused of these crimes can flee to the *ikulu* if he escapes the relatives of his alleged victims (who would otherwise kill him). Once there, the victims' kin can take no physical action against the accused, for no violence may occur at the *ikulu*. This is still a respected norm. Even minor violence, if it occurs at the *ikulu*, is very strongly condemned, where in other contexts it may be justified (such as legitimate wife-beating). The ritual leader acts as arbitrator, arranging an ordeal (*mhugu*) in the case of witchcraft accusation, or compensation (*ndesa*, for example) in the case of homicide or serious assault.[63]

The settlement of such conflict within the ritual area by negotiation constitutes its primary political function. Discussing both killing by witchcraft and by other, more direct means, an elder said:

[63] Refuge at the *ikulu* is not afforded those who are accused of cattle theft (*wuhizi wang'ombe*). All cattle thieves are said to come "from far away," and indeed they often do. But again, no violence must occur at the *ikulu*.

Long ago, if a person killed another who lived in the same ritual area (*munyawusi muyagwe*), the "words" [i.e. the case] could only be settled through the influence of the *mutemi*. So if a person has killed his fellow citizen, on one side the victim's kinsmen would gather their spears and shields and go to fight and avenge upon those who have killed their kinsman.[64] When the victim's kinsmen arrive, they find the others also ready armed with their spears and shields to protect themselves. Then that person who has actually killed, if he admits his guilt, will run to the *ikulu* and tell the *mutemi*, "I have killed a person." Then the ritual leader comes and stops the fighting and arranges compensation. . . .[65] One beast is eaten communally and the ritual leader says, "Go and live well again my children. This is indeed misfortune; but leave it (*mukatale!*) and live as you lived before."

Although witchcraft accusation is no longer public and witches cannot be killed, it is conceivable that a person suspected of homicide by any means could still escape the wrath of his accusers in the *ikulu* until the arrival of the police. A good idea of Gogo concepts of the *ikulu* is given in the case of a woman called Mahenje, who was accused of witchcraft during the period of the German occupation. After the accusation had been confirmed by several diviners, she fled to the *ikulu* . . .

. . . The people who were chasing her followed her right to the ritual leader's homestead. When they reached there, they stopped outside, and the people of the *ikulu* (*wanyikulu*) said, "What do you want?"

"We want our witch; she has escaped into your homestead." The people of the *ikulu* said, "Even if she has run into our homestead, will

[64] The plural is used here, as the killer's kinsmen are also held responsible. This responsibility is not confined to agnates; see Chapter VII.

[65] The action of separating (physically) people who are fighting, is *kulamula*. This verb is sometimes used now for "to judge." This usage is incorrect, however, and there is no office of "judge" in traditional Gogo society. An elder who is known to bring about good settlements of disputes may be referred to as *muling'anizi* (the equalizer). A *mutemi* is not necessarily a better *muling'anizi* than another elder.

you come into the *ikulu* and take her? You say, do you not, that she has 'escaped'?"

They said, "Ah, we shall not enter."

"Come on, enter, and we will show you."

They were afraid and went home.

After this, an ordeal was arranged through the services of an elder acting as intermediary. The ordeal did not confirm Mahenje's guilt, and she was left unharmed.

These cases are mainly historical in significance because these functions are no longer really in the hands of the ritual leaders. But they do illustrate that the role of *mutemi* concerns primarily the ritual peace and prosperity of his area and that any secular judicial and political functions he may have derived directly from his ritual status. No means of enforcing decisions are, nor ever were, available to him. Even his threats of supernatural disaster constitute only the possibility of its occurrence, not of its invocation.

It is said that in the past, captives taken in war became the "slaves" and dependents (*wawanda*) of the ritual leader; but I have shown earlier that any rich homestead owner now has such dependents. The primary military organization in Ugogo is based upon age-groups of warriors (*wazelelo;* lit., young men). Recruitment to these is through the ceremonies of circumcision and initiation, and the groups are named after Baraguyu age-sets.[66] Hence, although ritual leaders have some control over recruitment to such groups in their own areas, age-sets cut across the boundaries of ritual areas. Ritual leaders have little control

[66] Cf. Beidelman (1960). Gogo age-organization was set up explicitly for defence, in conjunction with the Baraguyu living in Ugogo, against the Kisongo Masai and Hehe. It is probable that the organization never "worked properly" and Gogo have forgotten about many of its functions. For a more successful adaptation of the formal aspects of the Masai age-set system to different functional circumstances, see the Arusha material: Gulliver (1963), pp. 25–27 *et passim.* Some Gogo ideas of "age-mate" and the age-sets are discussed in Chapters IV and VII of this book.

over their activities. Leadership within such groups is on the basis of personal qualities, and is acquired in a rather *ad hoc* manner.

"Military" organization is primarily for the defence of localities, although bands of young men might organize aggressive cattle raids. Also based upon the principle of locality which cut across ritual boundaries is the institution of the alarm call (*lwanji*). Whenever this call is heard, all able-bodied men *within earshot* should take up arms and run towards the call. Consequently, it depends upon the area where the alarm is given as to who participates in this posse. *Lwanji* still operates fully, primarily in cases of cattle theft (usually at night), although it has no official recognition in local government statutes. It also operates in cases of assault and offences such as the destruction of crops by negligent herding. *Lwanji* serves to institute legal action against offenders and provides witnesses for the subsequent proceedings (*vyalo*) at the informal local elders' courts. The latter are the primary legal institution of Gogo society and a great number of disputes are still settled in them. The jurisdiction of such courts is variable and very localized, and bears little relation to ritual boundaries. It is significant that the Bantu root commonly used in other parts of East and Central Africa for the political and judicial territorial unit (*calo* and its variants) is not used for ritual area (*yisi*) in Ugogo. It is only used for cases which come before the informal elders' courts (*vyalo;* sing., *calo*).

I have noted that Gogo ritual areas have definite boundaries, called *mimbi*. They can be described with fair accuracy by any resident in a ritual area. They are marked by rivers, hills, rocky outcrops and other fairly permanent natural features such as baobab trees (*mipela: Adansonia digitata*). For crop-fertility rituals the country forms the "unit." Medicines are placed at, or thrown toward, all six spatial aspects, the "six windows" (*ma-langa mutandatu*) of the land. These are the east, west, north and south boundaries and, in the center, up and down.[67] These spatial boundaries to the ritual area, particularly the four geographical ones, have distinct and explicit significances in all rituals beyond those confined to the homestead.[68] The unity of the ritual area is quite specific in these contexts. For example, rain medicines in their calabashes may not be placed upon the ground in a neighboring ritual area by the delegation returning with them from a diviner in another ritual area, lest their efficacy be transferred to that country. If the group must stop, the medicines should be hung secretly in a tree. The divination deputation (*wanyalamali*) may also be required by the diviner to "steal" rain from each of the ritual areas they pass through on their way home. This is effected by collecting ground-water in each such ritual area and putting it in the calabash containing the rain and fertility medicines. The mixture is then sprinkled at intervals once inside the home ritual area until the *ikulu* is reached. All this must be carried out secretly, of course, lest the "owners" of those countries find out and retaliate.[69]

Similarly, in purification rituals, the participants usually "dance" out or take the pollution (perhaps cattle disease or the ritual pollution engendered by events such as a breech delivery) to the western boundary of the country and "throw it out," pref-

[67] The six spatial aspects are fundamental to all Gogo rituals of whatever level of comprehensiveness, and in Gogo cosmology. See Rigby (1966a).

[68] The independence of the homestead unit from ties with the ritual area is expressed in the provision of medicines for human and cattle fertility and health, as opposed to crop fertility. This is of fundamental importance in the pattern of residential mobility and relations of ritual interdependence and is explored more fully in Rigby (1967a).

[69] Rain showers in Ugogo are usually very localized. Most of the rain comes in three or four main showers, each called *ivunde* (cloud) by Gogo. In one year a ritual area may have sufficient rain to produce a good crop, while a neighboring ritual area five or ten miles away suffers from drought.

erably into a water pan or pool so that it is destroyed (Rigby 1967a).

CONCLUSION

Only a few of the above-mentioned activities are "things of the past." I took part in three divination trips in 1962–63, as a *munyalamali* for a ritual area, and have participated in all the activities listed in connection with rain and fertility rituals. (There are many more.) This is not the place to expatiate on these aspects of Gogo religion. But they do illustrate the reality of Gogo ritual areas. Acceptance of residence in a ritual area implies conformity with the ritual leader's instructions, backed by those of a renowned rain-diviner. It does not depend upon clanship or any other agnatic group-membership. Most of the homestead heads and family groups in any area belong to clans other than that of the ritual leader. Cooperation and rights and duties in exploiting the resources of ritual areas are described in following chapters.

The ritual role of the *mutemi* is emphasized in its associations with that of the diviner (*muganga*). The ritual leader can take little action without the backing of a proven and accepted diviner. Consequently, the failure of some rituals performed for the country may be attributed to the inadequacy of the diviner, who may then be changed. The religious reputation of the ritual leader is preserved. The diviner may be dismissed; the ritual leader cannot be.

The relation between the two qualities of ritual leadership and divination power is articulated and expressed in terms of clan affiliation as well as role. The two qualities are, ideally, mutually exclusive in clans in particular localities. Theoretically, ritual leaders (and their clans) cannot have the powers of divination, and great rain-diviners should not have the powers of ritual leadership. Hence, a ritual leader's clan cannot provide rain-diviners for his own area, although a member of his clan may be a rain-diviner for another area, and *vice-versa*. A diviner expresses here the likeness, yet distinctness of his role and that of a ritual leader:

> We diviners are like *watemi*. When a *mutemi* dies there is no mourning,[70] but they [the people of his homestead] simply play a special drum-beat (*nhunhu*), and they dance special dances. And so it is with [famous] diviners . . . When a diviner dies, there is no mourning even for him . . . The diviner has no inheritance ceremony (*ipinde*) . . . People just say, "A dog has died." So too the ritual leaders of Cinyambwa do not have the *ipinde* ceremony . . .[71]
>
> Ritual leaders do not have divination power . . . but their countries do [because there are diviners]; and then the witches cannot do anything. The witch wishes the country to die, but the diviner wishes it to prosper and be built up (*yisi . . . yizenjece*).

This chapter has sketched briefly the background of ritual areas, clanship, and ritual leadership, the broader aspects of the social system within which the kinship system described in the following chapters operates. Gogo are dependent primarily upon agriculture for subsistence, and thus all activities concerning the ritual areas are of fundamental importance. Yet Gogo homestead groups are not tied to any area for their whole period of existence from founding to fission. The general pattern is one of widely dispersed clanship ties spread at each generation over a network of tiny ritual areas. Only the shallow descent group concerned directly with the possession of ritual control is residentially tied to its own ritual area.

But the homestead groups of diverse origin which reside within any ritual area and its neighborhood sub-divisions are

[70] Mourning, *cililo*. In some parts of western and central Ugogo there is no mourning for a *mutemi*. His death is kept secret for as long as possible ("for a year," says Mnyampala (1954), p. 101) or until an heir has been chosen. This may not be true of some areas to the east. The body is buried in the *ikulu* by the *wanyikulu*. Gogo say that a severe earth tremor (*ihuhuji lyetulo*) is a sign that a ritual leader has died somewhere.

[71] That is, no inheritance and succession ceremony of the usual kind given to the average homestead head.

linked to one another by a complex network of kin and affinal relationships. Having set the general pattern I now turn to a detailed examination of this network. The clanship and other descent affiliations described in this chapter provide the Gogo "theory" of kinship relationships on a broader scale; it is in the everyday relationships of cooperation and mutual rights and obligations in property that the "reality" of the Gogo kinship system exists. It is through an analysis of these relationships that the structure and process of Gogo kinship may be established, and it is to this that I devote the whole of the following analysis.

IV
Kinship and
Neighborhood

I have made reference to the high degree of spatial mobility of Gogo homestead groups, bearing in mind that they are a sedentary and not a nomadic people. In this chapter I analyze the reasons for this mobility and discuss its significance for Gogo social structure on the levels of neighborhood organization and that of local communities. One or two preliminary points must be noted. It has been shown in several recent papers and monographs that the structure of domestic groups cannot be understood by a purely synchronic analysis but must be examined in relation to a cycle of growth, development, and fission.[1] It is equally impossible to analyze Gogo neighborhoods and local organization except as part of a historical process of growth and development of a cyclical kind.[2]

[1] For example, Fortes (1949a), Chapters III and IV; (1949b); (1958); and Goody (1958); Gulliver (1955), Chapters III and IV; Gray and Gulliver (1964). The developmental cycle of Gogo domestic groups is analyzed in Chapter V of this book.

[2] That is, a statement of formal structure in terms, for example, of the relation between certain types of descent groups and land rights in certain localities is inadequate. A diachronic approach to the processes involved in a pattern of residential fluidity is necessary. In a recent study of Bemba village instability, Harries-Jones and Ciwale (1963) point out the cyclical processes involved. They suggest that a ". . . diachronic emphasis avoids the confusion of imposing a synchronic model on a constantly fluctuating situation and shows the importance of taking into account the whole life history of a village rather than deducing principles from only one part of that cycle" (p. 56).

I do not wish to suggest that the processes involved are of the same kind as those involved in the domestic cycle. This is obviously not so, for the neighborhood unit is not the "workshop . . . of social reproduction" as the domestic unit is.[3] Nevertheless, the changing pattern of settlement in Gogo local communities will be shown interrelated with the processes involved within the domestic group and its relation to, and exploitation of, its environment, both social and physical. But in this chapter I wish to stress that no analysis of Gogo neighborhood organization is possible without looking for the operation of certain principles through time. To this end, numerical data are essential, as are detailed case materials in the description of the growth of one neighborhood. The reasons for this will appear more clearly as the analysis proceeds.

THE NEIGHBORHOOD (*ITUMBI*)

In Chapter III, I outlined the significance of the definite boundaries to Gogo ritual areas (*yisi*). Each ritual area contains several neighborhoods, but occasionally may consist only of one. These neighborhoods (*matumbi;* sing., *itumbi*) are not usually identifiable as discrete geographical units, either with regard to the positioning of homesteads (*kaya*) within them, the fields cultivated by their residents, or the areas in which their livestock graze. In neighborhoods of average population density, Gogo homesteads are often some hundreds of yards apart, or in clusters with this distance between them.[4] These clusters are occupied by close kin and affines, the relationships among whom will be analyzed below. In areas recently occupied for the first time or those reoccupied after the regeneration of bush, the homesteads of one neighborhood or cluster are frequently not visible from the other. There is plenty of "bush" (*mbago*

---

[3] Hence, ". . . the domestic unit is the system of social relations through which the reproductive nucleus is integrated with the environment and with the structure of the total society" (Fortes 1958, p. 9).

[4] See Maps 2 and 3.

mbaha). But neighborhoods which have been occupied for some time and are in a mature phase of their growth become cleared of thorn scrub for fields, leaving only a few shade trees for humans and livestock. Distant homesteads are easily visible and such an area is called *ihala*.

Gogo do not inherit land. The definitive factor in obtaining usufructuary rights in land of any kind (except old homestead sites, which will be discussed later) is residence in a neighborhood near it and in the same ritual area, in order that these rights may currently be exercised. Hence, no permission is traditionally required, either in regard to the siting of a homestead or to the laying out of the fields and plots for cultivation, as long as rights currently being exercised by others are not infringed. Even fallow fields may be cultivated by anyone after a period of two years of fallow.[5] Gogo often have fields in neighborhoods other than their own, but they seldom cross ritual boundaries in order to cultivate, since the efficacy of rain and fertility medicines obtained at the annual ceremonies controlled by the ritual leader would be destroyed.

Grazing is unrestricted in Ugogo, even across ritual boundaries, as is the utilization of natural water sources. Homestead owners may fence off small grazing areas (*icito* or *mulaga*) for young or sick livestock when grazing becomes limited to distant areas during the dry season. Infringement of rights so established may on occasion be subject to compensation, but none of them are permanent. Neighborhood boundaries thus have little significance in the economic exploitation of resources, *except* in regard to the general availability of such resources at particular times, variations in which dictate residential movement. But cooperation in cultivation and in the institution of herding groups involve, as I have shown, neighbors within clusters in neighborhoods.

Gogo neighborhoods, however, are units of sociological sig-

[5] See Chapter II and cf. Cory (1951), ¶¶257–262 for other minor points.

nificance, named after geographical features which lie within
them. Hence, although homesteads within the sub-divisions
(*vitumbi*) of one neighborhood may be physically closer to
homesteads in adjacent neighborhoods than they are to each
other, they definitely "belong" to their own named *itumbi,* and
homestead owners will identify themselves as belonging to one
neighborhood. As in the case of the ritual areas, the administration set up by the British, with its hierarchy of village headmen
and chiefs, took little cognizance of these named Gogo neighborhoods. The boundaries of administrative "villages" (also called
matumbi) bore no relation to the "boundaries" between neighborhoods. Government headmen had official jurisdiction over
an arbitrarily designated minimum number of homesteads or
taxpayers. As a consequence, homestead owners often find themselves residing in one neighborhood, defined in Gogo cultural
and historical terms, and being considered a member of another
unit delimited by the government definition of "villages." Although the office of village headman has now been abolished,
these units still exist or have been modified, equally arbitrarily,
under the reorganized local government instituted since Tanzania's independence in 1961 (see Rigby, in press).

In Temanghuku neighborhood, which is the subject of the
detailed description in this chapter, Mujilima, the son of the
neighborhood founder Sandiya, was government headman for
nearly ten years. He had authority over only 14 of the 45 homesteads in his neighborhood; the other 100 or so fell within the
five other Gogo neighborhoods of Mugu, Musonga, Ncinila,
Mapamha, and Nghole to the east and northeast (see Map 3).
Due, however, to his personal qualities, all of which fit him for
authority in Gogo terms (see below), and the fact that he is
the senior son of the founder of Temanghuku neighborhood,
Mujilima fulfills the role of a leading elder (*munyamhala*[6] or

[6] The word *munyamhala* is etymologically cognate with the Swahili
mnyampara, which often means "soldier," "armed guard," etc., and is
used as such in other parts of Tanganyika: for example, in Nyamweziland
(see Abrahams, 1967). In Cigogo it does not have this meaning.

muwaha) in Temanghuku neighborhood. This role is expressed primarily in the settlement of disputes.

Even under the British colonial administration which only recognized chiefdom courts, the majority of disputes were settled at the neighborhood or inter-neighborhood level, by the unofficial courts of elders. This is still true under the new local government set up since Tanzanian independence. These courts are convened at any time and anywhere within the neighborhood. Every homestead head (*munyakaya*) is, by definition, an "elder" of the court. In Temanghuku the most common venue is a small shade tree and shelter (*cibanda*) outside Mujilima's homestead (homestead no. 1 on Maps 2 and 3), because of his official position and his status as "elder," but primarily because of the latter. One can infer this from the fact that the court which meets at Mujilima's homestead deals with cases from all of Temanghuku neighborhood, including those homesteads which fall under the official jurisdiction of other government heads. It is confirmed by the fact that, by legislation, the settlement of disputes is beyond the official capacities of village headmen, and now the newly-constituted village committees.

Cases involving persons from separate neighborhoods may be heard in either. The *ad hoc*, "localized" quality of judicial activity in the elders' courts may also be seen in the fact that many of the actions which come before them are instituted by the alarm call (*lwanji*) which bears no relation to neighborhood, official, or ritual boundaries. It is important for our purposes here, however, to note that Gogo distinguish between cases taken to these elders' courts (and therefore made public) and called *vyalo* (sing., *calo*), and those settled within a group of kin and concerning only them, called *maloloso* (from the verb, *kulolosa*, to explain or "make clear"). Although neighbors and homestead heads in the neighborhood are related one way or another in a complex network of links, in the informal elders' courts they are acting as elders, neighbors, and "citizens" (cf. Abrahams 1965). In this context, all the homestead owners in a neighborhood have a right to attend and express their views (and also an obligation to do so). But in *maloloso* discussions, only select elders who fall into specific kinship categories relating them to those concerned in the dispute, take part. They may come considerable distances. Neighboring homestead owners have no right of attendance or participation unless they can justify it in terms of their specific kinship connections with the disputing parties. In this context, the elders are acting in specific kin roles, and the operation of such roles (in relation to residence and distance) is analyzed in specific cases in later chapters.

For the purposes of the following discussion, then, it is only the neighborhood as recognized by Gogo in their own terms that will be discussed. The founder of a new neighborhood who clears new sites for his homestead and cultivations can be called *muzengatumbi* (lit., "the builder of a neighborhood"), and he takes some precedence, particularly in judicial matters, among those who follow him.[7] His position is one of *primus inter pares* among his fellow homestead heads, but only if he has the requisite attributes of personal authority. Among these are: substantial wealth in livestock, a large number of dependents in his homestead, a knowledge of Gogo traditions and law, the ability to speak well in court and put his arguments clearly, the supernatural power to use and combat witchcraft.[8]

---

[7] He might also be called simply *muzengakaya* or *munyakaya*, the builder of a homestead, as most kin or non-kin who follow him to settle in the neighborhood would live, for a time at least, in his homestead before establishing their own. This pattern will emerge clearly in the following description of the founder of Temanghuku, Sandiya, and an early co-resident of his, Nghopalo.

[8] Cory (1951, ¶262 n.) mistakes the settlement pattern in Ugogo and perhaps oversimplifies it, but he correctly reports the following information given to him by a group of distinguished Gogo elders: "The basic reason for giving important positions within the community to . . . [neighborhood founders] . . . is that only intelligent, strong and popular men are able to undertake such a hazardous adventure. If they are unable to stand the strain, they either return or perish; and if they are not popular, no one will follow them and no *kaia* [sic] (household community) will

The homesteads (and their occupants, both human and animal) of a neighborhood can be ritually protected by the planting of medicines at certain points on its ill-defined boundaries, which are called *mimbi*,[9] in the same manner as for ritual areas. But the ritual leader (*mutemi*) is not involved. The action is carried out by the elders of the neighborhood, or the neighborhood founder. This protection from supernatural attack for the neighborhood can have no influence in such important fields as crop fertility or the abundance and exploitation of natural resources; these are matters for the whole ritual area, or individual magic.[10] When a homestead owner changes the site of his homestead from one neighborhood to another within the same ritual area, he may take his building poles (*mazengo*) with him, but he may not do so if he moves to another ritual area.

The following case illustrates both the magical significance of neighborhood boundaries and the accomplishing of a move from one neighborhood to another, for although the homestead owner concerned crossed over a ritual-area boundary in his move, the subsequent rites performed as a result of a blunder concerned the protective boundaries of a neighborhood:

Molwa the son of Muzanje was living in Temanghuku neighborhood. He moved with his wife and children to Mbalawala neighborhood but could not take his building poles with him as this entailed a move over the boundary between Cilungulu ritual area and Ilindi. He chose a site for himself and put up a shelter while he collected building materials. Meanwhile, they harvested and winnowed the grain from their fields in the first neighborhood, which was only some two miles away. As the dry season wore on they saw that the site they had chosen

---

be founded. For instance, a man who has been forced by his neighbors to leave his home and community will have no following."

[9] Cf. Chapter III.

[10] Homestead heads also use protective medicines when they build their homesteads, and for particular reasons after this. These are probably among the most important medicines, but it will also be shown that these medicines are directed towards different ends and are different from those used for the neighborhood or ritual area.

was too bare (*ibalangu*) and would be marshy in the rains, so they moved a little distance to the north, to a new site. There was a marshy grass pan (*nyika*) immediately to the northeast, and as he was cutting and stacking building poles, he went and cut a *mukambala* tree [*Acacia nigrescens Oliv*] there. When it became known that he had done this, the *muzengatumbi* Kalungwana came to him and asked him, "Why have you cut this *mukambala* when we used it to protect the neighborhood [*capilimila'si*;[11] lit., used it to delimit, or encircle, the area.]?" This was because the *mukambala* tree had been smeared with the stomach contents (*wufu*) of a ritual goat, mixed with powdered medicines (*ndasimi*) obtained from the diviner Mwaja who lived way to the north at Mukondahi. The neighborhood elders told Molwa to pay a goat "to cool" (*kupoza*) the tree which he had cut. He had no livestock of his own but went to Cigongwe, about nine miles to the south, and traded some grain for a goat which he gave to them.

They killed the goat at the *mukambala* tree, skinned it, took out the stomach contents, and smeared the tree. They gave Molwa the hind leg and Kalungwana took the rest of the meat to his homestead to be shared out. No fires were lit at the *mukambala* tree to roast and eat the meat together on the spot, as is usual in other ceremonies. Molwa took his building poles and continued the work of constructing his homestead

The number of homesteads within neighborhoods varies a great deal, both between neighborhoods and in one neighborhood through time. I describe the cycle of growth of one neighborhood in detail in this chapter. The most important element in this pattern is the general mobility of Gogo homestead groups and individuals and it is to an examination of this factor that I now turn.

RESIDENTIAL MOBILITY

In respect of residence and residential mobility, there is a discrepancy between Gogo values and expressed norms on the one

[11] The word *yisi* (enclitic -*si*) basically means country or ritual area, but can also be used to denote the area of a neighborhood (as in this case) or "land" in general.

hand, and the pattern of events, engendered by the problems of survival of both men and livestock, on the other. For we have already seen that the Gogo live in what may be termed a "marginal" economic environment. Gogo move residentially quite often and over considerable distances, both as children and dependents, and as adults and homestead owners. But they maintain an attachment to, and a desire to return to, the neighborhood in which they were born or where they consider their clan area to be. Many mature homestead owners will list three or four neighborhoods or ritual area in which they have resided before their present area. They move from one to the other for a variety of reasons, but primarily because of drought and famine and witchcraft accusations; but they still talk of returning to "our place" (*kwetu*), which indeed they sometimes do. "Our place" is thought of as "better" and "safer" to live in than the present areas in which their homesteads may be established. At a distance this is expressed in terms of ritual areas, but may also apply to neighborhoods within a ritual area. A very young homestead owner who had moved some eighteen miles with his elder full brother from the place of his birth to Temanghuku neighborhood, where he had married, said (in 1962):

There at Matandala where we come from, to the east of Cigwe . . . is that not our place (*sikwetu*), where we came from at Hambaya [the 1946 famine]? Ah, let us return there to our home, to Cinyambwa. Here in Wugogo it is no good. Wugogo is hard!

He must have been 12 years of age when they moved, and he continually visits his classificatory sister's husband (*mulamu'-gwe*) there.

Majima, a homestead owner in Temanghuku neighborhood, was fifty-eight years old in 1962. He had come from Musalato, ten miles to the southeast, to Temanghuku neighborhood during the 1939 famine (*nzala yaJoni*), twenty-three years previously. In 1962 he returned with his dependents to build a new homestead at Musalato, in spite of the fact that his wife's father and mother (*wakwe'we*) had died at Temanghuku and were buried in his cattle byre. While building his homestead at Musalato he lived with his second wife's full-brother (*mulamu'gwe*) and the new homestead was built nearby.[12] Majima said that when he had moved from Musalato twenty-three years before, the land and bush there had been exhausted, and the general famine of 1939 had precipitated his change of residence. He now maintained that the Temanghuku neighborhood and its resources were exhausted, while at Musalato the bush had regenerated and was suitable for the clearing of new fields. He generalized this argument to account for the long-term movement of Gogo homesteads between neighborhoods:

People are leaving this area (Temanghuku neighborhood and Cilungulu) because the land has become old (*yisi yakombipa*). It is old because there is no longer any bush (*mbago*) to clear for new fields. So they move and go where they see good bush for clearing, to get new fields.

People generally clear a field one year and cultivate it. The next year they clear a little more, and again the following year. Then a person will leave the field he cleared the year before last and cultivate last year's field plus the newly cleared and burnt field (*nghangale*) . . . If there is enough bush he will clear (new areas) each year, leaving the old.

When bush is exhausted in any neighborhood and the cleared fields are no longer productive in spite of manuring, the homestead population begins to diminish. Homestead owners then move either to new areas or to old ones where the bush has regenerated. But although the argument of soil exhaustion and the scarcity of cultivable land is used here as a general one for residential mobility, individual homestead owners and other individuals usually give quite different *specific* reasons for their own actual moves, and Majima's case is unusual. The search for

[12] The significance of affinal relationships for residence patterns will emerge clearly later.

bush to clear for new fields explains to Gogo the evident cyclical rise and fall of population in specific neighborhoods, but individual moves are almost always the result of a search for grazing, or to avoid famines or witchcraft accusations. This is primarily due to the fact that land for cultivation is hardly ever *scarce*, and a very low value is placed upon it. I have already noted the idea of inheriting land appears ridiculous to Gogo. But I must now give evidence for the high rate of residential mobility with respect to a particular area.

TEMANGHUKU NEIGHBORHOOD AND POPULATION MOBILITY

For reasons of space the following analysis is restricted primarily to one neighborhood. I have information on adjacent neighborhoods and detailed data on another some eighty miles away from the one described here, which show that the pattern is general. Tables 5 and 6 provide numerical information on the spatial mobility of forty-four of the forty-five homestead owners of Temanghuku neighborhood,[13] with additional information on 115 other homesteads in other neighborhoods of Cilungulu ritual area in Table 5.[14] The first part of the table

[13] Information obtained from one homestead was too insufficient to allow its inclusion in some of the following tables. Where the information is available it is included and the total is then 45 homesteads.

[14] The information collected for the 115 homesteads outside Temanghuku neighborhood was not as detailed or extensive as that for the 45 homesteads within it. Also, in this and the following chapters I am concerned primarily with an analysis of Temanghuku neighborhood and its homesteads. Thus in most cases only the 45 Temanghuku homesteads are considered. But it will be seen that where the figures from both "samples" are analyzed separately, there is sufficient correlation between the figures to justify generalizations from the Temanghuku homesteads alone. I have already stated that other observations confirm this. In any case, the question here is not one of statistical validity, which would be necessary if the analysis rested upon statistical models, but one of illustration or "explicit criteria of verification and validation" (Fortes, 1949b, p. 58) for the general propositions made.

Table 5. Spatial mobility of homestead owners: place of birth and present residence, by age[15]

(a) Temanghuku neighborhood, Cilungulu ritual area

Approx. age category	Born in Teman-ghuku	Born in other neighborhood within Cilungulu	Born in other ritual area	Totals
15–29	—	—	1	1
30–44	2	—	14	16
45–59	1	—	16	17
60–74	—	2	6	8
75–	—	—	2	2
Totals	3	2	39	44
	(6.8%)	(4.6%)	(88.6%)	(100.0%)

(b) Other homesteads in Cilungulu ritual area

Age-sets	Born in neighborhood of present residence	Born in other neighbor-hood within Cilungulu	Born in other ritual area	Totals
(Dobola) Mesokile	1	2	3	6
(Kidotu) Menamba	10	8	22	40
(Ildwati) Balangati	2	10	29	41
(Kilanji) Kitumbotu	3	2	17	22
(Metemi) (Kishomi) Ngulumo	—	—	6	6
Totals	16	22	77	115
	(13.9%)	(19.1%)	(67.0%)	(100.0%)

[15] The significance of age in the status of homestead owner is discussed in Chapter V, where I also explain why the age categories of part (a) of this table are equated with the age-sets given in part (b).

shows that 93.2 percent of homestead heads in Temanghuku neighborhood were born outside the neighborhood, and 88.6 percent were born outside of both neighborhood and ritual area of present residence. The corresponding figures for the other neighborhoods of Cilungulu ritual area are 86.1 percent and 67.0 percent. It is very unusual for a man to become a homestead head under the age of about 30, and so the figures in this category are not really significant. But both parts of the table indicate that homestead heads are likely to reside in the neighborhood of their birth only until about the age of forty-five, by which time most of them have moved away to other neighborhoods. The structural implications of this are explored fully below.

Table 6 illustrates the number and proportions of moves of

Table 6. Number and proportion of residence changes of (1) dependents, (2) homestead heads, (3) 44 homestead owners within their own neighborhood, Temanghuku

	Number of moves						
Category of move	0	1	2	3	4	5	Totals
(1) Outside neighborhood while still dependents	13	18	7	2	4	0	44
	(29.5)	(40.9)	(15.9)	(4.6)	(9.1)	—	(100.0%)
(2) Outside neighborhood as homestead head	17	14	7	4	2	0	44
	(38.5)	(31.8)	(15.9)	(9.1)	(4.6)	—	(100.0%)
(3) Inside neighborhood, no. of homestead sites, (*matongo*)	14	13	10	5	1	1	44
	(31.8)	(29.5)	(22.7)	(11.4)	(2.3)	(2.3)	(100.0%)

residence accomplished by the present homestead heads of Temanghuku, both as dependents (as sons, younger brothers, or in other relationships to their homestead heads) and as homestead heads themselves (category 2), before their arrival in their present neighborhood. Category 3 indicates the number of changes in homestead sites they have completed within Temanghuku neighborhood and thus since their arrival there. The implications of this latter type of movement will be dealt with below; the importance of old homestead sites (*matongo*) has already been noted (Chapter II). The figures here are too small to distinguish sub-categories on the basis of age, or to separate categories 1 and 2 to give a clearer picture. Each category is relevant only within itself. Consequently the figures do not tie up with those in Table 5, for a homestead head may have moved a number of times outside the neighborhood both as dependent and as homestead head, or only as one or the other. Within such a repetitive pattern of residential mobility naturally a homestead head would have accomplished more moves the older he is, as we have seen in Table 5. But given such an age range as that to which these homestead heads belong, the number of changes of residence that Gogo homestead owners are involved in during their lives can be seen to be considerable. It may be added that of these homestead heads, fifteen (34.1%) moved to their present neighborhood of Temanghuku while still dependents, while twenty-six (59.1%) came when already homestead owners. We have seen that only three (6.8%) were born there. Thirty-one (70.5%) had moved one or more times *between* neighborhoods and outside of their present one, as dependents, while twenty-seven (61.5%) had moved one or more times outside of Temanghuku as homestead heads.

It is difficult to differentiate changes of residence caused by the search for grazing from those caused by the search for grain during famines. These, of course, often (but not always) occur together, and in some cases both causes may be present. There is no doubt, however, that the search for grazing and water for livestock during bad periods opens up new areas into which homestead groups may move, which both encourages and assists changes of residence. The relationships utilized by homestead heads during such changes of residence are, as we shall see, *kinship* links of various kinds; but often affinal ties are created anew by the exchange of cattle and women in each generation. The possession of livestock to be exchanged in creating such relationships is thus essential to the process and continuity of Gogo social structure and accounts partly at least for the pastoral ideology and system of values which pervade so many aspects of Gogo culture.[16] The two factors may be seen to be entirely interdependent: the survival of livestock is a primary (though not singular) cause for Gogo spatial mobility, and the possession of such livestock is essential to the successful accomplishment of such moves. In terms of Gogo social structure and its relationship to its ecological environment, both are necessary. Here I want to illustrate the relevance of these factors to the general residential mobility between neighborhoods and ritual areas by another case, which summarizes much of what has been said and what is to follow in this chapter:

Luzu the son of Gayilanga belongs to the Iheru clan who have ritual leadership in the Cahwa ritual area (about twenty-four miles to the east of Temanghuku). His father Gayilanga was born at Cahwa and moved as a mature homestead-owner to Mupunguzi, a distance of some thirty miles south, in search of grazing for his herd. At Mupunguzi he lived in the homestead of his wife's brothers (*walamu'ze*), one of whom was Munjire, until he built his own homestead nearby. Gayilanga died at Mupunguzi and his children moved to Mapanga, ten miles to the west, because of witchcraft accusations which occurred over the recognition of government "chiefs" by the German administration.

Luzu was born at Mupunguzi but brought up at Mapanga, where

[16] I am not implying by this that the passage of bridewealth in exchange for women is of primary importance only in intra-generational contexts. This is obviously not so, as bridewealth transactions almost always concern more than one generation and are of great importance in inter-generation relationships (see Chapters V–VII). I am here emphasizing the use of cattle to create new bonds facilitating residence in new neighborhoods, and the significance of this for spatial mobility.

he married and continued to reside until 1946, when he was about sixty years old. During the 1946 drought and famine he came to Temanghuku neighborhood in Cilungulu in search of grazing for his herd of some 170 head of cattle. [This type of seasonal trip is called *kudimiza.*] This entailed a journey of about twenty-eight miles. He came with the eldest son (then about nineteen) of his deceased second wife, his third and youngest wife Mondigwa, and her daughter [see Figure 4]. His first wife Mwilulya remained at Mapanga with her

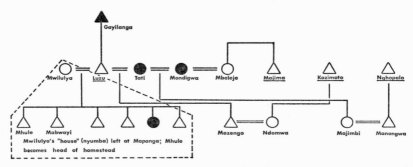

Figure 4. The case of Luzu (names underlined represent present or past homestead heads in Temanghuku neighborhood)

adult sons [that is, her "house," *nyumba,* remained there]. Also with Luzu was Nolo, another homestead head and unrelated neighbor from Mapanga, who also took up residence at Temanghuku later and died there. When they arrived in Temanghuku, they lived in the homestead of Nghopalo, to whom Luzu was not related at the time but who was a rich man and had a very large homestead in Temanghuku. Nghopalo later became Luzu's *muvwele muyagwe* [daughter's husband's father, denoted DHF] when Nghopalo's son Manongwa married Luzu's daughter Majimbi [see Figure 4]. While in Temanghuku on his supposedly temporary trip, Luzu traded some livestock for grain to take back to Mapanga. But when the local elders and head men, together with the government sub-chief, who was a close agnate [classificatory grandfather, *kuku'ye*] of Cilungulu ritual leader, heard that Luzu was taking away some grain and was herding 170 head of cattle in the area, they persuaded him to stay. Luzu then constructed a camp and cleared bush to build a homestead.[17] They thus remained in Temanghuku neighborhood and Luzu, who is now 76 years of age and a senior homestead head and elder in the area, established links with his new neighbors. Mwilulya the first wife stayed on in Mapanga and her sons, now middle-aged men, became homestead heads in their own right.[18]

The son Mazengo had been married at Mapanga. When he returned to Mapanga to get his wife, her father objected and said, "You have moved so far away, I'll take my daughter back and you may have your cattle." [They had married recently and there were no children.] A divorce was arranged. Mazengo then married the daughter of Kazimoto, who is the homestead head immediately adjacent to Luzu in Temanghuku [homestead no. 22, Map 3]. Thus Luzu and Kazimoto also became *civwele* [DHF/SWF].

Some time later, Luzu's third wife Mondigwa died in Temanghuku. Luzu again wished to return to Mapanga to his first wife Mwilulya, but Kazimoto also objected to Mazengo taking his daughter to live at such a distance. Mazengo told his father that he had destroyed one marriage of his by changing residence and he would not do it again, so he was staying on in Temanghuku. Luzu decided he did not wish to leave his son, so he resigned himself once again to staying. Luzu then married a fourth wife Mbeleje, in Temanghuku. She is the full-sister of Majima, a neighboring homestead head in the same cluster in Temanghuku [homestead no. 46, Map 3]. Luzu and Majima thus became full "brothers-in-law" (*walamu*). Subsequently he also married Lyamunze [not included in Figure 4], classificatory "daughter" (*mwana'gwe*) of Mbeleje, from the immediately adjacent neighborhood of Wangama [see Map 3]

This case illustrates several important principles which have general validity for Gogo residential patterns, mobility, and local organization. It shows the history of movement from neighborhood to neighborhood, with considerable distances involved each

[17] Luzu is now head of the homestead no. 7 on Map 3.
[18] This is a very common pattern of homestead fission and will be illustrated and discussed in Chapter V.

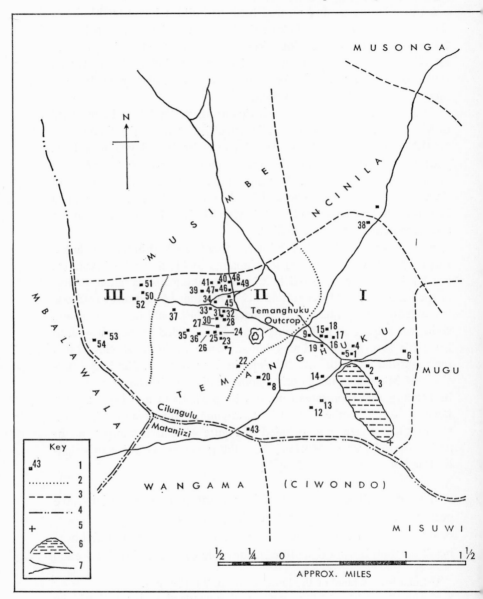

Map 3. Temanghuku and adjacent neighborhoods showing clusters and homesteads.

1: Homesteads (numbers refer to text and genealogies). 2: Distinction between clusters (*vitumbi*) I ("Kwilamba"), II ("Kwitunda"), III ("Musangambuya"). 3: Neighborhood (*matumbi*) boundaries. 4: Ritual area (*yisi*) boundaries. 5: Gravestone and old homestead site of neighborhood founder Sandiya, present venue for propitiation rituals for homesteads (nos. 1, 5, and 6). 6: Water pan (*ilamba*). 7: Cattle tracks (*mapalilo*) and foot paths (*nzila*).

time, in previous as well as present generations of homestead heads, to be a generally valid pattern.[19] Other factors illustrated by the case are: the general causes of spatial mobility such as the search for grazing, water, and grain, and avoidance of witch-craft accusations; the emotional attachment to the area of up-bringing and lengthy residence; the opposing necessities dictated by the inter-connections between economic survival, livestock herds and the values attaching to them; the precedence of deci-sions concerning livestock and herding over those in other spheres of activity, in spite of the general economic dependence upon grain crops for basic subsistence; the establishing of a new set of affinal bonds in new areas of residence by the exchange of livestock for women; the reluctance of close affines to agree to residential separation; and the utilization of affinal relation-ships to facilitate such moves. The case also illustrates one type of fission in domestic groups while the husband/father is still alive and in control of property; but this will be dealt with in Chapter V. I now turn to a rapid description, in case form, of the cyclical (historical) phases of neighborhood development, before considering in detail the relationships which exist among the heads of homesteads in one neighborhood.

THE FOUNDING OF A NEIGHBORHOOD [20]

First phase:

Temanghuku neighborhood lies within the Cilungulu ritual area in which ritual leadership belongs to the Deje clan of the

---

[19] Luzu's father Gayilanga must have moved from Cahwa to Mupun-guzi in the latter part of the 19th century (Luzu is now 76). This would have been before European penetration of any significance and thus prior to any disruptions and changes which have occurred as a result of colonial administration. I have other records confirming this pattern of residential change for even earlier generations.

[20] As in the case of the numerical data already presented, I am here concerned with only one neighborhood. I have detailed information on the historical growth of another neighborhood, Cidabaga of Loje ritual area, many miles to the south in southern Ugogo. This confirms the

Cisi *mulongo*. The founder of the neighborhood known as Temanghuku was, however, of the Pulu clan, who are "sister's sons" (*wehwa*) to the Deje.[21] He was Sandiya the son of Ngobito (see Figure 5). Ngobito was born in Ikogolo ritual

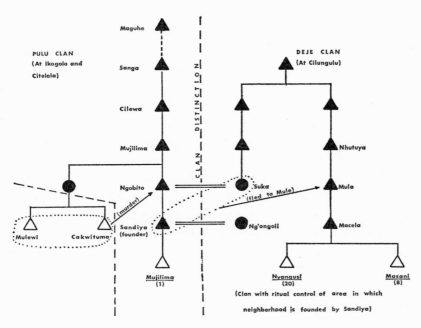

Figure 5. Sandiya and the founding of Temanghuku neighborhood (names underlined represent homesteads heads, Temanghuku; numbers refer to those used in Map 3)

area, where the Wanyikogolo, his maximal lineage (*mulango*), have ritual precedence. He moved to Citelela when the Germans fought the Gogo at Ikogolo. Ngobito married Suka, also of the Deje clan and the *mulongo* Cisi, who bore Sandiya. Later, two of Ngobito's sister's sons (*wehwa*) followed him to Citelela, and

---

general pattern described, although Cidabaga was a "younger" neighborhood and therefore at an earlier phase of its growth cycle.

[21] A "perpetual kinship" link: see Chapter III.

finding him at his homestead, they killed him with their spears. The reason for this heinous act is given by Pulu elders as follows:

Ngobito's sister's sons killed him because they quarrelled with him about their mother, who was very ill. They decided, "This mother's brother of ours (*Ayu kuku yetu*) is bewitching her [his sister]." When Ngobito moved from Ikogolo to Citelela, the embittered sons of his sister followed him there [both of them, Mulewi and Cakwituma] and they stabbed him terribly with their spears, and he died.[22] Suka fled with her child Sandiya to Misuwi neighborhood in Cilungulu, to the homestead of her classificatory brother [her patrilateral parallel cousin, *ilumbu'lye, wali cana cawasewo*] Mule.

Sandiya thus grew up in the Misuwi neighborhood at the homestead of his classificatory mother's brother (*kuku'ye*). He married Ng'ongoli, also of the Deje clan, and when his eldest son Mujilima was about four years old, he went to the water pan (*ilamba*) called Temanghuku, near the rocky hill (*itunda*) called Temanghuku, and cleared bush for a homestead. This was just after the 1918–19 Mutunya famine, and it was then that Temanghuku neighborhood was founded, at least insofar as those involved in its present cycle of growth are concerned. Sandiya did not move very far from this site until his death, and his gravestone (*citenjelo*) marks his last homestead and the spot where his sons Mujilima, Cosi, and Mhaka (homestead nos. 1, 5, and 6) now carry out their propitiation rituals (see Map 3).

When Sandiya and his two wives and children were established in this neighborhood, they cleared fields immediately to the east of the water pan. Three other homestead heads, Mataji, Ndilibe, and Cinyele, followed him there. Mataji constructed his own camp while building his homestead nearby, but both the others

---

[22] The structural implications of this incident are examined in the discussion of the mother's-brother/sister's-son relationship, below. It should be noted here that, because of the situation of witchcraft accusation between brother and sister, the ritual relationship between Ngobito and his sister's sons may, by inference, be seen to have broken down. They were thus forced into this action and there was no other course for retaliation.

attached themselves and their dependents to Sandiya's homestead as *wazenji* (builders of another's homestead).[23] By the time Sandiya died, several others had set up homesteads nearby in Temanghuku, including Nghopalo who has already been referred to in Luzu's case (see Figure 4) and who was to play a significant part in the expansion of Temanghuku. On Sandiya's death, Mujilima, the eldest son of the senior house (*nyumba imbaha*), became homestead head. Mujilima and his dependents subsequently lived at three other homestead sites, all on the eastern side of the *ilamba* and a few hundred yards from each other, until he built his present homestead (no. 1, Map 3) some thirteen years ago. Mujilima continues to live with his full brother Kamoga, their wives and other dependents (see Figure 6), although their mother Ng'ongoli is dead. Their half brothers Cosi and Mhaka set up their own homestead with their mother Mahungo who is still alive and lives with Mhaka (no. 5). Later, because of a quarrel, Cosi left his full brother and built his own homestead (no. 6) some distance away to the east, where he lives with his dependents.[24] This group of full and half siblings, sons of the neighborhood founder Sandiya, form the core of the homestead cluster and sub-division (*citumbi*) of Temanghuku neighborhood, known as Kwilamba (at the water-pan) (I, Map 3).

NEIGHBORHOOD SUB-DIVISIONS AND CLUSTERS (*VITUMBI*)[25]

Kwilamba, then, constitutes the oldest and original part of Temanghuku neighborhood, in which the first phase of its development took place. Some of the relationships that exist between the present homestead heads in this cluster are represented diagrammatically in Figure 6. The fact that it is the longest

23 The concept of *muzenji* is elaborated in Chapter V.

24 Fission in the unit of full brothers while their mother is still alive is very uncommon and occurs as a result of special circumstances which will be discussed in Chapter V.

25 *Citumbi* (pl., *vitumbi*) is the diminutive form of the noun *itumbi*, neighborhood, but is seldom used in Cigogo.

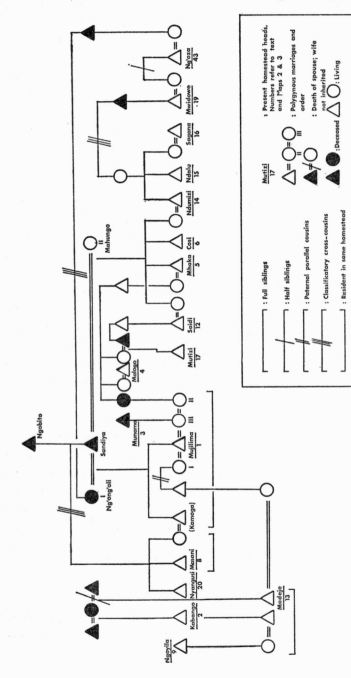

Figure 6. Some kinship and affinal links among homestead heads, "Kwilamba" cluster, Temanghuku neighborhood (see Maps 2 and 3)

established part of the neighborhood does not mean that all the homestead owners living in this area have been there longer than those in other sub-divisions of the neighborhood. It means simply that it is the area from which the whole neighborhood grew, and where the descendants of the founder and their closely related kin and affines reside.

We have seen that Mujilima (1), Cosi (6), and Mhaka (5), owners of three adjacent homesteads in the southeastern cluster of the neighborhood sub-division, are the core group of "children of one man" (*wana wamunhu umonga*). Malogo (4), who is poor and has no livestock, has also been in the neighborhood most of his life, but was born in another, close to the south in Matanjizi ritual area. He is classificatory "wife's father" (*mukwe*) to all three brothers.

Homestead owners Masani (8) and Nyangusi (20) are also a group of full brothers living in adjacent homesteads, who have been in the neighborhood for over thirty years. They belong to the Deje clan who have ritual leadership in Cilungulu ritual area (see Figure 5), and although they were born in the ritual area of Mukonze some twenty miles to the south, they came to Temanghuku with their father, who died there. They are related to the Mujilima group of siblings in a number of ways: they belong to clans which stand in a "perpetual kinship" relationship of "mother's brothers/sister's sons"; they are classificatory cross-cousins (*wali wuhizi*) (see Figures 5 and 6); and they are also "brothers-in-law" (*walamu*) because Kamoga, Mujilima's younger full brother, is married to the full sister of Masani and Nyangusi.

Munama (3) and Ng'oza (43) are also early residents of Temanghuku, having migrated there over thirty years before, with fairly large herds, particularly in the case of Ng'oza. In spite of the fact that they belong to the same clan (Pulu), have the same sub-clan name (but belong to different maximal lineages), Munama is also an affine to Mujilima and his group of siblings. Mujilima married his daughter and is therefore "son-in-law" (*mukwe mulima*) to Munama. But they were affines of another sort even before this marriage, because Kaega, Munama's younger brother who lives in Musimbe neighborhood three miles away to the northwest, had previously married Mujilima's full sister Henza. These two sets of siblings are consequently linked by two types of affinal relationships: as "WF/DH" (*mukwe/ mukwemulima*) and again as "WB/ZH" (*walamu*).

Among those who have lived in Temanghuku for some time and have not yet moved on elsewhere, are the homestead heads and their dependents who came to the area during the 1939 famine (*nzala yaJoni*), twenty-three years ago. In the *ilamba* cluster are Ngoyila (9), Mutizi (17), and Mwidowe (19) who belong to this category. After a series of broken marriages, Ngoyila, haunted by witchcraft accusations, came to Temanghuku with his cattle during the 1939 drought, to live with his classificatory mother's brother (*kuku'ye*) Nghopalo. Several of Ngoyila's classificatory cross-cousins are homestead owners in other parts of the neighborhood, and in Ncinila and Musonga neighborhoods immediately to the north and northeast (see Map 3), but all within Cilungulu ritual area. Having lost wives and children by death and separation, Ngoyila went to work for some time with Haji, an Indian who owned a small store in Temanghuku, in a part of what is now Ngoyila's homestead. Haji's son Sidi, whose mother is African, still lives there but no longer runs the store on any scale. While in Temanghuku, Ngoyila married a widow whose daughter by her previous husband is married to Muganga, the son of Kabango (2) (see Figure 6). Although the girl is the daughter of the dead husband, Ngoyila's relationship with Muganga and his father is based on the assumption that Ngoyila is her "father." He is thus *mukwe* ("WF") to Muganga and *muvwele* ("SWF") to Kabango.

Mutizi (17) who is also of the Pulu clan, came to Temanghuku from Nzasa, ten miles to the east in the heart of the ritual areas controlled by the Pulu. His father had died at Nzasa, and he came with his mother (who now lives with him) and younger full brother, also living with him at present. He brought his wife and two children, all of whom died in Temanghuku, and a small herd. His reasons for moving were a mixture of witchcraft fears and the quest for grazing. On arrival the family attached themselves to the homestead of Citojo, Mutizi's classificatory "father" (*sogwe*), who actually was his mother's elder full-sister's husband, and father of Mujilima's (1) second wife. Citojo was then living in Temanghuku, from which he moved to Musimbe neighborhood where he died in 1963.

Mwidowe (19) of the Nyanghwalo clan who have ritual leadership in Bahi, twenty-six miles to the west, is also in this category. His father Musote had died at Swaswa neighborhood in Dodoma, and Mwidowe came to Temanghuku with his two elder half brothers Biliya and Timba, his younger full-sister and brothers, and his mother. When the group of siblings arrived in Temanghuku they lived for three years in the homestead of Mataji, one of the earliest homestead owners with Sandiya. Mataji was classificatory "father" (*usewo*) to them, actually matrilateral cross-cousin to their father Musote. Mataji moved away to another neighborhood some time later and Biliya and his dependents built their own homestead, for Biliya was the oldest son of the senior house and became homestead head. Biliya and Timba died in Temanghuku and Mwidowe became homestead head himself, at the same time inheriting their wives. Apart from the links between Mwidowe and his neighbors shown in Figure 6, Mwidowe is "father-in-law" to the Mujilima (1) group, as Cosi (6) is married to the daughter of Biliya, Mwidowe's BD.

Second phase:

The next phase of population influx into Temanghuku (and one in which a large proportion of the present homestead owners of the kwitunda [II] part of the neighborhood arrived) was during the 1946 drought and famine called *nzala yaHambaya*. In this year large numbers of livestock died in Ugogo, but Temanghuku was probably less affected than other areas. This may be inferred from the fact that many homestead owners came to the area in search of both grazing and grain.[26] But apart from those now established in the "Kwitunda" area, Kabango (2), Madeje (13), Ndumizi (14), Ndalu (15), and Sagana (16) of the Kwilamba area also came to Temanghuku at this time. Kabango, an elder of about sixty-five years of age in 1962, and a moderately successful diviner (*muganga*), had come from Miyonwe in Cinyambwa, thirty-four miles to the southwest. He moved via Mhalanga in Luatu and Wuloga in Cipanga. The primary reason for his move was the death of his children and witchcraft accusations at Miyonwe; but he came to Temanghuku also to settle a case concerning the behavior of his full sister, the wife of Mwaja, who lived there. When Kabango came to Temanghuku, he liked the neighborhood, and his skills as a diviner were immediately recognized through some successful cases involving fertility medicines.[27] Madole, now a resident of the Kwitunda part of Temanghuku who had moved there from the same area, informed Kabango's wife and three sons that Kabango wanted to remain in Temanghuku, and so they moved there to join him. Arriving in Temanghuku, they attached themselves to Mwaja's homestead for several years, then to Mujilima (1), and later built their own homestead (2). Two sons married in Temanghuku, and as they had no livestock as a result of this, having given them all in bride-

---

[26] For example, see the case of Luzu, earlier in this chapter. I have already made reference to Gogo knowledge as to where grazing and water may be found at such times. Madeje (13), who came from Nhati to Temanghuku at this time, said, "We moved from where we were because of famine (*kusoko yanzala*). There was a great deal of grain in Cilungulu ritual area and in Mundemu, even as far as Musisi." Temanghuku (and indeed all the neighborhoods of Cilungulu) were affected by the 1953–54 drought to a much greater extent. This caused a major exodus of population and livestock. Worst affected was Mugu neighborhood, immediately to the east of Temanghuku (see Map 3), which lost most of its homesteads. Many went about 20 miles northwest to Lamaiti and in 1962 Mugu neighborhood had only 6 homesteads left from what everyone assured me was a large population, and the bush was regenerating.

[27] Diviners establish a wide reputation over the countryside for the efficacy of their own particular medicines, and a good reputation in any field of medicine would facilitate a move to many different areas.

wealth, Kabango became a stock trustee (*mukozigwa*) of Muji-lima (1) but also continued his diviner's practice. In 1962, Kabango's wife (who was now past menopause) moved back, with her youngest son who was about twenty, to her brother's homestead at Cigwambuga, eighteen miles to the southwest. At this, the homestead broke up, the eldest son Masaka went with his wife and child to live as an unrelated *muzenji* with Cosi (6); and Muganga went with his wife to live with Madeje (13), his classificatory "father" (*sogwe*). Kabango made several trips to other parts of Ugogo as a diviner, eventually joining his wife at Cigwambuga.

Madeje (13) came to Temanghuku with Kabango, who is his "elder brother" (*muwaha'gwe*): both were the children of the same mother but of different fathers (see Figure 6). They belong to different clans. When Kabango was born, his father Ihangha died, and there was no suitable man to inherit Kabango's mother. She then returned to her home at Isanza and was married again, bearing several children by Nyamusada, Madeje's father. Madeje was the youngest child (*muziwanda*). His mother and father died at Nhati, forty miles to the south of Temanghuku. He had no live-stock or property of any kind, so he attached himself to Kabango. When Kabango built his own homestead in Temanghuku, Madeje stayed on with Mujilima and later married Mujilima's classifi-catory "daughter" (*mwana'gwe*), actually his WBD. He thus became classificatory "son-in-law" (*mukwe mulima*) to Mujilima. This was accomplished with the aid, including livestock, of Muji-lima and Kabango, and Madeje set up his own homestead (13) some years later.

Ndumizi (14) was born at Cigongwe, a few miles to the south. He came to Temanghuku with his elder full brother Ndalu (15), full sister Majimbi, and her husband Sagana (16).[28] Wulaya, their mother's full sister's son (*wali cana canyina*), was living at Temanghuku at the time, and they came to the neighborhood on

[28] Actually, Ndalu and Ndumizi had different genitors but considered themselves the sons of the same social father, Mangwela, and thus as full brothers. This case is discussed later.

his instigation and lived in his homestead for two years. He then left Temanghuku and went to live in the nearby neighborhood of Musimbe, and the Ndumizi-Ndalu group lived with Timba, Mwidowe's elder half brother, until Ndalu married.[29] They then built their own homestead at the site of present homestead (15) and Ndalu became homestead head. Ndumizi went away to Tanga as a laborer for two years, and when he returned, married Malewo, Cosi's (6) and Mhaka's (5) full sister, with aid from Ndalu in bridewealth. A little later, Sagana (16) became the lover (*mbuya*) of Ndalu's wife, his own WBW. Although this arrangement is possible in Wugogo where they were then living, it is considered very bad in southwestern Ugogo from where the whole group had come.[30] There was conflict, and Ndalu accused his brother of aiding and abetting Sagana in his amorous activities. They came to blows, and as a consequence, Ndumizi moved away with his wife to build his own homestead at (14), taking the building materials of his own house (*nyumba*) at (15) away with him. This left Ndalu and Sagana in the remaining wings of homestead no. 15, which are in some contexts considered as one homestead, in others as two (15 and 16). Ndumizi's homestead grew. He was the youngest homestead owner (27 years of age) in Temanghuku and the only one of his age group to be so. In 1962, after further quarrels and violence, Sagana moved back to Matandala in Cigongwe, with his wife Majimbi, to live with his agnatic relatives, and Ndalu built himself a new homestead at a site some 200 yards from the old one and adjacent to his brother Ndumizi's homestead (14).

Third phase:

Finally, there are the homesteads which have been built by those who have come to Temanghuku more recently, within the

[29] Timba and Mwidowe were classificatory cross-cousins (*wahizi*) to the Ndalu-Ndumizi group (see Figure 6).

[30] The institution of *mbuya* and its consequences for marriage in Gogo are referred to in Chapter VI, and a detailed analysis of it is forthcoming.

past 10 years or so. Saidi (12) is one of these. He is of the Pulu clan and is forty-three years old. He is one of the few homestead owners whose father is still alive. His father Cihoma lives at Tinayi neighborhood, twelve miles to the north, from which Saidi had moved to Temanghuku four years before. He says he moved simply because he liked "the living" (*mukungwe*) at Temanghuku better than at Tinayi, but this is a clear case of the many in Gogo in which an adult eldest son of a senior house (as Saidi is) prefers to leave his father and other agnates to live with affines. In this case Saidi is living with his wife's brothers, Mujilima (1), Cosi (6), and Mhaka (5). When he arrived in Temanghuku with his wife and children, he lived with Ndumizi (14), his WZH, *mutozi muyagwe*, while building his own homestead on an immediately adjacent site.

I have described in some detail the histories of individual homestead-heads and their dependents in this section to illustrate the general pattern of movement in and out of neighborhoods, and the kinds of relationships utilized or created to facilitate this mobility. The general underlying principles have already been outlined, and I return to an analysis of the relationships operating in Gogo neighborhoods after a brief look at the expansion of the other clusters in Temanghuku.

NEIGHBORHOOD EXPANSION

It must be realized that, just as neighborhood boundaries are not clear-cut (they cannot actually be seen "on the ground"), so those between parts (*vitumbi*) of a neighborhood are more inferred than visible. Although in the previous section, and in Figure 6, I have considered in isolation some of the kinship and other links between homestead owners in the Kwilamba *citumbi* of Temanghuku (for want of a more convenient approach), these persons and their dependents obviously have numerous links with others, both in the other clusters of Temanghuku and in other neighborhoods and ritual areas.

The multiple-link complex which exists between homestead

heads (and others in their homesteads) in Gogo local communities inhibits the presentation of these links on genealogical diagrams, as may be seen from Figure 6. I therefore do not present in a similar manner the way in which the homestead heads in the other *vitumbi* of Temanghuku established themselves and the links which exist between them, but I later consider the frequencies of such relationships for the whole neighborhood. The general pattern may be assumed to be similar to that already described for Kwilamba cluster.

Nghopalo, a rich man, came to settle in Temanghuku in Kwilamba *citumbi* during the early years of its expansion, and built a homestead near Sandiya's (later Mujilima's) on the east side of the water pan. He had come from Mutumba, twenty-four miles to the east, looking for grazing. In the following years, particularly during the drought years of 1939 and 1946 already outlined, a large number of people came to Temanghuku, linking themselves to Nghopalo's homestead either as affines, cognatic kin, or unrelated dependents (*wazenji*). Having established themselves in the neighborhood, they built their own homesteads nearby. In the year following the 1939 famine, Nghopalo moved to the western side of the rocky hill called Temanghuku, and the other part of the neighborhood was established. This was all thick bush at the time and much clearing had to be done before homesteads and fields could be made. Thirteen of the present homestead heads in the Kwitunda and Msangambuya clusters (II and III, Map 3) have at some time been attached to Nghopalo's homestead, for varying periods, both before and after his move. As this number constitutes 44 percent of the homesteads in these clusters, the crucial role Nghopalo played in the expansion of this area may be appreciated. The homestead owners themselves tend to view their homesteads as having been "born of the one homestead" (*kaya zose zalelwa na kaya imonga*): that of Nghopalo, although others built their homesteads independently, or lived with others while they did so.[31] Nghopalo has now left the neighborhood and

[31] In contrast to this, none of the homesteads in these clusters (II and

moved to Lamaiti, twenty-two miles to the northwest. The manner of settlement and the relationships between the occupants of homesteads in Temanghuku, however, imply a sociological division between those Kwilamba on the one hand, and Kwitunda and Msangambuya on the other. The Msangambuya cluster is more recent and is said to be an extension of the Kwitunda cluster.

This division is further reflected in the frequency of kinship and affinal links existing between homestead heads, within and between these clusters. Of the total of 126 kinship and affinal relationships[32] existing between the forty-five homestead owners of Temanghuku, and considered as signficant by them,[33] ninety-four (or 74.6%) are intra-cluster links (i.e. between homestead heads living in the same cluster) and only one quarter (25.4%) are between homestead heads living in different clusters. This clearly indicates the relationship between such links and residence clusters within Gogo neighborhoods.

We are now in a position to reconsider the significance of neighborhood boundaries and the distinctions between clusters. The pattern may be stated generally as follows: although Gogo neighborhoods are not discrete geographical units in all respects and are not sub-divided by any marked boundaries, homesteads tend to cluster together in neighborhoods and within each neighborhood into clusters on the basis of cognatic kinship and affinal links. This pattern is "constant" in spite of the continual arrival and departure of homestead heads (and persons dependent upon them) within the situation of a generally high residential mobility.

III) were attached originally to Sandiya's homestead or to those of his dependents. Four of the present homesteads in Kwilamba *citumbi*, apart from Mujilima (1) himself, were "born of" the founder's homestead. Others had been attached originally to early residents and neighbors of Sandiya, such as Mataji.

[32] See Table 7 below for an analysis of these relationships.

[33] By this I mean that some may be related in ways other than those recorded in Table 7, but such links are not considered as significant, and therefore operative, by the homestead heads themselves. The problems which arise from this recognition of some links and the ignoring of others is explored further in Chapter VII.

Such links may pre-exist and facilitate the moves or may be established after settlement by the creation of new affinal ties, which are followed by ties of filiation and descent. Homesteads grow up adjacent to each other in which such ties continue to operate. Overall there is the pattern of cyclical growth of neighborhoods, and their eventual decline caused either by the exhaustion of resources or (more usually) droughts and famines which cause new homestead movements.

This pattern gives rise to two types of fission in Gogo domestic groups: (a) that which arises from internal forces as the polygynous family matures and "houses" break away, and (b) the constant separation (and accretion) of individual family heads and their dependents, related in a variety of ways to the homestead head. Both are intrinsically related to the operation of Gogo kinship relationships and the ecological environment and economic values of Gogo. The first type will be analyzed in Chapter V. Here it remains to consider the general pattern of the types of relationships which operate in Gogo neighborhoods.

KINSHIP AND NEIGHBORHOOD

It has been shown that the ties of patrilineal descent and clanship cut across neighborhood and ritual-area boundaries and have territorial significance only in respect of the stool-holding groups of the ritually dominant clans in each ritual area. As far as the operation of kinship relationships are concerned, as opposed to descent groups, it remains valid to isolate the neighborhood as a unit for analysis. All the more so since these relationships are predominantly of the kind established within each generation, or between individuals of two proximate generations, allowing the pattern of mobility and residence characteristic of Ugogo. This occurs within the context of the cross-cutting principles of (necessarily) dispersed descent categories and the broad significance of locality.

The forty-five homestead heads of Temanghuku are related as kin and affines by 126 links which they feel are significant in their everyday activities. These are set out in Table 7, by the frequency with which relationships of each type appear. Some notes of explanation are required before I set out to consider the significance of these frequencies.

Table 7. Frequency of links between homestead heads in Temanghuku neighborhood, by category of relationships

Relationship category	Basic description and sub-categories	"Primary"	"Classificatory"	Totals	Percentage
			No. of links		
Muwaha/ munakwawe	eB/yB; full siblings (*nyumba imonga*).	4	—	4	3.2
	Half siblings (*nyumba mitala*).	3	—	3	2.4
	Patrilateral parallel cousins (*cana cawasewo*).	3	2	5	3.9
	Matrilateral parallel cousins (*cana canyina*).	1	—	1	0.8
Sogwe/mwana'gwe	"Father/son"	1	4	5	3.9
Kuku/mwihwa	"MB/ZS"	5	4	9	7.2
Wuhizi	"MBS/FZS"	3	7	10	7.9
Mukwe/mukwe- mulima	"WF/DH"	2	22	24	19.1
Wulamu	"WB/ZH"	7	36	43	34.1
Watozi	"WZH/WZH"	3	6	9	7.2
Civwele	"SWF/DHF"	1	12	13	10.3
Totals		33	93	126	100.0
		(26.2%)	(73.8%)	(100%)	

First, they represent only relationships between the forty-five homestead heads (*wanyakaya*) and not between all the members of their homesteads, of which the total population is 413 adults and children, unless such links recognizably relate the homestead owners themselves. For example, the fathers of a married couple are linked in the *civwele* category, SWF/DHF. But links between dependents who are unrelated, or not significantly related, to the heads, are not represented. Second, the links are divided into "primary" and "classificatory." "Primary" indicates a relationship of the first degree in each category, such as "own" MBS/FZD or "actual" ZH/WB. All relationships in the "classificatory" column are those beyond the "primary" but which fall into these categories in Gogo kinship nomenclature. Thus, the children of full or half brothers would be "primary" paternal parallel-cousins, but their children would be in the classificatory column. Such distinctions would not, of course, apply to the sub-categories "full siblings" and "half siblings," which would all naturally be "primary."[34]

Third, the frequencies relate to the Gogo categories of kinship reference denoted by the terms in the first column, which are *not defined* by the shorthand descriptions in the second column. These are merely "genealogical positions concordant with the categories" (Needham, 1960, p. 93). For example, one's wife's classificatory "FZH" would fall in the Gogo category "father-in-law" (*mukwe,* "WF") and would be recorded in the *mukwe/mukwe-mulima* category. I do not here analyze the "meaning" of such categories as this is the subject of subsequent chapters. I merely wish to establish the frequency with which links of each category occur between homestead owners in Gogo neighborhoods, and which must be assumed, for the moment, to be "significant" in that the persons concerned address each other by the appropriate terms of address corresponding to these categories and whose behavior toward one another is defined by, or influenced by, their being linked in such relationships.

Finally, it is clear that the data presented in the table do not refer to "ego-oriented" relationships. All the categories are role or "double categories" in that they denote the relationship between two persons in each case. Where the terms of reference are

[34] It will be clear that I am not using the term "classificatory" in the sense that it is normally used to describe a system of *kinship terminology:* that is, a system in which terms for lineal kinsmen are also used for collaterals. I am using the terms "primary" and "classificatory" simply, in a descriptive way, to distinguish genealogical distance.

symmetrical, the relationship has been denoted by the one word in the Gogo category; where it is not, by both words denoting the relationship. This does not, of course, mean that the behavior implied by the former terms is symmetrical.[35] For present purposes, however, these distinctions need not be taken into account.

The first and most obvious point that arises from these frequencies is that agnatic links based upon patrilineal descent account for a total of only seventeen (13.4%) of all links between homestead heads in Temanghuku. Seven of these (5.6% of the total) are between full and half siblings, the "children of one man." It should be noted, however, that when full brothers live in the same neighborhood they often share a homestead, even when married, particularly if their mother is still alive.[36] But rarely in Temanghuku are there adult half brothers sharing the same homestead after the death of their father, although the case of Mwidowe (19) shows that this does occur. In only one case is a son living as a homestead owner near his father in the same neighborhood; Hata (32) has his own homestead a few hundred yards from the homestead of his own father Balidi (56). Hata's mother is dead, and he was the only son of his "house." He has thus been able to establish control over livestock allocated to his house. Balidi lives with his surviving junior wife and her daughters, and there is a running conflict between him and his son over the number of livestock Hata has the right to control. They herd together. All the other "Father/son" links are classificatory, indicating that when adult sons (even when married) live in the same neighborhood as their fathers, they usually live in their fathers' homesteads. But it will appear later that even in this case, the number of married sons living with their fathers is very small.

[35] As all the homestead heads are men in Temanghuku, the distinctions made when a woman is speaking are irrelevant here. Women can be homestead heads in Ugogo, but only in exceptional circumstances, some of which are examined in Chapters V and VI.

[36] The social composition of homesteads is discussed in Chapter V.

"Mother's brother/sister's son" links are as common as "Father/son" links, and if the classificatory links are added, account for nine (7.2%) of the total number. Such relationships are often used in Ugogo to establish common residence, and there are numerous cases in the individual life-histories of the residents of Temanghuku, including the founder Sandiya.[37] Mother's brothers and their sister's sons in Ugogo have a common interest in property (livestock) and strong bonds of ritual interdependence, which I describe later. This is also true of relationships between cross-cousins (*wahizi*) which account for ten (7.9%) of all links between homestead heads. As Evans-Pritchard clearly demonstrates for the Nuer, the co-residence of kin either in the "MB/ZS" or cross-cousin categories results not only from the return of mothers to their agnatic kin (their "brothers") for various reasons, but also from the co-residence of affinal kin in the previous generation. The signficance of this for residence, mobility, and the operation of kinship relationships in Ugogo (and thus for the whole structure of Gogo society and its relation to its environment) is far-reaching. But even with the co-residence of affines, which is a common pattern, the high residential mobility of Gogo homesteads and domestic units ensures that relationships based upon descent do not account for a high proportion of links between homestead owners within each neighborhood, or even in neighboring localities.

Consistent with the analysis which has been presented so far

[37] Gogo do not "convert" these ties in retrospect into patrilineal descent links after prolonged common residence, as do Nuer, by treating the mother as "a man" and thus re-ordering the genealogical connection to fit the "patrilineal principle." This is common in Nuer local communities and appears to be a device to compensate for the discrepancy between the principle of patrilineal descent and the resulting groups and their relation to residence. (See Evans-Pritchard, 1945, pp. 41 and 65; and 1951, p. 16.) It has been shown for Gogo that although the principle of patrilineal descent exists it has little import for residence and local communities. Thus such a device would serve no purpose. This has been shown to be true even for the genealogical history of clans with ritual leadership (see Chapter III).

in this chapter, these figures indicate clearly that the great majority of links binding homestead owners to each other in Temanghuku neighborhood (and as a general pattern throughout Ugogo) arise from affinal relationships of one kind or another. Eighty-nine (70.7%) of the 126 significant links belong to these categories. Links between "brothers-in-law" (*walamu*, "WB/ZH") make up the largest single number of forty-three (34.1%), although most of these are "classificatory," followed by twenty-four (19.1%) between "fathers-in-law" and their daughters' husbands (*wakwe mulima*), again mostly "classificatory." Relationships between men married to siblings or to women related closely in other ways (*watozi*), account for nine (7.2%) of the total, and the "fathers" of children married to each other (*civwele*, "SWF/DHF") for thirteen (10.3%) of the total, most of the latter in the classificatory category.

It is clear that in such a situation the homestead owners living in Gogo neighborhoods belong to a large number of clans and broader descent categories. Over time, the members of these descent categories become dispersed over large areas of Ugogo and have little or no contact with each other, although there are statistical preponderances of the members of certain clans in certain areas.[38] I show later why groups of agnates become dispersed, necessitating the increased importance of other kinds of relationships. The frequency with which these relationships occur has been analyzed. I now turn to a very brief examination of the way in which these appear in relation to residential clusters "on the ground."

KINSHIP AND HOMESTEAD CLUSTERS

Kin who form the core members of clusters within Gogo neighborhoods, and thus the units which are most important in the process of growth and fission in neighborhoods, are groups of half and full siblings, primarily men but women as well, whose

[38] The clan affiliations, sub-clan names, and avoidances of the Temanghuku homestead owners are given in Appendix C.

fathers have died or abandoned their control by moving on else-where. Full siblings are kept together while their mother is alive, for the herd allocated to their "house" may not be divided until she is dead. There is more in it than a mere rule sanctioning such a norm. It also ensures the continued interest of her brothers in her children and their herd.

Half brothers may remain in the same neighborhood to be near the gravestone (*citenjelo*) of their father, for this is crucial in contacting the spirits of the dead. The presence of the eldest sibling at such rituals is also important but, as we shall see, his control is far from great. As the heads of such homesteads mature the proximity to gravestones of their fathers become less im-portant and they begin to move apart, their homesteads begin to break up with adult sons setting up as new units of full siblings with their mothers. It only requires a drought or famine to cause the complete disintegration of the old agnatic groups in terms of residence.

A glance at Figure 6 and the previous discussion will show this to be true of the Kwilamba part of Temanghuku neighborhood. It applies equally to homestead owners born in the neighborhood and to later immigrants who settle in groups of full and half siblings. Links are established between these sibling groups by marriages, many of which take place within a restricted area, whether in the same neighborhood or between homestead clusters in immediately neighboring areas. Otherwise unattached home-steads are also linked up in the same way. Thus, in the Kwilamba *citumbi*, Mujilima (1), Cosi (6) and Mhaka (5) are a group of full and half siblings, together with Kamoga, Mujilima's younger full brother who lives with him. Mutizi (17) has his married full brother Nghangala living with him, and Ndumizi (14) and Ndalu (15) are full brothers living in adjacent homesteads; Sagana (16) was attached to them through his marriage to their sister. Nyangusi (20) and Masani (8) are full brothers and Masani has his two younger full brothers Saidi (married) and Mutinya (unmarried) living with him. These groups are in turn linked together by a complex of affinal ties in the same generation and by a variety of links through other generations. Malogo (4) is attached through marriage to a sibling group (mainly women) in the first ascending generation, and their children, most of whom are resident in the same area (see Figure 6). Mwidowe (19) originally lived with two half brothers in Temanghuku until they died, and he is attached by various affinal and cross-cousin links to the other units; and so on.

The same could be shown for other parts of Temanghuku neighborhood. Mukunya (33) and Madeje (49) are full brothers in nearby homesteads (see Map 3). Masenha's (34) senior wife Doga is the full sister of Madala, the wife of Cibu-maga (32). These two wives are the full sisters of Poga (54). Poga is also Mujilima's (1) cross-cousin (FZS, *muhizi*), as his mother is Mujilima's father's full sister.

In spite of these relationships, the affinal links established predominate and overshadow these groups in the context of the kinship network within the whole neighborhood. It is also clear, however, that this complex of affinal relationships has implications for the residence of kin and their spouses in the following generation, and at most (in the Gogo context) to the second descending generation from a given point. Spatial mobility is so high that these links have little meaning, in respect to residence, beyond this, and are invoked only if they happen to coincide with residence. Relationships which are current must constantly be expressed in the exchange of cattle and other goods and services, including ritual ones. How the system of inheritance and the distribution of livestock dovetails with this pattern appears in Chapter V. Marriages will be seen to be not the concern of patrilineal corporate lineages in which the ownership of livestock is invested (as in many patrilineal societies in the Bantu area), but rather of mobile small groups of kin with the herds in which they have mutual, if sometimes cross-cutting, interests. The patrilineal inheritance of livestock is differentiated by a house-property system and the interests of matrilateral kin in each herd. This results in small groups of kin with residential freedom and rights in livestock which enable them to manipulate or create relationships in the areas in which they settle.

CONCLUSION

The heads of homesteads which form the core of a cluster may comprise a shallow agnatic group (the "sons of one man") related directly to the founder of a neighborhood. Such homestead heads would naturally have closer historical associations with that neighborhood than those who arrive in later phases, and might take precedence in certain contexts vis-à-vis their fellows. But most of the residents of a Gogo neighborhood at any one time do not belong to any one descent group or category. On the contrary, they are of a great diversity of genealogical and geographical origins. In any neighborhood there is a constant process of accretion and loss of homesteads, although there may be overall phases of growth and expansion (or depletion) in any one neighborhood. This depends upon a variety of ecological factors. Shortage of land for cultivation is not, as yet, a major problem in Ugogo, except in some areas immediately adjacent to administrative centers. Consequently, it is not a major source of motivation for an individual homestead head to migrate, although it may be cited by Gogo in explanation of a constant cycle of population increase and decrease within neighborhoods generally, and the observable pattern of movement across the countryside.

Gogo distinguish between *wahamizi*,[39] who are thought of as being recent immigrants or "new-comers" to a neighborhood, from earlier residents; but the distinction is by no means a precise one in any particular case. The term may also be used to distinguish persons of clans other than that with ritual control in

[39] The word *wahamizi* (sing., *muhamizi*) is derived from the verb *kuhama,* to move residence some distance to a new place. (For moving a short distance within a neighborhood another verb is employed.) The noun is derived from the applied form of the verb, *kuhamila,* which denotes a move *to* a place, or *for* a reason.

any area, but only if they are also "recent" immigrants. A person of any clan who was born within a neighborhood or has lived there most of his life would not be considered a *muhamizi*. I have already shown that the Mujilima group in Temanghuku, who are the most strongly associated with the neighborhood, are not of the clan with ritual control in the area in which the neighborhood is situated.[40]

A young married man of about thirty-five who is Mukunya's (33) classificatory son and lives with him, summed up what is frequently mentioned by Temanghuku residents:

The only real residents (*wanyawusi*)[41] of Temanghuku neighborhood are Mujilima's group ("waMujilima," meaning Mujilima and his close kin and dependents), Ng'oza's group (43) and Masani's group (8 and 20). All the rest are strangers (*wajenzi*) only, newcomers (*wahamizi*).[42]

In other contexts, all of the homestead owners who live Kwitunda (II) and in Msangambuya (III) may be referred to as *wahimizi*, distinguishing them from those who live Kwilamba. This is because, it is said, the latter are the "founders" of the neighborhood, the other clusters being established later. I have shown that in terms of the length of residence of homestead owners taken generally, this is by no means true.

At any particular time, most Gogo neighborhoods are occupied by homestead heads and their dependents who may be classified into three basic categories: (a) those who are the

[40] Mujilima has actually usurped some of the ritual functions of the present *mutemi* in his area.

[41] The same word is used to denote members of clans with ritual precedence and the inhabitants of ritual areas, the "owners of the country" (see Chapter III). It is the context which distinguishes the particular reference.

[42] For several years dating from their arrival, homestead heads may measure the number of years they have lived in a neighborhood by the number of times they have hoed their fields for crops. In the past they would do this by the number of *masili* (lit., hoes) but the word *mwaka* (pl., *myaka*) is now in current usage.

"earliest" residents and are related to the founders, (b) more recent residents who have remained long enough to be linked by ties of descent and kinship links of various kinds and have closely knit obligations over livestock and other goods and services with those of the first category and between themselves, and (c) the real "newcomers," linked by a few ties of kinship to previous residents but whose main obligations center around newly created affinal links with their new neighbors. Common to all three categories is a complex of cattle transactions, which now link them in a further network of common rights and obligations in all further transactions, some of which will be exercised and fulfilled and others not.

Gogo also place a considerable value on the idea of neighborliness. Strangers (*wajenzi;* sing., *mujenzi*) are accepted into a new neighborhood during the early phase of their residence, either as members of the homesteads of others already there or as builders of their own. This is usually accomplished on the tacit recommendation of kin already there or the simple agreement of the other homestead heads and elders of the neighborhood.[43] It has been shown that the former is the more common pattern, but Gogo also say it is good to "build together," *kuzengana* (from *kuzenga,* to build), a verb form which has both a reciprocal as well as an associative meaning. It implies not only "building together" but also "helping each other to build." Those who do so may be referred to as *"wacizengane,"* "neighbors." And of course, in all neighborhoods at least some neighbors are not related in any other way, nor do they become so. But generally, such associations as neighborliness are soon converted into bonds through marriage and the creation of new links in the network of kinship.

[43] A stranger passing through a neighborhood and not intending to stay is also called *mujenzi* (which must be distinguished from *muzenji,* builder of another's homestead), toward whom certain highly valued canons of hospitality apply. Thus, where homesteads are rather isolated in thick bush, young men of the homestead will accompany a stranger many miles to put him on his path, after his physical needs have been satisfied.

The crucial point to be kept in mind, however, is that agnatic links (beyond those of half siblings) become spatially dispersed. They cease to be functionally relevant unless reactivated by common residence. This applies equally to common membership of clans and their sub-divisions, and the institutionalized links between these patrilineal categories, as set out in Chapter III. These provide the Gogo "theory" of kinship, not the basis for corporate interest and action. Instead, cognatic interpersonal kin and affinal relationships of other kinds become relevant in all spheres, material and ritual. These have constantly to be "kept alive" by the fulfillment of mutual obligations in livestock transactions and ritual interdependence, both of which, in a sense, may be termed "property relations." [44] Agnatic kin beyond the sons of one man do not have mutual interests in either of these. In any case they soon become so spatially dispersed as to make it impossible for them to sustain a continual interest even if they did have it. The categories of relationship that *are* sustained by such common interest are analyzed below, particularly in Chapters VI and VII.

In this chapter I have presented an analysis of a Gogo local community in terms of the reality of named neighborhoods (*matumbi*), and I have described the types of relationships which exist among the heads of the domestic units involved. It has been suggested that this is a pattern valid for most of Ugogo. The analysis has been set in the broader context of neighborhood growth, development, and the spatial mobility of homestead units. It has been impossible to avoid reference to the developmental cycle in domestic groups (which I examine in the next chapter) because neighborhood settlement is a function of the relation of such groups to their environment.

[44] Cf. Leach (1961), p. 305. The ephemeral nature of these relationships lies in the fact that they fall outside of the only permanent categories of relationship in Gogo society: those of patrilineal descent. How this pattern is expressed in terms of self-interest and the conflict of roles will be discussed later in this book.

V
Homesteads, Domestic Groups, and Property

The basic residential unit in Gogo society is the homestead (sing. and pl., *kaya*). It forms the unit about which the most marked "boundaries" are drawn on several levels: it provides physical and supernatural protection to life and property and demarcates the most fundamental units in the jural and political domain as well. Those living outside a particular homestead unit will view its members as a group with a named head, through whom all dealings that affect its members' legal and political status should be conducted.

Every Gogo person normally belongs to a homestead group (usually co-extensive with a domestic group) and those who do not are "outcasts," who "live in the bush" (*wekalaga mumbago*), outside the pale of society. This distinction is carried over into the world of the spirits, for all proper "spirits of the dead" (*milungu*) who have descendants to remember and propitiate them, have "homesteads": the gravestones in the cattle byres where they are buried or, if the homestead has moved, at the old homestead sites. Not all such shrines are remembered or have propitiation rituals performed at them because, as I have shown, Gogo homestead groups frequently transfer their residence over considerable distances; but the gravestones of close kin of the first ascending generation from the senior living generation are always remembered and utilized in rituals. Through them, all the spirits of the dead may be contacted.

The bodies of people who have died in a peculiar manner,

154

for example through being struck by lightning (*imuli*) or a contagious (*lona*) disease, used to be thrown into the bush or "buried" in the boles (*mapango*) of baobab trees, often associated with evil or capricious supernatural events and beings. The spirit of such a person has no "homestead" (i.e. gravestone, *citenjelo*)[1] and is not of the *milungu* spirits. He may become an "evil spirit" (*isoce*, pl. *masoce*) and "live in the bush . . . for *masoce* do not have homesteads, gravestones," *likalaga mumbago du . . . masoce gasina makaya, mabwe gevitenjelo*. But *masoce* are more usually associated with the activities of sorcerers and witches.

Hence, the concept of homestead group is fundamental to Gogo social structure and Gogo conceptual distinctions between beings which are a part of society and the community, and those which fall outside this category. That there are more inclusive groupings than the homestead group, based both upon territorial areas and descent, has already been shown in the chapters on clans, ritual areas, and neighborhoods. But I have constantly had to refer to the importance of homestead units in the organization of these. The domestic groups that constitute the core of Gogo homesteads are developmental groups, internally differentiating through a cycle from founding to fission and dissolution. I have shown how the developmental process is a partial factor influencing the fluctuating residential pattern in Gogo neighborhoods. This process and its relation to Gogo property relations and subsistence are the subject of the analysis presented in this

---

[1] The word *citenjelo,* gravestone, is derived from the verb *kutenga,* which is "to place a pot (of food or beer) on the ground," so that people may eat or drink. So, a husband may say to his wife, *"Unhenjelaje wugali!"* ("Put the food down so that I may eat!"). The applied form of the verb, *kutenjela,* from which the noun is derived, implies "to place food or beer for" . . . the spirits of the dead. Thus, *citenjelo* (the place at which food or beer for the spirits of the dead is placed). Food (*uwagali*) or beer (*uwujimbi*) are always prepared in pots (*nyungu*), although beer may be drunk from a gourd (*cipeyu*). The verb *kutenga* refers only to actions concerning pots; to place a calabash (*nhungu*) of, say, water in an upright position on the ground, is *kutuula.*

chapter; but it is necessary first to indicate the significance of homestead units in various spheres of social activity, and to describe their composition.[2]

ARCHITECTURE AND ORIENTATION

In my analysis of Gogo neighborhoods I pointed out that Gogo homesteads lie, either singly or in clusters, at considerable distances from each other, depending upon the population density and the stage in the development of the neighborhood.[3] All Gogo homesteads are built with more or less the same geographical orientation. This orientation, which I describe below, has implications for the placing of some of the houses (sing. and pl., *nyumba*) of the homestead, as well as for ritual, burial, and other more pervasive Gogo ideas about space in general. It is possible these days to find homesteads built with incorrect orientation, but there are usually specific reasons for this, such as proximity to modern roads, the ignorance of the homestead owner as to the reasons for this orientation, or his explicit rejection of these reasons on, say, religious or other cultural grounds.

Each *nyumba* ("house") consists of two rooms, an inner (*kugati*) and an outer (*ikumbo*), which are the domain of one

[2] Cf. Fortes (1949a, Chapters III and IV), (1949b), (1958); Goody (1958); Gulliver (1955, Chapters III and IV).

[3] In the Cinyambwa area of western Ugogo (see Map 1), near the grass-pan (*nyika,* swamp) of Sulungai, much larger conglomerations of closely-built homesteads are found, almost constituting geographical "villages." A good example is the neighborhood of Calicelisanga. Homesteads in this area are more permanent than in the rest of Ugogo, and rice production (primarily for sale), on the edge of the swamp, forms the basis of the economy of many homesteads. Rice is not made the basis of the subsistence diet, but sold to Indian traders (now co-operative associations) at nearby railheads such as Cigwe (see Map 1). The Gogo then buy sorghum or millet or maize grain for consumption. Cattle are grazed primarily on the grass-pan itself during most of the dry season. The reasons given above for the dispersal and mobility of homesteads in other parts of Ugogo do not hold with equal force for the Sulungai area, which I cannot describe in any sociological detail here.

married woman and her children. These sets of two-roomed *nyumba* are built in long, low, mud-roofed wings (*matembe;* sing., *itembe*)[4] around a courtyard which acts as a byre for mature cattle. Each *itembe* usually consists of only one *nyumba;* or, rarely, it may consist of the rooms of two women who share one "front room" in the middle but have their own inner rooms.

The first wing of any homestead is always built in a line north-south, with one door opening from the "front room" to the west. All subsequent *nyumba* are added to this one either in the same line to north or south or, more usually, at right angles to it at each end and running west of it, thus forming the sides of a courtyard around the byre. This may be completed by a fourth wing on the western side, leaving room for a gate or door so that livestock may go in and out of the byre (see Figure 8). In the case of smaller homesteads, the sides of the courtyard not closed in by *nyumba* will be enclosed with a stout palisade of poles and logs.[5]

Thus Gogo homesteads present the general pattern of rectangles or squares (*mapilima*) of rooms built around a byre and orientated to the four cardinal points. The main gate (*ideha*) is usually on the west, sometimes on the north or south. The eastern *nyumba* (*nyumba yecilima*), the first built, is usually occupied by the senior married woman in the homestead: either the mother of the homestead head or his senior (first) wife.[6] The first wife

---

[4] The word *itembe* has been used erroneously in many writings on Ugogo to denote the whole homestead building (*kaya*): cf. Claus (1911), pp. 5 *et seq.* Similar flat, mud-roofed structures are familiar in many parts of Tanzania: among the Nyaturu, western Kaguru, Iramba, Mbugwe, Isanzu, Sandawe, and so on. But the particular architectural layout as found in Ugogo does not seem to appear elsewhere.

[5] In southwestern Ugogo (Cinyambwa) the larger homesteads may have a number of concentric "squares" or rectangles arranged about the cattle byre. The outer series of *matembe* are called *mihali* (sing., *muhali*). This style of building (*kuzenga mihali*) is not found in other parts of Ugogo.

[6] This pattern is often varied by the fact that the homestead head is married while his mother is still alive. In such a case the mother usually

takes precedence in certain economic and ritual matters (see below) and in the confidences of her husband, functions which would be performed by his mother while she is still alive. None of the other wives are ranked, except numerically in the simple order of marriage, and consequently their positions are not reflected in the spatial configuration of the other *nyumba* in the homestead.[7]

When asked why they build their homesteads with this geographical orientation, Gogo give two answers: (a) the "wind" (*mbeho*) blows from the east (*icilima*) and (b) "you should not cut the land (country)," *sudahile dumula yisi,* which would apparently be effected by building in any other way.[8]

Now it is true that during the protracted dry season (*cibahu,* seven, sometimes more, months of the year) there is an almost continual easterly wind, laden with sand and dust particles, which at times becomes very strong. When the rains come, the winds veer to the northwest, although some light showers may come from the east. But it would be wrong to suppose that the physical reason of preventing the wind from blowing dust in through the door of the *nyumba* looms large in the Gogo explanation. Gogo ritual areas (*yisi*) are thought of as having six spatial aspects (*malanga;* lit., windows): north, south, east, west; up and down. In many senses, all space (particularly in the context of ritual action) is thought of in this manner by Gogo. A homestead also has these aspects although the four representing the cardinal geographical points are the most important. Thus, to build a homestead in any other way would disorient it in regard, generally, to the land and space and the ritual status of

---

occupies the eastern *nyumba* and the senior wife another. When the mother dies, the latter may remain where she is, and a junior wife or other married woman could then take over the eastern *nyumba*.

[7] As Gogo betrothals (*kubanya*) are very short, it is seldom necessary to distinguish order of betrothal from that of marriage. The exceptional cases where this may not be so are discussed in Chapter VI.

[8] Cf. Fortes (1949a), p. 51.

its inhabitants would be disturbed; they would have "cut the country."

I cannot here consider in detail the Gogo world view, but the east is associated in many action contexts with light, goodness, and fertility (see Rigby 1966a, 1967a). It is thus consistent that the eastern *nyumba* is the first built, the senior one. It is also the *nyumba* from which the *mukulo,* the tiny calabash of oil for anointing the new bride at marriage, comes. The west is associated with the opposite: death, darkness, and sickness. In all purification rituals involving the neighborhood or the ritual area, the sickness or contamination is always "thrown away" to the west (Rigby 1967a). The "wind" (*mbeho*) carries it away.[9] So, Gogo say, "It is because of the *mbeho* that we build our homesteads in this way; our fathers did so and told us this."

Whether the gate to the cattle byre is on the west, north or south, the area immediately adjacent to it, and outside, is called *mulazo*.[10] Theoretically, this may extend any distance westwards from the homestead, until the next homestead is reached, in fact. On the eastern side of the building, where ideally no door or gate permits entrance, the space nearby is referred to as *mhilimo,* best translated as "round the back." If a homestead is built contrary to these principles also, Gogo will remark on it. Thus Nceta, who lives in Busaka neighborhood in the extreme north of Ugogo, built the "western *nyumba*" (*nyumba yomwezi*) first, with the door facing east. His paternal parallel cousin Cinyele and his wife occupied a northern wing (*nyumba yesukuma*) running east from this. Nceta's stated reason was that he wished his byre gate to face a track which ran to the east of the site. There were no other *nyumba*. An elder said:

[9] The concept *mbeho* is multi-referent and very complex in Cigogo. The word is used to denote not only the "wind" which may be recognized by the physical senses, but also states of ritual well-being or danger, depending upon the context and the noun class in which the stem is placed.

[10] Cf. Cory (1951), Chapter VI.

Look at Nceta's homestead; they began by building the western wall (*luhengo lwomwezi*) first! So the cattle byre is on the "back" [*mugongo;* lit., back of animal or man] of the homestead. The cattle byre should have been on the west of it.

There are two main types of homestead construction in Ugogo, which differ only in the type of wall framework.[11] Both are found all over Ugogo, together with a layered, all mud construction (*ikuta*) which has only recently been introduced. All woodwork and construction is done by men, but women do most of the mud plastering except the roof, which men do (*kwesera*) while women pass up the wet mud to them in baskets. A final plastering of light clay (*kuhiliwa*), which may be smoothed or into which designs may be worked with the hands, is exclusively women's work and gives the walls a finished appearance.[12] Most of the heavy tasks (and there are many of them) are accomplished by communal work parties which are named after the specific tasks to be performed: thus, *wujimbi wesera* would be the "beer of the roof-sealing," and so on. For this reason, most building takes place during the early part of the dry season (April to June) when agricultural activity is over and there is grain for beer and enough water for the plastering operations. Kin of many categories, friends, and neighbors are invited and attend, much in the same way (though fewer people are involved) as for agricultural work parties.

Homesteads are built to last not more than about twelve to fifteen years, and my numerical data show that they are occupied without major reconstruction for an average period of about seven years. When a building begins to collapse, through excessively heavy rains or old age, a particular *nyumba* may

[11] Cf. Claus (1911), pp. 6–11 for basic description.

[12] It has been noted that Gogo depart from the general pattern of other cattle-keeping peoples by not using cattle-dung as a cement for building. Gogo do not use it because (a) all available dung is for manuring or is left for later planting beds, and (b) their homesteads are generally less permanent and do not need the stronger finish.

simply be rebuilt on the same site by just setting it a little farther back from the cattle byre. This is *kupula*. Or the whole homestead may be demolished and moved to a new site nearby within the same neighborhood (*kukata*), the same materials being used. The move may be to another neighborhood (*kuhama*), but if this entails moving to another ritual area the building materials must be left behind. This is quite a consideration in Ugogo, as the short thorn-scrub bush characteristic of the area makes the acquisition of building poles, particularly the larger ones, an arduous and expensive business. However, this does not generally deter the spatial mobility of Gogo homestead groups.

THE PROTECTION OF HOMESTEADS AND ITS SIGNIFICANCE

Although Gogo homesteads are inhabited by groups which are constantly differentiating internally, and which change their residence several times during the course of their existence, their distinctiveness in physical, social, and ritual terms cannot be overemphasized. They and their enclosed cattle byres provide physical protection from animal attack and human aggression to both men and their herds. The homestead, however, provides protection of equal, if not greater, importance from supernatural attack by evil forces of all kinds. It is necessary to examine this in some detail because it is in this sphere that the unity or internal differentiation of the domestic group is symbolized in different ways in different contexts. This is of fundamental importance in the process of fission that I describe later.

One of the most important observances in ensuring this protection is concerned with the ritual purification of the "fire" (*umoto*) used in the homestead for all purposes including cooking. When a new homestead is built and occupied for the first time, the homestead head must light a new fire with rubbing-sticks (*mhejeho*), which are then treated with medicines and buried in the cattle byre.[13] The following text, given to me in

---

[13] *Mhejeho* (sing., *lupejeho*) may be made from dry sticks of a variety of trees and shrubs, although in this case it is preferable to use a tree

conversation with a knowledgeable elder and confirmed by other statements and personal observation, admirably sums up the actions and reasons involved:

The firestick (*lupejeho*) which we bury in the cattle byre, when we have built a new homestead, *is* the *"mbeho"* [ritual purity] of the homestead, so that the children may have healthy bodies, and also the livestock (*mitugo*). It ensures that dangerous wild animals (*malimu*) will pass at a distance and not come near. You make a small hole in the ground and first put in powdered medicine [*ndasimi*, obtained from a diviner], then the firesticks with a small knot of medicine tied to them. It is this kind of firestick which is called "the firestick of the ritual state of the homestead" (*lupejeho lwambeho yekaya*). You cannot bring fire into a new homestead. That fire, it is as if you had left it at the old homestead and you had seen it was bad; that you should look for new [fire].

These preliminary precautions do not prevent the subsequent extinguishing of the fire in the homestead, on the direction of the ritual leader, and the carrying of new, ritually treated fire from the ritual leader to the homestead. Nor does it stop the women of the homestead, if their fires go out by accident, from "borrowing" some coals (*kupala umoto*) from a neighboring homestead or *nyumba* to relight their own at any time. These actions are outside the context of the ritual lighting of the first fire and the burying of the firesticks. The distinction is important, because it ensures the "ritual independence" of the homestead units in some spheres, in spite of their economic reliance upon crop production and consequent dependence upon rituals concerning the land and the ritual area as a whole. The fire obtained at the yearly ceremonies from the ritual leader concerns primarily the fertility of the soil, seeds and the rainfall; the fire of the homestead concerns

---

which belongs to the broad category *mupolo* ("non-poisonous," "non-bitter") such as the *musabi* bush (*Ficus* spp.), as opposed to the category *mukali* (poisonous, bitter). I have also seen firesticks made from the *muwelewele* shrub (*Strophanthus eminii*).

only the people and livestock living within it. These two spheres
are kept conceptually distinct by Gogo themselves:

That fire (obtained from the ritual leader) is "of the fields only"
(*wemigunda du*), not for the homestead. When you obtain medicine
from the *mutemi* (ritual leader), for example, to prevent birds from
destroying the crops, the "fire of that medicine" (*umoto wayo*)[14]
may be the prohibition of the collection of marrows (*mayungu*) or
green relish (*mboga*) on the day you sprinkle the medicine (*mwa-
minza miti*) on the plants. . . . But this is not connected with the
"fire of the homestead" (*sivihanjile nomoto wekaya*).[15]

Not only this, but the fire provided by the ritual leader is collected, together with other medicines, separately for each *nyumba*
of the homestead; that for the homestead includes all the constituent *nyumba* collectively and concerns the homestead as a
unit (see Rigby 1967a).

Apart from this, each *nyumba* may also have medicines to protect it and its inhabitants from a variety of specific dangers, particularly epidemic diseases. These must be provided by the hus-
band/father of each *nyumba,* or his heir if he is dead. He may
or may not be the homestead head. For example, the hairy outer
surface (*mbunywa*) of the roots of the *muwumbu* tree (*Lannea
stuhlmanii*) may be scraped off, wrapped with white, rounded
river-bed stones (*nzaga nzelu*) into a small piece of black cloth
(*civunje*) and tied above the doorway (*mulango*) of the *nyumba*.
Another similar object is buried at the threshold (*hacipimbira-*

[14] There is an interesting inference in the use here of the word *moto*
(fire): for *moto* also means "tradition" or "established custom." In this
case the informant is deliberately associating the use of the word for
"actual fire" (i.e. coals) obtained from the ritual leader, with the "tradition surrounding the use of the medicines"—that is, the promulgation
of the subsequent prohibitions (*miiko*).

[15] My informant used the indefinite subject concord -*vi*- in the verb
construction distinguishing these two "types" of "fire." This concord implies two things of totally different linguistic categories, although he was
talking about "fire" (*umoto*) in both cases, and (grammatically correctly)
could have subsumed both of them under the subject concord -*wu*-.

mulango). These, Gogo say, prevent the occupants of the *nyumba* from contracting smallpox (*idahi*) during an epidemic. Similarly, the whole homestead may also be protected from other diseases and misfortunes by a variety of specific medicines provided by the homestead head and obtained from a diviner.

The ritual unity and independence of the homestead in these fields extends also to the herd belonging to its members. The diligent homestead head and controller of the herd will obtain and use medicines to ensure the health and increase the animals in his byre. For example, he may, on the instructions of a diviner, take the seeds of the *musabi* shrub (*Ficus* spp.), crush them, spread them to dry in the sun, and grind them into a medicinal powder (*ndasimi*). To this he may add the similarly powdered leaves of the *ngeteteya*[16] creeper (*Commelina bracteosa*) to make cattle fertility medicine (*nghome yang'ombe;* lit., the cow stick). For this, a sheep is slaughtered and the fatty parts stuffed, with the powdered medicine, into the membrane of the intestine or pancreas (this combination is called *musunjilo*). It is then buried in a shallow hole in the byre, over which a fire is lit. The *musunjilo* burns until it bursts and the smoke circulates through the cattle byre and among the livestock. The crucial significance of this type of rite for the control a homestead head has over the herd in his byre will be referred to again in a discussion of homestead fission. The example given is just one of a number of actions which may be carried out privately by the homestead head. Cattle fertility medicine is secret medicine.

Finally, the ritual unity of the homestead is expressed in the propitiation ceremonies (*makumbiko*) to the spirits of the dead. It is necessary to note some aspects of them.

Members of senior generations such as the homestead head's

[16] *Ngeteteya* is the Baraguyu (Masai) name for this plant. I could not obtain the Cigogo name. Many diviners in Ugogo, both for rain and livestock medicines, are Baraguyu; or if Gogo, they have learned some of their knowledge of medicines from Baraguyu. The Gogo clan Temikwila, who claim to be descended from the Taturu (Tatog), are also said to have potent livestock fertility medicines.

father, mother, elder brothers, mother's brothers, or even his
wife's parents, may be buried in the cattle byre of a homestead
still occupied by their descendants.[17] In such cases the graves may
or may not be marked by gravestones, for the homestead is still
"their homestead." Only if it is moved must they be "given a
homestead" by marking the graves with stones. Minor beer
propitiation rituals (*wujimbi wemisambwa*) concerning all the
members of the homestead, are carried out in the front room
(*ikumbo*) of the senior married woman (wife or mother),
usually in the eastern *nyumba*. The trough made for the pouring
of the beer so that the spirits may "drink," is molded around one
particular beam pole (*isumbili*) in this room, at what is called
the "nose of the homestead" (*mhula yakaya*). Propitiations
affecting particular wives and their children will be held in their
own *ikumbo*.[18]

On leaving one homestead site to move to another, the spirits
of the dead particularly associated with it (i.e. those who died
there and are buried in its byre), and through them all the other
spirits that can be remembered, must be informed and asked for
assistance (but not permission). Thus, when Majima was moving his homestead from Temanghuku neighborhood to Musalato,
a distance of some ten miles back to where he had come from
twenty-three years before, he held a beer propitiation to the
mother and father of his senior wife, who had come to Tema-

[17] Gogo kinship rituals must await fuller analysis elsewhere. The central point to be kept in mind for the following discussion is that, except
in the case of rain rituals which concern the stool-holding agnatic groups,
Gogo propitiations are not directed solely to lineal ancestors. Usually,
lineal ancestors are remembered to only two or three generations. Thus,
the spirits of bilateral kin of senior generations to a shallow depth are
normally called, and may intrude upon the affairs of the living. The
spirits of the dead of anyone in the homestead or domestic group as a
unit are involved. Hence a man may even propitiate the spirits of his
wife's kin, his affines. This pattern of propitiation not concerned solely
with lineal kin is consistent with the lack of emphasis in Gogo society upon
patrilineal lineages as corporate groups.

[18] The orientation and architecture of the homestead feature directly in
the propitiation rituals.

nghuku with him and were buried in the cattle byre. The homestead had already been dismantled and two gravestones placed
on the graves, a few feet apart. Semwali, the son of those who
were to be propitiated (Majima's wife's full brother), had been
asked to come from Musalato where he had a homestead. Had he
arrived in time, a sheep would have been slaughtered and the
liver used in the propitiation, but he was late and beer only was
given. The genealogical connections of those involved are shown
in Figure 7. Early in the morning, before the livestock had been

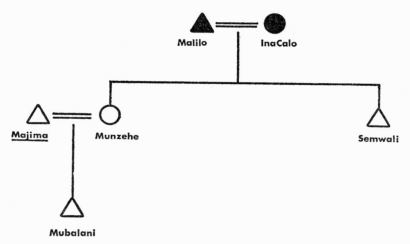

Malilo   InaCalo

Majima   Munzehe   Semwali

Mubalani

Figure 7. Majima's propitiation

taken out from the temporary camp to pasture, all the members
of the homestead group and several other neighbors and kin,
gathered around the stones with pots and gourds of beer. Majima,
his wife Munzehe and their son Mubalani (about 25 years of
age) came forward and addressed the spirits while pouring beer
on the stones, taking mouthfuls of the beer and spitting it
(*kufunyira*) in a fine spray over the assembled company, particularly the younger children. Majima addressed the spirits first:

Ale Malilo, mukwe wangu, mwaza nyenye mwagona baha,
So Malilo, my wife's father, you came and slept [died] here,

Naase mwikalo wewanhu, cikujenda, cikuyega.
And we, as is the way of mortals, we are going, we are wandering.

Alu ukuwona cimemile baba, camuletelenyi malenga genyu,
Now you see we have come together, father, and we bring you your "water," [19]

Ase catonga kuwuka, caza wuya kuzikwetu.
We are about to leave, about to return to our own place.[20]

Wose du muhulice, waInaCalo,
All of you listen, InaCalo and the others,

Malenga genyu gaga!
Here is your beer!

Then his senior wife Munzehe addressed her parents' spirits, carrying out the same actions:

Ale muwaha Malilo,
Oh great one Malilo,

Alu ahano nawa tela;
Now I move away from here;

Ukanghulile wana mabici kumwande!
Clear the path ahead for your children, of tree stumps and thorns!

Nawuka du ane.
I am leaving.

It is evident that belonging to a Gogo homestead, being a member of a particular domestic group, is not merely a matter of residence or relationship. It entails dependence upon, and acceptance of, a ritual unit in affairs which concern the well-being of both men and herds. It implies also an economic unit by common interest in the herd in the cattle byre, as I shall show, even though for crop-production purposes each *nyumba* of the homestead is virtually independent. Expulsion from a homestead, and

[19] In all ritual contexts, even when specific rituals are being referred to, beer (*wujimbi*) is always referred to as "water" (*malenga*).
[20] "*Kwetu*": see Chapter IV.

therefore from the group which inhabits it, is very serious (and was probably more so in the past). It means virtual expulsion from the community, and in such a case survival depends upon attachment to another homestead group (either as kinsman with associated status, or as a complete dependent, virtually slave (*muwanda*), especially in the case of a poor person), unless one has a family, property, and resources enough to build one's own. In cases of severe conflict between the members of a homestead, the homestead head might expel a dissident member, who is forbidden to return to the homestead (*kumulapila ciila*). Such a person is said to be *cinya laho*, or *cinya la'o*,[21] in regard to that homestead. This means exclusion from the physical as well as ritual membership and protection of the homestead group. Re-acceptance into it depends upon propitiation of the spirits by the slaughter of a sheep or goat, the blood from which must flow over the feet of those who have quarreled, within the doorway of their *nyumba*. This may occur between co-residents of a homestead related in any way, perhaps between husband and wife. An elder who was explaining procedure at the reconciliation of a young man with his wife, put it in general terms:

Perhaps if you have a child and you quarrel severely with him (*mwisonje nayo*), you would chase him away and would say, "You are banished. Do not come here to my homestead again!" [22] In that

---

[21] This means literally, "be with *laho*": in other words, a sheep or goat must be provided as an offering to the spirits of the dead before the expelled person may re-enter the homestead. This offering is called *laho* or *la'o*, derived from Sandawe *la'o*. Sandawe is a non-Bantu language spoken by a people whose territory borders on northern Ugogo. Mr. E. Tenraa has informed me personally that in Sandawe *la'o* is ". . . Derived from stem *la'*, meaning 'to destroy.' *La'o*: lit., the act of destroying, the act of causing disharmony, etc., and especially denoting anything destroyed by witchcraft or sorcery, e.g. destruction of social relationships by severe quarrel . . ." The word has come into Cigogo as *laho*, but the Bantu form for this banishment, *kulapa ciila*, is still more commonly used.

[22] Here my informant used the phrase literally, "So child, it is the foreskin and the road" (*nzunga nenzila*): a figurative way of saying, "You will not mature in my homestead." The reference to the foreskin

way you have ritually and physically expelled your child from the homestead (*wamulapila ciila mwana'go*).

This is a most unusual act, however, and most sons, younger brothers or other homestead members who leave the homestead as individuals or family groups when the process of fission begins, do so on their own initiative, even if the precipitating cause is conflict or strain. But this entails also the splitting of the herd. Setting up a new cattle byre symbolizes the surrender by the homestead head of his control over the deployment and fertility of the livestock which leave his byre. Conversely, a son or younger brother living in the homestead of his father or elder brother, although he has considerable control over the livestock allocated to his *nyamba* when he reaches maturity, accepts only partial control, particularly in ritual matters affecting the fertility and increase of the herd.

HOUSES (*NYUMBA*), PROPERTY, AND PRODUCTION

Each *nyumba* is the exclusive domain of a married woman and her children. The term refers to both the physical unit of two-room sets as well as the social unit of a woman and her children. These "matricentral cells" are the core units of Gogo domestic groups between which the lines of cleavage are laid from their founding until the domestic group reaches the end of its cycle of development, fission occurs, and it is replaced by other similar groups. Thus a person will identify himself by which *nyumba* he belonged to in a polygynous family: the senior house (*nyumba imbaha*), "second house" (*nyumba yekejete*) and so on until the junior house (*nyumba indodo*). In a family with three such houses, the middle one may be referred to as *nyumba yehagati*

---

is to pre-circumcision immaturity, and also links the act of banishing with that of a father disowning his son (*kuligita*), although he does not equate the two. Disowning or cursing a son, the father exposes his genitals to the son, saying in effect, "You are no longer my son or you would not see this." See analysis of F/S relations below and cf. Beidelman (1963d), p. 480.

(the house of the middle). The only significant position in this
numerical ranking is the first house, and this is so only in certain
very restricted circumstances. Other houses are considered as
equal in all spheres.

Most of the married women in a homestead are the wives of
the homestead head if he is a polygynist, or the wives of other
dependents, related or unrelated, living in the same homestead.
In the homestead of a fairly well-off man of mature years, such
as that of Mujilima described below, one or two *nyumba* may
be occupied by women or the wives of men only peripherally related to the head. There may be a constant turnover in the occupants of such *nyumba.* A mature homestead head with a
large homestead does not mind these comings and goings which
may eventually add to the size and prestige of his homestead.

Ikumbo, the outer room of the *nyumba,* is usually bare, and
into it the small stock and calves allocated to the *nyumba* are
locked at night. *Kugati,* the inner room, is where the wife keeps all
her possessions, including her granaries, and is her exclusive
domain.[23] The only door from *kugati* leads into the *ikumbo,* and
she often keeps this locked while she is out. Even her husband
cannot enter without her consent. Her hearth-stones (*mafigwa*)
and cooking utensils (*viya*) are symbols of this domain, and it is
at the hearth, for example, that a married woman and her husband receive her lover and his age-mate when an *mbuya* relationship is being arranged (see Chapter VI). This symbolizes her
consent and participation. The only door out of each *nyumba*
leads from the *ikumbo* into the cattle byre; thus the number of
doors (*milango*) usually denotes the number of *nyumba* in the
homestead, and indeed may be referred to as such. A homestead
head seldom has a room of his own and spends his time during
the day under the small shade tree usually left standing outside
the homestead, or in the cattle byre or the *igane,* the dormitory
room for boys and unmarried young men (see Figure 8).

Women together with their unmarried daughters sleep in the

---

[23] *Kugati* means literally "inside," from the root *-gati.*

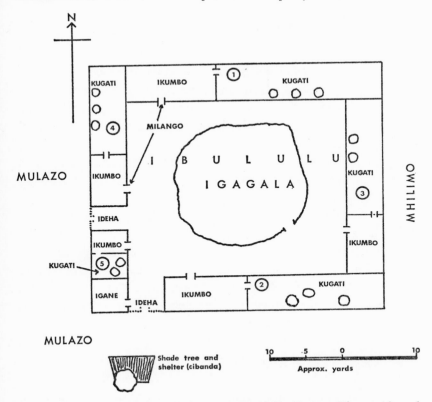

Figure 8. Plan of Mujilima's homestead, 1962–63 (see Figure 10 and text)

Key: *Ikumbo,* outer room; *Kugati,* inner room (*ikumbo* and *kugati* comprise the *nyumba*); *igagala,* inner ring of cattle byre; *ibululu,* cattle byre; *ideha,* gate; *igane,* boys' and young men's dormitory; *mulango,* doorway of *nyumba; mhilimo,* "back" of homestead (east); *mulazo,* milking area and place where livestock mill before and after going out to pasture; numbers refer to *nyumba* and circles within *kugati* represent granaries (*madong'a*) belonging to each married woman.

kugati, and a husband, if a polygynist, will divide his time between his wives. Each married woman has a bed (*wulili*), made either of a wooden frame of stakes and cross-pieces, or of a raised mud platform. On this is laid the large cow hide used as a sleeping skin mattress (*nhyingo*). A husband may also have a bed in one *ikumbo* if there are not too many small stock in the *nyumba*. Boys and young men sleep in the *igane* from the age when they begin herding, through puberty and circumcision, and until they are married and their wives have their own *nyumba*. Most large homesteads have an *igane* but boys seldom sleep in their own homesteads; they gather after the evening meal in one or other *igane* of the neighborhood to sing and tell stories and to sleep there. Before they are married, young men may establish *mbuya* relationships with married women or girls and sleep with them in the inner room. Strangers also sleep in the *igane,* where a fire is kept going all the night.[24]

The *nyumba* is an almost completely independent economic unit within the domestic group, for the production, storing, distribution, and consumption of the staple food crop of sorghum and millet, and all other agricultural produce. With regard to the principal inheritable property, livestock, the *nyumba* also becomes, at an early stage in its existence, independent vis-à-vis other like units. For a certain part of the homestead herd is allocated to every *nyumba* as soon as children are born. These livestock are utilized exclusively by the wife of that *nyumba* and her children, and will be inherited solely by her children, though they still form part of the common herd (*itewa*) of the homestead, and are primarily under the control of the husband/father, both in economic and ritual matters, until his death or unless he voluntarily abandons such control. But it will be seen that his control diminishes inversely with the increasing maturity of his sons. The economic independence of the *nyumba* is fundamentally important in the developmental cycle of Gogo domestic groups, their relation to their environment, and Gogo property relations and kinship structure. I return to a more detailed analysis of this in terms of livestock property later. Here I wish to

---

[24] Inside the *kugati* also a woman keeps a smoky fire burning all night so that the air becomes very heavy with smoke. This helps keep away mosquitoes and other insects but may make it very difficult for those unaccustomed to it to breathe or keep their eyes open.

examine some of its implications for food production and consumption.

Each married woman, that is, the owner of each *nyumba,* has her own fields (*migunda*) for the production of the basic crop of sorghum and millet, and her small garden patches (*vigundu*) for vegetable crops and small cash-crops such as castor and groundnuts for sale. She plants these fields with her own seeds from the previous year, though her husband must supply her with seed if she has none.[25] The husband is also obliged to clear bush (*kutemanga mbago*) for new bush fields for her, and to obtain fallow fields near the homestead. Most agricultural tasks are carried out through communal beer parties, but a husband is expected to spend equal amounts of his time and effort in the fields of each wife. Co-wives (*wasanji*) will help each other in agricultural work, particularly if they are closely related in other ways, but this is by no means obligatory and no sanctions can be applied if they do not do so. Very seldom, a husband will plant a field of grain (*wuhemba*) for himself, and then all his wives will help him cultivate it. This grain would be stored in a separate granary or in that of his senior wife or mother, and is used by him for his own purposes. He may also plant small patches of tobacco and so on, the produce and profit from which belong to him alone.

Every married woman has her own granaries (*madong'a* or *madongha*) *kugati,* and they are under her exclusive control, although she may not refuse her husband's reasonable requests for the use of the grain cultivated while she is with him. From these granaries she will feed her children and her husband, and take her reasonable share of providing meals and beer for her husband's guests and others who visit the homestead.

For propitiation rituals concerning all the members of the homestead, beer is made from the grain in the senior wife's

[25] If he borrows seed for this purpose from the *nyumba* of another wife, he must return it the following year or as soon as he can: see Chapter II.

granary, or from the husband's granary (if he has one), but more usually from grain contributed by all the women together. Beer for propitiation rituals concerning one wife or the children of one *nyumba* is made from her own grain store. A husband cannot use the grain from any wife's granary without her permission, just as he must consult with her and her adolescent or adult children over the use of livestock allocated to their *nyumba*.

The separation of each *nyumba* is seen further in the fact, already mentioned, that when crop fertility medicines are distributed by the ritual leader, each married woman with a *nyumba* will collect her own, for her own fields. So also with the ritually purified fire of her hearth. Thus, *nyumba* are separate entities primarily in relation to crop production, fertility, and the land (the ritual areas), while the physical and ritual protection of humans and livestock rest upon the homestead as a unit: a collectivity of *nyumba* under one jural and ritual head, forming one domestic group. This is consistent with the patrilineal inheritance of property and succession to major roles, and the economic basis of the society.

It follows that a married woman cannot perform her duties as wife or mother nor enjoy her full status and privacy unless she has a *nyumba* built for her. The great majority of marriages are virilocal, but there are often changes of residence during the course of a marriage. But even if a woman remains with her kin and a husband comes to live uxorilocally, he is obliged to build or otherwise provide for her a *nyumba* with *ikumbo* and *kugati* in whatever homestead she is usually resident. When he does so it entails his agreement to her residence in that homestead, and it is difficult for him to get her to change her residence after this against her will. Thus, husbands usually insist on their wives coming to reside with them in their own homesteads. Failure to provide a *nyumba* for a wife who has borne her first child, or within about a year from marriage, can lead to the wife's return to her kin and may be legitimate grounds for divorce if it can be shown that the husband is taking no steps to do so. But it is only a wastrel husband who would behave in this manner, for it is in a husband's best interests, whether he is as yet a homestead head or not, to keep his wives living near him and to provide them with *nyumba*. It would be a sad event if a mature man died while he had no *nyumba,* belonging either to one of his wives or, at a pinch, one of his sons' wives. His death would be compared with that of a young unmarried man or boy who "died in the boys' dormitory" (*mono yafwila mwigane*), for whom there is no proper inheritance ceremony (*ipinde*) or full mourning (*cililo*). It is in the innermost corner (*kunhuzi*) of the senior living wife's *kugati* room that a man's personal accoutrements, the symbols of inheritance, are guarded from pollution by witchcraft or sorcery after his death until they are inherited by his heirs.[26]

HOMESTEAD HEADS AND THE COMPOSITION OF HOMESTEADS

The status of homestead head (*munyakaya* or *muzengakaya*) is one of the few in Gogo society that confers the full prestige of maturity upon a man, and the only one which gives him full jural and political stature in the external domain. In spite of this, it is most unlikely that a man will become the head of his own homestead until he is over forty or forty-five. Furthermore, there is evidence that the age at which a man could hope to become a homestead head was higher in the past, when homesteads were much larger and held together for protection and subsistence to a greater extent than they do today. The figures set out in Table 8 indicate the age distribution of Gogo homestead heads[27] at one

[26] These consist primarily of his bow (*wupinde*), the main symbol of male inheritance, and all his other personal body ornaments, weapons and a particular stool (see below, Chapter VII).

[27] It will be noticed that I have alternatively translated the Cigogo noun *munyakaya* as "homestead head" and "homestead owner." The word has both these connotations in the way in which it is generally used: "homestead head" in relation to the other members of the homestead and those outside it, as a social group; "homestead-owner" in the context of his residence in a neighborhood, vis-a-vis the owners of other homesteads as units with a physical area and buildings.

point in time, both for Temanghuku neighborhood and other neighborhoods of Cilungulu ritual area. From these may be inferred the age at which Gogo may expect to become homestead heads. But first a note of explanation is required on the distributions in the two samples.

I was able to obtain with considerable accuracy the ages of the forty-four homestead heads in Temanghuku neighborhood and their dependents (413 persons altogether). Gogo have a chronology of famines dating back for the past eighty to one hundred years, and individuals often remember the years of births, circumcision ceremonies, first marriages, and so on, in relation to these named famines. Other base-lines were the arrival of the German administration in Ugogo, the railway-line at Dodoma, and the beginning and ending of the two world wars. But lengthy and detailed discussion of a person's life-history and those of his dependents is required in order to establish these fixed points. This was impossible to carry out systematically in the case of the sample of 115 homestead heads in other Cilungulu neighborhoods. It was, however, feasible to record their age-set names (*mazika*). Although there is considerable overlap in actual ages in relation to age-set classification, I was able on further knowledge of Gogo age-sets and the Temanghuku sample to equate with fair accuracy the age distribution of men in the various sets in 1962–63. Thus, the Mesokile (Dobola) age-set are the youngest warriors, mostly unmarried, whose eldest members are about thirty and whose youngest members are still being recruited at about fifteen, though it is near to being closed, by continual initiation ceremonies. The other age-sets ascend from this in approximate fifteen-year periods to the Ngulumo (Metemi, Kishomi) who are the senior elders of whom very few are left (1962–63).[28]

[28] The names and recruitment periods of Gogo age-sets (*mazika*) are derived from those of the Baraguyu. But there is no "closed period" of recruitment for the Gogo, who go on recruiting to the named set until the Baraguyu open a new one, when the Gogo change the name also and a new set begins. It is not possible here to examine the interesting problem

It is clear that, with the alignment upon internal evidence of the age-sets with the age categories in the two parts of Table 8,

Table 8. Age distribution of homestead heads, Temanghuku neighborhood and Cilungulu ritual area, 1962–63

Temanghuku			Cilungulu		
Age category by approx. age	No.	Percentage	Age-set membership by named sets[29]	No.	Percentage
15–29	1	2	(Dobola) Mesokile	6	5
30–44	16	35	(Kidotu) Menamba	40	35
45–59	17	39	(Ildwati) Balangati	41	36
60–74	8	18	(Kilanji) Kitumbotu	22	19
75–	2	5	(Metemi) Ngulumo (Kishomi)	6	5
Totals	44	99		115	100

there is a high degree of consistency in the percentage distribution by age of the homestead heads in each sample. The value of the figures would be enhanced if they could be compared with the age distribution of Gogo men in general. But from this and other evidence, it may be concluded that a man cannot expect to become a homestead head until he is over thirty, and probably not until he is over forty-five. The youngest homestead head in the Temanghuku sample was Ndumizi (homestead no. 14, see

---

of the incipient (and now very weak) age organization in Ugogo and its functions in comparison with the Kisongo Masai and Baraguyu systems. Some aspects of the Gogo concept "age-mate" (*muzika*, addressed as *laji*) will appear in Chapter VII. I am indebted to Dr. T. O. Beidelman and Dr. Alan Jacobs for information on Baraguyu and Kisongo Masai age-set systems which enabled me to make the above correlations with greater ease. See also Beidelman (1960), p. 262; Gulliver (1963), for Arusha age-sets and relation to Kisongo Masai; and Fosbrooke (1948) *passim.*

[29] The names in parentheses are the correct Baraguyu names for these sets. Those not in parentheses are the Cigogo versions of the abuse terms which can be used for the same sets. Gogo usually refer to age-sets by the Baraguyu terms, many not realizing the significance of them for Baraguyu.

Chapter IV), who is of the Mesokile age-set and twenty-seven years old. The six (5%) of the Cilungulu sample, who also belong to this age-set, all became heads through rather special circumstances, some of which will appear later. Most men in this set are not even married.

The majority in the Menamba (30–44 years of age) category are married, but many still live with their fathers (*sewo*). Men in the Balangati age-set (45–59 years of age) were, in 1962–63, elders at the height of their power, with large, growing homesteads. Some had children who were already married but not yet old enough to challenge seriously their authority. A man who is not a homestead head by this age has usually suffered some peculiar circumstance: either poverty or physical disability. If the fathers of men in this age category are still alive, as in some cases, they are rather old and losing their active interest in control over livestock (the symbol of authority). In any case all Balangati in the sample have moved their homesteads to areas other than those in which their fathers live and have thus effectively eliminated the latter's authority in most fields.

It may be taken then that the homestead heads in the Temanghuku sample of forty-four represent fairly well the general age-range of homestead heads in Ugogo in present conditions. Table 9 compares the proportions of homestead heads in this sample whose fathers are still alive with those whose fathers are dead, in relation to age-category and residence. Only six (13.7%) of the total have their own fathers still alive. Of these, four belong to the age-category 30–44, only one of whom lives in the same neighborhood as his father, another of whom lives in the same ritual area. The other two live in different ritual areas to their fathers. The two homestead heads of the 45–59 category whose fathers are still alive both live in different ritual areas from those of their fathers. Of the thirty-eight (86.3% of the total) whose fathers are dead, twenty-seven (61.3% of the total) have since moved from the ritual area in which their fathers died, and eleven (25.0%) are still in the same ritual area. Of these eleven who

Table 9. Residence and age of homestead heads whose fathers are still alive, compared with those whose fathers are dead (Temanghuku, 1962–63)

Age category	Father alive				Father dead			Total homestead heads in each category
	Living in same neighborhood	Living in same ritual area	Living in different ritual area	Totals	In same ritual area	In different ritual area	Totals	
15–29	—	—	—	—	—	1	1	1
30–44	1	1	2	4	7	5	12	16
45–59	—	—	2	2	2	13	15	17
60–74	—	—	—	—	2	6	8	8
75–	—	—	—	—	—	2	2	2
Totals	1	1	4	6	11	27	38	44
Percentages	2.3	2.3	9.1	13.7	25.0	61.3	86.3	100.0

have not yet moved from the areas in which their fathers died, seven are of the young age-category 30–44.

These figures further illustrate not only the mobility of homestead groups (homestead heads and their dependents) as discussed in Chapter IV, but also the fact that in the minority of cases where the father of a man who is himself a homestead head is still alive, the son will tend to move to another neighborhood, or even a greater distance to another ritual area, from that in which his father resides. The reasons for this are clear from the preceding analysis, where I have shown that a man can only attain full status in society and, most important, control over his own herd, when he assumes full responsibility, jural and ritual, for the people in his homestead and the cattle in his byre. This is difficult when one's father is still alive and resides close enough to be in daily contact, unless he is senile and practically out of the picture anyway. Further, when sons begin to marry and demand livestock for the bridewealth, and the father still wishes to marry more wives, conflict is almost inevitable, and spatial separation is a means of alleviating this. The cases given below to illustrate the process of development and fission in the domestic group will provide further illustration. I can, however, confirm the pattern established by these figures from observations made in other neighborhoods, both near Temanghuku and in other parts of Ugogo.

The homesteads of Temanghuku neighborhood contain domestic groups at all stages of the developmental cycle. Thus their composition and size vary to the extremes. Examples of each are given in a later section; but it is useful first to analyze the general composition of the domestic groups at any one point in time, in order to establish the broad pattern of relationships existing between homestead heads and their dependents.

It has been noted on several occasions that polygyny is highly valued by the Gogo. Every adult man, except the small but rapidly increasing group of young Christians, will agree that, *"Kutola mitala kuswanu muno,"* "It is a very good thing to marry more than one wife." Even the Christians, Gogo say, will have more than one wife if they can arrange it secretly, and I have recorded several cases where this is so, the second wife usually being acquired by inheritance from a close agnate.[30] But despite the high priority placed upon polygyny, the majority of Gogo men have only one wife at any given time. The figures set out in Table 10 indicate the number of wives the homestead heads in Temanghuku and Cilungulu have living with them, and the number of wives other married men, living as dependents of one sort or another in the Temanghuku homesteads, have living with them.[31] It must be emphasized that these figures refer only to the

[30] In this case the fact may not become generally known to the church hierarchy, although it is generally known in the community.

[31] Only in very exceptional circumstances would an unmarried young man be considered a homestead head, and even then he would probably have inherited wives when succeeding to the role of homestead head, even if he does not actually exercise his rights over these women. All of the homestead heads in Temanghuku were married, with wives living with them.

wives living at present (1962/63) with the men concerned, and do not include those left elsewhere with adult sons, or those separated from their husband by death, separation, or divorce, during the course of a total marital career.[32] Here I am concerned with those wives who constitute, with their children, the matri-central units of these homesteads as at one time.

It will be seen immediately from Table 10 that twenty-nine of

Table 10. Homestead heads and their married dependents, by distribution of wives living with them in 1962–63: Temanghuku and Cilungulu examples

Married men	No. of wives						Totals	Ratio of married men: wives
	0	1	2	3	4	5		
Homestead heads, Temanghuku	—	29	9	6	—	1	45	
Percentages	—	64.5	20.0	13.3	—	2.2	100.0	1:1.5
Dependent married men, Temanghuku	—	32	5	—	—	—	37	
Percentages	—	86.5	13.5	—	—	—	100.0	1:1.1
Homestead heads Cilungulu	2[33]	81	26	6	—	—	115	
Percentages	1.7	70.5	22.6	5.2	—	—	100.0	1:1.4

the forty-five (64.5%) Temanghuku homestead heads have only one wife living with them at present, and the corresponding figure for the Cilungulu sample is 70.5 percent (81 of the 115

[32] Rates of divorce and separation are discussed in Chapter VI.

[33] The two homestead heads in the Cilungulu sample recorded as having no wives living with them at present have been reduced to this state by the death of their spouses. In the case of the dependent men in the Temanghuku sample, I am here concerned only with those who are married. I have already noted that a large proportion of young men in the 15–29 age-category are not married; it is difficult to marry before the age of about 25–27, and was even more so in the past.

wanyakaya).[34] Given the wide age distribution of the married men in these samples, the proportion of polygynous domestic families is not too small. Sixteen of the forty-five Temanghuku homestead heads (35.5%) have two or more wives, of whom six (13.3% of the total) have three wives and one has five. Just under one-third of the Cilungulu homestead heads have more than one wife with them at present. The ratio of married men to their wives in Temanghuku is 1:1.5 and 1:1.4 for the Cilungulu sample. Although the figures are small, it is clear that married men who are not homestead heads have, on the whole, less chance of becoming polygynists.[35] Bridewealth is high in Ugogo and the transfer of bridewealth in most marriages puts considerable strain on the resources of most Gogo.[36] Agnatic and matrilateral kin who are obliged to assist a young man on his first marriage need not do so for subsequent marriages. A man thus has to be in control of a herd before he is able easily to become a polygynist. This usually necessitates being a homestead head. But it is also true that dependents are on the whole younger men.

It is to be expected, then, that polygyny is usually the prerogative of older, well-established homestead heads. In the Temanghuku sample, 43 percent of the homestead heads over forty-

[34] Lévi-Strauss (1956), pp. 267–268, writes, ". . . in all polygamous societies, the privilege of having several wives is actually enjoyed by a small minority only . . ." A comparison of the figures for the Gogo polygynous marriages with those for other societies in which polygyny is very highly valued shows few significant differences. Cf. Fortes (1949a), pp. 65–66; and Goody (1958), p. 89. It should be noted that the figures given for these societies include all men over the age of 18, not distinguished by their status as homestead heads or dependents. Cf. also Dorjahn (1959), particularly pp. 98–105, which shows that from available data on Sub-Saharan Africa, only 30%–40% of married men in most polygynous societies are polygynous, and the mean number of wives per married man is 1.5.

[35] For Cilungulu ritual area as a whole in 1963, the sex ratio for all adult men to women was 1:1.2; a ratio which corresponds almost exactly to that calculated for the whole of Ugogo (see: *Tanganyika Census, 1957*).

[36] See Chapter II, Table 2, and discussion.

five years of age had two or more wives living with them, while 57 percent had one wife. Three-quarters (76%) of the homestead heads under forty-five had only one wife each. These figures are almost directly comparable to those given for the Tallensi by Fortes (1949, p. 66). But even for older men the problem of bridewealth restricts the possibilities of acquiring more wives. As they reach the age of success, prosperity, and the accumulation of large herds, their sons reach maturity and begin to press for cattle for their own marriages. Only in very exceptional cases where the bridewealth needs of their sons and other dependents can be met and still leave a large surplus, are very rich men found with more than two or three wives. In some cases, a man may help his sons to marry a second wife to prevent them leaving. But the more usual pattern is conflict between father and sons over the limited livestock available for all their needs. In such conflicts, the mother and her brothers always take the side of the sons, emphasizing the rights of her own *nyumba*. This pattern will be seen clearly in the cases given below.

Despite the low figures for polygynists with wives living with them, it may be said that a typical Gogo man with a reasonably prosperous career may hope to have two and sometimes three wives, either together or at some time during his marital career. Thus, two *nyumba* are created, even among the descendents of one man (*wana wamunhu umonga*), and the seeds of fission are sown; for, as I have noted and as will be seen clearly from later examples, it is between the members of different *nyumba* in the domestic group that fission always occurs. But before I turn to an analysis of this process, we must look briefly at the relationships between homestead heads and their dependents other than their wives.

The total population, adults and children, of the forty-four Temanghuku homesteads of which I have sufficient detailed information, was 413 persons at the end of 1962. This gives an average population of 9.4 persons per homestead,[37] ranging from

[37] The figure for Cilungulu ritual area was 8.6 persons per homestead

two to thirty persons. Forty-four of this total were the homestead heads themselves. There were thus 368 dependents in these homesteads, of whom seventy-three (19.8% of all dependents) were "wives" of the homestead heads themselves, and their "brothers' wives." A further thirty-nine (10.6% of dependents) were related to the homestead heads with whom they lived as affines of other categories: eleven were *walamu* ("spouses' siblings") of whom five were wives' full brothers (3 married and 2 unmarried). The largest group amongst these affines were nineteen "daughters-in-law" (*wakwe mulima*, sons' wives) to their homestead heads, as opposed to only two "sons-in-law" (daughters' husbands).

Eight dependents were younger full brothers (*wanakwa'we*) of the homestead heads with whom they lived, five married and three not yet married; 171 (56.8% of all dependents excluding wives) were "children" (*wana*) of the homestead heads. Of these "children," seventy-seven were own sons (64 unmarried, mainly young boys, and 13 married); sixty-one were own daughters (59 unmarried and only 2 married); thirty-four were classificatory "children," of whom only four (all classificatory "sons") were married. Six "sisters" (*walumbu'ze*) were living with their brothers: four married full sisters, three of whom had lost their husbands while the husband of the fourth lived in the same neighborhood; one unmarried full-sister (a young girl); and one unmarried classificatory sister.

There were only eleven (3.6% of all dependents excluding

(from tax figures). In a survey carried out by the agricultural department in two Gogo neighborhoods in 1946, the average per homestead was 9.51 persons (5.85 adults and 3.66 "children"; i.e. unmarried) in Nagulo neighborhood in west-central Ugogo near the Sulungai grass pan. In Mulebe neighborhood in east-central Ugogo, in ecological conditions similar to those of Temanghuku, the figure was 9.65 persons (5.90 adults and 3.75 children) per homestead. These agree substantially with my own figures for Temanghuku and show that there has probably been little or no change in homestead size in the 16 years from 1946 to 1962. (See: *Dodoma District Book* and Rounce, 1949.)

wives) "sister's children" (*wehwa*) living with their "mother's brothers": four were full-sister's sons, only one of whom was married; four were full-sister's daughters, three unmarried; three were classificatory "sister's daughters," all unmarried. It is clear that this link does not often provide the basis for common residence *within* homestead groups.

Of the forty-four homestead heads, eight (18.2%) had their own mothers (whose husbands were dead) living with them; two of these women were the mothers also of the heads of homesteads adjacent to their own. Only one mother's brother (*kuku'ye*), in this case mother's full brother, was living as a dependent in the same homestead as his sister's son. He was married but had no livestock of his own and was generally regarded as a "poor" man (*mubi* or *muciwa*).

The only other significant group of dependents were twenty-six (8.6% of dependents excluding wives) "grandchildren" (*wezukulu*), all unmarried and mostly very young children, living with their grandfathers. Twelve were own sons' children, five own daughters' children, while nine were classificatory "grandchildren." Of the total number of dependents, twenty-four (6.5% of the total) were unrelated (*wewisa*) to the homestead heads with whom they were living, including six nuclear families of men with their wives, two women without their husbands, and the ten children of all of these.

It may be seen from these figures that the dependents living with Gogo homestead heads belong to a great variety of kin and affinal categories.[38] However, a general pattern emerges which substantiates and extends what has already been said about the

[38] As I have noted in a previous section, homesteads were probably much larger before colonial penetration than they are today. This was not necessarily correlated only with the possibly greater cohesion of kin groups then, but also because men with little or no property who may today set themselves up as homestead heads would not have been able to do so in the past. They would not have been able to marry wives as easily as they can today, nor would they have felt as able to survive physical and supernatural attack upon themselves and their herds.

social composition of homesteads and neighborhoods in previous sections of this chapter and in Chapter IV. Full brothers, whose father is dead, often live together in the same homestead or in adjacent homesteads with their mother (cf. Chapter IV, Table 7 and *passim*). But adult married half brothers whose father is dead very seldom remain in the same homestead for any length of time, or indeed even in the same neighborhood. There is no reason for them to share a homestead: their herds are separate, and there is often a tension between them. They are in no way economically dependent upon each other, although they may "claim" (*kukwega;* lit., "to drag") single animals from the bride-wealth given for each other's daughters and sisters. The only reason inducing them to remain in the same neighborhood or in nearby neighborhoods is the location of their father's gravestone. Cooperation between them is difficult and tense.

Extending this line of inquiry, the figures show that agnatic kin of any broader category than full and half brothers do not live together, either in the same homesteads or in the same neighborhoods. The tendency for married men to move away from their fathers as soon as they can has been demonstrated. Paternal parallel cousins (*cana cawasewo*), related through even two generations, do not usually reside in a common homestead or neighborhood any more than do other categories of kin. The agnatic principle, of importance primarily in the patrilineal inheritance of livestock, has no force beyond the group of the children of one man, and even within this group, property relations lay down the lines of fission. Correlated directly with this and the generally high residential mobility of Gogo domestic groups is the fact that there are seldom any *married* grandchildren (son's sons) residing in the homesteads of their grandfathers; by the time they reach maturity, their own fathers have usually long since moved away.

Incidentally, the figures presented above also indicate that marriage is primarily virilocal, or "patrilocal" in its earliest phases, as daughters marry out and sons bring their first wife to their father's homestead, for a time at least. These factors are examined in Chapters VI and VII. Having presented the general pattern, I now proceed to an examination, through specific cases, of the cycle of growth and fission in Gogo domestic and homestead groups.

CYCLE AND FISSION IN DOMESTIC GROUPS

The variations seen in the patterns of growth, fission, and dissolution of individual domestic groups can be reduced to order if they are seen as resulting from the operation of a limited number of sociological principles through time. I have in the preceding sections tried to establish some of these principles, but they may better be seen in operation in some specific cases.

The first case is provided by the homesteads of the descendants of Sandiya, the founder of Temanghuku neighborhood. Some aspects of these groups have been described in Chapter IV (see also, Map 3, homesteads nos. 1, 5, and 6). In domestic groups there are basically two types of fission that occur as a result of internal forces: (a) fission after the death of the homestead head and father, and (b) before his death, with the mutual if grudging consent of seceding and remaining groups. The case of Sandiya's descendants illustrates the first type.

Sandiya established himself, with his first wife Ng'ongoli and a fairly large herd which he had accumulated, in Temanghuku neighborhood after he had left the homestead of his classificatory "mother's brother" (*kuku'ye*), in whose homestead he had been brought up after the death of his father. He soon married a second wife Mahungo (see Figure 9). Two other non-related men and their wives and families joined his homestead as dependents (*wazenji*).[39] As Sandiya's homestead grew, these unrelated de-

___

[39] The term *muzenji* means literally "a builder." The noun is derived from the verb *kuzenga,* "to build." In Cigogo it refers to "one who builds another's homestead," meaning a dependent whose presence in a homestead is not explicable in terms of his relationship to the homestead head, for example as "son" or "younger brother." I have shown that residence in a homestead implies moral, jural, and ritual subordination

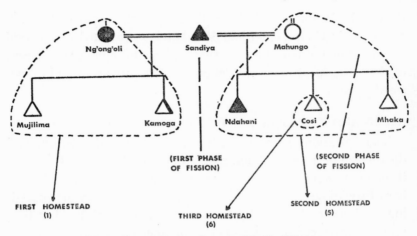

Figure 9. Fission between "houses"; sets of half siblings

pendents established their own homesteads nearby. Sandiya's sons from both houses married and remained living with him, for he was a comparatively rich man, was renowned for his powerful personality and as being a skillful diviner (*muganga*). He was also a "reasonable" man (*mupolo*), who helped his mature sons to marry and did not take more than two wives for himself.

When Sandiya died, his homestead was fairly large and included his own wives and children, and the wives and children of his eldest sons, plus some other *nyumba* containing kin related in a variety of ways (cf. Mujilima's homestead, below). Mujilima, the eldest son of the senior house (*nyumba imbaha*) and principal heir, became head of the homestead and inherited his father's bow (*wupinde*) and stool (*igoda*), the symbols of inheritance. This was in spite of the fact that the eldest son of the junior house (*nyumba indodo*), Ndahani, was older.

The homestead held together for a short time, Mujilima exerting his authority over his younger full and half brothers through

to the head. A combination of this subordinate status with no significant corresponding kinship link, implies low status in the external domain, in terms of wealth or prestige in political or jural matters.

the force of his personality, his ritual precedence in propitiations at the gravestone of their father Sandiya, and also through the fact of his periodic possession (*kutowwa macisi*) by Sandiya's ghost (see below). Then Ng'ongoli, the senior wife, died, and after a move of the homestead site, the junior *nyumba* broke off in its entirety and built a homestead some 200 yards away in the same neighborhood, Ndahani becoming *munyakaya*. Mahungo occupied the eastern *nyumba*. All the sons were married by this time, and Mujilima had two wives. He was keen to marry again. By this move, the full brothers of Mahungo's *nyumba* separated their herd by establishing their own cattle byre, and thus effectively consolidated their own control over its utilization. This was the first phase of fission.

I have stated that Mujilima is a resourceful and energetic man,[40] and he managed to build up his own herd and maintain control over his younger full brother Kamoga, who legally could have taken a share of their *nyumba* herd and set up his own homestead, as their mother Ng'ongoli was dead. Mujilima has three wives now, and Kamoga has two, although Kamoga's first wife lives with her full brother Masani (homestead no. 8, Map 3). She moved to Masani's homestead after conflict between her and Kamoga, and only Mujilima's intervention prevented them from breaking up the marriage. Although Kamoga has allocated to the *nyumba* of his own two wives sufficient livestock for their present needs, Mujilima retains effective control over the whole herd. The herd is considerably diminished since livestock were used for the later marriages of Mujilima and Kamoga, but primarily because of losses in the 1953–54 droughts. Nevertheless, Mujilima controls (1962–63) a herd of some fifty-five head of cattle and an equal number of small stock in his home herd (i.e.

---

[40] It has been recorded above that Mujilima not only became a successful village headman (government) under the British colonial administration, but also took over some ritual authority of the Deje clan ritual leader in part of his ritual area.

in the homestead byre), more or less equally divided between himself and Kamoga. He has a considerable number distributed among stock associates (*wakozigwa*) in his own and other neighborhoods. The livestock (including some in the herds of stock associates and therefore not in the home herd) are allocated between Mujilima's own three *nyumba* in the following way (see Figures 8 and 10):

	Cattle	Small stock
Nyumba of senior wife Ndudula	13	14
" of second wife Ngaga	24	12
" of junior wife Mbunda	12	13

Mujilima is about forty-six years of age and is at the height of his authority and prestige, both vis-à-vis the dependents in his own homestead, and the society at large. But even in this situation his control of his own property is severely limited by the autonomy of the *nyumba* to which they are allocated. His eldest son is Ndalu, of the second *nyumba* (the senior *nyumba* has two elder daughters). Ndalu is about twenty-three years of age, but is mentally retarded. However, Mujilima arranged a marriage for Ndalu, for which twenty-three head of cattle and fourteen small stock were promised as bridewealth (*cigumo*). But Ndalu is impotent (*yali mhinde*) and was unable to consummate the marriage. Mujilima then asked Ngaga, Ndalu's mother (see Figure 10), if she would let Tala (then about sixteen years old), the son of Ndudula (the senior wife), use the cattle instead to marry the same girl. There were insufficient cattle in the senior *nyumba* at the time, and she was a highly desirable girl. This would have necessitated the use of livestock in one *nyumba* by a member of another. Ngaga refused, the contract was broken off, the girl went home, and the livestock were returned to Ngaga's *nyumba*. Mujilima said, "So I just left it; after all, what could I do?" (*Hodu nghawa muleka; hambi alu noneza ci?*). But rumor had it that he had caused Ndalu's state through witchcraft in order

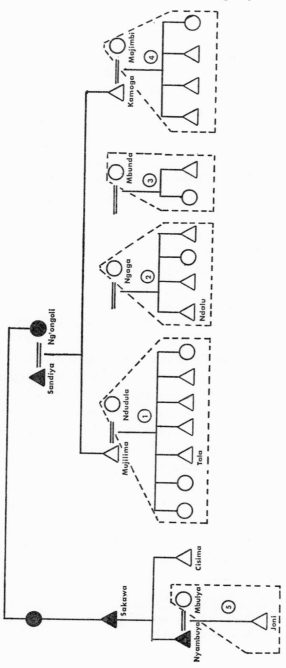

Figure 10. Present composition of Mujilima's homestead (each *nyumba* numbered as in Figure 8)

to maintain his wealth and prestige without challenge from his sons.[41]

Mujilima's domestic group provides a sample of one at the "middle" phase of its cycle of development, where the head is at the apex of his influence and just before his sons are mature enough to initiate the process of fission. The case nevertheless illustrates the independence and autonomy of *nyumba* within the domestic group and the difficulties a homestead head can have in maintaining his control of livestock in his herd. It is not merely an adage when Gogo say, *"Hono walela iwana, vinhu vyako vyose vyabokwa,"* (When you have children, all your things are snatched away).

The second phase of fission in this group occurred later between the full brothers Mhaka and Cosi (homesteads nos. 5 and 6, Map 3). Ndahani, the eldest brother of the *nyumba,* was homestead head but died soon after they split off from Mujilima's homestead. Cosi, the next eldest, became homestead head and inherited Ndahani's wife Nyigome. Nyigome had one son by Ndahani, but he too died, a young boy before his marriage. Cosi was already married and had one son Ngobito by this marriage, but his wife died soon after he had inherited Nyigome. He married another wife, the daughter of Biliya, who became the wife of the junior house, Nyigome now being the senior. But Nyigome soon came into conflict with her husband's mother (*mukwe'we*) Mahungo, who was living with them, and with her young co-wife Majimbi. What with the deaths of Nyigome's husband Ndahani, her own son, and Cosi's wife after Nyigome had been inherited by him, suspicions of witchcraft and sorcery soon became common knowledge against her, and were confirmed by various divinations. The process and causes of the fission which resulted in this domestic group are best described in the words of my informant, Mhaka:

[41] This case points to a crucial element in the Father/son relationship in Ugogo which, being within a patrilineal system, is of course characterized by a rather unusual form of the "holder-heir" complex.

We came into conflict with Cosi's wives,[42] and our mother Mahungo did also. Even now Nyigome, Cosi's senior wife, has forbidden herself (*yelila ciila*)[43] from even setting foot in my homestead [5]. But Majimbi, Cosi's junior wife, still comes.

It was because Nyigome began quarreling with our mother Mahungo and her co-wife Majimbi. We were all living together [in one homestead]. When they had quarreled and had finished, and a hen went by near her [Nyigome's] *nyumba*, she would curse it; she began to curse even the cattle and goats. This happened whoever she fought with in the homestead. But people knew she was not cursing the cattle or the goats, but the person she had been quarreling with.[44]

So Nyigome left and moved her *nyumba* to Malogo's at Musimbe [an adjacent neighborhood]. Then she moved to Mujilima's homestead [1], Cosi remaining here with me all the time. She lived a year at Mujilima's and Cosi stayed here. Cosi then decided that he did not like having one wife in one homestead and the other in another . . . He discussed it with me and said, "My younger brother, I cannot continue with one wife living here and the other there. I had better build my own homestead where they can live together; because if I say, 'Nyigome, come back and live with us in this homestead,' she will refuse. It is better that I build my own homestead and keep them together in one place."

Mhaka agreed and Cosi dismantled his two *nyumba* at homestead no. 5 and built his own at (6), where he lived with his two wives and his eldest son Ngobito, who was also married. Mhaka

[42] Here Mhaka uses the term "Cosi's wives" in general, in order to emphasize that the conflict was not with Cosi himself. Fighting among full brothers is considered very bad.

[43] *Kwilila ciila* is an alternative version of *kulapa ciila,* described earlier in this chapter. The reflexive form of the verb used here, thus implying that she "forbade herself," though with the mutual agreement of all concerned. This is in spite of the fact that she lives in a homestead only some hundreds of yards away.

[44] For wives to quarrel and cause the dissolution of the homestead is a very serious offence in Ugogo, for reasons which will have become apparent. It nearly always implies witchcraft or sorcery activities by the wife and is grounds for divorce.

remained with his wife, their mother Mahungo and his children at (5).

As Mahungo was still alive, however, Cosi could take the live-stock he had accumulated in his own wives' *nyumba,* but none of the herd held in common with Mhaka in the *nyumba* of their mother Mahungo. Even though Cosi was the senior sibling, it was he who was seceding; Mahungo, and the small herd left in her *nyumba* and received in bridewealth from the marriage of her daughters, remained at Mhaka's homestead. The two full brothers thus, paradoxically, have their own autonomous do-mestic groups even though their mother is alive, while Mujilima and Kamoga share one though their mother is dead.[45] Mujilima's authority over his half brothers is now practically nil, apart from that which he wields by virtue of his personality and position in the community at large. In spite of the fact that Mujilima still takes precedence at propitiation rituals to the spirits of the dead, Mhaka is now the favored medium for possession by Sandiya's spirit. The balance of power is thus equalized in favor of the junior siblings and the situation ratified by supernatural inter-vention. This influences considerably the cooperation between the sets of full siblings in economic and ritual matters.

I have described this case in some detail because it provides an example of fission in the domestic group set up in one generation and the kinds of groups that take its place. In the next genera-tion, the descendants of Sandiya will almost surely become dis-persed, and the system thus does not result in the creation of "expanded families" in localized clusters linked by ties of agna-tion.[46]

[45] The principles of the inheritance of livestock within one *nyumba* are further examined in Chapter VII.

[46] Cf. Fortes (1949a), p. 69. Also Gulliver (1955), pp. 100–123. The process of "structural amnesia" described by Gulliver for the Jie, which enables co-resident agnates to claim closer agnatic links than actually exist, leading to structural fusion and re-amalgamation, does not occur in Gogo. This is consistent with the Gogo pattern of the "hiving off" of house groups at each generation in a pattern of mobility which lies

An example of fission in domestic groups before the death of the father, and also of the composition of a domestic group at its earliest and simplest phase, is given by the case of Balidi (homestead no. 35, Map 3) and his son Hata (27). Balidi is a man of just under sixty years of age who arrived in Temanghuku neighborhood during the 1946 drought. He had married a wife Nghogwa by whom he had two children; both died. Nghogwa was troublesome (*mugazi*), and he divorced her. He then married Ngayo who bore him two daughters and his son Hata (see Figure 11). Both daughters died. Balidi came to Temanghuku with his son Hata, his third wife Ndekwa, and her three daughters. Hata's mother Ngayo had died before they came. Hata claims ten head of cattle were left in his (Ngayo's) *nyumba,* of which three were left in 1962. Balidi, however, wished to marry another wife and did so quite recently, but only after he had helped Hata to marry. He now says that there are no cattle left in Hata's *nyumba.* Hata decided two years ago at the age of about thirty, to leave his father's homestead. He built his own a couple of hundred yards from his father's, where he has only one *nyumba* (*ikumbo* and *kugati*) and a tiny byre for milk cattle (*nghamwa*). He lives alone with his wife and two young children in spite of the fact that his close agnate (paternal parallel cousin, *wali cana cawasewo*) Lusinde, whose father is dead, has his own small homestead (no. 26, Map 3) nearby.

Hata still has an interest in his father's herd and they form a herding group together. The dispute over the three head of cattle is not stressed, and neither man would think of taking it to the informal local elders' court for settlement. Balidi's herd now contains some eighteen head of cattle and twelve small-stock, all of which are allocated to Ndekwa's *nyumba* (the youngest wife Nongwa has run away; she has no surviving children). Hata has six head of cattle and four small stock in his wife's *nyumba;* only

---

somewhere between the more sedentary Jie homesteads and extended families, and the nomadic Turkana family units which have solved the problem in an entirely different way.

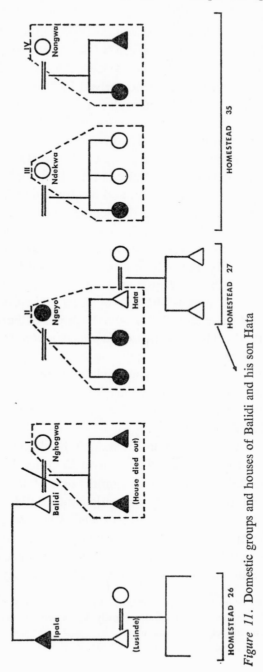

Figure 11. Domestic groups and houses of Balidi and his son Hata

one or two are kept in his own byre, the rest in his father's. It is clear that Hata established his own homestead in order to consolidate his rights in the livestock he has accumulated himself, as well as an attempt to do so in regard to the cattle he claims are left in his mother's *nyumba,* of which he is the sole surviving male member. He has not yet fully accomplished this. Not only does his father control most of the livestock (in both economic and ritual spheres), but Hata is still interested in obtaining more from his father's herd, although Balidi claims that these cattle belong to another *nyumba,* and therefore Hata does not have even legal rights of inheritance in them. But Balidi has no other sons and Hata would almost certainly inherit most of his father's herd on his death. The only way in which Hata could establish full control of his own herd, at least in economic terms, would be to move away to another neighborhood. This he is at the moment both unable and unwilling to do, for first he does not have enough resources himself to be entirely independent,[47] and second he feels he can still benefit from his father's inheritance. This arrangement is suitable for Balidi as Hata does most of the herding and other heavy work.

The case of Kazimoto (homestead no. 22, Map 3) illustrates another solution to the problem of inter-generational strain in the F-S/holder-heir situation. Kazimoto was seventy-two years old in 1962 and I heard when I had left the Temanghuku area that he died towards the end of 1963. He had been a rich man with over 150 head of cattle, but most of them had died during the 1946 and 1953 droughts and grazing shortages. In spite of his wealth, Kazimoto married only two wives. In 1962–63 the younger wife Ndayo (see Figure 12) was living with her full-brother at Ilindi, eight miles to the west of Kazimoto's home-

---

[47] Were Hata to move now to another neighborhood to live near, say, matrilateral or affinal kin, he would still have to have enough resources to set up his own independent homestead unless he was prepared to attach himself as a dependent (a lower status than his present one) to one or other of these kin.

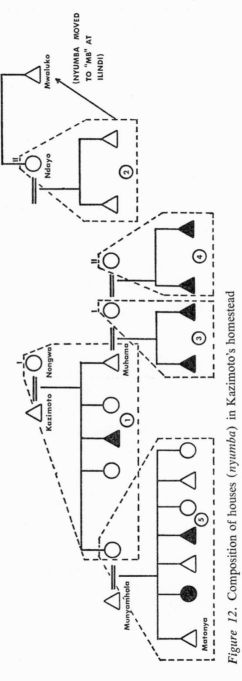

Figure 12. Composition of houses (*nyumba*) in Kazimoto's homestead

stead, with her two young sons, the eldest about eight years old (5 other children had died in infancy in the *nyumba*). Kazimoto himself had taken her there, and there was no question of divorce or separation; he visited her occasionally. The various *nyumba* of his Temanghuku homestead were constituted as set out in Figure 12.

Kazimoto lived in the eastern *nyumba* with Nongwa. All her children were married, and her eldest daughter and husband Munyamhala live in *nyumba* 5. Munyamhala is forty-six years old and came to live with his wife's parents (*wakwe'we*) from choice. He gave full bridewealth (15 head of cattle and 20 small stock) for their daughter and thus did not come as a poor son-in-law to do bridewealth service for his father-in-law (*kupanga:* cf. Cory (1954), ¶62; and below, Chapter VI). His son Matonya is now twenty-three years old and wishes to marry.

All Nongwa's other daughters are married out. Her eldest son is dead and Muhama, now thirty-two, has two wives but no surviving children. Kazimoto was considered a good man, who had held his domestic group together through his reason and unselfishness. But he was also considered lucky in that he had only one mature son who could have constituted an early threat towards fission. He had thus been able to give Muhama bride-wealth enough to marry two wives, and his eldest daughter and her husband and children lived with him (including two young men), increasing the size of his homestead and his prestige. It was also thought a sign of his reasonableness that he had per-mitted his junior wife to return to her kin, although her children would have full rights in the property allocated to her house.

Although Kazimoto was still an active man in 1962–63, a homestead head and a respected elder, he had virtually abandoned to Muhama economic control over the small herd left in the homestead. Muhama told me:

When the cattle were decimated by the grazing and water shortages, Kazimoto imposed upon himself an "avoidance" of anything to do with cattle.[48] He left that to me (*yandecela ane du*); even for [government] tax purposes my name is written.

The largest part of the herd is still of Nongwa's *nyumba* and will remain so until her death; but as Muhama is the sole surviving male in the *nyumba,* his virtual control over the livestock was not incompatible with the situation as it existed even before Kazimoto's death.

CONCLUSION

In this chapter I have attempted to show that Gogo homesteads and domestic groups are fundamental units in Gogo social structure, both in the external politico-jural domain and in property and kinship relations. The analysis was set against the immediate background of neighborhood organization and relationships between homesteads analyzed in Chapter IV. Viewed from outside the homestead is a corporate, jural unit, but its internal structure is implicit from its founding; and the cleavages which underlie this structure are the bases for later fission and dissolution. The rigid differentiation between houses, the matricentral units of one woman and her children, is shown in the autonomy of such units in the production and consumption of the basic subsistence commodity. As the houses mature, it is also shown in respect of the main form of inheritable property (livestock), which is inherited through the developed house-property system. The role of matrilateral kin, in particular mother's brothers, in the differentiation of houses, is examined in the following two chapters.

The domestic group is the corporate unit for rituals concerning the health and fertility of men and their herds, an autonomy which tends to hold such units together while allowing their residential movement, more or less *as units,* through different neighborhoods and ritual areas. But in the sphere of rituals for

[48] *Kazimoto yezila zing'ombe:* the reflexive form of the verb *kuzila* (to avoid) is used, implying a personal, voluntary avoidance, because he was upset by it all.

the land, crops and rain, the significance of the homestead as a unit is limited; the *nyumba* becomes the unit in relation to other like units. This is in spite of the fact that agricultural activity it-self is divided equally between men and women. It is consistent, however, as agricultural activities and produce are really outside the field of property relations and patrilineal descent. A married woman wherever she is will have her fields and granaries. But her sons will only have rights in property through their status in the patricentral domestic group, which is the core of the home-stead unit with its associated herd. The rituals directed towards the health and increase of livestock (strongly linked with that of humans) are domestic, kinship rituals; they are the secret of the homestead head and his close dependents, and not the con-cern of the broader ritual areas and their ritual leaders.

The analyses presented in these two chapters are closely inter-dependent: the structure of domestic groups and homestead units cannot be understood outside of their relationship with their social and ecological environment; and locality, the principles of local organization and kinship, cannot properly be analyzed with-out a consideration of the process and forces involved in the cycle of development and fission in domestic groups.

To add the third and final aspect to this general picture, I must now turn to an examination of marriage: its procedures, rela-tion to locality, and the kin roles involved. This will lend further insight into the role of livestock in the creation and maintenance of most of the significant relationships in the network of kinship.

VI
Marriage, Bridewealth, and Kinship Network

I have frequently referred to the structural importance of affinal links, in contrast to those of descent, in the operation of the Gogo kinship system. I now examine the implications of this in more detail with reference to locality and, later, the operation of specific kinship roles. But as the effectiveness of many kinship roles is virtually defined in terms of potential obligations and rights in livestock exchanges (the most important of which is the transfer of bridewealth at marriage) it is necessary to examine in some detail both marriage procedure and bridewealth transactions. I therefore confine this chapter to an analysis of marriage in its procedure, relation to locality, bridewealth transactions, and some affinal relationships.

Gogo have neither a preferential marriage system nor any unambiguously defined exogamous groups. Thus, neither clans, sub-clans, nor what I have called "maximal lineages" are actually exogamous groups, although the latter can theoretically trace common agnatic descent. This is consistent with the fact that, although they are based upon patrilineal descent, these groups are not corporate with respect to marriage, nor localized and therefore able to act as groups in any situation.[1] I also noted in Chapter III that a first response of Gogo informants is to state

[1] Cf. Fortes (1949a), pp. 114–115. The distinction between the categories of kin prohibited as marriage partners by the rules of exogamy and those who are prohibited in extra-marital sex relations by incest taboos is noted below.

that clans are exogamous, but when faced with the fact that many intra-clan marriages do actually take place, they always have a ready theory to explain their incidence. Other kin marriages are also common. Of 203 marriages, past and present, which I recorded, 144 (70.9%) were between non-kin (*wewisa*); forty-five (22.2%) were between kin; and in fourteen (6.9%) the pre-existing relationship between the spouses was not recorded. The largest group of "kin marriages" ("kin" here includes affines) were between persons who belong to the same clan (*mbeyu*). They constituted fifteen (33.2%) of all kin marriages, seven of which were between persons who shared only the same clan, six also shared a common sub-clan name (*mulongo*); and in two the spouses belonged to the same maximal lineage (*mulango*). Eleven (24.3%) were between classificatory cross-cousins and thirteen (28.8%) were between persons who were affines in the category *welizenjere,* "those whom we marry."

But the important point is that, in fact, marriages are never arranged on the basis of preferred kinship relationships. Although marriage with matrilateral cross-cousin and between joking-partners is culturally "preferred," such preferences are rationalizations given *ex post facto* by Gogo to explain the incidence of such marriages. These rationalizations are consistent with the patrilineal descent ideology and the relationships that exist between clans. But in fact, kin marriages are a function of the locality pattern of marriage, which I analyze in detail in this chapter. Most marriages take place within a limited spatial range, and as most people living in adjacent homesteads or common localities are related in one way or another, many marriages are bound to be intra-kin.[2]

As in most societies, the range of exogamy and the range of

---

[2] The locality pattern of marriage, which is of crucial importance in Ugogo, is of fundamental significance in the choice of spouse in most non-preferential marriage systems: see Lévi-Strauss (1963), pp. 293–294; Fortes (1962), pp. 6–7, 13; and further discussion below. See also Rigby (1967d).

incest rules in Gogo are not co-extensive. But the distinction between them is not the same as that found in societies with extensive corporate lineage organization.[3] In such societies, sex relations are permitted with distant agnates whom it is not possible
to marry, lest existing descent relationships be upset. Thus, marriage prohibitions are more wide-ranging than the rules of incest.
In the Gogo case, however, the procedure of "killing the kinship"
(*kuwulaga ndugu*) to allow *cifuta* marriages between certain
categories of kin (see Chapter III) permits sex relations between
persons within the marriage bond which would be considered
"incestuous" (i.e. witchcraft, *wuhawi*) outside of it.[4] Hence, it is
the regulative function of the rules of exogamy and incest for sex
relations in general within the local community that is structurally important, not the functions of such rules in maintaining
the structure of exclusive but dispersed descent groups. Exogamy
rules are linked by Gogo with the mutual obligations of close kin
in bridewealth transactions, and serve, they say, to prevent confusion in these obligations. I discuss them in detail below. Incest
rules are linked with the semi-institutionalized *mbuya* lover relationships, which function partially to control extra-marital sex
relations in local communities.[5] These three elements—livestock
obligations in bridewealth, *cifuta* marriages between close kin,
and the controlling influence of *mbuya* extramarital sex relations
—are built into the Gogo model of the rules of incest and
exogamy and serve to explain the distinctions between them.
Their importance for the localized Gogo marriage system and
affinal relationships will appear in the following analysis. First we

[3] For example, see Evans-Pritchard (1951), pp. 44–45; Fortes (1936)
and (1949a), p. 115. Also Radcliffe-Brown (1950), p. 61.

[4] For similar institutions among the Shona, cf. Holleman (1949), p.
29; or (1952), p. 53. Also Harris (1962), pp. 57, 62; La Fontaine
(1962), p. 107.

[5] A detailed analysis of the *mbuya* institution will be published elsewhere. A brief analysis is given in my paper (1963) in Conference Proceedings, Jan. 1963, E.A.I.S.R., Kampala.

must look quickly at formal procedures for setting up a marriage.

PREPARATION FOR MARRIAGE

All normal Gogo adults are married at least once during their lifetime. In the case of men, only a youth who is impotent (*yali mhinde*) because of some congenital defect and cannot consummate his first marriage, or who is a complete cripple, will not be married. Even boys who are totally blind (*wecibofu* or *mubofu*) from birth, or who have become so because of disease, usually can marry if they can collect sufficient livestock for bridewealth. But it is much more difficult for a blind girl to be married and the bridewealth given for her will be minimal.

The growth of a child is marked by certain distinctive physical operations, even before the most important of the rites of passage, circumcision, is reached. Most Gogo babies at a very early age (sometimes when only a couple of months old) have a scar (*inindi, ilindi,* or *cinindi*) burnt into the forehead as a part of protective or curative medicine for the eye infections very common in Ugogo.[6] At the age of about six to eight when the new teeth are growing, the two lower incisors are knocked out (*kutowa nyhende*). At about eight or ten years old, the lobes and the upper part of the ears are pierced (*kutobola makutu;* the upper holes are called *malomwa*) so that they may be extended for the insertion of attractive ornaments (*mitimbi* for girls, and *mindowi* and a variety of others for boys).[7]

Children before puberty and initiation play at being married. Young boys build tiny "homesteads" and "cattle byres" and clay cattle, and the girls help them in this and play at being wives. Sexual play among children before initiation is condoned as simply the result of childish ignorance. But sexual segregation in work and play takes place at an early age. As soon as boys

[6] Neighboring peoples in Tanzania distinguish Gogo by these marks, and it is very often the first thing they mention about the Gogo.

[7] Cf. Claus (1911), pp. 43–44; Mnyampala (1954), p. 92.

begin to herd small stock (at the age of about 7) they begin
to sleep in the boys' and young men's dormitory rooms (*magane*)
attached to many homesteads. They learn herding techniques,
games, and how to make and use such implements as bows and
arrows from their elders, and songs and stories in the evenings
(*cinyamaduwa*) from older children and their mothers. Toward
the age of about fifteen, boys begin to take an interest in dancing (*uwuvina*) and singing (*kwimba zinyimbo* or *membo*).
They attach themselves to the men's line in dance teams at
musunyunho, masembegu, and *nindo* dances to learn the steps
and songs. The young men whose company they now keep
joke about their uncircumcised state, calling them *walayoni*[8]
and threatening to cut off their foreskins (*nzunga*) with the
knives they carry. This makes boys of this age acutely embar-
rassed and eager to be initiated. It is virtually impossible for
uncircumcised boys to have heterosexual relationships, as it is
indeed for uncircumcised adults from areas who have come to
live in Ugogo; the girls and women simply laugh at them.

The age at which most boys are circumcised and initiated does
not correspond to that of puberty or any other single physical
stage of development. Puberty and the first emission of a boy is
not socially marked in any way as it is among many other Bantu
peoples, though a girl's first menstruation is (Rigby, 1967d).
In the past, boys were circumcised when they were between about
fifteen and twenty, but the age of initiation is rapidly decreasing

---

[8] The word *mulayoni* (pl., *walayoni*) refers to any uncircumcised
youth, who can only be rather young in Ugogo. It is derived from the
Baraguyu/Masai word *olayioni* (pl., *ilayiok*), "boy," "uncircumcised
boy," or "son." The Cigogo word for "youth," *muzelelo* (pl., *wazelelo*) is
now generally used to refer to initiated youths and young men, after
they have passed through the period of initiation, the several phases of
which have their own terms to describe the initiates. I have already
noted that the Gogo age-set organization was derived from and closely
linked to that of the Baraguyu, though very different in structure. The
Gogo word *muzelelo* may also be linked to Masai/Baraguyu *elelero*,
"youth."

8 Part of a bridewealth herd (*cigumo*) leaves the groom's homestead. Women from the groom's side, dancing and ululating, lead the herd a short distance.

9   Young men (*wazelelo*) cutting up a sacrificial ox

and youngsters of eleven to fourteen and even younger are now permitted to be circumcised. Gogo elders explicitly accept the earlier age at which boys are now initiated. Circumcision ceremonies (*sona zacigotogoto* or *kugotola*) can take place in any year when a good harvest coincides with a sufficient number of boys in a large homestead or neighborhood being ready for it. They may be promoted by any father, who is also a homestead head, for his own sons, whence others will join them, but it is a matter for the ritual leader's permission: he provides the religious sanctions necessary after consultation with a diviner, and ritual payments must be made to him. When the activities at the common circumcision camp in the bush (*cibalu* or *cibalwe*) are completed, the boys recuperate in shelters (*makumbi;* sing., *ikumbi*) near the homesteads which are shared by clusters of homesteads within each neighborhood.[9]

Gogo circumcision ceremonies are very rich in symbolism, and will be analyzed in detail elsewhere. After initiation and public acceptance of his change of status a Gogo youth begins to have legitimate heterosexual relations and to prepare himself for marriage. Because he is unlikely to be able to marry for some time due to the problem of high bridewealth, he might establish liaisons of some permanence with the young wives of older men through one of the *mbuya* relationships. Gogo youths are (and are expected to be) active and passionate lovers before marriage, and usually have a great number of affairs. They visit *mbuya* lovers or young girls in their homesteads at night (*kubita mbalani*), often taking considerable risks in entering the inner rooms (*kugati*) where their lovers are sleeping. It is, however, a very serious matter for an unmarried girl to become pregnant, and youths should take the more proper course of establishing *mbuya* relationships with the young wives of other men, in which the problem of the paternity of any children which may result does not arise. The husbands of wives with whom proper

[9] Cf. Mnyampala (1954), pp. 92–94; also Schaegelen (1938), pp. 531–544.

mbuya arrangements have been made should discreetly ignore (*kumutelela*) a lover of one of their younger wives.

Thus, the inception of a boy's search for a spouse and sexual activity is marked by the public act of initiation, in which several categories of his close kin are closely involved. A girl's initiation, however, in which similar kin roles are involved, comes before puberty at about the age of eight to eleven, and does not signify her immediate marriageability. Gogo draw this distinction between the initiation ages of boys and girls:

From time immemorial, girls have been initiated before puberty [that is, before first menstruation, *wakali nakalagala*]. But boys have been circumcised when they are grown up (*wawaha*), having "known about women" for some time. Before this, when a youth dreams and has his first emission (*hono yatunda "matunzi gakulela"*), others will not know; he will not tell them. He might inform his age-mates but will not tell the others. There is no fuss about it.

For the operation (*clitoridectomy*) and instruction (*mazimu*), the girls are also taken into the bush by the women operators and their helpers (*wanghunga*), but no camp is built. They merely choose a sandy spot or the dried-up course of a river, so that the blood may easily be covered over. The girls are immediately returned to their homesteads where they are secluded for the period of recovery in their mothers' *kugati*, inside room, and may not be "seen" by boys and men until they are cured. A girl at this transitional stage in her life-cycle is called *munyacipale* or *munyacinga*.[10] After the ceremonies are over and the

---

[10] The word *munyacipale* is derived from the root, *-pale*. The prefix *ci-* denotes 'quality of," and the *munya-* "possessor of": thus, "the possessor of the quality *-pale*." The root *-pale* appears to be (although to my knowledge this is not an explicit association made by Gogo) the same as that in the word *mhale* (prefix N + *-pale*) which means "circumcised penis" (the word for penis is *mbolo*). I have not been able to discover any tonal difference in the roots, and Gogo informants thought the association reasonable, though not, as I have said, generally stated. Thus the term may imply that a girl before clitoridectomy is one "who has the quality of penis." This interpretation is supported by the fact that the

ritual washing (*kuhovuga*) is completed, initiated girls go visiting the neighboring homesteads in twos and threes, sitting
silently and demurely while they are complimented on their
beauty and gentleness. But a girl is not marriageable until she
has reached puberty, although on rare occasions she may be
betrothed before then.[11] So it is necessary to mark a girl's first
menstruation, and it is accompanied by ritual seclusion and
public ceremony.

When a girl has her first menstruation (referred to politely
as *hono yatema ihamha,* "when she has cut the leaf"), she informs her mother, and it is made known generally in the neighborhood that she has now "grown up" (*yakalagala*). She is
secluded again in the *kugati* room of her mother's *nyumba,* and
given instructions in exclusively feminine topics such as child-
birth and the correct behavior toward a husband. She may be
instructed by any married women. There is a variation in the
period of seclusion, but it is usually between two weeks and a
month. As it nears its end, the women of the homestead brew
beer and invite (*kulalika*) neighbors and kin for the celebration.
Mainly women are invited, but men and boys tag along to
watch. Close kin of the girl who happen to be in the neighborhood are invited but, an important point, there are no specific
duties which kin have to perform at this ceremony. During the
last few days of the girl's seclusion, the women dance to drums
(*wakuvina uwuvina weng'oma*) for most of the day or even all
through the night.[12] Songs are usually very general in content

terms denoting the male and female sexual organs are reversed (*kusu-
taniza*) during the initiation period: *nghuma* (vagina) is used for "penis,"
and *mbolo* (penis) for the female organs. Cf. also Claus (1911), p. 45.

[11] Infant betrothal is uncommon in Ugogo and occurs only in extremely special circumstances. The betrothal period is usually a few days
only.

[12] Drumming and dancing to drums (*ng'oma*) is an exclusively feminine activity in Ugogo. A good drummer (*mutowi weng'oma*) has considerable prestige, and her technique and ability in composition is highly
praised and remembered even after her death. Men never dance "drum
dances" (*wuvina weng'oma*); their greater variety of dances are accom-

and each expert drummer sings her own compositions. One or two songs that have a didactic content may invariably be played on such occasions (see Rigby, 1967d).

When the dancing is over, the women are given beer. If they dance through the night (*wagula*) and the girl's father or guardian is well off, he slaughters a beast (*ng'ombe yomugulo*), and the ceremony is extended. The girl is ceremonially bathed (*yakuhovugwa*) that evening, still with only the women involved. In the morning she is bathed again, dressed in a new cloth, and they invest her with beads and ornaments (*wakumuvwika wihambo*) which she has been given. She remains in the *nyumba* but now may be visited by men, and she no longer "hides from people." The second day she is free to go wherever she wishes and do as she likes, and is ready to be actively courted.

Thus a girl, initiated and instructed and therefore already out of the phase of "childhood," is given public recognition as being marriageable after her first menstruation, by a public ceremony which concerns the neighborhood and locality generally. Kin are invited but have no special functions and those living at some distance are not specially informed as they are for the initiation ceremonies. The women who perform and rejoice may be related to her in one way or another, but this is not the reason for their presence. The statement of the girl's marriageability is made within the limited local group and is not the special concern of a dispersed kinship group. Offers of marriage are thereby invited from anyone living nearby, particularly those who are close

---

panied by singing and leg-bells (*nciinda*) only. However, on one occasion at the dancing for a girl's first menstruation ceremony, three men (all traveling diviners, *waganga*) from northeast Ugogo on the borders of Ukaguru ("Itumba"), took over some women's drums and danced and sang. Gogo know that Kaguru ("Wetumba") men drum and dance to drums, and it was accepted without comment. Also, all three were diviners, whose behavior is assumed to be unorthodox. The drum is often a feminine symbol, as is the calabash. Cf. also, Claus (1911), p. 45.

enough to attend. This is consistent with the locality pattern of marriage in Ugogo.

There are several ways in which the marriage contract may be established and completed in Ugogo. It is not possible to describe all of these, and in any case some either are unorthodox and very uncommon (such as infant betrothal as a pledge for borrowed livestock) or emerge from the more orthodox and common forms (as in the case of wife inheritance). I therefore discuss only those procedures which occur most frequently.[13] The point to be kept in mind is that, whatever the form of the initial approach to marriage, there are certain procedures and prestations to be carried out which symbolize the transfer of particular rights and the creation of particular obligations which are of crucial importance in conjugal and affinal relationships. It is upon these that I shall concentrate. But it must also be emphasized that the founding of a successful marriage is a process that stretches over a considerable period and must be analyzed as such, though there are one or two turning points which are jurally more important than the others.

The most common, and normatively "correct," type of marriage is betrothal marriage (*kubanya*). But if, in a betrothal marriage, the pace of negotiations is not fast enough, or the youth's father and kin refuse to initiate negotiations, he may force the issue by abducting the girl (*kupula*). The youth must nevertheless follow certain institutionalized procedures. He should have some of his own kin with him, particularly his female siblings, and the girl should be abducted with a companion of her own. This forces the hand of elders on both sides to begin negotiations, after which all of the procedures and prestations of a normal betrothal marriage are carried out, with the

[13] See also Mnyampala (1954), pp. 94–98; Cory (1951), ¶¶59–80.

modification only of some of the preliminary prestations. For example, the betrothal gift (*cibanyilo*) is not given, nor is the *luzizi* ("of opening the door"), but instead the following prestations are made by the suitor and his kin:

Cilatu ("the little sandal"), or *makwego* ("the dragging off"): a young ox (*nzeku*) or goat is given by the youth's kin to the girl's kin for having troubled them to send a messenger "to look for the girl."

Mabijili ("the painful grass-seeds"): one or two goats given for the painful trips which have to be made by the girl's kin as a consequence.

mwano: a goat provided for the girl's kin upon finding her, which is killed and eaten on the spot before negotiations begin.

If the girl's kin still refuse to consider the marriage, they will take the payments they have been given (and can claim in the elders' court), and the young man would suffer considerable ridicule. If they agree, the girl still returns home while the negotiations for bridewealth continue.

Kupula abduction as described must be distinguished from *Kutizya* (elopement; lit., "to run off with"), although the motivations and result of both may at times be similar. But in the case of *kutizya*, a young man runs off with a girl if he realizes that his chances of marrying her in any other way are hopeless: if, for example, he has no hope of obtaining bridewealth or the consent of her kin. The couple, usually alone, run off secretly to another ritual area or neighborhood, out of the reach of their kin. These days they may flee to another part of Tanzania or to the towns. There is often no intention of concluding the affair normally by paying bridewealth. *Kutizya* follows no rules and is a personal, "anti-social" act; *kupula* is an institutionalized method of initiating or speeding up negotiations. In the latter case, the girl is usually kept in the same neighborhood, or even next door, and kin on both sides often have prior knowledge of it and responsibility for it. In the case of *kutizya* the youth's kin are not responsible for his action unless the girl's people can establish proof, which would involve their finding the girl and youth and bringing them back—an often impossible task. In any case, both actions are based upon emotions and sentiment which make even more difficult the strained relations between potential affines (see below), and thus, Gogo say, do not augur well for sound affinal and conjugal relations and are so to be condemned.

A Gogo youth cannot usually hope to marry until he is about twenty-five, nearly ten years or so after circumcision.[14] When he can, he should look for a girl with qualities that will make her a good wife, and these are different from those that should make a good *mbuya* lover, although physical appearance is still important. Negotiations are opened for the betrothal (*kubanya*) marriage when the suitor arranges for a kinsman, either male or female, to present the betrothal gift (*cibanyilo*) of beads, chains, or other ornaments, to the girl and her mother.[15] If this gift is accepted, the elders concerned as kin of the suitor send one of their number "to cough" (*"kukolola"*) outside the girl's homestead. Her kin know what he has come for, and a day is arranged for the bridewealth negotiations (*kwiguma*) to begin. But it is essential that a young man inform his father (or his father's heir), or other agnatic kin, and his mother's brothers (*waku-ku'ze*), *before* arranging the betrothal for his first marriage. Those "on the father's side" (*wosogwe* or *wokulume*) and "on the mother's side" (*wokucekulu*) are intimately implicated, both economically and ritually, in the bridewealth transactions for a youth's first marriage, and negotiations may break down if they

[14] Under new economic conditions and with new avenues to wealth, Gogo youths can now marry at an earlier age than they did in the past.

[15] In one of the marriages I followed in detail, the *cibanyilo* gift was an "ivory" arm-ring (*mhogo*) plus three ten-cent pieces (*magobola madatu*) as the "arrow for opening the gate" (*"sonyo yedeha"*). The suitor, a young man of about 24, sent his matrilateral cross-cousin, a youth of the same age, as "messenger" (*mutumwa*). Both youths, and the girl he was seeking to marry, lived in three adjacent homesteads in the same neighborhood.

are not first informed. Consent of the kin on both sides who will be future affines is required, and the following case illustrates the importance of the correct order of procedure:

A young man Nyawombo, the son of Bozi, wished to marry as his first wife a girl who lived in a neighboring homestead. Bozi was dead, and Nyawombo's mother Mbeleje had been inherited by Bozi's classificatory "brother" [his FBS, *wali cana cawasewo*] Cidong'a, who lived in a neighborhood some three miles away. When Cidong'a moved his homestead to another neighborhood, however, Mbeleje and Nyawombo left him and came to live with her brother Mukwawa, near whose homestead they built a small one of their own. Nyawombo, who had a small herd of his own, sent a betrothal gift and arranged for a day to settle the bridewealth. He then in-

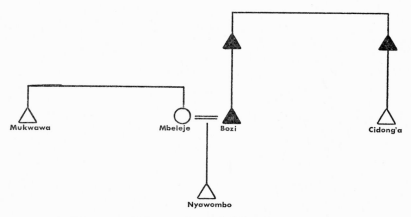

Figure 13. The case of Nyawombo and Cidong'a

formed Cidong'a what he had done and asked him to come and represent him as he was his "father" (*sogwe*). He also asked Cidong'a to contribute to the bridewealth. At the same time, he informed Mukwawa, his mother's brother. After the preliminary payments (*"vidodo-vidodo"*) had been arranged, it was discovered [at the bridewealth discussion at the girl's homestead] that Nyawombo had only five head of cattle available for the transaction. At first this did not unduly alarm the girl's kin as they naturally expected Cidong'a and Mukwawa to make up a sufficient number as they should [see below]. Cidong'a, however, was unwilling to contribute anything, on the plea that all of his cattle were already allocated to the *nyumba* of his own wives and sons, and that the latter would not agree to Nyawombo using any of them. Mukwawa was poor and could only give one heifer calf (*ndama*), but not immediately as it was still suckling (*nyonci*). Cidong'a was the chief negotiator for the suitor's party (*wanyakutola*), and during the heated and verbally hostile discussion characteristic of such negotiations, he was ridiculed for offering such a small bridewealth. He said to the girl's kin (*wanyakutolwa*), "Ah, my friends, this wedding defeats me. Look here, the lad who wants to marry is here, so you can see for yourselves that it is as if you had a boy who went and betrothed a girl without telling you. Would you like that? Well, he [Nyawombo] just came and told me, 'Father, I have betrothed a girl, let us go and arrange bridewealth.' I said, 'You have betrothed a girl, have you any cattle?' He said,

" 'Yes, there are some.'

" 'How many?'

"He said, 'Fifteen.'

" 'Oh, very well, I shall come. Indeed they are enough.'

"Now I came yesterday to his homestead, and his sister asks me, 'Look, where are the cattle?' I counted and there were only six. So what can I do? I am simply saying what he has."

The girl's kin said that, if the suitors could start with a basic ten, then there was something to argue about for the rest over the ten (*musapu*). The negotiations broke down and the marriage did not take place.

If, however, the suitor has ensured that he has sufficient preliminary support from his agnatic and matrilateral kin in his choice of partner and assistance in the bridewealth, the discussion over the number and types of animals involved in the bridewealth (*cigumo*) continues.[16] This always takes place at the

[16] In the case of an older man who is already married, most or all of the bridewealth is provided by himself alone, or he and his full-brothers. But he should never involve himself personally in the wrangle over the bridewealth (although a suitor is usually present at the discussion). He

girl's homestead, for reasons which will become clear. I noted that agnatic and matrilateral kin of both the suitor and his betrothed should be represented, and the elders also include a sprinkling of close friends and age-mates who act as witnesses. The suitor is usually present in his own group, but must not say anything. The girl should be with her mother or other close female relative with whom she is living in the *nyumba* concerned. The girl's mother is usually consulted (*kubita kwilungu*, see below) at some point during the discussions but can usually listen to all that is being said.[17]

The two parties face each other across the cattle byre at the girl's homestead, and this becomes the verbal battleground. The girl's father and his kin (*wanyakutolwa*) ensconce themselves firmly in a group in front of the doorway (*mulango*) of the *nyumba* to which the girl belongs. The suitor's party (*wanya-kutola*) sit the other side of the byre, towards the gate. As each elder speaks, he rises and walks some distance to the center of the byre and addresses the opposing group in a loud and formal voice. The form of the argument is stylized, and each phase of the negotiations and the particular prestations involved are referred to in allusive terms and phrases. Some of the personal innuendoes often border on the abusive. At intervals the married women of the homestead may run across the byre towards the suitor's party, ululating (*kutowa lujilijili* or *lucenze*) and telling

---

thus still needs the presence and support of elders related to him both agnatically and matrilaterally.

[17] Girls are not forced to marry a suitor they strongly object to. I have recorded cases where marriage negotiations at an advanced stage (after bridewealth has been transferred) have broken down because the suitor is unacceptable to the girl. This is in spite of the fact that Gogo recognize culturally the unwillingness of a girl's father and kin to see livestock, however few they may each get, slipping through their fingers. When a case of the girl's adamant refusal is brought to the elders' court, they will dissolve the marriage. But they will gently counsel the girl to be more amenable to her elders' wishes, while shaking their heads in sympathy with her father: "Yes, we know, wealth is indeed a difficult thing (*sawo nghamu muno*)! But what can we do?"

them rudely to go home: *Muwuye, mwamuleka!* ("Go home, you have left her!"). Although there may be no personal antagonism felt between the members of the two parties (and there should not be; indeed they are usually neighbors and often kin or affines), a formal hostility at this difficult stage of the bridewealth discussions is expressed and contained within the rules of procedure and symbolized in the spatial ordering and distance between the negotiating parties. If the negotiations break down at this stage (as they often do), the suitor's party should leave at once and no bitterness should subsequently affect relations between the members of the two parties.

Every beast in the preliminary prestations (*vidodo-vidodo*, lit., "the little things") and the main bridewealth (*litoto*, "the conical grain-basket"; or *mahikwi*, "the marrows") is disputed, and a promise extracted from the suitor's guardian or other kin. This includes much discussion in whispers (*kwiheha*) within each group as each point is conceded. When the last few beasts in the main prestations are at issue, the discussion is usually forced into an impasse: the suitors refuse to add any more and the girl's kin are still holding out. The former should then say, *"Ale, mubite kwilungu, ase cina umusunho,"* ("Go to the girl's mother and ask her; we are in a hurry"). Although the "kinsmen of the mother's side" (*wokucekulu*) are represented in the negotiating group, often by the girl's mother's full brother himself who will claim a considerable portion of the bridewealth, the girl's mother alone is considered the final arbiter at this stage, representing the matricentral segment of her own house (*nyumba*). Two or three individuals of the girl's group go into the inner room of the *nyumba* to consult her. This usually provides the *wanyakutolwa* with an opportunity to compromise gracefully over the last few animals in the bridewealth. But the role of the girl's mother at this point is conceptually important to Gogo and symbolizes her ritual and economic concern in the marriage of her daughter. I therefore analyze it a little further.

The consultation with the mother is called *kubita kwilungu;*

lit., "to go to the *ilungu*." The stem *ilungu* is apparently the same as that which appears in the word *milungu*, "spirits of the dead" or "ancestral spirits." The stem is used in the form *ilungu;* pl., *malungu*, "spirits of the dead" or "ancestral spirits." The stem is used in the form *ilungu* (pl., *malungu;* noun classes 5/6: Meinhoff),[18] when it implies spirits which are angry or malicious, interfering with the living. Thus, the mother here also stands for the relationship of ritual interdependence between a mother's brother and his sister's children. Although the latter may himself be present, he is not a part of her *nyumba* in this context, which exists as such only by virtue of its association with the husband/father in the patricentral domestic family of which it is a part. The livestock that remains after the distribution of the bridewealth will go to her *nyumba*, and her sons (if any) will use them for their marriages or inherit them. Hence the economic unity and partial autonomy of the *nyumba*, in the field of property relations concerned with livestock, is situationally combined with its ritual distinctiveness; it has a different set of "mother's brothers" from other like units in the patricentral domestic group. So although women cannot normally *own* livestock (there are exceptions), they play a crucial role in its distribution in relation to their *nyumba*, in both the economic and ritual spheres. Gogo cultural recognition of this is illustrated by the following text:

The father of a girl does not [in the situation of marriage negotiations] have more "power" (*vilungo;* lit., "strength") than the mother. So when you "go to the *ilungu*," you do so because while you were arranging bridewealth she did not hear, so you go to the *nyumba* to tell her. That is called *"ilungu."* It is called that because she herself cannot come to this part of the wedding negotiations (*lusona*) . . . so she sits in the *nyumba,* listening and waiting and knowing

---

[18] Noun classes are given according to Meinhoff's (1899, English edition with Van Warmelo, 1932) classification of Bantu noun classes on morphological criteria. Within localized culture areas Bantu noun classes also have sets of distinctive semantic associations.

that when they have finished arguing they will come and tell her how many animals have been offered, and she will agree or not. If she agrees, the wedding will proceed to its conclusion (*lusona lwomalika*). If she refuses, it collapses (*lusona hodu lwofwa*) . . . The reason for this, some people say, is because the mother of a person is much "harder" [*mukamu*, i.e. difficult to negotiate with] than the father [over livestock concerning her *nyumba*]; so they call her *"ilungu."*

When the size and composition of the total bridewealth has been fixed (or nearly fixed)[19] and the elders are tired of wrangling, the opposing hostility of the negotiating groups is replaced by one of familiarity and friendly joking. This is physically expressed by the two groups coming to sit together at this phase of the discussions, called *kuhanza* (lit., "to mix in"), either inside the byre or outside the homestead under a shade tree (*wakubita kuhanza kunze*). Sitting in groups of threes and fours, the elders go over the discussions, confirming each stage. Many are agemates (*wali izika*) and kin, and joke accordingly. Those closely related to the suitor and his betrothed may now address each other as *"muvwele muyangu"* or *"civwele,"* the reciprocal terms used between "parents" whose "children" are married, and the atmosphere is one of easy though formalized familiarity which should exist between affines. A time, some two or three days hence (depending upon the distance between the respective homesteads), is arranged for the actual selection and transfer of the livestock.

Most marriages in Ugogo take place within a day's easy walking distance, many within the same neighborhood or between adjacent neighborhoods. Thus, a party of elders and young men can easily be assembled again by the bride's father or guardian to go and collect the bridewealth cattle; for it is the girl's kin

---

[19] It is not necessary here to describe in detail all the prestations involved and the reasons for each. The jurally and economically more significant ones will be noted in their contexts, and the average number of livestock involved is analyzed with examples in the section on the distribution of bridewealth, below.

who go to the suitor's homestead (where he should have assembled most of the livestock) to select the cattle and drive
them home.[20]

The transfer of the bridewealth livestock (or nearly all of it)
is the central act in the transfer of jural rights and obligations
between the potential spouses and the groups of kin concerned.
But it is by no means the definitive act in establishing a marriage,
for the girl is at this stage still living with her father or other
agnatic kin, and the contract is still provisional. A number of
procedures and a considerable period remain before a complete
and stable conjugal relationship is established. Primarily, upon
the transfer of bridewealth, the husband receives exclusive rights
in genetricem. In the event of his death, his close agnatic kin,
mainly his full and half brothers, can take these rights, but the
wife may be inherited by other agnatic kin if she is willing. As
a mother of adult or adolescent sons, she can refuse to be inherited at all, and no bridewealth is returnable. At this early
stage (i.e. after bridewealth has been given but the marriage
is not complete), certain rights *in uxorem* are also transferred
to the husband (such as rights over the disposal of her sexuality),
but others (for example, her domestic services) only arise later.

When the livestock are driven away by the girl's kin, a day

[20] In Cinyambwa (southwestern Ugogo) the girl's kin do not go to
drive home the bridewealth cattle but must await the suitor's kin to select
and drive them over, on the basis of the verbal agreement. An illustration
from central Ugogo is provided by one of the groups I went with to drive
back (*kuhwaga*) the bridewealth livestock. It consisted of: the girl's own
father (*sogwe*); his full brother's son (*mwana'gwe*)—his own son was
off herding that day; his classificatory son (son of his agnatic parallel
cousin), all of whom lived in the same neighborhood as the girl's
father himself; also the *suitor's* maternal parallel cousin (*wali cana
canyina*) who also happened to live in the girl's neighborhood. The last
member of the party was the girl's "brother-in-law" who was married to
her sister (i.e. her father's son-in-law) and lived in a neighborhood some
six miles away. We walked seven miles to the suitor's father's homestead, leaving in mid-morning, selected the herd with a great deal of additional argument, and drove the animals the seven miles back to our
neighborhood by late evening.

is arranged for the next major act, which is the ritual washing (*kuhovuga*). This is set for some days hence, or even a week or two, to give both parties time to brew beer and collect the numerous other objects of mutual exchange which must be transferred before and after the *kuhovuga* ceremony. On the day decided, the youth goes with male and female kin, elders, and age-mates, to the girl's homestead. The youth and an age-mate stay outside, a little distance from the homestead, while the others go in. The women of the party, after various token payments have been made, go into the room where the girl "is hiding" (*kono yehundice*), singing formalized songs. The girl's female kin go out and carry the youth and his friend in, singing of his qualities.[21] The *kuhovuga* ceremony is primarily concerned with the fertility of the marriage, both in a physical and ritual sense. The youth is taken into the inner room (*kugati*) of the girl's mother and sat on a stool next to the girl. The girl's female kin (including affines) are present. She takes off her cloth and sits naked. The man does the same and they are sprinkled with water by one of the elder women (*mudala*). The man should have an erection (referred to as "the homestead has arisen," *kaya yema*). If he does, the elder women begin to ululate and say, "Our child is married by a man" (*mwanetu yatolwa newacilume*). There is no cause for breaking off the marriage should he not, but there is no ululating.[22] The ritual washing

---

[21] These formalized activities concerning the groom are omitted in the case of an older man's second or subsequent marriages.

[22] Impotence which prevents the husband from consummating the marriage is ground for dissolving the marriage, although a decision is not hurried as it is recognized that it may be a temporary condition, especially if he has other wives and children to prove his virility. But it is interesting to note that, in the case of a young man's first marriage, there is this "physical" test of his virility in this patrilineal society. Concern by the bride's kin in their daughter's (or sister's) husband's virility is more common in matrilineal societies where they maintain an interest in her procreative potential. In patrilineal societies in which rights in women are transferred in marriage to the corporate lineage to which the husband belongs, and into which she is fully incorporated both jurally and

should be carried out by those "who have in-law-ship" (*wulamu*) with the girl or the youth; for example, her "mother's brother's wife" (*mama'ye*) (cf. Rigby, 1968a). One condition is that the women who perform this task should be those whose first-born children (*wana walongozi*) are still alive. The bride and groom then exchange clothes and dress again.

The couple are taken to the midden heap (*cugulu*) outside the homestead to the west, and the elders in turn narrate the clan histories of the four "sides" (*zimbavu zose ine;* lit., "four ribs") concerned in the marriage: the "fathers" (*wasogwe*) of bride and groom, and the clans of their mothers (*wokucekulu*), so that "wherever they are, they may know this." There follow various mutual feasts; but the bride and groom must be given compensating gifts (*zakulila* or *"ndigwa";* lit., "food") before they will eat in each other's homesteads.

At this stage there is usually no *nyumba* yet for the new bride at her husband's homestead. She is taken with ceremonial re-luctance, being given token gifts at each stage, to live in the *nyumba* of the husband's mother if she is alive, or to that of his senior wife. The marriage is consummated, and she continues living and helping in this *nyumba* until her first pregnancy.[23] The bride then returns to her father's or "brother's" homestead to give birth to her first child. As will have by now become clear, a woman never severs her ritual ties with her own kin, partic-ularly her full brothers, and this is one of the factors in the

---

ritually, this interest in the husband's virility is seldom exhibited. This is yet a further indication of the non-corporate nature of patrilineal lineage groups at marriage in Gogo kinship structure, as well as of the continued interest of the bride's kin in her and her children's welfare, both social and ritual. I return to this point again. It should be noted that both female barrenness and male sterility are recognized as possible causes in an unproductive marriage.

[23] There is a great deal of variation in the details of marriage pro-cedures throughout Ugogo, particularly between east and central Ugogo on the one hand, and southwestern Ugogo (Cinyambwa and related areas) on the other. Nevertheless, the crucial points are generally much the same.

desirability of the co-residence of affines for as long as possible (marriage being virilocal; see below). There are no corporate ritual functions of lineal groups beyond that of the sons of one man; a wife is thus not "absorbed" ritually into her husband's patrilineal group as she is among many patrilineal peoples with a similar type of social organization, for example the Jie of Uganda.[24] This even includes to some extent her children; the ritual dependence of a woman's children upon her brothers has already been indicated. This is so even when the former are adults, and it is in the "mother's brothers'" interests to maintain a close relationship with at least one of his "sister's children," who will provide the ritual sheep which preserves the continuity of inheritance within his own family (see below, Chapter VII).

When a girl gives birth to her first child at her "father's" homestead, he must kill a goat for her to provide her with medicinal "soup" (*muhuzi*) which restores her energy (*kumudesa*). It is up to her husband to go to a diviner and obtain the small medicine object (*mhiji*, usually a bead or piece of medicinal plant) that is tied on to the baby to ensure the correct closure of the fontanelle suture (*yakwimila cidosi cilece kunga*). But the wife is still dependent upon "her own" spirits of the dead (*milungu*) and always will be to some extent; so too they may influence her husband. Traditionally, the skin of the goat given at birth was cured and used by the mother as a carrying skin (*sambo*) when she carried her child on her back (*kupapila mwana*). Now a father should provide his daughter with a cloth for the same function. The husband should provide the

---

[24] See Gulliver (1955), p. 228, and (1953), p. 151. The Jie ceremony *lokidor* is held when a wife ". . . and her children are ritually incorporated into the man's clan, and give up their former affiliation to her father's clan, entirely and permanently." Fallers (1957) argues that, for a society (the Soga) with corporate patrilineal descent groups, non-incorporation of a wife into her husband's patrilineal group is a factor causing a high divorce rate. The divorce rate is very low in Ugogo, and its reasons and correlates will be discussed below.

ndesa goat and the carrying cloth for all of his wife's subsequent children.

By the time she has borne her first child, the husband should have constructed for her a full *nyumba* of two rooms, inner and outer. He may be fined if taken to court for having no intention of doing so, and, considered neglect, it is also ground for divorce. Even if the wife has not borne a child, he should provide a *nyumba* within the first year of marriage.[25] If the marriage is to continue as a properly established one, she must have her own *nyumba* for her own granaries, utensils, and the livestock allocated to her *nyumba;* she must have her own domain. This is usually at the husband's homestead, or that of the agnatic kin with whom he is living. Marriage is both normatively and statistically virilocal when it has reached the stage of a stable conjugal union.

If it is the husband's first marriage, the new wife will live for a time in his mother's *nyumba* before she is given her own. In a polygynous family if the husband's mother is dead, the new wife will live in the *nyumba* of his first (senior) wife, who is now called the female "owner of the homestead" (*munyakaya*) in place of his mother. It is from one of these houses that livestock will be allocated to her *nyumba*. Even if a husband marries a third, fourth or more wives, they are all attached to the senior wife's *nyumba* until they have their own and, ideally, should have livestock allocated to them from that *nyumba*. There is no pairing of wives and linking of *nyumba* into dichotomous categories, as there is among several other patrilineal peoples,[26] and this is consistent with the non-ranking of wives, apart from the first wife.

[25] Barrenness is not *a priori* a ground for divorce, although most divorces take place in the first two or three years of a marriage (see below), and the lack of children may contribute to the dissolution of a marriage.

[26] For example, among the Arusha (see Gulliver, 1961, *passim*); the Baraguyu (Beidelman, 1960, pp. 270–271); and among several southern Bantu peoples.

The relation of a new wife to the *nyumba* to which she is attached before she has her own is symbolically expressed in the ritual anointing with the *mukulo* bark and oil. The senior married woman of the homestead takes the sweet-smelling pow-dered bark and oil (*mukulo*) and smears it ("*kukula*") on husband and wife, both for the ritual good of the union and because "it smells nice (*wukunungha mhanhi*)." The *mukulo* for the wife of a younger man who is still dependent, say, upon his elder brother, may come from the *nyumba* of this full brother's senior wife. This again expresses the community of interest of the brothers in the livestock given for her bridewealth, as well as the *nyumba* from which livestock is allocated to hers.

THE COMPOSITION AND DISTRIBUTION
OF BRIDEWEALTH (*CIGUMO*)

Gogo bridewealth transactions usually involve a comparatively large number of livestock and constitute the largest single trans-action in the Gogo exchange system.[27] The general wealth in livestock of a group does not determine, except in a limiting sense, the size of bridewealth usually given; there is no clear correlation between the number of head in the average herd in a particular society and the number of stock in a bridewealth

[27] It has been alleged that the use of the term "bridewealth" instead of "bride-price," established as a result of a protracted controversy over terminology in the early thirties, obscures the "economic implications" of bridewealth transactions: e.g. Gray (1960), p. 53 *et passim*. This may be true of some analyses of bridewealth systems, but Gray's case for the re-introduction of the terms "wife purchase" and "sale" seems totally unjustified and appears to arise out of the peculiar Sonjo custom of "selling" wives and children to their hostile and more powerful Masai neighbors (1960, p. 42). There is no doubt that the bridewealth trans-actions of the Gogo are "economic" or "exchange" transactions; but the terms "purchase" and "sale" are singularly inappropriate for *any* "traditional" transactions involving livestock or women or both. Certainly, the Gogo terms for "buying" and "selling" objects, including livestock, in the modern markets (*kugula* and *kuguza*) could never be employed for the exchange of livestock for women (*kwiguma*). Gray fails to report the Sonjo terms for the various types of exchange they practice.

herd. Thus, among the Jie of Uganda, whose wealth in livestock averages from about three to four head of large stock and four head of small stock per person, the bridewealth averages about fifty cattle and one hundred twenty-nine small stock.[28] Among the Gogo, who are about half as poor in livestock, the average bridewealth is about fifteen head of cattle and about ten small stock (see Table 11). But among the Masai (Kisongo) where the ratio of cattle to humans is about fourteen to one, seldom more than five head of cattle are given for bridewealth, the same amount normatively given by the Arusha, where the ratio of livestock to humans is much smaller, being rather less than one to one.[29] Numerous examples could be cited.

There may be, however, a correlation between the number of stock given in bridewealth and the type and implications of the transaction in a particular society, expressed in its composition and distribution. It is possible that where the relationships within a network of kinship are activated by mutual obligations and rights during bridewealth transactions, and their effective range may even be determined by this (as among the Jie, Nuer, and the Gogo),[30] the bridewealth must naturally be made up of a number of parts (usually head of livestock) so that claims and obligations can be met. Gogo often say, after an unsuccessful trip to claim a beast given in the bridewealth for a kinswoman, "there were too few, so I did not get it." Such a situation, where bridewealth must consequently be fairly large, may be compared with the other where bridewealth obligations and claims do not play this role in the kinship network, and kin relations in the context of marriage and bridewealth are defined more in terms of links between two unambiguously circumscribed corporate descent groups.

[28] Gulliver (1955), pp. 38, 228–242.

[29] Gulliver (1963), pp. 14, 242.

[30] Among the Nuer, the *ideal* bridewealth consists of 40 head of cattle. The importance of bridewealth transactions in defining fields of kinship is demonstrated by Evans-Pritchard (1951), pp. 49, 74–99 *et passim.*

Be this as it may, I have noted that the bridewealth for a young man's first marriage is composed of contributions from many sources and is distributed among the kin of the girl. The transfer is not a profit-making transaction for those concerned; even the father of the girl may be left with only a couple of head by the time the distribution is over. In fact, Gogo say that they prefer sons to daughters, for in spite of the problems of providing them with a part of their bridewealth and the potential conflict between father and adult sons over property, with understanding and tolerance sons remain with their fathers and increase their influence and prestige, at least in theory. Girls marry out and "are lost," although they still make claims for protection, both economic and ritual. A Gogo informant told me:

When you have sons, they are yours. If you have daughters, they do not remain yours for long; they are like the seeds [fruits] of the *mubevu* tree [*Bussea massaiensis*]. Because when the *mubevu* bears offspring, they become mature and explode, and the seeds jump a great distance: one goes there and the other in another direction. They do not fall at the foot of the tree (*hesina lyamubevu*). When you search for the *mbevu* seeds, look far away from the trunk and you will see them. So with daughters: they are married, one in one place, another in another, away from each other.[31] So we say they are like *mbevu* seeds.

The main part of Gogo bridewealth is still normally given entirely in livestock, except among the very small minority of Christians where the bulk may be given in money. These days, some of the preliminary prestations (*vidodo-vidodo*) may be given in cash, but it is extremely difficult, if not impossible, to marry a young girl unless one has sufficient livestock for the major prestations. The bridewealth may be given entirely in cattle, or in a combination of cattle and small stock, which is the most usual. Small stock may be substituted for prestations

[31] This refers to the domestic groups and homesteads to which they belong as wives, and not necessarily the spatial distance involved, which is desirably limited.

that should be given in cattle (*kubumunda* or *kujela*, "to make up for" or "to make equivalent to") and vice versa; but the equivalence of values between the cattle and livestock in these transactions bears no relation to the cash market value of each at the numerous livestock markets (*minadi*) where Gogo sell their animals.[32] This is consistent with the fact that it is virtually impossible to substitute money for livestock in bridewealth transactions, although Gogo know full well the cash value of their livestock at any particular time.

The size of bridewealth given varies not only with the individual qualities, age, and attractiveness of the girl concerned, but also the subsistence conditions extant at the time of its transfer. When discussing the size of bridewealth given in past marriages, a small total is often explained by the fact that the marriage took place in a famine year. There is also considerable variation between localities. But other factors also count, including the economic capabilities of the suitor and his kin, whether the couple had forced the issue by abduction or elopement, whether the girl is already pregnant (*waamula kutumula*), and so on. Whether the couple are related or not does not usually affect the number of livestock given.

Again, bridewealth payments in Ugogo are seldom entirely completed. Out of a total of, say, eighteen head of cattle, two may be left "to be given later" (called *muganda;* pl., *miganda*). Gogo say that to leave *muganda* is very bad and causes ill-feeling, but most exchanges do; and although the debt is inherited, it is seldom settled. The "loose ends" of bridewealth transactions form a complex of "perpetual debts" that are never caught up with. A very high proportion of litigation involves the giving or return of bridewealth, but an even larger number of nearly-fulfilled contracts never come to either the informal elders' courts or the *baraza* (local government court).

[32] It is not usually possible to give a bridewealth herd entirely in small stock (sheep and goats); a balance must be struck with a bias toward the cattle.

The normal bridewealth for a young girl should be over twenty head of cattle and sixteen to twenty small stock, but can be as much as thirty head of cattle. It is said to have been higher in the past.[33] The average number of livestock given for 120 recent marriages, for which I was able to obtain information, is set out in Table 11. The averages may be seen to be considerably lower than the ideal. In view of the importance of this transaction for Gogo social structure and economic system, some explanation is required.

Table 11. Average size of bridewealth herds (*cigumo*), by agreed number, those said to have been given by wife-receivers, and those claimed to have been obtained by wife-givers

Transaction	Average no. of head	
	cattle	sheep and goats
A. Livestock claimed to have been actually transferred by 90 wife-takers	15.9	10.8
B. Livestock claimed by 30 wife-givers to have been actually transferred to them	12.8	10.8
C. Total transactions (120)	15.1	10.8

The figures in all these categories include those for marriages in which bridewealth was small for special reasons. For example, in one case only four head of cattle and five small stock were given because the woman "was old" (*kusoke yakombipa*) and before her marriage had had several children, who had been

[33] This means the "Gogo past," in the sense that the elders conceive it in its heyday, before the penetration of colonial rule, and does not necessarily include the past of some clan histories which state that high bridewealth paid in cattle only arose when they came into Ugogo and became "Gogo" (see Chapter III). Some clans, which say their founders came from Uhehe and Ukaguru, have clan histories which state that only chickens or hoes were given as bridewealth before they became "Gogo."

claimed by her various lovers (a possible claim only because she was still unmarried). In another, twelve head of cattle and fourteen small stock were given for a woman who was already married. The new husband gave the bridewealth to her previous spouse. A young couple in another marriage forced the girl's kin to capitulate through her pregnancy, because the young man could obtain too few head for the correct *cigumo*. The total transferred was eight head of cattle and ten small stock.

The discrepancy in the average number of cattle claimed to have been transferred by the wife-takers (A) and the wife givers (B) (15.9 to 12.8 head) does not point to unreliability in the information obtained on the transactions. The average difference of two head is explained by the fact that one or two head in the *cigumo* herd are slaughtered by the wife-givers for the communal feasts during the ceremonies. These animals are called *isaye* or "*tumbako*" and are included as *cigumo* given by the wife-takers, but naturally excluded by the receivers of the bridewealth.

An example of the composition of *cigumo* is given by the case of Mwidowe. When he arranged his first marriage, Mwidowe was a young man of about twenty-five; his father was dead but his mother still alive. They were living as dependents in the homestead of his elder half brother. He gave a total of twenty-four head of cattle and twenty-one small stock, all of which were handed over (Figure 14). The bridewealth, as usual, consisted of *zokulume* ("those of the male side") and *zokucekulu* ("those of the female side"). Mwidowe's mother's full brother, who contributed the ritual *itambi* goat and four head of cattle, lived some nine miles away and had previously taken the share allotted to matrilateral kin (*zokucekulu*) for the marriage of Mwidowe's full sister. The mother's brother cannot keep all of the cattle he claims, but he must share them between his agnates if they claim them, particularly among his full brothers. Similarly, he will be assisted by his agnates in providing his share for the marriages of his sister's sons.

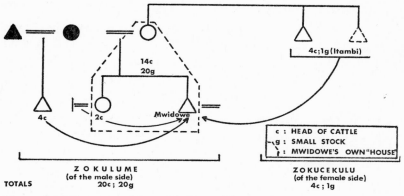

Figure 14. The composition of bridewealth, a case

The distribution of the bridewealth is along much the same lines. Both composition and distribution usually involve a much wider range of kin than those involved in Mwidowe's marriage. The bride's father's full and half brothers also "claim" (*kukwega*) one head each, even after the death of their own mother (i.e. the dissolution of their own natal *nyumba*). Thus, at the marriage of Pelanze, the daughter of Mugonela, the distribution of bridewealth was as in Figure 15.

Married full brothers of the bride, the sons of one woman, whose father is dead but whose natal *nyumba* is still extant be-

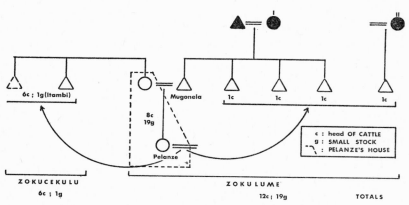

Figure 15. The distribution of bridewealth, a case

cause their mother is alive, can claim for their own wives' *nyumba* one beast each from the *cigumo* given for their sisters. The rest will go to the herd of their mother's *nyumba* held jointly by them all. Half brothers may also claim one head each at the marriages of their half sisters, and will succeed if there are sufficient available. In fact, a great variety of kin may attempt to claim (*kukwega;* lit., "to drag away") single animals given in a bridewealth. They will succeed only if they have been in close contact with the parties concerned and have fulfilled their obligations as kinsmen in other contexts. This usually implies fairly close residence, or co-residence in one neighborhood. Thus, the effective range of kinship relationships tends to be localized at any one point in time, and defined in terms of mutual claims and obligations during bridewealth transactions. This is particularly so in defining the effective, intimate yet delicate, relationships with matrilateral kin, primarily "mother's brothers," and Gogo are most concerned over livestock obligations in this context.

Ideally, "mother's brothers" should contribute one-quarter to one-third of the *cigumo* cattle for a sister's son's first marriage and receive a similar proportion from the marriages of their sisters' daughters. They are also the givers and recipients of the ritual *itambi* goat in the marriages of their sisters' children (see Chapter VII). In theory, these obligations apply to all "mother's brothers" and "sister's children," particularly in the case of mother's full brothers (*wanyumba imonga*). In practice, only those mother's brothers who have fulfilled their duties during the upbringing of their sister's children, giving animals during their initiation ceremonies and when they are ill, and so on, have effective obligations and rights. As I have noted, this implies residence close enough to bring them into frequent and easy contact. Residential proximity to matrilateral kin of course it-self implies, in a virilocal marriage context, the desirability of the prior residential proximity of affines. That this is in fact the pattern that exists in Ugogo, in spite of the relatively high residential mobility of homestead groups, will be demonstrated in the following section. But first I record a case that illustrates how the mutual interdependence of a man and his closest affines, his wife's full brothers (*walamu'ze*), who are also his childrens' closest matrilateral kin in the senior generation (mother's full brothers, *wakuku zawo*), is expressed in terms of obligations in bridewealth transactions and affected by distance (see Figure 16):

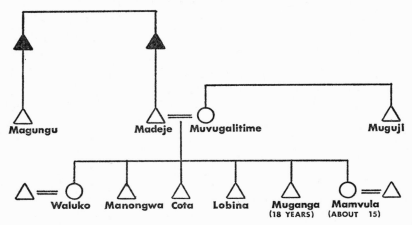

Figure 16. The case of Madeje and Muguji

Muguji lives in Mutumba neighborhood, some twenty-four miles away from that of his full sister's husband Madeje. Madeje was born in and used to live in Mutumba neighborhood himself, near his brother-in-law, but twenty-three years ago came with his wife and children to the neighborhood in which he lives at present. His youngest children were thus born and most of them brought up in this neighborhood, including his daughter Mamvula who is about fifteen years old. When Mamvula was married, Muguji heard and came to Madeje's homestead to claim six head of cattle from the *cigumo* as "those of the mother's side" (*zokucekulu*). Muguji had already received five head of cattle and the *itambi* ritual goat for the marriage of Waluko, Madeje's eldest daughter, who had been married while they were still at Mutumba. Now Madeje absolutely refused to let

Muguji have any animals from the *cigumo* of twenty-two head given for Mamvula. Muguji decided to make a case (*calo*) of it and brought it to the informal court of neighborhood elders.

Madeje said, "When my sons Cota, Lobina, and Muganga [now about twenty-six, twenty-four and eighteen years old] were circumcised and my daughter Mamvula initiated, Muguji did not come with the various things he should have brought [for example, *ngholo yemafuta*, 'the sheep of the fat' to provide soup for the children so that they would recover quickly; *myenda yakuhovujila mwana*, 'the cloths for wearing after the ritual washing of the children at the end of the circumcision ceremonies,' and so on]. Now Muguji comes to ask for *cigumo?* I cannot look upon him as related to me or my children; it is as if he were a stranger, a non-relative (*yawa nha sindugu yetu, mwiwisa du hodu*)."

The elders then told Madeje that everyone knew that he and Muguji were brothers-in-law, and so how could he say that? He could complain in any other way, but not that. Madeje retorted that as Muguji did not help his [Madeje's] children at all, what sort of "mother's brother" was he to them? In court, Muguji agreed that he had not done so.

Muguji was told to bring one head of cattle to compensate for the payments he should have made at the initiation ceremonies of his sister's children. He was also instructed to bring the "things from the mother's side (*vinhu vyokucekulu*)" to give the bride Mamvula, before he could claim a share of the *cigumo*.[34] After

---

[34] When a girl is married and goes to live (after the birth of her first child) with her husband, she should already have been given the following things. By her father and his agnates she should be given "things of the father's side" (*vinhu vyokulume*): a sleeping skin (*nhyingo*), grain-seeds (*mbeyu*) for planting her first crop, a hoe (*isili*) presented to her husband but for her use, some gourds (*mheyu*) and pots (*nyungu*); by her "mother's brother" who comes to collect the *cigumo* share, a conical grain-basket (*nhoto*) and sometimes also a winnowing basket (*luheneko*), stool (*ligoda*), a large cloth for wearing (*mwenda mutote*), and "*citonga*," a small stoppered calabash (nowadays a bottle) of oil for anointing herself. The "mother's brother" may then claim his portion of the *cigumo* herd, plus *itambi*, usually a full-grown female goat which has not yet had a kid (*nhogota*), and "*vumba nemalenga*," (lit., "the sweet scent and the water"), a goat with its first kid still sucking

further lengthy discussion, Muguji was awarded four head of cattle of the *cigumo* as suitable, relative to the size of the bridewealth and the distributions already made by Madeje (who had hardly any stock left since Manongwa, his son, had already used most of it for his own bridewealth). Muguji held out for six head and told the elders that he would take the case on to the local government court (*baraza*). But Muguji did not have the ready cash on him to pay the court fee. He was told by the local magistrate (*hacimu*) to go home and get the fee. During the course of the discussions, Muguji wished to call Magungu, Madeje's FBS, who was witness to the bridewealth transaction, to give evidence. (He had had nothing out of it himself.) Madeje strongly objected to what he felt was Magungu's partiality towards Muguji.

The case was allowed to drift for some time. The local court said that Mamvula was too young by modern regulations to be married anyway, and Madeje was jailed for three months after being instructed to dissolve the marriage and return the bridewealth. This never would have happened without Muguji's action. When he came out of jail, Madeje accused his wife Muvugalitime of selling grain from her *nyumba* in order to give money to her brother Muguji to help him in the case. Madeje could not dissolve the marriage as he did not have enough livestock to return. Muguji went home in high dudgeon, and the relationship between the brothers-in-law, some elders felt, was damaged beyond repair.

It is clear in this case that the elders were throughout attempting to get the two men to perform the obligations and fulfill the duties normal to their relationship.

MARRIAGE, LOCALITY, AND KINSHIP NETWORK

I have repeatedly stressed, from different points of view and in different contexts, a set or "constellation" of factors in Gogo kinship organization. The interrelations between these factors are of fundamental importance for Gogo social structure. Among them are the mobility of homestead groups, over fairly long in-

---

(*ngadada yina mwana*), both of which symbolize the role of the "mother's brother" in the fertility and ritual welfare of his "sister's children."

tervals, dictated by ecological conditions, the structural importance of affinal relationships, the related co-residence of
affines and kin of a variety of categories, and the rights in livestock and the house-property inheritance system, associated
with the definition of effective range in the kinship network in
terms of cattle-exchange obligations.

I have also noted that, although kin marriages are "recommended" between certain categories of kin (which could only
be explained in terms of the maintenance of alliances between
lineal descent groups), the kin marriages which *do* take place
are often simply the result of a network of kin links within
localities. The culturally desirable though not very frequent
marriage with a matrilateral "cross-cousin" may be seen to be
logically the result of a patrilineal descent system and consistent
with its ideology, but not *structurally* important in the Gogo
marriage system. What *is* structurally important is that Gogo tend
to marry within a very limited spatial range, co-operate a great
deal with close affines (even in the rearing of one's own children and their ability to inherit), and manipulate claims and
obligations over livestock to maintain such relations.

Although marriage occurs within a limited spatial range, I
do not mean that there are endogamous local groups. I mean
simply that, as it is the man among the Gogo who usually initiates
negotiations, he tends to marry within a limited spatial radius
from his residence as center-point. There is thus, in social and
physical space, what may be conceived of as a series of overlapping individual "marriage circles," necessarily resulting in a
network of closely-residing affines and the consequences of this
fact for residence in the first descending generation, but always
within the context of the general fluidity of residence pattern.

It has been shown for several non-prescriptive marriage systems that certain factors limit the choice of spouse. Geographical
(spatial) propinquity is a major one of these factors. Thus,
among the Taita, the "high degree of local endogamy" is related to land acquisition and political status; only elders of

established status marry wives who come from distant communities.[35] So too, among the Gishu of Uganda, the spatial distribution of affinal links is of crucial structural importance.[36] In the Gogo case, differential political status is not a factor, but the close residence of close affines is essential for their continued cooperation, in economic and ritual spheres. Since this is a crucial point in the analysis of Gogo kinship structure, it is necessary to demonstrate the relation between locality and marriage.

In certain contexts, Gogo express what appears to be an explicit desire to live *at a distance* from their close affines. They say:

To live at a distance from your "fathers-in-law" (*wakwe'wo*) is good, because there can be painful situations (*kowuli wusungu*) . . . If you live near your *wakwe* and then come into conflict with your wife [when you might abuse or even hit her] and your brother-in-law is there, you might come to blows with him over the pain it caused him when you hit or abused his kin. So usually we like to live away from parents-in-law.

This immediate reaction, and it is very common, is recognized, however, as being founded only upon knowledge of the frequent conflict between husband and wife in the domestic situation, and designed to prevent conflict in the delicate relationship between brothers-in-law, *walamu*, and so protect this relationship from damage. There is, for example, restraint, but not avoidance, be-

[35] Cf. Harris (1962), pp. 58, 78–86.

[36] La Fontaine (1962), pp. 106–113. Also Fortes (1962), p. 6: "Structural propinquity between the parties is conducive to marriage because it facilitates continuity and consistency between the network of status relations in which they and their kin were placed before their marriage and the status arrangements that are the result of the marriage. Local intra-marriage is but a special case of this more general principle. At its simplest, it may make it easier for both spouses and their kin to manage their mutual affinal relationships without detriment to the loyalties and obligations that persist from their pre-marital social and personal relations."

tween a man or woman and their parents-in-law (*wakwe'we*). Certain types and topics of conversation are improper. Relations between brothers-in-law, however, should be intimate and friendly, although there is an element of institutionalized joking and therefore strain.[37] Brothers-in-law (*walamu*) address each other as *mbuyane*, a term derived from the same root as *mbuya*, which I have already noted has the connotation of emotion and potential disruption and is therefore delicate. Gogo have an adage, which one man discussed:

"Brother-in-law has finished the meat while it was still in the fire," (*Mbuyane yamaliye inyama mumoto*). The reasons for this, you would say, is that when your brother-in-law asks you for something,[38] you should never refuse, because he is your brother-in-law. You have affection for him as you have for your wife, his sister. And in another way, you may even call him "my wife" (*mucekulu wangu*), yet he is a man. This is because you are married to his sister and even though he is a man you call him your wife because of this . . . And so if he asks you for anything, if you have it, that is all there is to it; you see that you had better give it to him, because you think, "He is my *mulamu*, I'll have to find another of these things for myself."

But elders also realize that, in fact, one does tend to live near one's affines and that there are very good reasons for this. In the same discussion in which I was assured that, as far as having a row with your wife is concerned, it is better to live at a distance from your affines, my informants nevertheless added:

[37] See Rigby (1968a). In general, unspecified contexts, in-law relations are usually referred to as *wulamu*. The fear that conflict with a wife may cause more damage if she can easily flee to her father or other agnatic kin is common in many societies: e.g. the Soga of Uganda; see Fallers (1957), pp. 113–114.

[38] Note that, although this relationship has elements of joking about it, it does not include the "stealing" or indiscriminate taking of one's joking partner's property which is characteristic of joking relationships proper, such as between cross-cousins or clan joking-partners (*watani*). One must "ask" a brother-in-law. The emphasis is upon "unlimited giving" rather than "privileged taking."

10 An elder admonishing the heir at an inheritance ceremony (*ipinde*)

11 The principal heir (*muhazi*) receives the symbol of inheritance, the "great bow" (*ipinde*). He sits in the cattle byre on the skin of a freshly slaughtered ox while his patrilateral cross-cousin sits on his left and receives the "bow" with him.

But on the other hand, to live near your in-laws is not bad, but
good; because if you are beset by certain duties at your homestead
[e.g. in the initiation of your children, funerals, marriages, etc.],
there always appear certain jobs which must be done by "those on the
woman's side" (*zikwijela milimo zinji zokucekulu*). Now if you are
far away from your in-laws it is difficult to undertake a journey to
inform them quickly that they should come and fulfill their obligations (*waze kwituma mulimo wawo mbela*), and things become de-
layed and mixed up. So it is bad to live away from close affines.

These norms are frequently repeated in many contexts and are
not simply isolated, individual ones. I have already quoted a case
where distance, and therefore limited contact, between affines
was instrumental in the breakdown of the relationship.

But apart from the norms involved, what is the actual pattern
of affinal relationships "on the ground"? I have already indicated
the high incidence of both primary and classificatory affinal relationships in intra-neighborhood kinship network. An analysis
of the residence of spouses at the time of marriage, in a sample
of 192 marriages where the information was available, adds supporting though not conclusive evidence to the pattern already
described. Not conclusive because the figures take no account of
subsequent moves by the homesteads concerned, which would
naturally affect the distances between the residence of affines. But
I have shown in Chapters IV and V that in fact individual homestead and domestic groups move two or three times during their
cycle of existence, with intervals of fifteen or twenty years or so
between moves, and that in any case, in each new locality these
groups are linked to each other by a complex network of ties in
which affinal links predominate over those of other kinds. Thus,
the figures presented on the limited spatial range of marriage in
Tables 12 and 13 offer convincing support in another aspect of
the pattern described.

The total number of marriages was divided into (A) those still
extant or "recent" in that one spouse was still alive and could act
as informant; (B) those where both spouses were dead but their

Table 12. Spatial range of marriage, by residence of spouses at marriage, with reference to neighborhood and ritual area

Category of marriage	Intra-neighborhood	Between neighborhoods within same ritual area	Between ritual areas	Totals
(A) Extant marriages and "recent" marriages in which one spouse is dead	55 (33.8%)	31 (19.0%)	77 (47.2%)	163 (100.0%)
(B) "Historical" marriages remembered by descendents of spouses	4 (13.8%)	7 (24.1%)	18 (62.1%)	29 (100.0%)
(C) All marriages (A) and (B) on which information was obtained	59 (30.7%)	38 (19.8%)	95 (49.5%)	192 (100.0%)

Table 13. Spatial range of marriage, by residence of spouses at marriage

Category of marriage	Approximate distance in miles between residence of spouses at marriage				Totals
	0–4	5–19[39]	20–39	40–over	
(A) Extant marriages and "recent" marriages in which one spouse is dead	100 (61.3%)	50 (30.7%)	12 (7.4%)	1 (0.6%)	163 (100.0%)
(B) "Historical" marriages remembered by descendents of spouses	12 (41.4%)	8 (27.6%)	7 (24.1%)	2 (6.9%)	29 (100.0%)
(C) All marriages (A) and (B) on which information obtained	112 (58.3%)	58 (30.2%)	19 (9.9%)	3 (1.6%)	192 (100.0%)

[39] An original sub-division of this distance category into 5–9, 10–14, 15–19 miles showed no significant differences over the range. I have thus placed them in one category; under 5 miles being crucial for very close neighborhood ranges, and within 20 constituting an important outside limit (see above).

residence at time of marriage (together with other things) was remembered by descendents. Most of the latter were lengthy, successful (and therefore remembered) marriages whose offspring are now adults, and took place at the turn of the century or the early part of this one. I thus attempted to establish any difference in pattern over the past few years of colonial administration before independence. Category (C) records all of these, (A) and (B), together. In all cases the specific neighborhood and ritual area in which the spouses were residing at the time of marriage were established and those marriages for which the information was not available were excluded. The distances recorded in Table 13 were obtained by later plotting on maps, combined with other information for areas in which I had actually been myself.

The distances given in Table 13 are, of course, very approximate. Further, the information on distance in both tables do not coincide at any point in the distance categories used. Thus, not all marriages within five miles need be within the same neighborhood, and vice versa; some may, in fact, be between ritual areas. The figures in Table 13 indicate "spatial network"; those in Table 12, the spatial range of marriage in relation to areas with known "boundaries."

Taken together, however, the tables indicate that most marriages take place between members of homestead groups that are resident within a highly restricted spatial range. About one-third (30.7%) of all marriages in the sample were within one neighborhood, and one-half (50.5%) within the same ritual area (which I have indicated are very small in geographical terms; see Chapter III). But the figures in Table 13 are more significant. Nearly two-thirds (58.3%) of all marriages took place within a radius of five miles, and virtually all (85.5%) within a radius of twenty miles; a range which is critical if the obligations and rights of kin and affines are to be effectively maintained. Although the figures are approximate, I think the general pattern is substantiated.

It appears that marriages are more localized now than in the past. Marriages in category (B) seem to be generally over a wider geographical range than those in (A). This may be due to several factors. The first is that population densities are much higher now than at the beginning of the century; hence, one may expect more marriageable partners to be residing within a more limited spatial range. Also, a number of marriages among the earlier ones in category (B) took place during the first fifteen or twenty years of this century when tremendous upheavals caused by conflict during colonial penetration, World War I, and the famine of 1918–19 caused considerable population movements and may account partly for the wider geographical range of marriage.

Nevertheless, the pattern indicated in the preceding analysis is clear. Highly localized marriage is structurally interrelated with the close residence and strong interdependence of affines as an important factor in the operation of the Gogo kinship system.

MARRIAGE STABILITY AND AFFINAL RELATIONS

If, however, affinal relationships are so important and fundamental, they must be relationships built upon fairly firm and permanent foundations, not fleeting and ephemeral ones. For, unlike other kinship relationships which are determined by descent, affinal relationships, can be made, broken, or weakened by the state of the conjugal bond about which they revolve. They are ephemeral in the sense of having to be re-created in each generation, but they must be firm within it if they are to provide a basis for cooperation. The answer to this problem for Gogo social structure provides one further insight into the constellation of factors already outlined.

The divorce rate in Ugogo is very low.[40] The figures for 136

[40] By "divorce rate" I mean "Ratio C" as defined by Barnes (1949): "The number of marriages ended in divorce expressed as a percentage of all marriages except those that have ended by death" (p. 44). The figures given here for the Gogo may be compared with those provided by Barnes. Cf. also Lewis (1962), p. 34. The significance of the Gogo

marriages on which data is available are given in Table 14. The few marriages that end in divorce (i.e. with the return of all or some of the bridewealth) do so in their early phases (after an

Table 14. Extant and recent marriages, divorces, and separations: Temanghuku (male and female informants)

Status	No.	Av. no. of years of marriage
Extant Marriages	116	—
Divorces	13	3.3 years
Separations	7	31.9 years
Total	136	

Divorce Ratio C = 9.6
Separation Ratio[41] = 5.2

average of 3.3 years) and before they are properly established. Gogo say that once a woman is divorced she is "that type of woman" (*musenca*) who will go on through a series of marriages, never settling down. Even after divorce, however, all the children born during the marriage belong to the ex-husband, the *pater,* and go "where the cattle came from" (*kono zalawa izing'ombe*). The father will continue to treat his ex-wife's kin partly as

data for the general problem of marital stability cannot be considered here (cf. Gluckman, 1950, in Radcliffe-Brown and Forde, 1950; Fallers, 1957, and so on). I am more concerned with the implications of the low divorce rate for Gogo social structure, rather than the question of linearity and marriage stability.

[41] I have called "separation ratio" here a similar percentage of marriages ending in separation except those ended by death. "Separation" means the discontinuation of the co-residence of the spouses concerned. The average duration of marriage was 31.9 years. Almost all of these separations are the result of a wife's moving away from her husband when she is no longer productive and going to live with her adult sons, in the pattern described in Chapters IV and V. The figures are only significant insofar as they illustrate this pattern and have little bearing on the problem of the stability of marriage.

"affines," for "are they not still my children's 'mother's brothers'?" They continue to be concerned in the bridewealth obligations and ritual welfare of the children.

The "affinal principle" is pushed to its logical conclusion in the rare case where a man impregnates an unmarried girl and does not marry her, but claims the child as his by giving (after the fine for "fornication") the *ndima* payment (lit., "herding payment") for the child's upbringing to the girl's father or guardian. When the child is old enough, usually about six or seven years of age, it goes to live with its "father" (in this case both *pater* and *genitor*) and is attached to the house of one of his wives, where it will inherit. The following case illustrates this:

Mujilima, then a young man of about thirty, impregnated the daughter of Magungu before she was married and while she was still living with her father. She bore a daughter and Mujilima paid a fine (*wutumu*) to her father of one head and *ndima* payment of two head of cattle. The mother was later married to someone else and the girl, Mwenzemulo, came to Mujilima's homestead where she is attached to the *nyumba* of one of his wives. She is about seventeen, and when she is married, her mother's brothers will claim their share of the *cigumo*. "Affinal" ties are set up, although there is no marriage. One of Mwenzemulo's mother's brothers had a daughter who is married by Mwaluko. Mujilima refers to Mwaluko as "my son-in-law" (*mukwe mulima wangu*), as if he were Mwaluko's WFZH. The relations between Mujilima and Mwenzemulo's mother's brothers are as cordial as those which should exist between brothers-in-law, *walamu*.

Apart from this exceptional circumstance, bridewealth is necessary to establish the paternity of children and it transfers entirely the genetricial rights in a woman to her husband and his close agnates. The *mbuya* lover of a married woman can never claim any children she may bear, and would be considered a fool to try even if he could prove he were the *genitor*. No quasi-affinal ties are set up over an *mbuya* relationship with a married woman.

The close network of kin and affinal ties as analyzed in this and previous chapters is functionally interrelated with the *mbuya* (permitted adultery) relationships. These semi-institutionalized relationships tend to regulate extramarital sex relations within the local group and the network of kinship, and probably also contribute to the stability of marriage. In a situation where there are no clear-cut rules for exogamy, related to exclusive and unambiguous descent groups, *mbuya* relationships define the field of incestuous relations by explicitly permitting extra-marital relations outside of these categories.

CONCLUSION

Gogo have a saying (*nonga*) which explicitly and admirably sums up the significance of the new relationships that are set up (or the old ones that are modified) by each successful marriage:

"Mukwega isanzu nemapalala" ("You drag the thorn bush along the ground and all the objects which come with it"; i.e. the bits and pieces). If you go somewhere and marry the child of others, then all your wife's relatives become your relatives, because you have married their "child," and so you will love even them (*kokwenda nawo*).

In this chapter I have tried to take one step further the analysis of kinship network in relation to locality and mutual obligations in livestock transactions and their significance. The structural importance of affinal relations has been stressed, and the importance of the continued cooperation that exists within them for the first descending generation. In a situation where agnatic relations beyond the second descending generation become weak and spatially dispersed, affinal relations in each generation and matrilateral links in and between adjacent generations assume primary importance. This is expressed not only in economic cooperation in local communities, but also in strong ritual ties, linked with specific kin roles outside those of agnation beyond the sons of one man.[42] It is to an analysis of the content, operation, and structural relations of the crucial roles involved that I now turn.

[42] Affinal relations are, of course, "critical" in all societies, ". . . because it is through them that the structurally discrete conjugal unit is fitted into the external systems of political, juridical, economic and religious institutions and arrangements": Fortes (1962), p. 6.

VII
Kinship

In this chapter I examine some of the jural norms and "conventional attitudes" concerned with kinship. The roles analyzed are those whose structural importance and articulation with other areas of social structure have been brought out in the preceding analysis. I have argued that, although the Gogo kinship system is characterized by the "ideology" of patrilineal descent (and descent is a "fundamentally jural concept"),[1] descent ". . . does not serve as the constitutive principle of corporate group organization."[2] Kinship roles other than those defined by unilineal descent come into play and may be said to have "structural primacy" in the Gogo kinship system. It is the morphology and structural relations of these roles (whose operations in various contexts has already been discussed at some length) that I propose to analyze here.

Such an analysis necessarily involves an examination of the terminological system designating these roles, although, of course, it cannot simply be reduced to a description of kinship nomencla-

---

[1] Cf. Fortes (1953); Radcliffe-Brown (1935), reprinted in Radcliffe-Brown (1952), pp. 32–48.

[2] In this sense we are restricting the term "corporate" to common rights and control of "the most valued productive property of the society": (Fortes, 1953), where it is also noted that in such societies as the Bemba, Tonga and Lozi of central Africa, descent does not provide the basis for corporate groupings, although ". . . it still takes primacy over all other criteria of association or classification of persons in the regulation of social life." The broader descent groups, described in Chapter III of this book for the Gogo, are "corporate" only in the sense of possessing "an exclusive common name": Fortes (1959), p. 208.

ture. Kinship terms are but one part of one aspect of these relationships. In the analysis of kinship systems (as in the analysis of
all social institutions) several "quite different orders of reality"
must be taken into account.[3] One of these is the "system of terminology" (for kinship terminologies do constitute systems) and
another is a system of prescribed attitudes; both of these are aspects of kinship roles.[4] Between these two systems there exists a
relationship of functional interdependence, but by no means a
one-to-one type of correlation.[5] But the problem arises: which
kinship roles require analysis in order that the important structural relationships may be revealed?

Gogo distinguish terminologically between kinsmen (*ndugu*)
and non-related persons (*wewisa;* sing., *mwiwisa*). But the distinction is relative, for the values of kinship (including affinal
relationships) are pervasive in social relations of all kinds. Non-
related persons who constantly come into contact and cooperation

[3] Lévi-Strauss (1958), pp. 45–47 (trans., 1963, pp. 37–39). Cf. also
Beattie (1959), p. 47.

[4] This does not imply that these are the only, or even the most important "orders of reality" inherent in kinship systems. The "statistical"
facts of kinship are another level (see preceding analysis). I take the
meaning of "statistical" here from Leach (1961), p. 9. Kinship terminology systems are, on one level, systems of ideas, of ideal relationships, based upon (in the Gogo case) such ideas as theories of procreation, spatial and genealogical propinquity, stock owning and exchange,
and so on, as intrinsic to such relationships. As such they may function
to enforce certain basic patterns of behavior. And particularly with classificatory systems of terminology such as the Gogo one, they also have
mnemonic functions. However, kinship terminologies, on another level,
are also "logical systems," susceptible to analysis as such; for example,
componential analysis of their meaning (e.g. Wallace and Atkins, 1960).

[5] See Lévi-Strauss (1958), p. 46. But also cf. Radcliffe-Brown (1961),
in Radcliffe-Brown (1952), p. 62 *et passim*. Kinship terms are obviously
an aspect of the jural definition of kinship roles, which derives from the
external politico-jural domain. This influences (if not determines) the
"conventional attitudes" or "affective bonds" of kinship roles in the
domestic domain, the realm of interpersonal cognatic kin relationships
(e.g. see Fortes' brief discussion of MB/ZS relations in Fortes (1959), p.
208). It is the latter we are primarily concerned with here.

with each other because of common residence, place themselves in some convenient kin or affinal category (more frequently the latter) and anyway probably soon become related in some way or another by the creation of new ties. Of course, such persons would be distinguished as "non-relatives" were it important in any context to do so; even the category classifications of genealogically related kin may be modified by the context.

All kin and affines are classed in certain contexts as *ndugu,* but there are further broad sub-categories into which particular relationships are placed. All cognatic kin of the same generation as ego may be referred to as *wandelwa* (sing., *mundelwa*),[6] a term that covers most relationships of "consanguinity" but excludes specific "relationships of descent" (such as father/son)[7] or filiation. Neither does *wandelwa* include affines (*welizenjere, wakwe,* or *walamu*—see below). Gogo distinguish as follows:

I am *ndelwa* with my maternal parallel cousin (*alayo*), with my paternal parallel cousin (*alaba*), with my cross-cousin (*baguma*), and so on. But I am not *ndelwa* with my father or grandfather, or even my mother's brother or my mother herself; we are not *ndelwa* but we are *ndugu.* Then again, I am *ndugu* with my father-in-law (*mukwe*) or brother-in-law (*mulamu*), even a person who has married close kin of my wife (*mutozi muyangu*). . . . But I am not *ndelwa* with these people.

All kin and affines are *ndugu,* but not all *ndugu* are *ndelwa.* Cognatic kin of a man's generation tend to be classed as *ndelwa.* But this distinction, once made, need not detain us any longer here. I shall be discussing roles that are classed as both *ndelwa* and *ndugu,* and those that are only *ndugu.*

[6] The term *mundelwa* is derived from the verb *kulela,* "to bear a child," in its passive form *kulelwa,* "to be born." Thus it denotes "those who are born of kin" in all lines. In other words, filiation, which is "bilateral" (Fortes, 1953), is emphasized, not unilineal descent.

[7] In the sense used by Lévi-Strauss in distinguishing types of "family" relationships that must exist for kinship structures to exist: (1958), p. 56 (trans. p. 46).

The relationship categories that I shall consider are those designated by the terms for father/son; brother/brother and brother/sister ("siblings"); brothers-in-law; mother's-brother/sister's-son; and cross-cousins. This means then that I shall not be discussing relationships within "the family" as distinct from other kinship relationships; on the contrary, I discuss the role categories in general designated by these terms in the Cigogo system of terminology.[8] But I shall show that, for example, in the system of attitudes, prescribed behavior between full and paternal half siblings is sharply distinguished, as it is between paternal half siblings and agnatic parallel cousins, although the same terms may be used to refer to them all in some contexts. Hence, my remarks apply, as do those of Gogo themselves when they discuss these problems, to the behavior of persons actually involved in these role pairs, as "mother's full brothers" and "full sister's sons," for example; although in the event of genealogically close kin being unavailable, more distant kin in the same categories may take over the full functions of any particular role.

I have already shown that relations in the external politico-jural domain do not depend upon lineage organization in Gogo, for lineages are not corporate groups as they are in many other African societies (for example, the Nuer).[9] Hence, no strong distinction is drawn by Gogo between lineal and non-lineal kin except insofar as I have already outlined in previous chapters. Analysis in terms of kinship network and relation to *locality* elucidates more clearly Gogo social structures. It is in terms of

[8] This set of roles contains within it the kin roles that constitute what Lévi-Strauss has termed the "unit of kinship" (*l'élément de parenté*) in kinship systems; the structure of the "global system" containing these relationships comprises the "basic kinship structure": Lévi-Strauss (1958), pp. 56, 51 (trans. pp. 46, 42). I discuss these separately in the final section of this chapter. See also Lévi-Strauss (1949).

[9] The *political* implications of lineage organization are emphasized: e.g. Evans-Pritchard (1940) and (1951), pp. 177–178. Fortes (1953) states: ". . . the way a lineage system works depends on the kind of legal institutions found in the society; and this, we know, is a function of the political organization."

this type of organization that I now wish to analyze some structural relationships between the crucial kinship roles.

IDEOLOGY AND TERMINOLOGY

The central concept of Gogo kinship ideology is that of patrilineal descent. This is embodied in the concepts of clan, sub-clan names, and avoidances. But the Gogo system of nomenclature is not greatly influenced by this patrilineal bias, and terms for kinship categories are cognatically equally elaborated. Thus, the principle of the "unity of the lineage" [10] does not overlay the differentiation of kinship terms by generation, relative age (order of birth), and sex, particularly in one's own generation and the first ascending and descending generations. At the second ascending and descending (alternate) generations and beyond, the terms merge with those for "grandparents" and "grandchildren," again with equal force in all lines. But the Gogo terminology system has some features that have considerable bearing upon the problem of the "functional interdependence" which, as I have already noted, exists between systems of attitudes and systems of terminology. One of the most important of these factors is the radical difference that exists between the terms of reference and the terms of address for a number of key relationships (all of which are set out in Appendix D). Terms for certain categories may be reciprocal (symmetrical) in address but asymmetrical in reference, as in the case of the mother's-brother/sister's-son relationship. Or the terms used may change in different contexts: for example when cross-cousins (*wahizi*) of opposite sex refer to each other as "brother" and "sister" (*ilumbu*). Further, terms that are symmetrical in both the address and reference systems may denote relationships that are qualitatively distinguished in the system of attitudes, as in the case of matrilateral and patrilateral cross-cousins. Each of these distinctions will be considered when the separate relationships are analyzed, but they do point to

[10] Radcliffe-Brown (1950), pp. 33, 35 *et seq.*

some interesting aspects of the problem of kinship terminology and behavior systems.

It is now generally recognized that Radcliffe-Brown placed too much emphasis on the causal relation between kinship terminology and kinship behavior. Some investigators have taken the opposite position by suggesting that there is little significant relation between the two systems.[11] If this were the case, it would be important to analyze only the system of attitudes, and the system of terminology would become irrelevant. But this is not the case, for the people who act in terms of a kinship system explain their behavior by use of the terminology. There must be, therefore, *some* kind of "relation of interdependence" between the conceptual system embodied in the terminology and the system of prescribed attitudes and behavior.[12] But the fallacy of assuming, for example, that where kinship terms are reciprocal, the relationship must necessarily be symmetrical in terms of behavior is obvious;[13] or else how can we explain relationships that are "symmetrical" in terms of address and "asymmetrical" in terms of reference? When discussing kinship terminology we must therefore carefully distinguish (a) *context:* whether the terms are reference or address, in which case different aspects of the same relationship may be emphasized (for example, when joking); and

[11] See Radcliffe-Brown (1935), p. 531 and (1952), p. 62. But cf. Lévi-Strauss (1958), pp. 46–47; (trans.), p. 38.

[12] This is but one aspect of the wider and more complex problem of the relation between language and culture and the elucidation of a structural pattern for both that might illuminate this relation. Cf. Lévi-Strauss (1958), Chapters III–V; particularly pp. 90–91 (trans. pp. 79–80). For an earlier discussion of kinship terms and kinship behavior see also Firth (1936), Chapter VII; particularly pp. 247, 256–257, 261, 270–271 etc.

[13] Radcliffe-Brown (1950), p. 32, states: "Terminology can also be symmetrical or asymmetrical . . . Where terminology in a relationship is symmetrical it is *frequently* an indication that the relationship is thought of as being approximately symmetrical in respect of behaviour" (my italics). This may be true of the cases he cites, but the danger of arguing from such a premise has already been pointed out and the type of reasoning involved is unacceptable.

for what purpose the explanation is being made; (b) *situation:* the social situation of the speaker who uses the term (age also accounts for changes in the same relationships); and (c) *order:* particularly in address, when reciprocal terms may be used but are distinguished by the order in which actors of differential status may have to use them.[14]

The distinctions between the Gogo systems of reference and address may be explained partly by the fact that different aspects of the same relationship are brought out in the address/reference contexts. This will be discussed below for some particular cases.

Many of the terms of address in the Gogo system are "borrowed" (some inaccurately) from the Baraguyu, who have lived in Ugogo and been in contact with the Gogo for a considerable period.[15] They have a terminology system similar to that of the Masai. But the borrowing in itself cannot explain the differences between the two systems in Cigogo; in some relationships the terms are not borrowed and are nevertheless different. Such is the case with the term of address *mbuyane,* used reciprocally between "grandfather/grandson" (*kuku/mwizukulu*) and "brothers-in-law" (*walamu*). The "borrowed" terms have been completely Gogo-ized and absorbed into the terminology system, and may be considered "Gogo" in the present context.

A significant number of these terms involve Baraguyu cattle terms and denote relationships in which cattle have been, or can be, exchanged.[16] For example, the reciprocal term of address, *lamutani,* between classificatory (in some parts of Ugogo also "actual") "wife's father/daughter's husband" (terms of reference: *mukwe/mukwemulima*) is derived from Baraguyu *olaputani,* "male affine," including brother-in-law.[17] The more com-

[14] Cf. Malinowski (1929).

[15] See Beidelman (1960) and (1962).

[16] A general list of these terms and their equivalents are given in Appendix D.

[17] For information on Baraguyu and Masai terms I am indebted to Dr. T. O. Beidelman and Dr. Alan Jacobs. There is a great deal of variation in the use of these terms in different parts of the Baraguyu area. I was

mon reciprocal term of address between WF/DH in Cigogo is *ndawo* or *wandawo*.[18] This is derived from the Masai *entawuo* (heifer), which is used as a quasi-kinship term in Baraguyu for agnates who have mutual obligations over livestock, particularly between a father and his married son.[19] Similarly, the third alternative Cigogo form *ngishu* or *wangishu* is derived from Baraguyu *inkishu* (milch cows; sing., *enkiteng*).

It is apparent that these "borrowed" livestock terms are most common in affinal relationships where exchange of livestock is the major principle in the creation of the tie.[20] The use of such terms in Cigogo is not, however, limited to affines, although the notion of mutual obligations or interest in livestock is always present. Thus, mother's-brother/sister's-son (*kuku/mwihwa* in reference) address each other as *bulayi,* which is the Gogo version of Baraguyu *olapu* (genitive, *apulai,* "my mother's-brother/sister's-son"). It should be noted that all of these terms of address are reciprocal and used in situations where the terms of reference are asymmetrical.

A final distinction between contexts of reference and address is of structural significance. This is in the *obligatory* use of personal names instead of kinship terms of address in certain re-

---

able to confirm some of them from Baraguyu living in Ugogo (most of whom know Cigogo).

[18] The prefix *wa-* in these terms of address in Cigogo *does not* denote a plural, as the use of this prefix normally does in Cigogo and other Bantu languages. It is probably more closely related to the "honorific plural" prefix, which has been designated class 2a in other Bantu languages. So also with the terms *walaji* and *wangishu* (see Appendix D).

[19] That is, a father who has given his son some cattle to marry with. The term of address used by Baraguyu between WF/DH is *pakiteng* or *pakishu,* "those who have exchanged milch cows."

[20] One further important usage has a bearing upon the relationship between brothers-in-law. This is the use in Cigogo of *latalai* as an alternative to *mbuyane* between brothers-in-law (ref. *walamu*). *Latalai* appears to be derived from Baraguyu/Masai *elatia* (genitive, *latialai?*), "neighbors" (see Tucker and Mpaayei, 1955, p. 261). The implications of this for the close residence of affines in these categories, which I have already discussed at some length, will be obvious.

lationships, and primarily concerns the terminological distinction Gogo make between full siblings, paternal half siblings, and paternal and maternal parallel cousins. All of these "siblings" refer to each other as *muwaha* (elder) and *munakwetu* (younger) if they are of the same sex (see Appendix D). Full and half siblings of the same sex address each other by their personal names only. Paternal parallel cousins, however, address each other as *alaba* and maternal parallel cousins as *alayo*. If one wishes to specify these relationships in reference one can refer to paternal parallel cousins as *cana cawasewo* (lit., "the sons of their fathers"), and maternal parallel cousins as *cana canyina,* "the children of their mothers." The term *alaba* is composed of the elements *ala-* ("the son of") and *-aba* (classificatory father; FB) and means literally "son of my classificatory father." The term *alayo* is similarly constructed from *ala- + -yeyo* ("my mother"), and thus means "son of my mother." [21] These usages are almost universal between actual FBS/FBS and MZS/MZS respectively, but Gogo say men in these categories should not use this terminology, but personal names instead, so that they may be more "like brothers," the "children of one man" (*iwana wamunhu umonga*). This argument is also applied to address usage between "real" cross-cousins of the same sex (MBS/FZS), who normally address each other as *baguma* but who should, Gogo say, use personal names. In the case of primary agnatic parallel cousins, use of the term *alaba* instead of personal names is thought to indicate a lack of cooperation and solidarity between close agnates, a theme to which I return below. [22]

[21] These terms should be used only between men, although female parallel cousins may use them jokingly, and they may be used between parallel cousins of opposite sex, who normally address each other by name. The term *yeyo* for "my mother" is Baraguyu. The Cigogo word is *yaya,* and in reference *nyina yangu.*

[22] In southwestern Ugogo (Cinyambwa), where homestead groups are much less residentially mobile, agnatic parallel cousins tend to be neighbors more so than in other parts of Ugogo (i.e. agnatic groups of greater depth tend to be localized). It is said that in this area, actual

Having noted some of the distinctions and variations in the address and reference systems of terminology, I now turn to an analysis of some of the kinship relationships that I have suggested are crucial for the elucidation of certain levels of Gogo kinship structure. As a point of departure I take certain patrilineal relationships, particularly father/son, which we have already considered in various contexts.

FATHER/SON RELATIONS AND AGNATION

The paternity of children is established primarily by the transfer of most of the bridewealth in marriage. Lovers of married women can never claim their offspring, even from a properly established *mbuya* relationship. The role of *pater* is entirely distinguished from that of *genitor,* who in *this context* may be said to lack any socially defined role whatsoever. It is only the case of an unmarried girl's pregnancy, where she is not married before the birth of her child, that a lover can claim the paternity of a child he has begotten, by paying the fine for "fornication" and the payment "for the upbringing" of the child (*ndima*).[23] In such a case the role of *genitor* merges with that of *pater.*

---

paternal parallel cousins use personal names in address as is considered desirable. I have not been able to verify this. But I have noted that the use of the term *aba* for one's father's half-brother (classificatory father) is quite common in central Ugogo. This usage is frowned upon in Cinyambwa, where he should be called *baba,* the proper address for "father" (see Appendix D).

[23] If a husband who has just given bridewealth for his wife comes to know that she was pregnant before he married her, he must nevertheless accept paternity of the child. The lover has no claim to the child after the mother is married, even if he can show that he is most probably the *genitor.* When the husband consummates the marriage, he is said to have "squeezed" or "pressed against her" (*yamubandiciza*), i.e. against the womb, and so accepted the paternity of the child who must then have full rights in her mother's *nyumba* in the homestead of her husband. In one such case, Sona was pregnant when Saidi betrothed and married her. The marriage was consummated and Saidi later learned that she must have been pregnant already. Everyone "knew" that the child's *genitor* was Masaka, who lived in an adjacent homestead. Saidi tends to maltreat

In the very rare case when the lover of a pregnant unmarried girl can neither be traced, persuaded to marry her, nor to give the *ndima* payment to establish the legal paternity of the child, it will belong to the mother's agnatic kin. The child will be given its mother's clan (usually referred to as "mother's brother's clan," *mbeyu yokuku'ye*), sub-clan name and avoidance, and will be attached to the house (*nyumba*) of one of her brother's wives, where he will have (theoretically) full rights of inheritance. There is no concept of "illegitimacy" in Gogo law where a child may have no clan affiliation or rights of inheritance, nor belong to a "house" (*nyumba*), due to being unable to establish a *pater*. This is illustrated in the following case:

A young girl was made pregnant by an Arab storekeeper from a nearby trading post. He neither paid bridewealth for her, nor an *ndima* payment for the paternity of the child. The Arab left the area and the girl was married by a Gogo man, but long after the birth of the child, a boy. Her husband was thus not obliged to accept the paternity of the child. The boy is now about 15, and very "non-Gogo" in appearance. When strangers ask him what "clan" (i.e. *mbeyu*) he is, he gives a Gogo clan name and says he is Gogo. When this is doubted because of his physical appearance, Gogo elders support his claim. They say that the physical appearance of a person does not establish his clan. The boy is said to belong to his mother's clan, and should have full rights of inheritance in one of his mother's brother's homesteads. This is in spite of the fact that the mother has subsequently been married [after his birth] by another man of a different clan.

In these rare cases, the mother's brother is jurally obliged to assume the role of *pater* of his sister's child.

---

this child Nyanjizi, a girl, who is now about 13. He favors his "own" children whom he has subsequently had by Sona. This is considered very bad behavior on Saidi's part: "She [Nyanjizi] is Saidi's child, because Saidi is the one who married Sona and gave the bridewealth herd," elders say. When a lover claims a child with the *ndima*, when he is in the position to do so, he is said *kutema umwana mutozo*, "to put a [brand] mark [as used on a calf] on the child." Cf. Cory (1954), ¶¶184–206.

All Gogo men are known throughout life by their own personal names (*litagwa lyanhili,* "the name of the [weaning] gruel"), given them soon after birth. The name is always followed by the father's (*pater's*) name in the form "son of so-and-so" (*ala nhendu*). Thus, "Cisima the son of Sakawa" is Cisima ala Sakawa. When Gogo meet for the first time, it is not impolite to ask, when one has heard a man's name, "The son of whom?" On the contrary, it indicates interest and friendship when two men meet, and might lead to their discovering some common relationship. These days, when some men are reluctant to reveal their father's name to people they have just met, elders might say, "Why should you not state (*kutambula*)[24] the name of your father? Are you ashamed of him?" A girl, when referred to by her own personal name, is known as "the child of so-and-so" (*mwana wanhendu*) and her father's name is also reiterated. Boys give each other nicknames but these are known and used only within one age-set (*izika*). Middle-aged and older men and women are given, or give themselves, nicknames (*matagwa ganzwaji*) by which they may be generally known, but never lose their correct personal names.

In the normal course of events, then, paternity of the children of a married woman lies exclusively "whence the bridewealth herd came" (*kono zalawa izing'ombe*). Rights *in genetricem* and rights in the disposal of a wife's sexuality are transferred exclusively *to the husband* alone. Though any agnatic kinsman may theoretically inherit a wife (if she consents), community of interest in her reproductive capacities extends as far as the full brothers of her husband.[25] Half brothers never interfere with the marital rights and affairs of half brothers, because they have "married with different herds," even if they have married before

---

[24] The normal word for "to greet each other" (*kwitambuza*) includes the connotation of "making each other narrate one's genealogy," if it is not already known, and is the reciprocal/causative form of the verb *kutambula,* "to state," or to "enumerate."

[25] Cf. Cory (1951), ¶¶512–529.

the death of their father. Once a marriage is complete and the rights transferred, a husband's full brother may, however, act to preserve such rights over a woman were the marriage endangered by divorce. This is particularly so if an elder brother has assisted his younger full brother with bridewealth, and if the *mukulo* anointing oil symbolizing their community of interest in the marriage has come from the *nyumba* of the elder brother's senior wife.

There is no levirate in Ugogo. Even if a man inherits the wife of a full brother, any children she has by her new husband will consider him their *pater*. The *pater* of the children of a married woman is her husband at the time of their birth.[26] As an heir who inherits a wife also inherits the assets of her *nyumba* (unless her sons are mature, when she would not be inherited in any case), the children he begets belong to one *nyumba* with their maternal half siblings: hence, the children of one *nyumba* may have different *paters*. If the wife is inherited by a classificatory "son" of the dead husband, the maternal half siblings in one *nyumba* may even belong to different "generations." Gogo elders make up puzzles for each other that deal with the kin terms people will use in such situations, and the joking is endless. The confusion of generation identifications is one of the most common elements in joking between kin, and the ambiguities caused by wife inheritance fall into this category.

In the following discussion of relations between father and son in Ugogo, all remarks apply to those that exist between a boy and his *pater,* in the sense defined above, who is normally his *genitor* but by no means need necessarily be so.[27] It is always

---

[26] Legally, the heir must be an agnate of the husband. If there is no suitable agnate, and the wife is inherited by a non-agnatic kinsman (such as a son of the dead husband's sister), the children born subsequently may consider as their *pater* their mother's dead husband. But this is an unusual occurrence.

[27] The rules I have described here and in Chapters III and VI for establishing the *pater* are universal in Gogo law, in spite of the fact that Gogo ideas of procreation postulate firmly that an individual's entire

the child's "mother's husband," however, except in the single case
of giving birth before marriage where a "mother's brother" assumes the role of *pater*. To some extent the norms described as
applying to relations between "father and son" also apply to
relations between a person and anyone in the parental generation
to whom he refers as his "father" (*sogwe*). This may include
father's agnates (e.g. FB), father's cognatic kin (e.g. his cross-
cousins) or even affines of that generation (e.g. FZH). In fact,
the term *sogwe* includes all related males of the parental generation except those classified as "mother's brothers" (*wakuku'ze*),
including non-related age-mates of "father." But relations with
real *pater* are sharply distinguished from those with other kinds
of "father" by the presence of the "holder-heir" complex only in
the former. I have shown how rights in the primary form of inheritable wealth (livestock) are rapidly segmented in each generation by the house-property system. But it is also clear that
sons cannot attain full control of the herds allocated to their
respective *nyumba* until the death of their father or until his
voluntary abandonment of control. This means almost always the
spatial separation of father and sons who have reached "elder-
hood" (i.e. 35 years and over) by the latter setting up their
own homesteads (and thus their own byres). They usually would

---

physical make-up, blood, flesh, bones, skin and all, are derived exclusively
from the *genitor*. When I inquired about this, at different times and
places, knowledgeable informants who had any ideas about the subject
all confirmed that, "When a person is being 'created' (*yakuwumbwa*),
the blood (*sakami*), bones (*mafupa*), skin (*nghuli*) and so on, all come
from the *genitor* (*vyose vikulawilila kosogwe yamunhu du*)." The mother,
the "womb" (*muda*), is likened to a round bark-box (*mutundu*) or
"something to put things in" (*muwici*). In contrast, however, a child is
said to be able in his character traits to follow either paternal or maternal
characteristics. The character a person develops has nothing to do with
the *genitor*. This, together with Gogo ideas of paternity outlined above
(and the institution of *mbuya*), indicates the complete distinction Gogo
make between social paternity and biological fatherhood. The role of
the sexual act and semen is fully recognized in the biological process of
procreation.

move away to another neighborhood to be outside the orbit of their father's remaining influence, both economic and ritual. Rights in the *nyumba* herd cannot be exercised by individual full brothers until that *nyumba* ceases to exist as a unit: that is, on the death of their mother. Thus, full brothers always live, or move away, together, with their mother.

Normatively, however, sons should never move away from their father's homestead until his death. Even when they are married, if he has helped them, as he should have, to achieve this status, they should remain in his homestead under his jural control, economic, political and ritual, and so "build his homestead" and prestige in the community. The filial piety of a son towards his father should be an element in their relationship while the latter is alive, and even after his death. A son should always show his father respect (*loga*), do his bidding, and "fear him" (*kumogopa*). In fact, this is seldom the case when the son reaches maturity.

A father should be affectionate and sympathetic to his sons, help them marry, and give them an early share in the control of their common property as soon as they are adult. This sometimes is the case. But more usually, if a man has one or two wives, several sons, and only average wealth in livestock, conflict is almost inevitable between them over the use of the livestock in bridewealth. Married sons begin to chafe against the authority of their father and wish to move away. But to do so is a serious moral offence, though no legal action can be taken by a father to prevent it. He can only withdraw his support and assistance, both economic and ritual. The sons are said to be "killing the homestead of their father" (*wakumuwulajila sewo ikaya*), and it is thought of in the same light, and as related to, the wickedness of bad wives who wish to destroy their husband's homestead by witchcraft. Nevertheless, it is a frequent occurrence, and an illustrative and detailed case is given in Appendix E. Where adult sons do leave their father in this manner, Gogo commonly express the conflict in terms of the sons' attraction to their mother's brother: their matrilateral kinsmen instead of their agnatic kin. When sons move away with their mother, they frequently go to reside near their mother's full brothers. If they leave without their mother, they are said to go to live near their own affines, their wives' kin. But as the sons' mother's brothers and even affines usually reside nearby, they may move and build their own homesteads only a short distance from their father's. This situation might continue until the son moves away altogether to build near kin or affines who live at some distance. But the point is that in Gogo theory the process is thought of in terms of the differential attraction of the son toward his agnatic, matrilateral, and affinal kin. And this is an additional Gogo argument for having all of these kin living near each other (see case, Appendix E).

Gogo think of the father/son relationship as a developing one. A father is usually very affectionate with a small son, calling him *"baba"* (father) and playing with him with remarkable patience and gentleness.[28] Even when they are older, a father, together with his wives' brothers—his children's mother's brothers—will go to great lengths to ensure the health and prosperity of his children. Thus:

Ndahani, whose son of about 6 years old is a deaf-mute (*wacibwibwi*), took his son to all the local diviners. They could do nothing, so he took him to the government hospital in the local town of Dodoma some 30 miles away. He was turned away from there as hopeless. Ndahani then took him 80 miles to a diviner at Mhamvwa, but this too was no good. He returned home to Cikola and heard of another diviner called Canzi who lived at Musonga. Ndahani, on foot, carried his son 23 miles to Canzi's homestead. He stayed with the child at Canzi's homestead for two months, and then carried him back to Cikola only after the diviner had given up the attempt at a cure.

[28] He calls his son *"baba"* because he identifies his son with his father (his son's grandfather, whose name the child may even bear) through the principle of the identification of alternate generations. (See further discussion below.)

I have recorded several cases of fathers helping mature married sons in this manner who were still living with them in their homesteads, or nearby.

But as soon as sons become adolescent, strain begins to appear in their relation with their father. Gogo elders spend a great deal of time talking and worrying over the constantly evident discrepancy between values and behavior in the relationship between fathers and mature sons. And so rigid is the house-property principle in the inheritance of livestock, that even if a father curses (*kumuligita*) for good reason a disobedient and unmanageable adolescent son, he cannot by doing so deprive that son from his right to inherit a share of the property allocated to his mother's *nyumba*.[29] For no one will take the responsibility of upholding the father's decision, after his death, against the claims of his son. An informant put it this way:

When a person curses his son, even if he banishes him from his homestead, when he dies the son can return and inherit, even the bow (*wupinde*) and other things, simply because his father is now dead. Who would press his claims against him?

Sometimes the elders will call back a son who has been banished and tell the father, "Remove the curse; you have spoiled him [your son]" (*Ubehe umwana; wamutalila gwegwe*). If he has any sense, the father will remove the curse so that his son may remain with him until his death. So a person is not able to say, "This son of mine is useless, he must not inherit my wealth." He will simply return

---

[29] A father curses and disowns his son by banishing him from his homestead and exposing his genitals to him as a curse. I recorded only one such case: Munama, now about 63 years old, had been cursed and disowned (*yakaligitwa*) by his father for stealing livestock from others when they were a comparatively rich family themselves. The father had been injured in a battle with the Sandawi, and although he lived for several years with a piece of barbed arrow (*mhagali*) in his shoulder, he died before withdrawing the curse (*kubeha umwana*). Munama came back at his father's funeral and, as the eldest son, was the principal heir and inherited the bow (*wupinde*).

and the elders will even give him the main inheritance if he is the eldest.[30]

This is a further indication of how little control a father has over the eventual distribution of most of his property, which is determined by the considerable autonomy of the houses in the house-property system. Even though inheritance must be seen within a patrilineal context, the house-property system differentiates potential rights in property within each generation before inheritance, and at the same time incorporates the interests, both economic and ritual, of close matrilateral kin.

In this situation, Gogo reluctantly recognize the incipient conflict between father and son as inevitable (particularly with the eldest son, *mwana mulongozi* or *muwaha*, in each house). Witchcraft accusation is rife (or imputed to occur) between them. Also in this context, the youngest son (*muziwanda*) of each house, but particularly the junior house, is thought of as being in a special position. He is usually too young seriously to challenge his father's position or control while the latter is alive. Gogo say that youngest sons frequently stay on with their fathers when all their elder brothers have left. They help their father with his cattle and homestead, and may even inherit the building (*ikaya*) after his death although they normatively cannot become principal heir and inherit the bow (*wupinde*), which is reserved for the first son of the senior wife.[31]

[30] *Kuligita* can be used to mean the deprivation, with supernatural sanctions, of the reciprocity any kin or non-kin may expect from any particular relationship. Thus, between partners in a blood covenant (*ndugu yalusale*), if one fails to fulfill his obligations, the other may curse him over it (*kumuligitiza*). "The cursed one will then be [supernaturally] prevented from increasing his wealth in any way" (*Yuyo mono aligitwa, sikowa sawa*).

[31] This Gogo "model" of relations between father, elder son, and youngest son is also illustrated in a great number of Gogo stories and folk tales. In several of these tales the content and detail may vary, but the relationship pattern involving these roles remains constant. The tales portray the disobedience of elder sons. They disobey their father's instructions in such activities as herding and hunting, which eventually

Breaches in harmonious relations between father and son should be handled by a gathering of closely related cognatic kin, usually elders who are both close kin and live nearby (see Appendix E). These are "kinship matters" and should be settled in discussions (*maloloso*) where only kin are concerned. They should not become *vyalo* (cases) by bringing them to the "public" courts of elders in the local community.

Most of the points I have made in this and previous chapters about the father/son relationship in respect of the norms concerning it, the frequent discrepancy in the behavior and practice, and the concern of Gogo about it generally, are illustrated in the detailed case given in Appendix E; it is too lengthy to include in the text. When relations between father and son break down, the elders try to restore amity by persuading the two to take up their rights and duties in normal behavior toward each other. Compensation is restricted to payments for misdeeds that could be perpetrated against anyone, kin or non-kin: for example, payments for defamation (*kutema lulimi*) or assault (*ndesa*). The values of the solidarity of the patricentral homestead group,

---

leads to trouble and the loss of the herd or other wealth. The youngest son (*muziwanda;* lit. "the one who 'closed' the womb") solves the difficulties, saves his father's livestock and so on, and becomes the hero of the day. Not all of these tales are simply didactic. Where the F/S relationship is not directly involved, the youngest son appears as a culture hero (very common in folk tales from widely scattered areas). In one widespread non-didactic tale, matrilateral kin are included by the presence of the MB (to whom dissident sons are said to defect; see above). In this tale the *muziwanda* saves all his kin, but his actions lead to the slaying of an uncooperative, unreasonable, and ungrateful mother's brother. This is surprising in a society where the relationship with MB is conceived of as based upon intimacy and mutual ritual dependence (see below). But the implication is clear if we consider the tale in the light of Gogo theories of the relations between father, elder sons, youngest son, and the latter's mother's brother. Cf. also Carnell (1955b). Much of what Lévi-Strauss says on the structural study of myth may be applied to oral literature in general: (1958), p. 254; (trans.), p. 229. Lévi-Strauss explicitly criticizes the type of "representational approach" I have used in this note; but see also p. 231; (trans.), p. 209.

father/son and brother/brother are constantly reiterated. So too are the values of solidarity and cooperation in wider groups including affines: the father's brother-in-law, his sons' matrilateral kin. It is clear that these values are reiterated because of the latent conflicts over property and authority which are evident in the domestic family. The F/S relationship is discussed by Gogo only in terms of the other relationships that are functionally related to it, such as WB/ZH, MB/ZS, and relations between siblings. I try to show later in this chapter that it is, in fact, in this functional interdependence of roles (of which the Gogo are aware) that the important structural relations lie.

The inter-generation conflict over rights and obligations in property is transposed to the intra-generation level primarily in the relations between paternal half siblings. In terms of the ideology of patrilineal descent, Gogo say, one should make no distinctions between full and half siblings because they are all the "children of one man." This is reflected in the terminology identity, in both address and reference, between full and half siblings. The cleavage and opposition between paternal half siblings, however, is not only implicit in the structure of domestic groups but also expressed constantly in various institutionalized values and usages. From an early age, half brothers are separated from each other and brought closer to their full brothers. For example, they usually eat separately because *nyumba* are separate production and consumption units. Although they may be circumcised together with their half brothers, some of the animals which are slaughtered at different times during the ceremonies are supplied by different sets of matrilateral kin, "mother's brothers." Although they call all of their father's wives "*yaya*" and refer to them as *nyina* (mother), children are taught very early that their own mother is quite distinct. She is the head of their own *nyumba* and links them to a whole network of important matrilateral kin to whom their half siblings are not related except in a very vague and unreal sense, "unreal" because such relationships lack the basis of cooperation and reciprocity. They are relationships in terminology only. But above all, half siblings know that the property they will use to marry and will inherit is quite distinct, except for token obligations involving one head of cattle in each case. They consequently feel that they are, in a sense, competing with each other for the property and favors bestowed upon them by their father, within the polygynous family and domestic group.

Gogo thus think of relationships between the sons of different houses (*wana wanyumba mitala*) in terms of these factors, however much they theorize about the significance of being the "sons of one man." Witchcraft accusation and competition for ritual precedence (after the father's death) is expected to be an intrinsic element of inter-house relationships.[32] Co-wife hostility and witchcraft accusation are explained not in terms of jealousy over the sexual and other attentions of the husband, but in terms of the property and privileges wives wish to attract to their own *nyumba*, to the advantage of their children.[33] Co-wife hostility is an intrinsic part of inter-*nyumba* hostility, and the strain between them and the strain between half siblings (particularly brothers) are but two sides of the same coin. It does not explain, nor is it explained by, anything else.

Hence, the solidarity of agnatic kin, which is desirable in terms of the ideology of patrilineal descent, is fragmented at a low level in terms of two major structural factors: common rights in property and common residence. This is embodied in the very early fission between "house groups," the children of one *nyumba* (*wana wanyumba imonga*). Even relationships between full brothers may be subject to strain, particularly in the sphere of the authority of elder brothers. But they usually remain to-

[32] Some aspects of witchcraft accusation have been noted in the description of fission in Sandiya's domestic group after his death (Chapter V). Others will be noted in the discussion of MB/ZS relations below.

[33] In an otherwise unperceptive article, Beverley (1903), pp. 206–207, shows that he is one of the few writers on Gogo ethnography to have realized the forces at work in the fission between houses in the domestic group, at least in their outward manifestations.

gether in the same homestead or adjacent homesteads while their
mother is alive, and even after. Normatively, these relationships
should be close and cordial throughout life. Relations between
full brother and sister are discussed below. Full sisters, and even
their children (*wali cana canyina*), continue to cooperate and
visit each other throughout life. In one case:

Muhawi, a homestead owner in Cilungulu, whose mother lives with
him, went 25 miles to Nghong'onha to arrange for his mother's full
sister to come to Cilungulu. She has tuberculosis of the spine and
he arranged for her to be treated by a diviner in Cilungulu. [Muhawi
would refer to her as *nyina mudodo*, "little mother," MyZ.] She
came to live with her sister, Muhawi's mother, in one homestead.
Her husband also took up residence until she could be cured or
the treatment finished. The two old ladies' younger full brother
Lubeleje also has a homestead nearby and he was instrumental in
arranging for the treatment.

Relations between close agnates beyond the children of one
man are also influenced by these norms and values, if sometimes
negatively. Relations between paternal parallel cousins (*wali
cana cawasewo*), who address each other as *alaba*, are expected
to be more cordial than those between paternal half siblings.
They are not directly involved in competition for property or
authority. Neither is there any competition over ritual precedence, for they have the separate gravestones of their fathers at
which to propitiate. Examples of cooperation between paternal
parallel cousins are given in Appendix E (e.g. the roles of
Magungu and Cedego in the case between father and son);
but they are often reluctant to involve themselves in each other's
affairs. In any case, they seldom live in the same neighborhood
throughout their lives and have no corporate interests in livestock, though they can "claim" (*kukwega*) single beasts from
the bridewealth given for each other's full sisters and daughters.[34]

[34] Lack of solidarity and cooperation between paternal parallel cousins
is also the pattern among the Nuer. For the ambiguities in their relationships, see Evans-Pritchard (1951), p. 159.

Due to this lack of corporate interest (and in this case competition), yet close relationship, paternal parallel cousins living
at a distance from each other may cooperate when herds must
be moved during droughts and grazing shortages. They provide
shelter and assistance for each other's herds and herders when
they go considerable distances to find adequate grazing and
water. But they would not, for example, cooperate in cattle-
trusteeship (*kukoza*) contracts, for they might be tempted (being
close kin) to make claims upon each other's herds which would
not normally be their right.[35] There is no fusion of more distant
agnates in local or residence groups, through the merging of
separate grandfathers by "structural amnesia" in genealogical
reckoning, as there is for example among the Jie.[36]

The rather strained sibling relationship between "brothers"
(except, perhaps, between full brothers) as described here does
not occur between brother and sister, particularly between full
brother and sister. Brother and sister refer to each other by the
reciprocal term *ilumbu lyangu* ("my brother/sister") and address each other by name.[37] Sexual segregation in work and play
between brother and sister occurs early in life, but they usually
(and normatively) have friendly and easy relations with each
other throughout life. There are few taboos in the relationship
outside that of incest. A sister may even cook for her brother

[35] In fact, cattle trusteeship contracts are much more common between affines or unrelated persons than agnatic kin. This appears also to
be the case with the "stock guardianship" contracts of the Taita: see
Harris and Harris (1964), p. 127.

[36] Gulliver (1955), pp. 108–117.

[37] Another version of this term, *kalumbu*, is used as a term of address
between the children (of opposite sex) of two men who are "blood-
brothers" (*ndugu yalusale*). This is the only context in which the form
is used. Children of men who are party to the blood covenant may not
marry. Their sons address each other as *"alaba,"* the term of address between paternal parallel cousins. The prefix *ka-* in the work *kalumbu* may
be connected with the Bantu diminutive prefix *ka-*: thus, *kalumbu,* "little
brother/sister." But *ka-* does not normally occur in Cigogo as a diminutive prefix except in some extreme southwestern dialects that border on
Kikimbu. Its place is taken in Cigogo by the prefix *ci-*.

and sit chatting nearby while he eats, as a mother may do for her son or a wife for her husband. Even linguistic usage is not strictly controlled between brother and sister; I have heard a man indulging in ribald joking with a joking partner, within the hearing of his sister. Gogo say that there would be no embarrassment in such a situation, for no one would desire his sister. The close and sentimental relation between brother and sister is also illustrated in the context of affinal relations, where Gogo imply that a man should have as much affection for his wife's brother as for his wife, because of the relationship between one's wife and her brother.

Even when married, a girl continues to visit her parents' homestead and meets her brothers there, or at her brothers' homesteads when her parents are dead. Younger brothers who are not yet married often go on extended visits to their married full sisters' homesteads. I have already shown that, although marriage is virilocal, the restricted spatial range of marriage and the continued close residence of affines ensure that brother and sister live within easy visiting distance. Brothers assist their full sisters in sickness, when the latter often leave their husbands' homes and come to live with their brothers until they have recovered. Brothers have strong moral and jural obligations to fulfill these duties, in cooperation with their sisters' husbands.[38] Even later in life, when sister and brother may be separated by considerable distances due to the movements of their respective homesteads, they continue to visit each other. In a typical case:

Kabango is an elderly homestead head of about 65, who lives in Temanghuku neighborhood. His full sister (who is about 45) lives with her husband at Cinhinghu, some 40 miles away, where they moved during a famine (Kabango also moved to Temanghuku during a famine). She came to visit him, together with one of her married

[38] In one case: Petelo's sister came some 8 miles to his homestead from her husband's homestead at Ilindi. She was ill with complications in her second pregnancy. Petelo took her to the local government hospital and paid the costs of her transport and treatment until she recovered.

daughters, and stayed about a week. She does this fairly regularly each year.

Such cases could be multiplied. Also, a widowed mother with young children, if she is not or refuses to be inherited, may come to live with, or near, a full or classificatory brother, especially if some incident causes disruption with her deceased husband's kin.[39] If she has adult sons, she stays with them in their homestead, but they quite frequently wish to reside near their mother's brothers.

The crucial point to note here is a sister's continuing reliance upon at least one of her full brothers, or a classificatory brother if she has no full brother, in the upbringing and marriage of her children. These mutual obligations between brother and sister concerning her children are, of course, fulfilled in cooperation with her husband. The bonds between brother and sister are functionally tied to relations between mother's brothers and sister's sons, and those between brothers-in-law. One aspect of the structural relations among these sets of relationships is the tie between brother and sister. It has therefore been necessary here to examine the norms and attitudes concerning this relationship. The free and easy B/Z link is in sharp contrast with the more formal and sometimes difficult relations between husband and wife, in spite of the low rate of divorce which has already been analyzed (see Chapter VI); both jointly indicate the structural importance of the complex of affinal relationships in Gogo social organization.

HUSBAND AND WIFE

A husband refers to his wife as *mucekulu wangu* or, in more formal circumstances, *mugolece wangu*.[40] She refers to him as

[39] An historical example is given in Chapter IV in the case of the founder of Temanghuku neighborhood.

[40] *Mucekulu* means literally "mature woman," i.e. "married woman." (A girl before marriage is *muhinza*.) *Mugolece* is a more respectful term, often used for a first, or senior, wife, or for the wife of an elder when a

mulume wangu ("my husband"). A husband addresses his wife
by the name given to her by himself or his kin on marriage
(*litagwa lya komulume,* "the name of the husband's place").
This name is made up of a boy's name prefixed by *Ina-,* "mother
of": thus, InaMutemi, "The mother of Mutemi." The giving
of this name by the husband does not depend on the birth and
name of the wife's first child, or first son. The name is simply
chosen from one common among the husband's bilateral ancestors, because "they may at some time name one of the wife's
children by that name." A husband will, of course, always know
his wife's own personal name (*litagwa lyanhili* or *lyokwawo;*
lit., "the name of her own place") and may sometimes refer to
her by it. A wife always addresses her husband by his own personal name and no honorific prefixes or affixes of any kind are
used. No special ceremonies are performed at the giving of
such names, though token gifts usually accompany naming of
all kinds.

A wife is never "fully incorporated" into her husband's "patrilineal group." She maintains throughout life ties of cooperation
and ritual community of interest with her own kin (particularly
her full brothers), through the desirable and frequent close residence of these kin, as well as frequent visits if they live at a
distance.[41] Normatively, a husband should never interfere in his
wife's relations with her own kin, as long as they do not unduly
affect her duties and obligations toward him. But his brothers-
in-law, due to the ideal closeness of their relations with him, may
ask him to do so:

------

younger man is speaking. The root *-gole-* is very common in other eastern
Bantu languages, such as Nyamwezi and Sukuma. In Lunyoro the word
may mean simply "bride," or be used by a servant of his "mistress."

[41] Personal mobility through the different ritual areas of Ugogo was
probably just as easy in the past as it is now. Unless marred in very
localized areas by recent cattle raids or hostilities, Gogo could move
through most of the country making use of the widely dispersed network
of kinship links, clan relations and joking partnerships, for safe conduct.
Residential mobility of homestead groups was just as high, or higher, in
the past as it is now.

Kamoga's first wife Nyamusice lives with her full brother Masani. She went to live there after conflict with her husband, but due to the intervention of Kamoga's elder full brother, there was no divorce. Nyamusice has a *nyumba* in her brother's homestead and Kamoga frequently visits her there, as the homesteads are only about three-quarters of a mile apart. Some of the cattle allocated to her house by Kamoga have also been moved to Masani's byre, so that she may easily benefit from the milch cows (*nghamwa*). Recently she came into conflict with her brother Masani over herding responsibilities and the duties of her children. This directly concerned Kamoga as their father, but the quarrel developed into a personal one between full brother and sister. This was considered in itself very bad and Kamoga was asked by his WB to come and arbitrate. Mujilima, Kamoga's elder full brother, was discussing the case with a junior elder Madinda:

Mujilima: Listen Madinda, if your wife is continually fighting with her own kin and you are called to help settle the dispute (*maloloso*), would you go?

Madinda: I would not say a thing, but simply indicate to them that "I don't know, it is your business. You are both close kin."

Mujilima: Yes, I would say, "You are of one blood" (*sakami imonga*).

Kamoga adhered to others' advice and did not become actively involved.

Although there are rare exceptions to the rule, one of the central features of the conjugal relationship is the co-residence of the spouses in one homestead, primarily that of the husband. This is borne out by the normative and statistical incidence of virilocality. The obligations of a husband in providing a *nyumba* for his wife have already been discussed. He is also legally obliged to provide her with various household goods, either with the assistance of his father in the case of a first wife, or on his own for subsequent wives or if his father is dead.[42] In return, a wife is expected to reside with her husband, except at certain

[42] She must also be provided with certain household objects by her own agnatic and matrilateral kin.

specified periods such as during the birth of her first child or during visits of reasonable duration and frequency to her own kin. She is expected to cultivate with him sufficient grain and other crops to feed him, herself, and her children, perform her other domestic duties regularly, and be responsive to her husband's wishes and orders.

Owing to the political and jural significance of the homestead and domestic unit the husband's jural authority over his wife is only fully expressed by her permanent residence in his homestead. A husband would be thought of as lacking full control over his wife in all fields, economic, political, and ritual, were she to reside in another's homestead. Only after she has passed the menopause and has her own adult sons, or the husband is impotent through old age, is residential separation between husband and wife the norm. Only in the case of service marriage (*kupanga*) does a husband necessarily reside, for the early years of the marriage, with his wife's kin: or in the few cases where a husband may choose voluntarily to live with his wife's father even if he has given full bridewealth. However, husbands may often build their own homesteads near those of their wives' kin, when, for example, they move away from their own fathers' homesteads.

Serious conflict between husband and wife may result in his banishing her from his homestead. This can be resolved only with the inclusion of ritual sanctions concerning the *kulapa ciila* and *la'o* procedures already described. Most conflicts within the homestead lead to witchcraft accusations. One of the gravest accusations a husband can level against his wife is that she is "destroying his homestead with witchcraft" (*yakumuwulajila kaya nowuhawi*).

I have indicated too (see Chapter VI) that a man should not choose a wife on the basis of physical attraction and emotional attachment alone, although these may play a part. He should choose her for her industry, obedience, and potential child-bearing capacity. The latter is indicated by other characteristics such as freedom from contagious or venereal diseases, and her family's freedom from ritually dangerous diseases such as small-pox and leprosy. Passionate love affairs should be reserved for extra-marital relationships controlled by the formalized *mbuya* ties already referred to. In Gogo theory, extreme emotion does not augur well for stable conjugal links, which provide the basis for highly valued and structurally important links in Gogo society.

The formal values and norms which are embodied in the con-jugal relationship characterize it as distant, formal, and relatively rigidly defined by external jural and moral forces.[43] The obe-dience of the wife and the authority of the husband are under-lined, although they are also considerably diminished as the marriage matures and the wife has adolescent sons. An example of the norms concerning conjugal behavior is given in the following case:

A husband brought his wife to the elders' court, for he alleged that she threatened to break up his homestead by witchcraft and other means. They had been married several years, had several children, but the husband wanted a divorce. The elders managed to avert this and reconcile the two. The wife's parents had to pay a fine for her, "*yakutema lulimi*" ("of cutting the tongue," for saying defamatory and dangerous things). The husband had sent her away to her parents, so another goat (*mhene yala'o*) had also to be provided. This was slaughtered in their *nyumba*, the blood spilling on their feet, for ritual reconciliation. When giving this judgment, the elders addressed the woman:
"Mother (*mudala*), you wished to bring destruction and trouble upon your husband, so you must give *kutema lulimi;* you will pay a goat for it. Now, he married you, so you must listen to whatever

[43] This does not mean that affection and love do not play an im-portant part in Gogo marriages. I have noted the remarkable stability of marriage. It is after a marriage is firmly established and children are born that affection grows between the spouses. Gogo norms about marriage are only concerned to show that the passionate (and ephemeral) affairs of youth should not be the basis of the conjugal relationship.

he says. If he says, 'The sleeping skin has bed-bugs in it, take it outside and spread it in the sun so that they will leave,' you will take it and spread it. You will listen to your husband!'"

Another elder added, "*He* came to betroth *you* [when he married you]; *you* did not betroth *him*."

The formality and distance in the conjugal relationship are contrasted with the free and easy behavior between lovers (*wono wali mbuya*) and brother and sister. (In the case of close cross-cousin marriage, where a relationship approaching that of joking existed between the spouses before marriage, the formality of the conjugal relationship ousts the former one.) The formality of this relationship does not, however, affect the close, intimate, and egalitarian relations between brothers-in-law. The distance and authority involved in the conjugal relationship is thought of by Gogo as simply ensuring its stability, upon which other relationships of cooperation are based. It is to a consideration of the norms which concern these other affinal relationships that I now turn.

AFFINES: *WAKWE* AND *WALAMU*

I first consider relationships between affines of different generations. A man refers to his wife's father and mother as *mukwe wangu* (pl., *wakwe*); a woman refers to her husband's parents by the same term. The relationships distinguished by the sex of the speaker have different modes of address (see Appendix D). Correspondingly, both SW and DH are referred to as *mukwe-mulima* (pl., *wakwe-mulima*), although again distinctions are made in the form of address. The term means literally, "the in-law of proximate generation (*mukwe*) who hoes," because the element *mulima* is derived from the verb *kulima*, to cultivate.[44]

[44] The word is a compound noun and the element *mulima* is not an adjectival qualificative, qualifying the noun *mukwe*. This is shown by the fact that the prefixal element *mu-* of *mulima* does not change to *wa-* in the plural form. Thus, "sons-in-law" are *wakwe-mulima*. The word has been hyphenated to emphasize its structure, but must be treated as a single, compound word. The reciprocal emphasis is on the word *mukwe*.

This does not imply that service in the form of agricultural labor is part of the bridewealth, except in the case of service marriage (*kupanga*) where the groom and his supporting kinsmen have insufficient livestock. It implies rather the norm that affines, who reside near each other, should cooperate in most activities, and cultivation is one of them. The junior should assist the senior, but the obligation is mutual.

A son-in-law is morally obliged (though not legally required) to come with a party of his kin and age-mates to hoe his wife's parents' fields. This kind of hoeing party is called *kulima cikwemulima*, "to hoe in the manner of sons-in law." The obligation is particularly strong in the early stages of a marriage, but can continue indefinitely while the husband's *wakwe* are still alive. The son-in-law's party (*wakwe-mulima*) are given a separate part of the field to work on. But if they do this, the wife's father is equally obliged to provide the *wakwe-mulima* party with a sheep or goat to "bring them back from the field" (*ngholo* or *mhene yakuwagomolela iwakwe-mulima*) when the work is over. Or at very least, he must provide them with a special and exclusive pot of beer.[45] The obligation of mutual cooperation is thus emphasized, even though the "in-laws" (*wakwe*) are of different generations. It is not obligatory service by a junior for a senior.

This cooperation between *wakwe*[46] extends to other areas of

[45] If a father-in-law is mean about this and does not provide the gift, the *wakwe-mulima* party can ridicule him and make it publicly known by not returning to the homestead from the field until he reciprocates in some way for their labor. On one occasion I observed this when the *wakwe-mulima* party continued hoeing and singing in the field, into the night until about 9 o'clock, when it was too dark to see what they were doing. Homesteads for some distance could hear them. The father-in-law had then to face the risk of having them hoe up his crop with the weeds in the dark, and he only persuaded them to return to the homestead by sending a large pot of beer to them. They drank it at the field, then returned to the homestead for their share in the beer normally consumed at such parties.

[46] DH/WF can generally be referred to as "being *wakwe*," without the need to distinguish the different generations.

activity as well, such as in the sharing of herding duties, and the very common practice of forming cattle-trusteeship (*kukoza*) ties between them. House-building (*luzengo*), the other major labor-requiring activity, is also a field for cooperation between *wakwe*. Sons-in-law help their fathers-in-law, again for recognized rewards.[47] Gogo insist that these mutual exchanges should be, and traditionally were, viewed in the light of reciprocity and cooperation between affines, and not as profitable to one party or another. The values involved in cooperation between affines of different generations are illustrated in the following incident:

Masaka, a rich diviner with a large herd and homestead (he has five wives and several dependent *nyumba*), moved his homestead to a new site in the same neighborhood. He is about 60 years old. He asked some of his own daughters' husbands to help him in the considerable task of building the new homestead. Six responded, all of whom lived fairly close by. The building of a large homestead is an extended business, and some of the young men were living with Masaka's family in shelters on the site. Others who lived in the same neighborhood returned each day. Apart from food and beer which they consumed as the work progressed, Masaka would give them a large ox (*nghongolo*) at the end. The *wakwe-mulima* can do with this ox as they please, but normatively it should be slaughtered on the spot and eaten by all present. Some meat is then taken to the various homesteads concerned.

While visiting Masaka one day, I heard the following conversation, which took place between a junior elder and one of the sons-in-law:
Junior elder: (to son-in-law) When Masaka gives you the ox, will you have a feast on it or take it to the cattle market?
Mukwe-mulima: We'll take it to the market.
Junior elder: Why won't you eat it?
Mukwe-mulima: Now, if we slaughter it, all these youngsters, our wives' brothers (*ivilamu vyetu*), will come and ask us to cut off

[47] All of this is further confirmation of the desirability of close residence of affines, for which a considerable weight of evidence has been adduced in the preceding analysis.

pieces and give them meat, and we'll have to do so.[48] So we want to sell it and get the money. Then we would only give the "chest and stomach meat" (*inghwa du*, i.e. a few shillings, a token payment only for the share he and his family should receive from the beast he has given them) to our *mukwe*.

Junior elder: But you young men are doing extreme wrong. That is why the elders these days no longer wish to call you youngsters to come and work with them, so that they can give you animals. Because the father-in-law knows, "If I give them a beast, they will take it to the market." It is you young sons-in-law who are doing the wrong, so elders are reluctant to give you things. Elders in the past used to like calling their sons-in-law and giving them the animal. They used to kill it, there in his byre, and eat it together . . . Because he knew when he gave his sons-in-law an animal they would kill it in his byre and so propitiate the spirits of the dead at the new homestead. And then even the spirits would see that, "Indeed, our child is caring for his youngsters (i.e. *wakwe-mulima*)"; so they used to be happy. But if you *wakwe-mulima* take it to the market, even if you come and give your father-in-law money, there is no propitiation.

Mukwe-mulima: Ah, we'll kill the small goat he gives us for "the dust and dirt of the labor" (*cipene cemanghundi*) and propitiate with that.

Although based upon this idea of mutual cooperation, the relationship between DH and WF may be seen to be an unequal one. Certain kinds of services go in one direction and certain kinds of goods in the other. Yet the continuation of the proper relationship through time rests on reciprocity and moral norms, not legal coercion. The asymmetrical element in the affinal relationship is caused by the generation difference. This "structural asymmetry" is important in reference situations and is embodied in the reference terminology (*mukwe/mukwe-mu-*

[48] The diminutive form *vilamu* ("little brothers-in-law") from *walamu* "brothers-in-law." The implication is that only youngsters would actually *ask* for meat from their brothers-in-law (*walamu*) in such a situation, instead of its being given voluntarily.

lima) which refers, incidentally, to the agricultural basis of Gogo subsistence. In the address situation, face-to-face relationship, however, the emphasis is on the fact that cattle have been exchanged. DH/WF address each other by self-reciprocal terms which refer to cattle exchange, the commonest of which is *wandawo* (see pp. 253–254). This is consistent with the Gogo conception of the activation (and evaluation) of all important social relationships in terms of cattle exchange rights and obligations.

Relations between individuals of opposite sex, between WM/DH and HF/SW, who stand in the *mukwe/mukwe-mulima* relationship are governed by more complex norms. They are also thought of as developing relationships, as the marriage about which they center matures. The crucial point is the birth of the first child of the marriage, when the conjugal bond is thought to be firmly established and affinal relationships to crystallize.[49] I shall first take the case of a man and his WM.

In the early phases of marriage, he may address her as *yaya* ("mother") or by her "married name" (*litagwa lyo komulume*). Before a child is born, she will address him as "*wana'nye*" (lit., "you child") and after the birth of a child by his name or as "*wanyamhala'nye*" (lit., "you elder").[50] There is no physical avoidance, but certain topics and types of conversations are taboo, including topics dealing with general values of life, love, and sex. Such conversation is called *muduwo*. Thus Gogo say, "*Munhu yasina muduwo nonyina yomucekulu wakwe,*" "A person has no general conversation with his wife's mother." He will

[49] The low rate of divorce, particularly after the first three years, confirms this.

[50] The use of the prefix *wa-* in these address terms is almost certainly connected with the honorific plural prefix already discussed (see footnote 18). It is quite consistent that it is also used for an affine of junior generation. DH is treated with elaborate formality by his wife's parents, especially during marriage negotiations and just after marriage. A girl's father will even give up his stool to his DH when the latter visits, however young the youth and old the WF.

also step aside (*kumutelela*) on a path; but they greet each other along the normal, formalized pattern (*kwitambuza*). When a child is born of the marriage, a man addresses his WM as *wadala'nye* (lit., "thou elderly woman who has borne children"). Relations ease between them and they can even indulge in a mild form of joking (*nzwaji*).[51] The introduction of the third generation effects the identification of alternate generations, which brings about this familiarity in relations between proximate generations. If the child is a boy, the WM (to whom the child is "grandchild," *mwizukulu*) jokingly calls him "my husband" (*mulume wangu*); in the joking context, her *mukwe-mulima* (DH) thus becomes her "husband's father" (*mukwe*), and the generation difference is "reversed." So too, if the child is a girl, she jokingly calls it "my co-wife" (*musanji muyangu*), because it is her husband's granddaughter, and therefore also "his wife." The generation identification is still reversed.

Much the same situation obtains between a girl and her husband's father, whom she addresses as *"wanyamhala'nye"* (elder) or *"baba"* (father). He addresses her as *"wana'nye,"* or her name "of the husband's place" (*litagwa lyo komulume*) before the birth of her child, but *"wadala'nye"* [52] after she has borne her first child ". . . because, when she has borne a child [who is then the grandchild of her HF] the HF calls the child [if a girl] 'my wife' when joking; and so his *mukwe-mulima* (SW) becomes his *mukwe* (WM)." This again is the limited joking (*nzwaji*) already described.

Hence, relations between close affines of different generations, though formal and somewhat difficult (particulary in the early phases of a marriage), by no means approach the total avoidance and rigid taboos on behavior found in other patrilineal Bantu societies. Particularly relations between a man and his wife's

[51] *Nzwaji* is mild joking, not of the kind that exists between clan joking-partners or in proper joking relationships, which is called *maligo* (lit., swearing). See Rigby (1968a).

[52] Cf. usage between DH/WM, above.

father are based upon mutual (albeit not symmetrical in kind) duties and privileges. The term *wandawo* used in address between these male affines is very frequently used between non-related men who come into frequent contact and whose age puts them in "proximate generation" roles towards each other. Gogo say, "Might not the younger man marry the daughter of the older and thus make him his *mukwe?*"

Relationships between affines of the same generation are, on the other hand, completely egalitarian. I have already devoted considerable attention to various aspects of these relationships and their structural significance, particulary that between wife's full-brother and full-sister's husband. I shall here examine briefly the significance of the terminology used between them, together with further analysis of their structural importance and relations with other roles. [53]

Brothers-in-law refer to each other as *mulamu* and address each other as *mbuyane*. I have described the implications of the term *mbuyane* as denoting an intimate "joking relationship," which is also used between men in alternate generations. The emphasis is on affection, but tempered with potential strain. The relationship is thought of as delicate and easily disrupted by conflict between husband and wife; that is why the latter must be firmly controlled and formalized. But at the same time it implies cooperation that

[53] Leach (1961a), pp. 106–120 *et passim,* demonstrates the structural importance of the relationship between brothers-in-law over that of full brothers in a Ceylon village. This is in a very different context where rights in fixed land units and agricultural cooperation are at stake, whereas in the Gogo situation these factors do not occur. (Relations between brothers, sharply distinguished as between full and paternal half brothers, are characterized by interest in easily movable and divisible property, viz., livestock.) Thus the incidence of factors such as that of uxorilocal (*binna*) marriage, which is so important a feature of brother-in-law relations in Ceylon, do not arise in the Gogo context, where the inheritance system is designed to distinguish as soon as possible in each generation rights in movable property (often necessarily moved), in an area where ecological conditions make population density low and residential mobility fairly high.

is significant not only for brothers-in-law themselves, in their own generation, but also for their respective children. Brothers-in-law should reside close together; even if they do not, they should visit each other, paralleling the norm implicit in full brother/sister relations.[54]

Brothers-in-law are also tied by strong mutual obligations of a ritual nature to each other's children. A's wife's full brother B is his children's MB. I have referred on several occasions to the ritual content of the latter relationship and do so again below. But B also requires the continued ritual cooperation of the son of at least one full sister throughout his life, to ensure the ritually pure continuity of inheritance within his own family. For when B dies, his full sister's son (*mwihwa*), his own sons' patrilateral cross-cousin (*muhizi'we wokulume*), must provide a sheep (*ngholo yakwemela wupinde*) whose stomach contents are used to rub the bow of inheritance and cleanse it of the contamination of witchcraft and death. I discuss this further below but refer to it here to emphasize the subsidiary structural complex of inter-dependent relationships involving ZH/WB, ZC/MB, and MBS/FZS, the latter two of which stem from the structural importance of the first. The structural significance of each can only be seen in its relation with the other two. A full understanding of all is required before an analysis of the more central structural complex is possible. I therefore give a brief analysis of the terminology significance and norms relating to MB/ZS and cross-cousin relationships.

---

[54] Although Gogo do not make the explicit association, it is of interest to note that the verb "to visit" or "to greet" is *kulamusa,* and "greetings" are *mulamu.* The tonal structure of these roots is roughly the same as that for *mulamu,* "brother-in-law." Thus:

    mulamu (brother-in-law) = LHL (i.e. low-high-low)
    mulamu (greetings)   = LHL
    kulamusa (to visit)   = LHHL

I have already noted the use of the term *latalai* (neighbors) as an alternative form of address between *walamu* (see footnote 20).

MOTHER'S BROTHER AND SISTER'S SON

The general problem of MB/ZS relationships is highly complex.[55] It is beyond the scope of the present work to examine in detail the significance of the Gogo material for this problem in general. An explanation in terms of unilineal corporate descent groups, residual property rights within which are expressed in the MB/ZS relationship, is not feasible in the Gogo case, due to the house-property inheritance system and the non-corporate nature of descent groups. Neither do Gogo have a preferential or prescriptive alliance system in which this crucial relationship is involved. I have, however, tried to show, at various points in the preceding analysis, that the structural importance of the MB/ZS relationship must be explained in terms of (a) its interrelations with other relationship pairs involved intimately in economic and ritual cooperation and cattle exchange, and (b) the significance of this structural complex for the broader aspects of Gogo social structures, economic and political. The two structural complexes of kin and affinal relationships I consider to be important in an explanation of the MB/ZS relationship are further discussed in the concluding section of this chapter.

A man refers to his mother's brothers, both "actual" and classificatory, as *kuku yangu*. The term is the same as that used for both paternal and maternal grandfathers. Thus, it may be said that in reference terminology, MB is placed in the second ascending (alternate) generation; this implies a close and intimate relationship, involving "joking." [56] However, in the system

[55] For example, see: Radcliffe-Brown (1952), Chapters I and IV; Radcliffe-Brown (1950), "Introduction"; Goody (1959); Leach (1961); Lévi-Strauss (1949) and (1958), Chapter II; Needham (1962); Fortes (1959); Homans and Schneider (1955); and so on.

[56] It does not imply, however, that Gogo kinship terminology is of the "modified Omaha type" as described by Radcliffe-Brown (1950), pp. 34–35. For MBS is not referred to as *kuku* also, but *muhizi:* a reciprocal term of reference between MBC/FZC. The principle of the "unity of the lineage," which explains the Omaha type of terminology, does not operate in Gogo nomenclature for matrilateral kin.

of address terminology, *kuku* (grandfather) and *kuku* (MB) are distinguished. For grandfather/grandson address each other as *"mbuyane"* ("brother-in-law") but MB/ZS address each other as *bulayi*.[57] The term *bulayi* is exclusive to the MB/ZS relationship.[58] Also, the two kinship categories referred to as *kuku* are distinguished in the system of reference by distinct terms referring to the other two elements in the role pairs. A grandson is referred to as *mwizukulu* but a ZS is *mwihwa*.[59]

At first sight it appears that there is little significance in assuming a connection between the terms *kuku* (grandfather) and *kuku* (MB); and indeed, in terms of the behavior and attitude system, except for the common element of equality and light joking, there is little in common between the role pairs. However, the reference terminology equation, as long as the filial generation is taken as starting point, is consistent insofar as MBW is also *mama yangu,* the term used for both paternal and maternal grandmother. The terminology equation is reinforced by the fact that a man may also joke with MBW and call her *"mucekulu wangu,"* "my wife," and she responds with "my husband," just as may occur between grandmothers and grandsons. But again, in reference terminology, the complementary roles are distinguished: MBW refers to her HZS as *mwana'ngu* (my child), not *mwizukulu wangu* (my grandchild).

The ritual interdependence and the limited though important mutual economic interests (primarily in bridewealth herds) which are an important part of the MB/ZC relationship, have been stressed at many points in the preceding analysis. This is particularly so in the case of men (MB/ZS); the interdependence is

[57] See text at note 20 and Appendix D.

[58] Gogo now also use the Swahili term *mjomba* in the MB/ZS context, as an alternative address term, which is also reciprocal. This does not alter the implications of the usage, for it is considered as a direct translation of the Gogo term *bulayi*.

[59] A woman also refers to her MB as *kuku'ye* and he to her as *mwihwa*, but they do not address each other as *bulayi*, unless in a very light joking context which is not consistent. They address each other by name.

embodied in their affectionate use of the term *bulayi* to each other.[60] Although adult men seldom live in the same homesteads as their mother's brothers, they often visit them, with their mothers when they are children, and alone later in life. They often live near each other in separate homesteads; this is desirable and is the direct outcome of the close residence of brothers-in-law. I have recorded one or two cases of inheritance of MBW by ZS, in the event of a suitable agnate being unavailable as heir. But this is unusual and not normatively correct, although the possibility of such inheritance is an element in the joking relationship between cross-cousins (see following section). In Chapter III, I recorded two historical cases of the ritual leadership (*wutemi*) of particular ritual areas passing into the clan of "sister's sons" (*wehwa*), and the linking of clans in "perpetual-kinship" relationships in these categories. But yet a third relationship, that between cross-cousins, is closely linked in a structural complex with MB/ZS and must be examined before explanation is possible.

CROSS-COUSIN RELATIONSHIPS

All cross-cousins refer to each other by the symmetrical term *muhizi* (pl., *wahizi*); two men who stand in the relationship address each other as *"baguma."* Female cross-cousins or those of opposite sex address each other by name only, except in joking when they also may use *"baguma"* (see Appendix D). Although it is not desirable for primary cross-cousins to marry because of the confusion this causes in rights and obligations over bridewealth, such marriages occasionally occur. It is "desirable" to marry classificatory cross-cousins, particularly matrilateral cross-cousins, for they are already "those who are married" (*welizenjere*). The proportion of cross-cousin marriages in kin marriages

[60] They may also use personal names. The term *bulayi* is very commonly used between non-related men who are very close friends and who wish to express their dependence upon each other, both emotional and in practical affairs.

is relatively high, but the real incidence of such marriages is low. They may logically be explained as "desirable" by the Gogo in terms of the ideology of patrilineal descent. But their incidence is a function of locality: the strongly localized pattern of marriage and the co-residence of affines in the previous generation.

In what follows, I refer primarily to relations between male cross-cousins (MBS/FZS). Ritual interdependence (such as at inheritance ceremonies) between these kin has already been noted. But I have also shown that this aspect of the relationship is partly a function of the interdependence of MB/ZS and WB/ZH. The structural explanation of none of these relationships is complete without the others. The MBS/FZS relationship therefore requires further analysis in terms of the terminology and attitude systems which refer to it.

The relationship between cross-cousins is characterized by Gogo as being a particular type of joking relationship (Rigby, 1968a). But one does not "swear at" (*kumuliga*) a cross-cousin as one may with clan joking-partners (*watani*) or age-mates (*wazika wayagwe*). One jokes with him in a much more subtle and clever way (*yakumwizawisa* or *kumuzwajiza*). In Gogo theory, distant cross-cousin relationships become the basis of some instances of clan joking-partnerships (*wutani*). One also jokes with cross-cousin's wife.

On the level of "physical joking," cross-cousins take things from each other without permission. The similarity between the term of reference for cross-cousin (*muhizi*) and the word for "thief" (*muhizi*) is sometimes referred to explicitly by Gogo, but *only* in the context of funerals and inheritance ceremonies. Although this association is not always made, the comparison is highly illuminating for the way in which Gogo conceive of the cross-cousin relationship between men. In a discussion, one informant expressed it as follows:

I think the term *muhizi* comes from the context of funerals and inheritance ceremonies (collectively termed *mafwa;* sing., *ifwa*). When a man dies and he has his own children (*wana*) as well as his

sister's sons (*wehwa*), on the day of the inheritance ceremony they
cannot "bring out the bow" (*kulavya wupinde*) if the deceased's ZS
is not there [the heir's FZS].[61] They wait for the ZS to come and
"bring out the bow" and give it to them. Then they can give it to
the son who is inheriting the bow. . . .[62] But if the [deceased's] ZS
is not there, they cannot bring out the bow and give it to anyone.
And when the elders who have assembled ask each other, "Why
have you not brought out the bow?" they reply, "Because the
'owner-of-the-bow' [*munyawupinde*, i.e. deceased's ZS] hasn't come
yet; *we* cannot bring it out." But when they say that, they know that
the bow is not really his, the ZS's. The person who will inherit the
bow (*munyakuwuhala*) is the son of the dead man. But when the
elders talk like that, they know that, when the *mwihwa* arrives with
his sheep,[63] he will call out "It is my inheritance!" But it is not really
his and he knows it is not his.

Now, when the *mwihwa* is cunningly using his words [and the
threat of withholding the cleansing sheep], he wants to "steal"
(*kuhiza*) the inheritance of his MB (*kuku'ye*). And indeed, if his
MBS's are fools, he will trick them of the inheritance. He overcomes
them with words only, when they are narrating the clan histories
(*hono wakukomanghoma*).[64] But even if he does snatch away the

---

[61] When a man dies, his personal weapons and accoutrements, principally his bow (*wupinde*), stool (*igoda*), sticks (*nghome*), machete
(*hengo*), arrows (*sonyo*), sandals (*malatu*), and spear (*mugoha*) are
tied together and placed in the back corner (*kunhuzi*) of his first wife's
inner room (*kugati*). All of these objects together are referred to collectively as *ipinde,* "the great bow," and are handed ceremonially to the
principal heir as the symbol of inheritance. Before this is done, the corner
in which they are kept is frequently swept clean by an affine (*welizenjere,*
often the deceased's BW) who is appointed "to guard the bow" (*mono
yakulindiliza ipinde*) from further witchcraft and sorcery. The *ipinde*
must be "cleansed" with the stomach contents (*wufu*) of the sheep brought
by the heir's FZS, before it can be inherited.

[62] This rule is always adhered to except in the ceremonies for some
Christian converts. It is not possible here to go into further detail of the
symbolic roles played by various kin at these ceremonies.

[63] "The sheep for cleaning the bow" (*ngholo yakwemela uwupinde*).

[64] At inheritance ceremonies, the elders of the deceased's clan and
those of the clans of his ZS's have a night-long, ritualized verbal battle

inheritance, he goes to sit with his clan group. Then the elders
will go over and plead with him and say, "Bring out our bow!" And
he will do so. But the elders have to plead with him . . .

While the ZS is strutting around (priding himself on his victory)
the other elders laugh at the dead man's sons and say, "He'll snatch
your inheritance from you, if you mumble (*mukuvumamvuma*)
when you speak! He will steal it from you, he is your cross-cousin
(*muhizi wenyu*)! . . ."

He brings out the bow and gives it to them, but he does not
then go back to his own clan group. He sits there in the clan group
of his MB, and he sits together with the heir who will inherit the
bow. And when the elders actually give the heir the bow, they give
it to him together with a heifer (*ndama*); and the cross-cousin from
whom they have taken it back, they must give him a young ox
(*nzeku*) as well . . .[65]

"for the bow of inheritance." Naturally, if a man has more than one
full sister, the ZS's may belong to several different clans. It is usually only
those with whom he has been in close contact and cooperation who will
play this dramatized role, but to Gogo it is quite conceivable that ZS's
of several clan affiliations may come with their own elders and add to
the "battle." The verbal tussle consists in the elders of each clan showing
off their superior skill in narrating clan history in great detail. At the
same time they incorporate a story that will "justify" their claim to the
bow of inheritance. Although the outcome is never in doubt (ZS's never
inherit unless there are absolutely no suitable patrilineal heirs), the
elders who put on the best show at big funerals are talked about ad-
miringly, and are said to "have defeated" (*wawasuma*) their opponents.
(In any case, the weapons and other accoutrements which are the subject of the tussle are primarily symbolic and of minor economic importance when compared with the livestock that is already divided up
among the houses of the dead man, whose sons know exactly their inheritance.) At inheritance ceremonies, membership of the patrilineal
descent categories (clans and sub-clans) is crucial, and the mourners sit
in groups by clan affiliation. But there is still no question of corporate interest in property rights, and it is the actual sons, full brothers and
mother's full brothers, etc., who act the roles, while the elders ensure
that old debts are settled and contamination removed.

[65] When the elders hand over the *ipinde* to the heir and admonish him
to live well and uphold his obligations, he sits, together with his FZS, on
the skin of a freshly slaughtered ox, in the cattle byre.

Hence, it may be seen that, although the terms of reference and address are symmetrical between MBS/FZS, the relationship of interdependence between them is asymmetrical in content.[66] This asymmetry is further brought out in the most common institutionalized form of joking between them, which may be summarized briefly as follows:

When a person wants to joke with his *muhizi* who is his MBS, he calls him *"bwabwa"* [67] and says "You are my child" (and therefore not equal to me). But that cross-cousin in turn says, "I am not your child," and he responds by calling his FZS *"bulayi,"* saying, "You are my ZS (*mwihwa*), and I am your MB (*kuku'yo*)." The reason for this is as follows:

A says the wife of my MB (C) is "my wife" (when joking). Therefore her child (B) is my child (*mwana'ngu*) and so I call him *"bwabwa."* B says, on the other hand, when my father (C) dies, I succeed to his position. Therefore my FZ becomes my own Z (*ilumbu lyangu*), so her son is my ZS (*mwihwa wangu*) and I'll call him *bulayi*. Furthermore, when C dies, A goes to B for bridewealth cattle from "the mother's side" (*ng'ombe zokucekulu*). So he "admits" that B is his "MB" (*kuku'ye*). And so on; so they joke together. [See Figure 17.]

Thus, asymmetrical usage in the joking context indicates the asymmetry (though reciprocity) in the relations of ritual interdependence between male cross-cousins. This in turn is entirely inter-linked with the form and norms of the MB/ZS and F/S relationships. Cross-cousin relationships constitute one aspect of

[66] In another context (which belongs to an analysis of Gogo witchcraft) MBS also plays a crucial ritual role in relation to his patrilateral cross-cousin. This is in the case of the death of FZS which results in a particular person being accused of witchcraft. If the accusation was serious enough (in the past) to precipitate an ordeal (*mhugu*) of the accused, the MBS *of the victim* was designated to look after the alleged witch until the ordeal could be arranged. This person was obliged not to leave the accused until the outcome was known, and to go through the (boiling water) ordeal with him. He was known as *wecinamata* ("one who clings, or sticks, on").

[67] See Appendix D for the use of this term in other contexts.

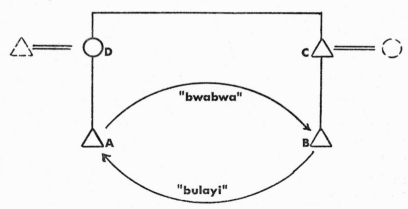

Figure 17. The joking context between male cross-cousins (*wahizi*)

the structural complex linking the role pairs that have been discussed in this chapter.

CONCLUSION

I have tried to analyze the central role pairs in Gogo kinship structure within the context of the terminology system and attitude system that relate to them. The operation of these roles in the broader social and economic spheres has been referred to in earlier chapters. For the structural explanation of these roles, one must isolate two analytic levels. The first is that of the two structural complexes of which these roles are intrinsic and indispensable parts; the second is the integration and articulation of these structural complexes with the broader areas of social organization. Thus, the relationship between MB/ZS has not been viewed simply in opposition to F/S relations, nor solely in terms of a patrilineal descent system, though undoubtedly these two factors are of basic importance. I have tried to examine each relationship as a part of a structural system that includes all of the others. The first step was to approach the sub-system of the mutually dependent roles of WB/ZH; MB/ZS; and FZS/MBS. But this is only one side of the coin. I chose to analyze these role pairs interdependently not because they form the central structural complex (F/S, for example, is omitted), but because this procedure illuminates, by exposing a subsidiary structural complex, the important elements in each of the roles. Once these are established, we can profitably look at the structural relationships between other roles in the Gogo kinship system, in terms of the structural complex suggested by Lévi-Strauss. The predictive value of the relation MB/ZS:B/Z::F/S:H/W has been illustrated by many examples.[68] The proposition is designed for "unilineal descent systems";[69] the Gogo system is characterized by an ideology of patrilineal descent, although lacking a corporate lineage system, and thus the proposition can profitably be applied in the Gogo case.

Denoting intimate, free, and "equal" relations by the sign +, and "unequal," formal, and reserved, or antagonistic ones by −, the data presented in this chapter indicate the configuration as valid for Gogo kinship structure in Figure 18.[70] However undesirable it is to reduce to a set of two single symbols relationships that are complexes of attitudes, rights, and duties as described in this chapter (and Lévi-Strauss specifically states this difficulty himself), the relational structure postulated for these role pairs by Lévi-Strauss is clearly upheld.[71] In the Gogo case the

---

[68] Lévi-Strauss (1958), pp. 50–55 (trans. pp. 42–46); Needham (1962), pp. 33–35; (1963), pp. 146–148; and so on.

[69] Needham (1962), p. 35.

[70] I made clear at the beginning of this chapter that, although I am dealing here with the "effective bonds" of these relationships in this structural complex, in the domestic domain of interpersonal relations, they derive from the jural definition of these roles in the external domain. But apart from this, I have tried to show in previous chapters that these roles are also structurally linked with the broader politico-jural domain by the "statistical facts" of their incidence and importance for cooperation in all spheres of social action.

[71] ". . . it is not enough to study the correlation of attitudes between *father/son* and *uncle/sister's son*. [Cf. Radcliffe-Brown, 1952, Chapter I.] This correlation is only one aspect of a global system containing four types of relationships which are organically linked, namely, *brother/sister, husband/wife, father/son,* and *mother's brother/sister's* son . . ." Lévi-Strauss (1958), p. 51 (trans. p. 42).

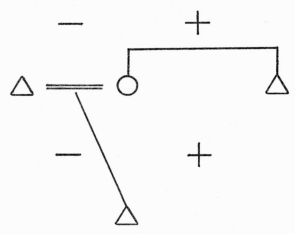

Figure 18. "Conventional attitudes" in Gogo kinship relations

MB/ZS relationship is further illuminated in its functional inter-relationship with WB/ZH and FZS/MBS as a sub-system. The former is contained within the central structural complex; the latter arises directly out of it.

I have also attempted at several points in the preceding analysis to demonstrate the structural importance of affinal relationships (particularly between brothers-in-law) over those of descent (but not filiation), *and* the consequences of this fact. From the data presented in this chapter this may now be more clearly seen on the "levels of reality" embodied in cases and the terminology and attitude systems involved. The incidence of such relationships has been analyzed in previous chapters. The "fluidity" in kinship relations that results from this pattern is an integral aspect of the system described in this chapter and previous ones.

One further note may be added on the significance of kinship categories for corporate groups. This is in the field of collective responsibility in cases of homicide, witchcraft accusation, and other conflict. Agnatic kinsmen (even full brothers) are not held solely responsible for a non-minor's misdeeds in Gogo law. I have already noted that this is so in the case of a man who elopes with another's daughter, sister, or wife to a distant area (Chapter

VI). In the case of homicide or witchcraft accusation also, the culprit alone is personally responsible, although in the case of witchcraft the stigma would attach also to close kin, as it can be inherited.[72] But in the past, through the arbitration of a ritual leader, a homicide, or person accused of witchcraft could be saved from execution by the payment of (a very large) compensation by his kinsmen, to the victim's kin. The responsibility for this lay equally with agnatic and matrilateral kin, who were obliged to provide animals to make up the compensation herd. Here, affines (of the accused) were legally exempted from responsibility, but could contribute if they wished (*kwehewa lyawo du*). Again, the responsibility of kin is defined in terms of an ego-orientated network activated by obligations over livestock, not an exclusive kin group bound by the rule of unilineal descent.

[72] Even the head of the homestead to which the accused belongs (his jural and political head), although responsible for all dealings affecting the jural and political status of the individual, cannot be held responsible for producing the wrongdoer if the victim's kin do not do so themselves.

VIII
Conclusion

This study of Gogo kinship has been concerned primarily with the processes involved in the domestic domain of kinship relations. To this end I have analyzed in some detail the structural interconnections between property rights and exchange, and kinship and affinal relationships. But to establish some of the essential variables on this level of kinship analysis it has also been necessary to examine the broader economic adjustment of Gogo domestic groups within the general ecological conditions in which they find themselves. This in turn has necessitated an analysis of residential groups; the most significant of these are the neighborhood and its clusters of homesteads. I have shown that neighborhoods are characterized by the clustering of homesteads, related by kinship and affinal links, about certain points, while the boundaries between them are indistinct. The structure and social processes involved in these wider units of neighborhood (and the ritual areas within which they lie) may properly be said to belong to the "external" politico-jural domain. The latter presents some problems of definition, which I examine later.

I have had to keep in mind throughout the analysis the general question postulated at the beginning: what kind of structural articulation exists between the domestic and politico-jural domains in Gogo society, given that the structure of the latter is not characterized by a segmentary lineage system of corporate unilineal descent groups? The subsidiary question immediately arises: what are the structural characteristics of the politico-jural domain to which we must relate the processes involved in the domestic domain of kinship relations?

As I noted in Chapter I and elaborated in Chapters III and IV, what we have called the external domain has, in Gogo society, two characteristic aspects: (a) the "structural units" based upon patrilineal descent and (b) the system of bound ritual areas and the fluid composition of neighborhood groups that are contained within them. Both aspects are recognized in the Gogo conceptualization of their own kinship system, (i) in the theory of patrilineal descent and the dispersed groups, or categories, based upon it, and (ii) in the awareness of Gogo themselves of the necessity of activating a network of cognatic and affinal kinship relationships in the different localities through which homestead groups move, within the pattern of residential mobility. The only locally anchored and ritually corporate agnatic descent groups are the shallow lineages with direct control of the ritual concerned with the whole of each ritual area.

The structure of the first aspect (the dispersed descent groups or categories) lies in the Gogo model of kinship relations, based upon their ideas of patrilineal descent. This is essentially an "equilibrium structure." [1] The structure of the second aspect can only be elucidated through a model constructed by the investigator, who must isolate the operation of a number of structural principles through time; this is essentially a "structural process," or set of structural processes.[2] But the fluidity of local groups and

---

[1] I use "structure" here in the sense of a set of interrelations between Gogo verbal concepts: cf. Leach (1954), Chapter V, and "Introductory Note" (p. xii) to the 1964 reprinting; Lévi-Strauss (1958), *passim*, and particularly Chapter XV.

[2] This is consistent with the previous interpretation that "social structure" is essentially a conceptual abstraction from observed events, either by the people themselves or by the external investigator. Hence, the "structure" of kinship relations in Gogo local groups can only be established through the analysis of the "statistical" facts of kinship through time: cf. Fortes (1949b); Leach (1954) and (1961a). That there is no inherent contradiction between structural analysis and the inclusion of the "time dimension" has been demonstrated by several writers in different contexts: for example, Nadel (1957), Chapter VI, particularly pp. 127–134.

the network of kinship relationships involved in them is also built into and expressed in Gogo ideas about those relationships that provide the most important structural bonds. I have thus tried to show in this study that the point of articulation between the domestic and external domains can be elucidated only by an analysis of kinship on these different levels. The theory of descent provides the jural definition of the crucial relationships involved (those analyzed in detail in Chapter VII). Further, the processes underlying neighborhood organization are closely interrelated with the processes underlying the development of domestic groups and their relation to the broader social and economic environment. The analysis of kinship relations on several levels becomes necessary before suitable structural models may be established.

In this study, the emphasis has been laid upon the operation of a network of kinship and affinal relationships in the context of locality and cooperation. The operation of the kinship system, in terms of the basic facts of close residence and cooperation in the economic, political, and ritual spheres, is limited directly by spatial and temporal considerations. Through the system of dispersed descent groups the potentiality of kinship relationships is extended over the whole of the Gogo area and all of its local groups. But it is through an analysis of the mutually dependent processes involved in domestic groups and localities that I have been able to establish the point of structural articulation I have been seeking. I conclude in this chapter by highlighting very briefly the significant points which have arisen at each stage of the preceding analysis, in an attempt to integrate in a more coherent form the models I have tried to establish of structure and process in Gogo kinship relations.

KINSHIP AND PROPERTY RELATIONS

I have indicated that some of the crucial variables in interpersonal, cognatic kinship relationships may be isolated by viewing them as relationships concerned with rights and obligations in the most important form of property.[3] In Gogo society this property is primarily livestock, although other forms of property (such as homesteads and food crops) also play a significant, if subsidiary, part. The most important negative point to be made is that there is no sustained attachment to any type of land, arable or grazing, by kin groups or individual persons, other than that of current usufruct of fields and two years of subsequent fallow. Old homestead sites constitute a rather special category in this connection, and rights in them may be inherited, but this is primarily because of their manure content and the fact that very often the immediate ascendants of the present senior living generation lie buried in them. They are exceptional, not as a category of land, but by their association with a recently dissolved domestic group, or the previous living site of an existing one, with all its bound and exclusive characteristics of livestock ownership, legal and political unity, and exclusive ritual status in the field of human and livestock fertility and health. This is so in spite of the internal structure and differentiation of these units, whose significance was fully explored in Chapters IV and V.

Thus, through the fact that property relations in Gogo are primarily concerned with rights in livestock (which are easily divisible and differentiated in each generation), the attachment of large-depth patrilineal descent groups to the "most valued type of productive property" becomes irrelevant. The more general ecological conditions of periodic drought and famine ensure a residential mobility of herd-holding groups (domestic/home-

---

[3] I do not mean, of course, that this is the only way in which they may be viewed, or that kinship relationships may be *reduced* to other kinds of relationships. Kinship relationships cannot be analyzed as constituting a system complementary and comparable to systems of other types of relationships, such as "political," "economic," or "religious." Rather, in some societies, kinship is the idiom in which all such relationships are expressed. All important structural relations are thought of as kinship relations; kinship provides the idiom through which the persons involved "order their experience" (cf. Beattie, 1959).

stead groups) and consequently the spatial dispersion and eventual atrophy of "active" agnatic ties. However, such homestead groups are not economically independent, and therefore must establish ties of economic (and ritual) cooperation with other groups of the same order in the areas into which they move. This is a condition of survival and results in the importance and maintenance of affinal and cognatic ties within each, and between generations, bolstered by a highly localized marriage pattern which ensures the close residence of affines, and cognatic kin in subsequent generations, at least until ecological or other conditions enforce a dispersal of homestead groups yet again. The cohesion of local groups is expressed in an overlapping network of kinship and affinal ties, the incidence and characteristics of which have been fully examined in preceding chapters.

It is worthwhile here to look briefly at what is meant by "cohesion" in this context. It is a mere metaphysical assumption to state that "cohesion" in local or kinship groups (or any other kind of group, for that matter) is a kind of necessity, without stating the basis for such cohesion. Why should Gogo homestead groups not move freely and entirely independently through the countryside, exchanging women with each other but not bothering to cluster into local groups with particular kinds of kinship and affinal ties which provide the bases for cooperation?[4] Some of the factors which may be indicated in answer to such a question have been brought out in this study. They may be summarized as follows:

a) Subsistence is basically agricultural in Ugogo and the labor required to produce sufficient crops in each year cannot be provided by single domestic groups.

[4] I do not seriously propose this question for answer when we are primarily concerned with functional interdependence between structural complexes. However, I have phrased a question in this way simply to show that to make the teleological assumption that the end of all functional relations is "social cohesion" is merely to beg the main issue. I use it here to highlight what I think are some of the basic factors influencing Gogo social structure.

b) Given the fact of necessary cooperation between such (independently) mobile units, the firmest ties are established through the exchange of livestock for women, with the creation of new conjugal units and complexes of affinal relationships, which in the next generation become close cognatic ones.

c) The agnatic basis of the cattle-holding group (the patri-central domestic group) is necessarily small in order to ensure its independent mobility. Hence, bridewealth transactions (except sometimes in the case of a second marriage by a rich man, and not always even then) cannot be completed by a single cattle-holding unit. I have shown that the average bridewealth herd is larger than the average homestead herd, and rights in the latter are even further sub-divided by the house-property system. The cooperation of both agnatic and matrilateral kin is necessary for the completion of this major transaction.

d) The whole complex of kinship relationships involved in such transactions is further underlined by a fundamental set of ritual interdependences in a religious system that minimizes the role of lineal ancestors and maximizes the role of bilateral ancestors and even affinal "spirits of the dead." It has not been possible to treat this aspect fully in the present work; the religion of the Gogo and its relation to witchcraft and sorcery beliefs will be analyzed elsewhere. But the ritual content of many of the crucial roles has been referred to, particularly in the context of funerals and inheritance ceremonies.[5] This is the kind of progression of factors that gives body and content to the "cohesion" engendered by Gogo kinship relations.

The analysis of kinship relations mainly in terms of property rights and obligations is not new.[6] I have already noted that such an analysis must be handled with caution lest the investigator reduce kinship relations to property relations. The point that must be kept in mind, however, is that, within a given type of

[5] For example, see Chapter VII.
[6] Cf. Gulliver (1955); Goody (1959) and (1958); Gray and Gulliver, (1964).

ecological situation, the different *kinds* of property that are "economically" important constitute a crucial variable in the operation of kinship relations, although it is not always the only or necessarily the most important variable. This "economic" importance applies not only to the property which is most "valuable" in terms of subsistence, but also to those kinds of properties that may be most easily accumulated and are valued for their role in exchange transactions. But even from a subsistence point of view, livestock are important, particularly at the "crisis points" of the economic cycle. For I have indicated that, during the periodic (usually localized) famines, livestock play a central subsistence role (a) in being exchanged for grain crops obtained from more fortunate areas and (b) in being the means by which new relationships are created, or existing ones "activated," in the new neighborhoods to which homestead groups move.

It is this type of factor that led me to examine some of the connections between ecological conditions, economic adjustment, and kinship structure, through the linking role of property relations.[7] In Ugogo, rights in livestock are rapidly differentiated within each generation and within the basic stock-holding group, the domestic group. Although the father and head of the domestic group theoretically has full control over its property resources until his death, his powers are seriously curtailed with the birth of children, particularly sons, in the house of his wife or each of his wives. As the domestic cycle proceeds, and the

---

[7] In a recent symposium of papers (Gray and Gulliver, 1964) on the role of property in the domestic domain of kinship relations ("family structure"), Gray states (p. 5): "Natural resources are major points of ecological contact between human communities and their physical environment, and in tribal societies the ecological processes of exploitation occur mainly in a family milieu. The labor and skills necessary for exploiting the natural resources are funneled through the family in actual application, while the goods consumed are distributed through family channels . . . The family is a principal locus of ecological processes." Although this involves an extended use of the term "ecological," the interconnection Gray establishes, and which I have tried to indicate in the preceding analysis, is clear.

sons (and their houses) mature, the control of the husband/ father is progressively diminished. When the sons are mature, they may reject entirely the control of their father and move away as a set of full brothers with their mother, or as individuals, to set up their own homesteads. For it is only in the status of homestead head that a man reaches full maturity in the jural and political domain, and thus in respect of control over property. However, even if sons have their own homesteads, they have not reached full ritual maturity if their father is still alive. After his death, the necessity of contacting the spirits of the dead through his grave-stone has the effect for some time of keeping sets of half brothers residentially together, usually in adjacent homesteads, although they now have only the most tenuous common interest in prop-erty transactions. But when their own homesteads mature, even this impediment against distant residential separation becomes weak; and, in fact, the principal heir, the eldest son of the first house, seldom maintains his ritual precedence over his junior (usually younger) half siblings.[8]

This rapid differentiation of property rights in each generation has the effect of permitting the residential mobility of the new domestic units, independently of their close agnates.[9] The gap left by the necessity (economic, political, and ritual) of cooperation with wider groups of kin than those contained within the domestic group, is filled by matrilateral and other cognatic kin and affines. To demonstrate this, I analyzed in some detail the fundamental role of matrilateral kin (particularly "mother's brothers") in the

[8] For example, see Chapters V and VII.

[9] In the volume already cited (Gray and Gulliver, 1964), Gray com-ments (p. 28): ". . . against the tendency for sets of full brothers in a polygynous family to form separate lineages there is a countervailing tendency to preserve the genealogical integrity of developing patrilineages, and this would require that the distinction between half brothers of the same father be minimized or ignored. Which of these tendencies prevails in any given society is probably determined mainly by the system of property rights."

differentiation of houses within the patricentral domestic group.[10] Linked with this in Ugogo is a structural complex of interdependent cognatic and affinal roles whose operation is critical in certain major contexts, such as inheritance, marriage and circumcision ceremonies, and the property transactions of bridewealth.

In Chapter I, I referred to some of the postulated sociological connections between economic and kinship systems. Without subscribing in any way to a theory of "economic determinism," I have tried to show a close structural interdependence in the processes involved in Gogo kinship relations with economic processes and underlying ecological factors, through the mediation of the central property relationships involved. In fact, far from assigning the role of "prime mover" or determinant to any one factor, I have tried rather to indicate the interrelations among various factors, given the *choices* available in such spheres as residence and economic cooperation. These choices are limited by the ecological conditions in which Gogo society operates. I noted at the beginning of this chapter that this necessitated an examination of structural units broader than the domestic group, and an approach to the problem of the structural articulation between the domestic and politico-jural domains of kinship.[11] I

[10] Fortes in his analysis of Tallensi kinship (1949a) and in later work emphasizes the role of matrilateral ties as the "individuating factor" in lineage relationships, through the principle of complementary filiation. Contrasting lineage and other kinship ties among the Tallensi (1949a), pp. 341–342, Fortes characterizes relationships of patrilineal descent as the "chief centripetal force" and matrilateral ties as the "chief centrifugal force" in Tallensi society. Among the Tallensi the former principle dominates in the localized and corporate segmentary lineage system; among the Gogo it is reduced to a force commensurate with those exerted by other types of kinship and affinal relationships, at least on the level of the everyday, "statistical" facts of kinship.

[11] In his introduction to the study already cited (Gray and Gulliver, 1964), Gray notes that the papers presented neglect "one of the major theoretical problems" posed by this type of analysis, and one that was

turn now to a summary of the points relevant to this problem
which arise from the Gogo material.

STRUCTURE, PROCESS, AND THE LOCALITY FACTOR

Clearly, there is a problem of definition concerning the distinction between the domestic and politico-jural domains. I have
suggested that, in Gogo society, the Gogo theory of descent and
the clan system, as well as the structure of local (neighborhood)
groups belong properly to the latter. It could be argued that, because relationships within such local units are based upon
cognatic interpersonal kin ties, these belong properly to the
domestic domain. I suggest that there is, in fact, a conceptual
overlap here, and that the type of structure of Gogo local groups
which I have postulated is a "structural bridge" between domestic
kinship relations proper, and the broader political and legal
spheres.

I have stressed the fact that the role of homestead head is the
critical one in the politico-jural domain, as well as in the domestic domain. Thus, "inter-homestead" relations may, in certain
contexts, be considered as political relations. Yet such groups
are also linked by cognatic, interpersonal kinship and affinal ties.
The pivotal role is that of homestead head. In this respect, the
role of homestead head in Gogo society resembles that of the
village headman in some of the centralized political systems of
Central African peoples, which Gluckman has called "inter-
calary" and Richards "intermediate."

I have suggested in this study that the conceptual tool that
clears up the problem of "overlap" in the different domains of
kinship in Ugogo (that is, the problem of the structural articulation of the two spheres) is that of "process analysis": the introduction of the time factor into the analysis of structural units
more comprehensive than, but including, domestic groups. For I

---

dealt with in Goody (1958); that is, "the relation between the family
group and society at large, or, as Fortes phrases it, the 'domestic domain'
and the 'politico-jural domain.' "

have tried to show that the structure of domestic (homestead) groups and that of local (neighborhood) units are to be viewed as partially interdependent developmental processes, within the general pattern of the extant economic processes and ecological conditions of Gogo society.[12] In both cases we have to consider what might be called "cyclical processes" or "recurrent processes," rather than "directional processes" or those of "structural change."[13] However, from the material presented on Gogo kinship structure, a tenuous link may be established between the two kinds of process. This link lies in the fact that, because of changes in the politico-jural domain and economic conditions, the inherent process of fission in domestic groups in Ugogo may have been accelerated since colonial penetration in the area and the imposition of a broader political structure. The changes lie in such facts as greater security and thus greater survival potential for smaller homestead groups, slightly increased variety of avenues to wealth in livestock for younger men, and the related diminution of the ritual monopoly held by the father/homestead head over his sons and other dependents in the sphere of human and livestock health and fertility. It may thus be said that the recurrent process of domestic group fission is related to the directional process of a tendency toward earlier fission and toward the crea-

[12] It has been recognized for many societies without segmentary lineage systems that the structure of groups wider than domestic groups cannot be explained simply in terms of a formal description of the relation between certain kinds of descent groups and territorial units, or political structure. Hence these structures must be described as sets of processes, which may constitute cyclical phases or not: for example, Fortes (1949b); Turner (1957); Harris, G. (1962); Harris and Harris (1964); Harries-Jones and Chiwale (1963); Colson (1962), Ch. VI.

[13] Cf. Vogt (1960), pp. 21–22 *et passim;* Nadel (1957), Chapter VI. Vogt's analysis is directed mainly at "cultural processes," but the logic of his argument may be applied with equal force to "social processes." The problem of the time-scales involved in the different levels of "process analysis" has been considered by Lévi-Strauss (1958), pp. 318–319; trans. (1964), pp. 289–290; and Nadel (1957), pp. 134–135 *et passim:* cyclical processes concern "micro-time" and directional processes concern "macro-time" scales.

tion of smaller domestic groups. However, this contention cannot be shown to be statistically valid;[14] it relies primarily upon
the testimony of older men[15] and the impressions of early travelers
in Ugogo,[16] as to the generally greater size and stability of homestead groups in pre-colonial times.

But we are concerned here primarily with "micro-time" and
"micro-space," and the recurrent processes described for the
structure of homestead and neighborhood groups in Ugogo. The
central issue is that it is only through the analysis of such
mutually dependent processes that the structural "bridge" may be
established for the articulation of the domestic domain with the
broader politico-jural domain of kinship relations.

One further theoretical point to which the material presented
here has relevance is that of the nature of descent and affinal
relationships

DESCENT AND AFFINAL RELATIONSHIPS

In the preceding analysis I have frequently stressed the structural importance of affinal relationships in the Gogo kinship
system, as against those of descent. One of the central factors
promoting the economic and ritual cooperation of persons involved in a fluctuating set of cognatic and affinal relationships is
spatial propinquity, while spatial separation tends to reduce the
maintenance of agnatic descent links. This occurs within the
general pattern of an overall residential mobility of domestic
groups over fairly lengthy periods. The factor of descent does not
produce cooperating (or corporate) groups beyond the "sons of
one man." But the affinal and resulting cognatic relationships,
set up in each generation and between proximate generations, do
provide strong localized bonds upon which cooperation in all
spheres, including the economic and ritual, is based. The network
of kin relationships involved in such cooperation is in each case

[14] Cf. Nadel (1957), pp. 143–144.
[15] For example, see in the case of Cedego and Lubeleje, Appendix E.
[16] E.g. Southon (1881); Stanley (1890); Speke (1963).

an ego-oriented one. It does not provide the basis for groups with corporate rights in property. But the individual persons involved have mutual rights and obligations in each other's property which must be fulfilled as a condition of the proper functioning of the various roles through which they are related to each other. The broadest corporate property-holding group is the patricentral domestic group, progressively subdivided into its constituent matricentral house groups. Conventional attitudes and affective ties indicate the actor's conscious, "homemade" model of the relevant kin categories (cf. Lévi-Strauss, 1958, p. 309; trans. p. 282; Ward, 1965, 1966).

Hence, although patrilineal descent is a basic element in Gogo kinship relations and theory, the emphasis in the Gogo system lies more upon relationships derived from successive steps of filiation (always "bilateral")[17] and affinity. I have shown that Gogo marriages are comparatively stable. The affinal relationships which center on these strong conjugal bonds are considered essential to the continuing cooperation of cognatic kin in the next generation, and hence the relationships between proximate generations. Nevertheless, although relationships of filiation ideally derive from marriage, the emphasis is not solely on the conjugal bond but on the legal status of the children, which unites the different categories of kin in each case. Paternity is usually established by the fact that a man is a woman's legal husband at the time that the children are born, and the complex of affinal relationships should be, and is normally, based upon established marital bonds. But, in the case of an unmarried girl giving birth to a child, the child's *genitor* may establish his rights as *pater* by the payment of the fine for fornication and the payment for the "up-bringing" of the child. In this case, although there is no conjugal bond, quasi-affinal relationships are set up between the child's *pater* and its mother's kin. Affinal terms of address come into use, and the child's "mother's brothers" should cooperate with its father at all stages of its upbringing: at circumcision,

[17] Cf. Fortes (1953), (1959), (1963).

marriage, and in the livestock transactions involved. Thus, the affinal relationships, and in the next generation the cognatic kin relationships, are created, not by the payment of bridewealth and the creation of a conjugal bond, but by the establishing of a legal claim to a child's paternity.[18] However, this is an exceptional case and does not reduce the emphasis Gogo place upon the stability of marriage and its significance in maintaining the most important affinal relationships created anew in each generation.

We may give, then, the factors of filiation and affinity important and equal weight in the operation of the Gogo kinship system, although they may not in *all* cases be based upon a marital bond. Relationships of descent, on the other hand, are operationally important only at a "shallow" level commensurate with the other two. After this level, descent relationships constitute what is primarily only a *part* of the Gogo theory of descent, and provide the basis for the potential extension of certain types of kin relationships to spatially and socially remote sectors of Gogo society, from any given point. Such an interpretation has involved an analysis of both the "statistical facts" of Gogo kinship and Gogo concepts of kinship relations in general. The analysis has been necessarily restricted to certain aspects of the Gogo kinship system, but an attempt has been made to sketch in the main lines. The Gogo kinship system is an aspect of a highly fluid, mobile, and egalitarian society. I have tried to put into perspective in an operational context what could in other ways be viewed as a considerably elaborate theory of patrilineal descent.

[18] Cf. Fortes (1959), p. 194.

Appendix A

Provisional List of Gogo Clans, with Areas and Other Associations Where Known

Mbeyu[1] (clan)	Ndawililo (area of origin)	Mulongo (sub-clan name)	Muzilo (avoidance)	Mulango[2] (nghungugo: maximal lineage)	Yisi (ritual area)	Watani (joking partners)	Cilahilo (clan oath)
Aca	—	—	—	—	Itiso	—	—
Balasalo (Ng'omvia)	Ng'omvia	Munyambwa	Funo	Mayamaya	Mayamaya (Maseya)	—	—
Bahago	—	Munyambwa	Ndunghu	Solowu	Solowu (Hombolo) (Itiso)	—	—
Bamuko	Mbugwe (Ng'omvia)	Munyakongo	Msomha	Hombolo	Hombolo	—	—
Bena (Cimbilizi) (Nyamululu)	Sagala	Semwali	—	Solowu	Solowu	—	—
Bezato (Ng'omvia)	Bulunji	Munyatoma	Wufuli	Selije	Selije (Canene)	Nyalindi	Selije
Bohola	—	—	—	Nghogwa	Nghogwa (Mwiticila)	—	—
Bulunje	Fyomi	Munyambeyu	—	—	Itiso	—	—
Bulunje	—	Munyambwa	Ndunghu	—	—	—	—
Catila	Kamba	—	—	Miganga	Miganga	—	—
Cimbu	Kimbu	—	—	—	—	—	—
Cinya	—	Munyagwila	—	—	—	—	—
Cungu	—	—	—	—	—	—	—

309

Appendix A (*continued*)

Mbeyu[1] (clan)	Ndawililo (area of origin)	Mulongo (sub-clan name)	Muzilo (avoidance)	Mulango[2] (nghungugo: maximal lineage)	Yisi (ritual area)	Watani (joking partners)	Cilahilo (clan oath)
Deje	Hehe	Cisi Munyiwe	Muhanga Cituwacamhene	Isitu Isitu (Mutumba) (Ipelemehe)	Cilungulu Mutumba	— —	Isitu (hill) —
Dimangholo	Masai (Kisongo)	—	—	—	Ipelemehe	—	—
Donghwe	—	Nyanzaga	Mbofu	Bwibwi	Ilazo (Dodoma)	Pulu	Isima lyebwibwi
Gwazo	Ng'omvia	Nyapumbuye	—	Zangha	Zangha	Ng'omvia (WanyaWuselya)	—
Gonanze	—	Munyambwa	Mbala	Musamalo	Musamalo	—	—
Gugumizi	Hehe	Mulombo	—	Mulowa	Mulowa	—	—
Hanila	—	—	—	—	Ng'anda	—	—
Hehe	Hehe	Mufyomi Lukanzi Nyigahi Kwama Mufwamba	Muhanga Mbofu — — Mulungulungu	Cididimo Mafwemela Igoji Mutela Mulimu	Cididimo Mafwemela Igoji Mutela Mulimu	— — — —	No Mufyomi'ne — — — —
(Wategete Muluguto) Hiru	Nyaturu	Munyanghali Munyanghali	Mbofu Mbofu	Nzinje Nondwa	Nzinje Nondwa	Nyomi —	—
Ibago	Ng'omvia	Munyambwa	Ndunghu	Musanga	Musanga	Pulu (WanyaMadako)	—

Icinga	—	Munyitongo	Ndunghu	Naye	Naye (Hombolo)	Mhalala	—
Icinga (Waciwaye)	—	Ng'anzagala / Temaluji	Mbofu / Wutumbu	Miganga Goligoli	Miganga Goligoli (Ludi)		—
Idoga	Itumba	—	Mbala	—	—		—
Igongo	Hehe	Munyakongo	Ciswagumbi	Isece	Isece	Nyagatwa / Igongo-WanyIhumwa	Kwidole (citunda)
Igongo	Hehe	Munyanduli / Muzigula	Mbala / Nyungumhya	Isece / Nghwandali	Isece / Nghwandali	Itumba (Wanyacunyu)	—
Igoso	Itumba	Muzigula	Nyungu yono yikali nazigula	Ilanji	Ilanji	Igongo (WanyIsece)	—
Iheru	Hehe	Muzigula	Nyungu yono yikali nazigula	Ihumwa	Ihumwa		—
Ijidu	Hehe	—	Mbala	Cunyu	Cunyu (East of Ilindi)		—
Ikando	Hehe	Ciwaye(m)[3] / Nyambuce(f)	Finga yanhete-tele imonga (Citumba)	Cahwa	Cahwa		Citunda ca Nguji
Ilanji	Ilanji	Mulombo / Munyagwila	Nhongolo	Makang'wa / Mwiticila	Makang'wa / Mwiticila		—
Ilewela	—	Munyagwila / Munyambwa / Sembuce(m) / Inambuce(f)	Nhongolo / Ndunghu	Cifukulo / Wafucu / Nghong'onha	Cifukulo / Nghong'onha		—
Inyelu	Hehe	Seng'unda(m) / Inang'unda(f)	—	Idaho	Idaho		—

Appendix A (*continued*)

Mbeyu[1] (clan)	Ndawililo (area of origin)	Mulongo (sub-clan name)	Muzilo (avoidance)	Mulango[2] (nghungugo: maximal lineage)	Yisi (ritual area)	Watani (joking partners)	Cilahilo (clan oath)
Inzelu	Itumba	Munyambwa	Nomvi	Igandu	Igandu (Cikombo)	—	Igandu (cigongo)
Itega	—	Ciwaye	Cilama	Nghungu	Nghungu	—	Itega (itunda)
Itiliko	Hehe	Ciwaye	Muhanga	Nzinje	Nzinje	—	—
		Muzigula	Nyungumhya	Lukole	Lukole	—	—
		Munyanghali	Itoga lyang'ombe	Cikola	Cikola (Mhamvwa)	—	—
		Munyanghali	Itoga lyang'ombe	Ngalamilo	Ngalamilo	—	—
Itumba	Kaguru	Senyhina(m)	Muhanga	Iganhu	Iganhu (Cunyu)	—	Cunyu (itunda)
		Inanhyina(f)					
		Inanhyina(f)	Cisunha cadede	Ihogolo	Ihogolo	—	—
		Ncanda	Mbofu	Cunyu	Cunyu	—	Cunyu (itunda)
		Nyagatwa	Cituwa camhene nhitu	Cunyu	Cunyu	—	—
		Munongwa	Mhene nhitu	Cunyu	Cunyu	—	—
		Munyanghali	Mbala	Nghumbi	Nghumbi	—	—
		Munyanghali	Mbala	Ilazo	Ilazo	—	—
		Ihelu	—	Ihogolo	Ihologo	—	—
		Sewando(m)	Mbala	Cunyu	Cunyu	Igongo (Munyakongo Wanyisece)	Cunyu
		Inawando(f)					

Itumba	Sagara	Nyacunyu Ncanda Sembuce(m) Inambuce(f) Senyagwa(m) Inasenyagwa(f) Fyomi Fyomi Nyasenga	Nghwale — — Mbofu Mbala Mbala Muhanga	Igowe Musalato — Cunyu Cisambo Nghong'onha Ilonga	Igowe Musalato — Cunyu Cisambo Nghong'onha Ilonga (Cilosa)	—	—
Itumba	Hehe	Semwali(m) Inamwali(f)	Mbofu (mhene)	Nzuci	Nzuci (Cunyu)	—	—
Izizimiza	—	Munyacituli	Fumbu Iyang'ombe	Ng'anda	Ng'anda	—	—
Jibalo	—	Munyacituli	Fumbu Iyang'ombe	Mulece Nondwa	Mulece Nondwa	—	—
Koyisata	Ng'omvia	Munyambwa	Ndunghu	Ikoya	Ikoya	—	—
Kamba	Kamba	Munyatoma	Wufuli	—	—	—	—
Kami (Walekacende)	Hehe	Oncela	—	—	—	—	—
	Bena	Ciwaye	Finga yanhetele imonga	Ihezela	Ihezela	—	—
Limba	—	Muhanga	Muhanga	Ibeleje	Ibeleje (Mhavwa)	—	Ibeleje (citunda)
Limilanhemo	—	Nyanzuga Munyambwa Munyanghali	— — Mbala	—	—	Nyalindi	—
Manghala	(Earliest Gogo inhabitants)	Munyambeyu	—	—	—	—	Iguluwi (Itunda lyeGuluwi, in Mbulu country)

Appendix A (*continued*)

Mbeyu[1] (clan)	Ndawililo (area of origin)	Mulongo (sub-clan name)	Muzilo (avoidance)	Mulango[2] (nghungugo): maximal lineage	Yisi (ritual area)	Watani (joking partners)	Cilahilo (clan oath)
Menda		Muzigula	Sunhamahenje (cidunghu)	Wunyagwira	Wunyangwira	Nyalindi	Iguluwi
Mhalala (Gwazo)	Ng'omvia	—	Muhanga	Ibihwa	Ibihwa	Nyalindi	Iguluwi
		Ihimbila	—	Ipala	—	Pulu	—
		Mufyomi	Nzoka	Mahoma	Ipala	Ibago	—
		Munyalivwa	—	Ipala	Mahoma	—	—
		Munyanzoka	Nzoka	Mahoma	Ipala	—	—
Mhanga	Hehe	Munyanghali	Nomvi	Idodoma	Idodoma	—	Itunda lyemaje
		Muwemba	Cima camhene	Ipagala	Ipagala	—	Itunda lyemaje
Mima	Hehe	Ciwaye	Ciswagumbi	Mima	Mima	—	—
		Munyakongo	Ndunghu	Ibeleje	Ibeleje	—	—
Nangwalo	Ngulu (Nguu)	Isongo	Nzanagwayo (fudi)	Itiso	Itiso	—	—
		Munyanzoka	—	Itiso	Itiso	—	—
Ngalamilo	Taturu	Yegongo		Cigongwe	Cigongwe	—	Benamapinde (citunda)
Nghuta	—	—		Bweseti	Bweseti	—	—
Ng'omvia	Zigula (Bulunje)	Munyangwira	Fumbu (yang'ombe yoyose)	Wuselya	Wuselya	—	Cibuga (citunda)
(Wahunduka-simba)		Gwazo	—	Cihanga	Cihanga (Mahoma)	Gwazo, Wanya-Cihanga, Ng'omvia, Wanya-Wuselya	—

Clan	Group						
Nunga	Itiliko (Hehe)	Munyanzoka Muhenga	—	Mahoma Wota	Zangha Wota	—	—
Nyacipegulu Nyacituli	— —	Munyanzoka Munyatoma	—	Cipondwa Nzuguni Nzinje	Cipondwa Nzuguni Nzinje	—	—
Nyadumalo	—	—	Muhanga Cise Cisunha (cidunghu)	— Nzuhe Muhalala Cikombo	— Nzuhe Muhalala Cikombo	Igongo (Wamunya- kongo)	—
Nyaganza	—	—	—	Sagala Ibwijili Matanjizi Loje	Sagala Ibwijili Matanjizi Loje	—	—
Nyagatwa	Hehe	Sembuce	Mbofu Mbofu	Wanyika Luatu	Wunyika Luatu	—	—
Nyagundu	Nyamwezi	Sembuce Munyambwa Munyanduli Muwemba (Munyanghali) Himbalukondo Munyambwa	Mbofu Cise	Mugunduko	Mugunduko	—	Mhumbwa (itunda)
Nyalindi	Kimbu Sandawi	Munyambwa Munyatoma — Munyilanga Munyambwa	Cise Cise Cise Ibangho lyanjili; kuhanga ikumbi	Isanza Nghongho Lindi	Isanza Nghongho Lindi (Fwadi)	Manghala Bezato	Nghonghobila (itunda)

Appendix A *(continued)*

Mbeyu[1] (clan)	Ndawililo (area of origin)	Mulongo (sub-clan name)	Muzilo (avoidance)	Mulango[2] (nghungugo: maximal lineage)	Yisi (ritual area)	Watani (joking partners)	Cilahilo (clan oath)
Nyambwa	Hehe	Munyatoma (Wanghalunga)	Mbala	Cipanga	Cipanga	—	—
		Munyatoma	Mbala	Misuwi	Misuwi	—	—
		Munyatoma	Mbala	Caali	Caali	—	—
		Munyatoma	Mbala	Igongo	Igongo	—	—
		Munyatoma	Mbala	Ikasi	Ikasi	—	—
Nyamuzula	Hehe	Munyambwa (Wota Semwali)	Mbala	Mvumi	Mvumi	—	—
Nyang'anga	Kimbu	Munyanguluwe	Mbala	Wunyangwila	Wunyangwila	—	—
		Munyanguluwe	Mbala	Muhalala	Muhalala	—	—
Nyanghali	Kimbu	Munyilanga	Fumbu	Nghongho	Nghongho	—	—
Nyanghwalo	Nyaturu	Munyambwa	Fumbu	Bahi	Ibahi	—	—
		Munyambwa	Fumbu	Citalalo	Citalalo	—	—
		Munyambwa	Fumbu	Ng'anda	Ng'anda	—	—
Nyang'onje	Ngulu (Ng'omvia)	Muzigula	Mbala	Mahamha	Mahamha (Musanga Cilonwa)	—	—
Nyangwe	Hehe	Munyambwa	Nomvi	Huzi	Huzi	—	—
Nyanzaga	Fyomi	Munyanzoka	Nzoka	Bwibwi	Bwibwi (Idodoma)	—	—
Nyomi	Sandawi	—	—	Goima (Nzinje)	Goima	Hiru	—
Nzeyago	—	—	—	—	Musanga?	—	—
Pomo	—	—	—	Cahwa	Cahwa?	—	—

Pulu		Munyambwa	Ndunghu	Madako	Nhyemianga	Ibago (Wanya-Musanga)	Kwimbuli nghasuka (citunda)
	Sukuma Konongo	Munyambwa	Ndunghu	Igoji	Igoji	Ibago	Kwimbuli nghasuka
		Munyambwa	Ndunghu	Ikogolo	Ikogolo	Ibago	Kwimbuli nghasuka
		Munyambwa	Ndunghu	Citelela	Citelela	Mhalala Wahimbila (WanyIpala)	—
		Munyambwa	Ndunghu	Ciale	Ciale	Donghwe (WanyIlazo)	—
		Munyambwa	Ndunghu	Madako	Makutupora	—	—
		Munyambwa	Ndunghu	Mucemwa	Mucemwa	—	—
Sagala	Sagara	Sembuce	—	Gulwe	Gulwe	—	—
		Mujegwa	—	Muyowe	Muyowe	—	—
		Semwali (Wacilama)	Cilama (Nzimba mbaha)	Sagala	Sagala (Kongwa)	—	—
Sambala	Hehe Bulunje	Munyambwa	Sunha	Migoli	Migoli	—	—
		—	—	Mukondahi	Mukondahi (Hombolo)	—	—
Sangu	Sangu	—	—	Mudaburo	Mudaburo	—	—
Sembegu	Itiliko	—	—	Ludi	Ludi	—	—
Sukuma	Itusi	Fulamubitu	Nomvi	Iguluwi	(Cinyambwa)	—	Iguluwi
Suluho	Ng'omvia	Munyanghali	—	Wuselya	Wuselya	—	—
Suwako	Ng'omvia	Muzigula	Ndigwa zono zasigala	Mukoye	Mukoye (Hombolo)	—	—
Sigani	Hehe	Nyazuni	—	Wusawanga	Wusawanga	—	Idugala (citunda)
		Nyazuni	—	Cidamala	Cidamala	—	—
		Nyazuni	—	Huzi	Huzi	—	—

Appendix A (*continued*)

Mbeyu[1] (clan)	Ndawililo (area of origin)	Mulongo (sub-clan name)	Muzilo (avoidance)	Mulango[2] (nghungugo: maximal lineage)	Yisi (ritual area)	Watani (joking partners)	Cilahilo (clan oath)
Tazilo	Hehe	Munyanghali Munyanghali	Nomvi Mangu (ndeje yamatunda)	Manhumbulu Mukonze	Manhumbulu Mukonze (Manhumbulu)	— —	— —
(Ijidu) Temaluji	Icinga	Mulombo Ciwaye	— Wutumbu	Makang'wa Goligoli	Makang'wa Goligoli (Ludi)	— —	— —
Temikwila	— — Taturu (Baradiga)	Munyanghali Munyambwa Munyatoma	Mbala Mbofu Mbofu	— — Mhang'we	— — Mhang'we	— — —	— — —
Tiganda	—	—	—	Cigongwe Ilumbu	Cigongwe Ilumbu	—	—
Taturu	Taturu	Nyang'ombe	—	—	Mulimu	—	—
Tejete	Hehe	Mufwamba	Mulungulungu	Membe (Hombolo)	Membe	—	—
Zaganza	Ng'omvia	Munyang'wira	Nhongolo			—	—
Zigula	Nyaturu	Nyiguluwi	Mhene yembala	Iguluwi	—	—	Iguluwi'?

[1] Clan names are recorded under the first consonant or vowel of the root. The prefixes *mu-* (sing.) and *wa-* (plural) are omitted. In certain cases, when the stem commences in a vowel, the addition of the prefix in Gogo usage might alter the vowel. Thus, the Igoso would become Wegoso in the plural, and Mwigoso in the singular.

[2] All the *mulango* names recorded would be prefixed in Gogo usage by *Wanya-* ("the owners of"): thus Nghogwa would be Wanyanghogwa. This has been omitted for brevity; thus most *mulango* names are reduced to the name of the ritual area.

[3] In these cases of *mulongo* names, (m) denotes that used by men; (f) denotes that used by women. In all *mulongo* names beginning with Se- and Ina-, the former is used by men (*se-*, archaic form of "father,") and the latter by women (*ina-*, "mother of").

Appendix B
Shortened Version of the
History of the Pulu Clan
(See Figures 2 and 3, Chapter III)

Maguhe, the founder of the Pulu clan, came from Usukuma. He fled from there because he became involved in serious conflict.[1] There in Sukuma he had married a woman, Goli, who bore him a son, Mutalijembe, who grew up and became a fine boy. But when he had been weaned, the woman ceased to bear children. Maguhe went to consult many diviners, and as a result his wife began to bear again, but always twins. The old midwives of the

[1] In a more detailed version given at a funeral, one elder went further back in time with the following account: "Iguluwi [Hanang mountain] is where we come from, at the place of the Nyawu zebwasi, from the Owners-of-the-cattle-troughs, where the stones are piled in cairns (*vinhenyela*). Cifulung'unyi killed Daha, his elder brother, in Utaturu [a place between Usukuma and Ugogo], at Iguluwi, during a quarrel over their common watering trough for cattle (*mulambo*) which had been destroyed by Cifulung'unyi's donkey . . . Their father gave the alarm call (*lwanji*) at the homestead and said, 'Catch him [Cifulung'unyi] and kill him also; I might as well be completely bereft' [that is, have no sons left at all]. So Cifulung'unyi fled. First he went west, then changed direction and went south. He passed through Uhanyaci and went through Usinzang'ombe (where he had many adventures) and came out at Ikonongo, the country of the Konongo people of the Sukuma, the blacksmiths who make hoes. He was utterly alone; he had rejected his friends and his kin when he fled, and his father had cursed him and disowned him. Indeed he was lost! When he arrived at Ikonongo . . . he lived in the chief's homestead (*ikulu*) and engendered a child by Goli, the daughter of the chief, there in the *ikulu*. This child was Maguhe . . . who was given this name because he had his ears lopped off through the ignorance of his father [*kubuha makutu:* cut off part of the ear]." (Note that in this version, Goli is Cifulung'unyi's wife not Maguhe's. Such variations are common in Gogo clan legends.) From here on Maguhe is involved in the same adventures in the version given above

area would secretly kill the children and tell Maguhe that they were stillborn and premature.[2] This happened six times, and then Maguhe, who had counted the months of several pregnancies and had taken great care of his wife, became suspicious. One old lady told him what was happening and he became so angry that he killed all the midwives concerned. At this, the husbands and sons of the women raised the alarm call, and for fear of their lives, Maguhe fled with his wife and son Mutalijembe who was then old enough to be able to run away as well. The men from Usukuma came after them. They passed through Taturu country and at each place they stopped and told the people what had happened. The Sukuma came on behind to each place and learned that Maguhe was ahead.

From here, Maguhe turned southeast towards Cilimanhinde, where he and his family met no one. They followed the ridge of Cilimanhinde to the west of the Sulungayi grass pan (*nyika*)[3] and then down to Cinyambwa.[4] Maguhe went straight to the ritual leader's homestead (*ikulu*) there, and after Maguhe had explained his position, the ritual leader (*mutemi*) of Cinyambwa gave him, his wife, and son asylum.

When the pursuing Sukuma arrived and explained their quest, the Nyambwa asked them what was the sub-clan name (*mulongo*) of the Maguhe they were looking for. They said, "We are looking for Maguhe whose *mulongo* is Muhanyaci, of Iguluwi, at the sky

[2] The Gogo do not kill twins (*wana wematundu*) and consider this is a terrible thing. But purification ceremonies are held for the area and twins have a special ritual status and special tasks to perform in communal rituals, as directed by a diviner. See Rigby (1966a), (1967a).

[3] The Sulungayi grass pan (swamp in the rainy season) is called *nyika ya Sulungayi* by the Gogo and the "Bahi swamp" by others: see Map 1.

[4] The longer and more detailed version, quoted in footnote 1, includes references to several other areas through which Cifulung'unyi (sometimes called Cifulukunya), the father of Maguhe, passed. He taught the people of Usinzeng'ombe how to make and use knives, for he found them skinning cattle with their fingers. In that version, Maguhe marries in Ikonongo, where the episode in which he kills the midwives takes place. He flees with his son Munyamakumbulu (not Mutalijembe), who was named after the diviner who provided the medicines for his wife, a common Gogo practice. He does not take his wife in the longer version. The first place he arrives at in Ugogo is also the *ikulu* at Cinyambwa.

rock which is like a house." [5] The Nyambwa replied, "We have a Maguhe here, but he is of our place and his *mulongo* is Munyambwa." So the thwarted Sukuma turned south, still trying to pick up the trail of Maguhe. Thus the Pulu acquired the *mulongo* Munyambwa, from Cinyambwa.

Maguhe stayed on at the *ikulu* at Cinyambwa for several days, and a beast died in the *ikulu*. While the people were preparing to cook the meat, the boy Mutalijembe ran off with a piece of it (*yakapula nyama*), and he and his father ate it raw in the bush. This behavior so shocked the Nyambwa that they said, "Oh, you are 'Mapulu' [awful things which run off with people's property]." They called the Sukuma back and together decided to punish Maguhe. But, sensing danger, Maguhe fled again with his family, with the Nyambwa pursuing this time. But from the raw meat they had eaten, the Pulu acquired their clan avoidance which is "redness" (*ndunghu*), and from the Nyambwa accusation of theft, they took the name "Pulu" for their clan. [6]

Maguhe now followed the paths again and reached Cikanga, in Mvumi ritual area. There they found some seemingly unattended goats. The boy Mutalijembe was so hungry by this time that he began to suck milk from the teats of a lactating animal (*mhene yigahile*) which thus had a lot of milk. But they were observed and the herder gave the alarm call. Maguhe fled but his wife and son Mutalijembe were caught and killed by the people of Mvumi. [7] Now Maguhe was alone.

[5] Some versions simply give Maguhe's *mulongo* at this point as Munyatoma, a common *mulongo* among several Gogo clans, and the *mulongo* of the clan called Nyambwa.

[6] Many Pulu clan members know that their avoidance is *ndunghu* but say that they do not know what it means, "For how can one avoid 'redness'?" Some suggest that it is a particular rare animal, like the hyrax (*mhimbi*), which lives in rocky outcrops. Perhaps this is a suitable place to note that these mythical histories require systematic structural analysis of the Lévi-Straussian kind (Lévi-Strauss, 1958; 1962b; 1964); cf. Willis (1967). However, this is not the place for such an analysis.

[7] In another version, Maguhe goes into the *ikulu* and stays a long time. He brings ritual danger upon the place by becoming the lover of one of the ritual leader's wives. He has to flee again and does so after being warned of danger by an omen (*ndeje*, lit., bird; cf. Beidelman, 1963a).

His pursuers followed him through Mvumi, Cikombo, Ibwijiri, and Nhati,[8] until he reached Musanga, the place of the Ibago clan; he again went straight to the *ikulu* of the ritual leader. There he came upon several people playing *wusolo* [a board game like checkers]. He was very tired by this time but the Ibago saved him by hiding him under the old shell of a wooden beehive (*musiku,* or *ipugu,* in this case), upon which they were seated as they played *wusolo.*[9] When the pursuers arrived, they asked for Maguhe of the Pulu clan and the *mulongo* Munyambwa.[10] The Ibago tricked them by saying that there was a Maguhe but he was of the Ibago clan, and anyway he was a young boy with one eye. The Nyambwa demanded to see this boy, and when they realized it was not the Maguhe they wanted, they gave up and went home.

Maguhe now lived at the *ikulu* of the Ibago clan, where he fell in love with the beautiful daughter of the ritual leader. But as he was considered a dependent, nearly a slave (*muwanda*), he did not know immediately how he could win her. Then he had an idea. He cut the tail off an ox and, going some distance west of Musanga to Makutupora, he partly buried the tail in the ground. Then he gave the alarm call and all the people from north, south, east, and west gathered, including the ritual leader Cimwaganje. Maguhe told them that he had just taken the ox from a relative and it was his, and he had been letting it drink here in their country when it had been

---

He goes to Musamalo, where the goat-suckling incident occurs. In this version, Mutalijembe alone is killed by the people of Musamalo. The ritual leader of Mvumi is identified as Cilimbogo.

[8] These are all ritual areas in present day Ugogo and are known throughout the area.

[9] In a more detailed version, Maguhe asks the Ibago to show him the way to the hills north of Musanga. They tell him he cannot go into these hills because there are strange beings there called Nghunduhi, which kill and eat people. This, one elder told me, might have been a reference to the Ng'omvia clan called the Gwazo who live in that area and are reputed to be able to turn into lions (*wahundukaga simba*). They hide him under the beehive and his pursuers are also persuaded to give up the chase because of the Nghunduhi.

[10] In an alternative version, the pursuers ask for Maguhe of the Munyatoma *mulongo.* The Ibago, after tricking them, give Maguhe the Munyambwa *mulongo,* which is also their sub-clan name.

swallowed up by the ground. The people were upset and tried to pull the tail which came out all bloody, but no ox. They dug and dug, but in vain. Maguhe then told them that they should compensate him, as it was into *their* country that his animal had disappeared. Cimwaganje and his people admitted their responsibility and offered Maguhe five head of cattle, then one hundred, then a thousand head, saying that each homestead owner in the country would contribute one head. Maguhe refused all these offers and Cimwaganje, with his special knowledge of the ways of ritual leadership, saw that Maguhe really wanted ritual leadership in the country where his ox had disappeared. So Cimwaganje explained to the people how Maguhe had sought refuge in his *ikulu* and how he had saved him from his enemies; thus he was his "son" (a fact to which Maguhe readily agreed). Since Maguhe was his "son" he would compensate by giving him the ritual leadership (*wutemi*) of this area, as well as his daughter in marriage.[11] This was settled, and Maguhe was married again. He lived in that area for a year.

After this, he had a dog called Nyanghasejere with which he went hunting, to the west, then to the north, until he found the little hill of Mbuli. They moved there. Maguhe had three sons. Masi, the eldest, went to take over the ritual leadership in Madako; the other son went to Nzasa, and the youngest of the junior house established Pulu precedence in Citelela.[12] The grandsons of Maguhe, one of whom

[11] Through this trick, the Pulu established their ritual precedence in the Makutupora ritual area, which later grew to five ritual areas. Thus the myth serves "its function." Also through these incidents and historical associations with other clans and areas, joking partnerships are established, in this case between the Ibago and Pulu clans. "For did not the beehives of the Ibago bring forth the Pulu clan?" elders say. See Rigby (1968a) for further comment.

[12] This is different from the version represented in Figure 2. For the latter, I use a more likely version, in which Maguhe is said to have had five sons by his wife from Musanga: Liati, Mudunghu, Mutalijembe (another, not the one killed on the way to Ugogo), Masi, and Mulumbisi. (There are at present five Pulu ritual areas.) Liati took a ritual stool to Citelela, Masi to Ikogolo, Mudunghu to Ciale, Mutalijembe to Nhyemianga, and Mulumbisi (the youngest son, *muziwanda*) took over the senior stool at Madako, after Maguhe's death. These areas constitute the five at present under Pulu ritual control. The expansion of ritual control

was Mulumbisi, established Pulu control in the rest of the five Pulu areas, and from them the present stool-holders directly trace their descent.

Some Pulu informants added, "And that was how the areas of the Pulu were established and how the name of the Pulu came from Cinyambwa; also, they have the *mulongo* Munyambwa. The Pulu are many [i.e. have many ritual areas] but the senior house is that of Madako. And our family name (*nghungugo*) came from there! We are Sukuma."

In a more detailed version of this story, Maguhe does not play a trick on the Ibago to gain the ritual control in Madako, but takes and expands this area by war, fighting over grazing and water for cattle, first against the Jibalo to the northwest of the present Pulu area, then the Itomboligwa in the center of the country, the Donghwe in the south, and the Mhalala in the southeast. The battles with the Donghwe and the Mhalala were incidental to the main conflict with the Jibalo. Through this, the Pulu established joking-partnerships with the Ibago (Rigby, 1968a), from whom they had usurped the area by force, and with the Donghwe and Mhalala from the conflict. This version is corroborated by Mhalala clan history.

---

into new areas by brothers who are the sons of previous ritual leaders is common. I recorded a much more recent and better remembered case in Loje, in southern Ugogo. See also Figures 2 and 3.

Appendix C

Clan Affiliation (*mbeyu*), Sub-clan Names (*mulongo*), and Avoidances (*muzilo*) of Homestead Heads, Temanghuku Neighborhood, 1961–62.

Sub-clan names[1]	Avoidances	Bamuko	Deje	Hehe	Igongo	Iheru	Ikando	Ilanji	Itumba	Mhanga	Ng'omvia	Nyagatwa	Nyagundu	Nyanghwalo	Nyangwe	Pulu	Sagala	Sukuma	Tazilo	Tejete	Temikwila	TOTALS
UKANZI	(mbofu)			5																		5
IWAYE	(finga)				1																	1
ISI[2]	(muhanga)		2																			2
IMA	(mbega)			1																		1
IUFWAMBA	(mulungulungu)																		1			1
IUFYOMI	(mbala)								1													1
IUNONGWA	(mhenenhitu								1													1
IUNYAKONGO	(ciswagumbi)				1																	1
	(msomha)	1																				1
IUNYAMBWA[3]	(ndunghu)							1								7						8
	(cisi)										1											1
	(nomvi)												1									1
	(sunha)														1							1
IUNYANGHALI	(mbala)								1													1
	(nomvi)																		1			1
	(mbofu)									1												1
UNYANZOKA	(nzoka)																	2				2
UNYASENGA	(muhanga)							2														2
UNYATOMA	(mbofu)																			1		1
UNYIWE	(cituwacamhene)	1																				1
UZIGANI	(fumbu)												1									1
UWEMBA	(nomvi)									1												1
UZIGULA	(mbala)								1													1
MWALI	(mbofu)								2													2
NG'UNDA	(muhanga)				1																	1
NHYINA	(sunha)								1													1
NYAGWA	(mbofu)								2													2
WANDO	(mbala)								1													1
TOTALS		1	3	6	1	1	1	1	11	1	1	1	1	1	1	7	1	1	2	1	1	44

[1] *Mulongo* names which differ in usage between men and women are given in the masculine form (Se-) only; cf. Appendix A.

[2] The Deje, Cisi (Muhanga) are the clan with ritual leadership in the area in which Temanghuku neighborhood lies.

[3] The founder of Temanghuku neighborhood belonged to the Pulu, Munyambwa (Ndunghu) clan and sub-clan.

Appendix D
Kinship Terminology:
Reference and Address Systems

Note: The relationship categories given for each term do not define the term, nor do they cover all possible categories that may be described by the term. They denote the most common genealogical positions referred to by the term.

Terms of reference	Sub-categories	Terms of address	Relationship categories
lumbu	—	(name)	(Sibling of opposite sex): Z(m.s.); B(w.s.).[1] FBD(m.s.); FBS(w.s.) MZD(m.s.); MZS(w.s.). (Cross-cousins of opposite sex when referring to third person, particularly an affine): FZD(m.s.); MBD(m.s.). FZS(w.s.); MBS(w.s.).
muwaha	—	(name)	(Elder sibling, full and half, same sex): eB(m.s.); eZ(w.s.).
	cana cawasewo[2]	*alaba*	eFBS(m.s.); eFBD(w.s.) when joking
muwaha	*cana canyina*[3]	*alayo*	eMZS(m.s.); eMZD(w.s.) when joking.
munakwetu	—	(name)	(Younger full and half siblings of same sex): yB(m.s.); yZ(w.s.).
	cana cawasewo	*alaba*	yFBS(m.s.); yFBD(w.s.) when joking.
	cana canyina	*alayo*	yMZS(m.s.); yMZD(w.s.) when joking.
muhizi	—	(name) *baguma*	FZD; MBD. FZS(m.s.); MBS(m.s.). FZD(w.s.) when joking. MBD(w.s.) when joking.

326

Appendix **D** (*continued*)

Terms of reference	Sub-categories	Terms of address	Relationship categories
sogwe, sewo	—	*baba*	F; FeB; FyB; FZH; sometimes MZH.
		(recip.) *aba, abayo*	MZH; Father's age-mate.
		(recip.) *bwabwa*	FFBS; FMZS.
		(recip.) *lebaba*	FMBS/FZSS; FFZS/MBSS, etc.
nyina, nyoko, etc.	—	*yaya*	M; MeZ; MyZ; FW; FBW.
nyinahenga	—	*yaya*	FZ; Father's female clan-mate of same generation.
		(name) or *yaya*	FFBD, etc.
mwana	—	(name)	(Child): S; D; BC; ZC (w.s.); MBSC; MBDC(w.s.); WZC; WBC; HBC; ZC (in certain contexts); HZC (in certain contexts).
		mulume	HZS when joking.
	(cf. *mwizukulu civu*)	"*mwana*"	great grandchild (address only).
mwihwa	—	(recip.) *bulayi*	ZS(m.s.);
		(name)	ZD(m.s.).
			HZD (in some contexts).
kuku	—	(recip.) *bulayi*	MB(m.s.); MB(w.s.) when joking.
		(name) or *kukuye*	MB(w.s.).
		kukuye or *mbuyane*	FF; MF.
		mabuya	Grandfather's age-mate; gF in naming relationship (*ndugu yalitagwa*).
		mulume	FF; MF (w.s.) when joking.
mama	—	*mamaye* or *mama*	FM; MM; MBW.
		mucekulu	FM; MM(m.s.) when joking. MBW when joking.
		(name)	MBW.
mwizukulu	—	(recip.) *mbuyane*	SS; DS(m.s.).
		(name)	SD; DD(m.s.); SS; DS (w.s.).
		mucekulu	SD; DD(m.s.) when joking.
		mulume	SS; DS(w.s.) when joking.
		(recip.) *mabuya*	gS's age-mate.
mwizukulu civu	(cf. "*mwana*")	(name)	SSC; SDC; DSC.

Appendix **D** (*continued*)

Terms of reference	Sub-categories	Terms of address	Relationship categories
mulume	—	(name)	H; HB.
mucekulu	—	(name)	W; BW(m.s.); BW(w.s.) when joking.
mulamu	—	(recip.) *mbuyane* ⎱ *latalai* ⎰	WB; ZH(m.s.); ZH(w.s.) when joking.
		(name)	BW; WZ; BWZ; ZH(w.s.).
		(name) or *wifi*	HZ; BW(w.s.).
		ala mbuya	Wife's male cross-cousins; wife's male parallel cousins.
mukwe	—	(recip.) *wandawo* ⎫ (recip.) *walaji* ⎬ (recip.) *wangishu* ⎭	WF; WFB.
		(recip.) *lamutani*	WMB; WF's cross-cousins, WF's parallel cousins.
		baba or *wanyamhalanye*	HF; HFB.
		wadala, yaya (name)	WM; WFZ; WMZ.
		yaya (name)	HM.
mukwemulima	—	(recip.) *wandawo* ⎫ (recip.) *walaji* ⎬ (recip.) *wangishu* ⎭	DH; DHB(m.s.).
		(recip.) *lamutani*	ZDH.
		wananye ⎱ *wanyamhalanye* ⎰	DH(w.s.).
		(name) *wananye* ⎱ *wadalanye* ⎰	SW(m.s.); BSW(m.s.).
		(name)	SW(w.s.).
mutozi	—	*njalai*	WZH; HBW when joking; WBW, joking; HZH, joking.
		(name)	WBW; HZH.
musanji	—	(name)	(Co-wife): HW.
muvwele	—	(name) or *civwele*	SWF; SWM; DHF; DHM.

[1] The symbols used in this list are conventional: Z = sister; (m.s.) = man speaking; (w.s.) = woman speaking. Where not specified, either man or woman speaking: e = elder; y = younger.

[2] *Cana cawasewo* means, "having the quality of being the children of their father."

[3] *Cana canyina* means, "having the quality of being the children of their mothers

Appendix E
The Case of Lubeleje and
Cedego: Father/Son Relations
(See Chapter VII)

Lubeleje, a young married man of twenty-three, is the son of Cedego, who is about fifty-seven years old. Cedego's elder sons Mate and Manongwa, who are also married, have already moved away from their father's homesteads for reasons which will appear. They moved to neighborhoods some fifteen and twenty miles respectively from Cedego's.

Lubeleje had a child by his young wife Nyawukali. She went away on a visit to her father's (Matonya's) homestead a few miles away in an adjacent neighborhood, and the child died there. The diviners stated that, as the child had not even been ill, the cause of death must be witchcraft. They accused the wife of Lubeleje's elder brother Manongwa, and she moved away to her kin at Gubangholo. Manongwa left his father's homestead to follow his wife and to live with his affines. Lubeleje's wife bore another child which also died soon after birth, again at her father's homestead. Matonya then began putting the story around that Lubeleje's and Cedego's people must be witches.

Cedego sent his cross-cousin Ngoyila (also an elder of about 60) to the diviners to see if he could find out the reason for the deaths. The diviner said to Ngoyila, "There are no witches among you, it is your 'child' [i.e. Lubeleje's wife, Nyawukali] who has the 'defect.'" (He did not specify whether this "defect" was physical or implied witchcraft, but he suggested that she could be cured.) This information was passed on to Cedego and Matonya, the girl's father. The latter was deeply shocked.

Later, Mate's wife fell out with her husband's mother, Mulya, as the latter said she was greedy and pilfering (*cancila* or *ibugu*). This

329

brought Mate into conflict with his father Cedego, and the young couple moved away to live with Mate's affines. There were also implications of incest between Cedego and Mate's wife, his daughter-in-law (see below).

Some time later, Cedego began moving his homestead to a new site about a hundred yards away in the same neighborhood. Relations between him and his son Lubeleje had been very bad, and Lubeleje's wife still had no surviving children. Lubeleje decided to build his own homestead very nearby. His mother's brother, Mhalanyuka, has his own homestead a few hundred yards away to the west. Lubeleje thus left his father, mother, and younger unmarried brother, Musemune, alone to build the new homestead. Father and son began to build their homesteads simultaneously, using the building poles from the old one they had shared. Lubeleje began to uproot poles which he said belonged to his brother Mate's old *nyumba* before the latter had moved away. Lubeleje claimed that Mate had "given" them to him.[1] Cedego contested this and a quarrel broke out. Lubeleje hit his father and, when Mulya (his mother) tried to separate them, he hit her too.

Magungu, Cedego's paternal parallel cousin who lives in an adjacent neighborhood some three miles distant, knew of the long period of strain between father and son. When this erupted into violence, he assembled the elders Ngoyila (Cedego's classificatory cross-cousin who lived nearby), Malagala, and Mhalanyuka (Mulya's full brothers and therefore Cedego's brothers-in-law). Mhalanyuka has a homestead immediately adjacent to Cedego's and Malagala resides in the same neighborhood. Mutaze and Mude, Malagala's sons-in-law (senior and junior elders respectively) were also present at the discussion for settling the dispute (*maloloso*). They both live in the same neighborhood as Cedego and Malagala and are also Cedego's classificatory "sons-in-law" (*wakwemulima*) according to Gogo kinship categories. Mujilima, the son of the founder of an adjacent neighborhood, was also asked to attend.[2]

[1] Mate was asked about this later, but denied having given the poles to Lubeleje. He did not, however, take sides. He told Lubeleje, "I did not *give* them to you. Say rather that you took your elder brother's poles for yourself. But do not say that I gave them to you."

[2] I failed to enquire whether Mujilima was in attendance as a related elder and what this relationship was, or whether he was there simply in

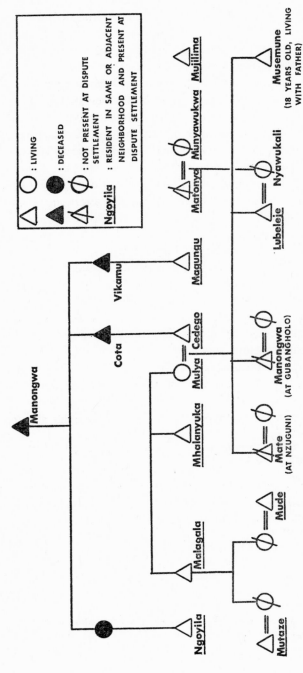

Figure 19. Genealogical relationships of those involved in Cedego's case with his son Lubeleje

The elders assembled at Cedego's homestead on the appointed day and began to discuss the case before either Cedego or Lubeleje had themselves arrived. It was stated that Lubeleje had gone to a diviner with his wife's father, Matonya, without informing Cedego. This implied that Cedego was the witch who was killing Lubeleje's children and inflicting Nyawukali with *mhepo* disease.[3] For not only had Cedego's son not informed him of the divination, but also his son's wife's father (*muvwele muyagwe*) Matonya had said nothing. (Relations between those who are *civwele* are supposed to be very close and friendly.) Lubeleje had come to take a goat from the homestead to use in the divination, and even this had not prompted him to inform his father. This was a clear accusation, by implication, of witchcraft against the latter.

Cedego brought a counteraccusation that in fact it was his son's wife's parents (*wavwele wayagwe*) who were destroying his homestead for him, not his sons. All this was discussed by the elders before the arrival of father and son.

When they did arrive and the discussion began formally, the elders tried to limit it as much as possible to the immediate cause of conflict: the argument over the building poles.[4] Cedego explained how they had come to blows and how his sons had hit him, upon which he exclaimed, "Kha, Lubeleje my son! And I am the one who gave you the marriage herd for your wife and now you hit us, your mother and me?"

Lubeleje was asked to give his version, which he also confined

---

his capacity as *munyamhala* (distinguished elder). I have no record of any relationship between him and Cedego's group, except through Ngoyila.

[3] *Mhepo* is a disease which causes pains in the chest and head, and fainting spells. Cured by dance possession, it is always thought to be caused by witchcraft.

[4] This is unusual in the settlement of disputes in Ugogo, where the whole relationship among persons between whom there has been a breach is relevant and should be taken into account. All evidence concerning their relationship is admissible, whatever the precipitating cause of the conflict. However, if another action arises from such evidence, it must be brought separately. It is probable that in this case the elders tried to limit the discussion because too many incidents had affected relations between father and son.

to the argument over the building poles, saying that he could not cover all the problems that had arisen between himself and his father; there were just too many (*sinogasuma ane, makani menji gakatali, sinogasuma*). After hearing Lubeleje's version, Mujilima suggested that it was not he who had caused the trouble, but Matonya and his daughter (Lubeleje's wife), by persuading them to go to a diviner and to accuse Cedego of witchcraft. Then Lubeleje and Cedego were asked if they would agree that the elders present should try to settle the case between them. Both agreed, but Lubeleje implied that they would not be successful as it had dragged on for three years now (since the death of his first child).

Mude suggested that Lubeleje should keep the building poles which he had already taken, for he had not done wrong. They were Cedego's poles and therefore were also Lubeleje's poles. He drew an example from wealth in cattle: "If you have a herd and you give your son cattle to milk, on the day that your son says, 'Father, I am going to build my own separate homestead,' would you take back the cattle you have divided among the 'hearthstones'? No! You would not take them back." [5]

This was agreed and a division of the poles settled. The discussion then turned to the wrong committed by Lubeleje in hitting his parents. The elders suggested that Lubeleje should move back and live with his father again. This Lubeleje categorically refused to do, and they could bring no pressure to bear on him in this. But Mujilima admonished him and told him that he must begin herding his father's cattle again, for he had heard that he had stopped doing this.[6] Lubeleje readily agreed, saying that it was in fact Cedego who had prevented him from herding, not he himself who had refused.

Mude then addressed Lubeleje: "Lubeleje, the problem of the poles is finished now; let us follow up the other thing. There, when

[5] Mude uses the word "hearthstone" (*ilifigwa*) here figuratively to denote "house" (*nyumba*), for each married woman has a separate hearthstone. He implies that once cattle have been given by a father to his son's wife for her *nyumba* (or any *nyumba*), he cannot claim them back. So too with the building poles.

[6] That is, to resume his duties towards his father and thus establish a *moral* right to inherit part of his father's herd upon his death. The legal right could not be upset by this conflict.

you were angry over the poles, you hit your father and mother. Now you have called us [elders] here, and we are very upset by this and think you should be fined (*ce kutya uli mutumu*). When you saw you were going to have an argument over the poles, you should have called the elders, Magungu perhaps, and Mhalanyuka [Lubeleje's classificatory father and own mother's brother respectively]. So we say you should be fined." Lubeleje was fined a goat.

Mujilima, however, said that this fine should be rather for the wrong Lubeleje committed by implying that his father, who had brought him up and cared for him and given him cattle, was a witch. Thus, the fine should not be *ndesa* (for assault) but "*kutemalulimi*" (lit. "to cut the tongue," for defamation). This was agreed. Mulya, Lubeleje's mother, who was sitting nearby, was asked what she thought. She agreed to the settlement after confirming more or less what had already been said about the conflict. Mujilima again addressed Lubeleje: "And you Lubeleje, don't be afraid to go to your mother's *nyumba*. Even if they give you food, you must eat there and not be afraid. What do you say?" Lubeleje said he agreed, but it was difficult to eat in a *nyumba* where people are angry with you (*wakusimbiye du*).[7]

The elders then admonished the two to behave towards each other as father and son should, not listen to other people's gossip (*maheho*), and discuss things openly together. Ngoyila added: "Over that issue we are all extremely annoyed. Look, here is Cedego's homestead and there next door is Mhalanyuka's, and nearby is Lubeleje. If the alarm call (*lwanji*) were sounded at Cedego's, would Lubeleje not come?[8] And if Cedego is away, should not Lubeleje come to sleep at his homestead to look after it until his return?"

[7] In such a case, where the father has one wife and the sons of the *nyumba* split up residentially, the mother usually remains with her husband. Relations between mother and son, which I have not discussed here, can become quite strained.

[8] The obligation to help when the alarm call is sounded lies upon all who hear it. For Lubeleje not to come because of his rift with Cedego would be a negation not only of the relationship but also of common residence and the fundamental rules of neighborliness. Such behavior is inexcusable for unrelated neighbors, let alone kin as close as father and son.

Lubeleje sent a young lad for the goat he had been fined. It was approved, slaughtered, and eaten by the elders present. Some meat was given to Mulya and some to Nyawukali, who was in the shelter of her partly built homestead about 100 yards away. It was reiterated, by Cedego this time, that the goat was not for assault but for defamation.

At the end, Mude addressed Lubeleje and the other elders: "Now you see why they hate each other, Cedego and his son? It is because of Munyawukwa [Lubeleje's wife's mother]; it is she who is causing it all. And Lubeleje is fool enough (*mulele*) to listen to the words of his parents-in-law (*wakwe'we*) instead of his father's." (He then again went over the story of how Lubeleje went with his parents-in-law to the diviner, who accused Cedego of bewitching Nyawukali.)

There followed a discussion of how unreliable diviners are, and it was emphasized that their statements should be taken with discretion. Mujilima again addressed Lubeleje: "Lubeleje, we are about to disperse. Live well with your father, herd the cattle, and care well for each other. If he has work and you the time, you should come and help him. If you have work, he will also come and help you. Greet each other when you meet, and the trouble will be forgotten . . . Talk to each other when you meet, as normal people do . . ." Magungu added a similar adjuration and concluded: "Our forebears used to have huge homesteads. We used to live, a great many in one homestead, yet we never saw conflict like this." [9] Mude also took up this theme: "Truly, now when we see you all living like this in three homesteads, do we not think of them really as one? This one is Mhalanyuka's (your mother's brother, Lubeleje) and that is of your father Cedego. People should not say of your homestead, 'That is the homestead of Lubeleje' and not mention your father's name. That is forbidden. They should say, 'The homestead of the son of Cedego.' "

Magungu reminded Lubeleje: "When Cedego is dead, and we

[9] That is, sons used to live with their fathers and there was harmony in the large homesteads. I have suggested that homesteads used to be much larger in the past (see Chapters IV and V) because it was much more difficult to set up an independent homestead. But there is no evidence to believe that there used to be less conflict between father and son in the past.

relatives say, 'Let us drive away his cattle and take all the things from his homestead,' would you, Lubeleje, agree to that? No, you would refuse! And could we be perverse and come and take them? If we wanted something of Cedego's property, we would ask it of you. And if you agreed, you would say, 'Yes, take this thing.' "

The settlement was unsuccessful. Lubeleje soon ceased building his homestead and moved away completely to live with his full brother. Cedego and his wife were left alone with their youngest son Musemune

Gogo interpreted much of this conflict in terms of competition between father and son over the use of livestock for bridewealth. This was brought out in several places, the first when Cedego called out that he had been struck by a son to whom he had given cattle to marry a wife. Later, Ngoyila emphasized this when he told me: "All the children Lubeleje had by his wife have inexplicably died . . . Now they do not have any. People say that Cedego bewitched his son's wife because he wanted to sleep with her, and she refused. That is why Lubeleje left his homestead. He used to live with his father; now he has begun to move away. He does not even know where he wishes to live. [That is, his mother's brothers are nearby, so he cannot go to them. So are his affines.] He began building his homestead nearby, but now has left even that and wishes to go away completely."

It is incest (*wuhawi,* witchcraft) to sleep with one's son's wife. This only made the situation appear even worse, but only such heinous behavior can explain to Gogo the complete disintegration of a man's homestead by the departure of all his married sons, Cedego's sad fate.

Bibliography

Works that refer principally to the Gogo

Note: This is by no means a full list of references to the Gogo, as it is restricted to works cited in the text. It does, however, contain most of the major works upon which sociological analysis may be based.

BEVERLEY, J. E.
  1903. "Die Wagogo," in *Rechtsverhältnisse von eingeborenen Völkern in Afrika und Ozeanien*, ed. S. R. Steinmetz. Berlin: Julius Springer. Pp. 203–217.
CARNELL, W. J.
  1955a. "Sympathetic Magic among the Gogo of Mpwapwa District," *Tanganyika Notes and Records*, XXXIX, 25–38.
  1955b. "Four Gogo Folk Tales," *Tanganyika Notes and Records*, XL, 30–42.
CLAUS, H.
  1910. "Die Wangomwia," *Zeitschrift für ethnologie*, XLII, 489–497.
  1911. "Die Wagogo." *Baessler Archiv*, II, 1–72. Berlin: Reimer.
COLE, H.
  1902. "Notes on the Wagogo," *Journal of the Anthropological Institute*, XXXII, 305–338.
CORY, H.
  1951. *"Gogo Law and Custom,"* unpublished MS, Library of University College, Dar es Salaam, and Makerere Institute of Social Research Library, Kampala.
CULWICK, A. T.
  1931. "Ritual use of Rock Paintings at Bahi, Tanganyika Territory," *Man*, XXXI, No. 41, 33–36.

Dodoma District Book, District Office, Dodoma, Tanzania.

HARTNOLL, A. V.
  1932. "The Gogo Mtemi," *South African Journal of Science,* XXIX, 737–741.
  1942. "Praying for Rain in Ugogo," *Tanganyika Notes and Records,* XIII, 29–60.

MNYAMPALA, M. E.
  1954. *Historia, Mila na Desturi za Wagogo wa Tanganyika.* Dar es Salaam: The Eagle Press.

PAULSSEN, F.
  1922. "Rechtsanschauung der Wagogo," *Baessler Archiv,* VI, 161–175.

RIGBY, PETER.
  1962. "Witchcraft, Kinship and Authority in Ugogo," *East African Institute of Social Research Conference Proceedings* (roneo). Kampala. E.A.I.S.R.
  1963. "The Mbuya Relationship and Marriage in Ugogo," *East African Institute of Social Research Conference Proceedings* (roneo). Kampala: E.A.I.S.R.
  1966a. "Dual Symbolic Classification among the Gogo of Central Tanzania," *Africa,* XXXVI, No. 1, 1–17.
  1966b. "Sociological Factors in the Contact of the Gogo of Central Tanzania with Islam," in *Islam in Tropical Africa,* ed. I. M. Lewis. London: Oxford University Press for International African Institute.
  1966c. "The Tale of the Ungrateful Grandfather" (with Gideon Senyagwa), *Transition,* No. 28.
  1967a. "Some Gogo Rituals of 'Purification': an Essay on Social and Moral Categories," in *Dialectic in Practical Religion,* ed. E. R. Leach. Cambridge and New York: Cambridge University Press.
  1967b. "Changes in Local Government in Ugogo and the National Elections," in *One Party Democracy,* ed. Lionel Cliffe. Nairobi: East African Publishing House.
  1967c. "Time and Structure in Gogo Kinship," *Cahiers d'études africaines,* VII, No. 28, 637–658.
  1967d. "The Structural context of Girls' Puberty Rites," *Man,* (N.S.), II, No. 3, 434–444.

1968a. "Joking Relationships, Kin Categories, and Clanship among the Gogo," *Africa,* XXXVIII, No. 2, 133–155.

In press. "Politics and Modern Leadership Roles among the Gogo," in *Profiles of Change: The Impact of Colonialism on African Societies,* ed. V. W. Turner. Cambridge and New York: Cambridge University Press.

SCHAEGELEN, THEOBALD.
1938. "La Tribu des Wagogo," *Anthropos,* XXXIII, No. 1, 195–217; No. 2, 515–567.

SOUTHON, E. J.
1881. "Notes on a Journey through Northern Ugogo in East Central Africa," *Proceedings of the Royal Geographical Society,* III, 547–553.

Other references cited in the text

ABRAHAMS, R. G.
1965. "Neighbourhood Organization: A Major Sub-system among the Northern Nyamwezi," *Africa,* XXXV, No. 2, 168–186.
1967. *The Political Organization of Nyamweziland.* Cambridge and New York: Cambridge University Press.

APTHORPE, R. J.
1967. "Nsenga Social Ideas," *Mawazo,* I, No. 1, 23–30. Makerere University College, Kampala.

BARNES, J. A.
1949. "Measures of Divorce Frequency in Simple Societies" *Journal of the Royal Anthropological Institute,* LXXIX, Nos. 1 and 2, 37–62.

BASCOM, W. R., AND HERSKOVITS, M. J. (eds.).
1959. *Continuity and Change in African Cultures.* Chicago: University of Chicago Press.

BATES, M. L. Z.
1962. "Tanganyika," in *African One-Party States,* ed. G. Carter. Ithaca: Cornell University Press.

BEATTIE, JOHN.
1959. "Understanding and Explanation in Social Anthropology," *British Journal of Sociology,* X, 45–60.

1960. *Bunyoro: An African Kingdom.* New York: Holt, Rinehart and Winston.

BEIDELMAN, T. O.

1960. "The Baraguyu," *Tanganyika Notes and Records,* LV, 244–278.

1961a. "A Note on Baraguyu Housetypes and Baraguyu Economy," *Tanganyika Notes and Records,* LVII, 56–66.

1961b. "Beer Drinking and Cattle Theft in Ukaguru," *American Anthropologist,* LXIII, No. 3, 524–549.

1961c. "Hyena and Rabbit: a Kaguru Representation of Matrilineal Relations," *Africa,* XXXI, 61–74.

1961d. "Right and Left Hand among the Kaguru," *Africa,* XXXI, No. 3, 250–257.

1962. "A Demographic Map of the Baraguyu," *Tanganyika Notes and Records,* LVIII, 8–10.

1963a. "Kaguru Omens: An East African People's Concepts of the Unusual, Unnatural and Supernormal," *Anthropological Quarterly,* XXXVII, No. 2, 33–52.

1963b. "Further Adventures of Hyena and Rabbit: the Folktale as a Sociological Model," *Africa,* XXXIIII, No. 1, 69.

1963c. "The Blood Covenant and the Concept of Blood in Ukaguru," *Africa,* XXXIII, No. 4, 321–342.

1963d. "A Kaguru Version of the Sons of Noah: a Study in the Inculcation of the Idea of Racial Superiority," *Cahiers d'études africaines,* XII, 474–490.

1963e. "Kaguru Time Reckoning," *Southwestern Journal of Anthropology,* XIX, 9–20.

1964. "Intertribal Insult and Opprobium in an East African Chiefdom (Ukaguru)," *Anthropological Quarterly,* XXXVII, No. 2, 33–52.

1965. "Some Baraguyu Cattle Songs," *Journal of African Languages,* IV, 1–18.

1966. *"Utani:* Some Kaguru Notions of Death, Sacrifice and Affinity," *Southwestern Journal of Anthropology,* XXII, 354–380.

BURTON, R. F.

1860. *The Lake Regions of Central Africa.* New York: Harper.

BUXTON, J. C.
1963. *Chiefs and Strangers*. Oxford: Clarendon Press.
CAMERON, V. L.
1877. *Across Africa*. 2 vols., London: Daldy, Isbister and Co.
CHRISTIANSEN, J. B.
1963. "Utani: Joking, Sexual License and Social Obligations among the Luguru," *American Anthropologist*, LXV, 314–327.
COLSON, E.
1951. "The Role of Cattle among the Plateau Tonga," *Rhodes-Livingstone Journal*, XI, 10–46. (Reprinted in Colson, 1962, Chapter V.)
1962. *The Plateau Tonga of Northern Rhodesia: Social and Religious Studies*. Manchester: Manchester University Press for Rhodes-Livingstone Institute.
CUNNISON, IAN.
1956. "Perpetual Kinship: a Political Institution of the Luapula Peoples," *Rhodes-Livingstone Journal*, XX, 28–48.
DORJAHN, VERNON R.
1959. "The Factor of Polygyny in African Demography," in *Continuity and Change in African Cultures*, eds. Bascom and Herskovits. Chicago: University of Chicago Press.
DYSON-HUDSON, N.
1966. *Karimojong Politics*. London: Oxford University Press.
EVANS-PRITCHARD, E. E.
1940. *The Nuer*. Oxford: The Clarendon Press.
1945. "Some Aspects of Marriage and the Family among the Nuer," *Rhodes-Livingstone Papers*, No. 11. Livingstone: Rhodes-Livingstone Institute.
1951. *Kinship and Marriage among the Nuer*. Oxford: Clarendon Press.
1962. *Essays in Social Anthropology*. London: Faber and Faber.
FALLERS, L. A.
1957. "Some Determinants of Marriage Stability in Busoga: a Reformulation of Gluckman's Hypothesis," *Africa*, XXVII, No. 2, 106–123.
FIRTH, R.
1936. *We, the Tikopia*. London: Allen and Unwin.

1951.   *Elements of Social Organization.* London: Watts and Co.

1957.   (ed.). *Man and Culture.* London: Routledge and Kegan Paul; New York: Harper (1964).

FORDE, C. DARYLL.

1947.   "The Anthropological Approach in Social Science," *The Advancement of Science,* IV, No. 15, 213–224.

FORTES, M.

1936.   "Kinship, Incest and Exogamy of the Northern Territories of the Gold Coast," in *Custom is King: Essays Presented to R. R. Marett,* eds. L. Buxton and H. Dudley. London: Hutchinsons Scientific and Technical Publications.

1945.   *The Dynamics of Clanship among the Tallensi.* London: Oxford University Press.

1949a. *The Web of Kinship among the Tallensi.* London: Oxford University Press.

1949b. "Time and Social Structure: An Ashanti Case Study," in *Social Structure: Studies Presented to A. R. Radcliffe-Brown,* ed. M. Fortes. Oxford: The Clarendon Press.

1953.   "The Structure of Unilineal Descent Groups," *American Anthropologist,* LV, 17–41.

1957.   "Malinowski and the Study of Kinship," in *Man and Culture,* ed. R. Firth. London: Routledge and Kegan Paul; New York: Harper.

1958.   "Introduction," in *The Developmental Cycle in Domestic Groups,* Cambridge Papers in Social Anthropology, No. 1., ed. J. Goody. Cambridge: Cambridge University Press.

1959.   "Descent, Filiation and Affinity: A Rejoinder to Dr. Leach," *Man,* LIX, article nos. 309, 331.

1962.   "Introduction," in *Marriage in Tribal Societies,* Cambridge Papers in Social Anthropology, No. 3., ed. M. Fortes. Cambridge: Cambridge University Press.

1963.   "The 'Submerged Descent Line' in Ashanti," in *Studies in Kinship and Marriage,* ed. I. Schapera. London: Royal Anthropological Institute.

1966.   "Totem and Taboo," (Presidential address). *Proceedings of the Royal Anthropological Institute,* London.

FOSBROOKE, H. A.

1948.   "An Administrative Survey of the Masai Social System," *Tanganyika Notes and Records,* XXVI, 1–50.

FREEMAN, J. D.
 1961. "On the Concept of the Kindred," The Curl Bequest Essay, *Journal of the Royal Anthropological Institute,* XCI, No. 2, 192–220.

GLUCKMAN, M.
 1950. "Kinship and Marriage among the Lozi of Northern Rhodesia and the Zulu of Natal," in *African Systems of Kinship and Marriage,* eds. Radcliffe-Brown and Forde. London: Oxford University Press for International African Institute.

GOODY, J.
 1956. *The Social Organization of the LoWiili.* London: Her Majesty's Stationery Office.
 1958. (Ed.). *The Developmental Cycle in Domestic Groups,* Cambridge Papers in Social Anthropology, No. 1. Cambridge: Cambridge University Press.
 1959. "The Mother's Brother and the Sister's Son in West Africa," *Journal of the Royal Anthropological Institute,* LXXXIX, No. 1, 61–88.

GRAY, R. F.
 1953. "Positional Succession among the Wambugwe," *Africa,* XXIII, No. 3, 233–243.
 1960. "Sonjo Bride-price and the Question of African 'Wife Purchase,'" *American Anthropologist,* LXII, No. 1, 34–57.

GRAY, R. F., and GULLIVER, P. H. (eds.)
 1964. *The Family Estate in Africa,* London: Routledge and Kegan Paul.

GULLIVER, P. H.
 1952. "The Karamajong Cluster," *Africa,* XXII, No. 1, 1–24.
 1953a. "Jie Marriage," *African Affairs,* LII, 149–155.
 1953b. "The Population of Karamoja," *Uganda Journal,* XVII, 178–185.
 1955. *The Family Herds.* London: Routledge and Kegan Paul.
 1961. "Structural Dichotomy and Jural Processes among the Arusha of Northern Tanganyika," *Africa,* XXXI, 19–35.
 1963. *Social Control in an African Society.* London: Routledge and Kegan Paul.

HARRIES-JONES, P., and CHIWALE, J. C.
 1963. "Kasaka: a Case Study in Succession and Dynamics of a

Bemba Village," *Rhodes-Livingstone Journal,* XXXIII, 1–67.

HARRIS, A., and HARRIS, G.

1964. "Property and the Cycle of Domestic Groups in Taita," in *The Family Estate in Africa,* eds. Gray and Gulliver. London: Routledge and Kegan Paul.

HARRIS, G.

1962. "Taita Bridewealth and Affinal Relationships," in *Marriage in Tribal Societies,* ed. M. Fortes. Cambridge Papers in Social Anthropology, No. 3. Cambridge: Cambridge University Press.

HOLLEMAN, J. F.

1949. "The Pattern of Hera Kinship," *Rhodes-Livingstone Papers,* No. 17. London: Oxford University Press for Rhodes-Livingstone Institute.

1952. *Shona Customary Law.* London: Oxford University Press for Rhodes-Livingstone Institute.

Iringa District Book, District Office, Iringa, Tanzania.

KUPER, HILDA.

1947. *An African Aristocracy.* London: Oxford University Press.

1950. "Kinship among the Swazi," in *African Systems of Kinship and Marriage,* eds. Radcliffe-Brown and Forde. London: Oxford University Press for International African Institute.

1954. *The Swazi.* Ethnographic Survey of Africa. London: International African Institute.

LA FONTAINE, F.

1962. "Gisu Marriage and Affinal Relations," in *Marriage in Tribal Societies,* ed. M. Fortes. Cambridge Papers in Social Anthropology, No. 3. Cambridge: Cambridge University Press.

LEACH, E. R.

1954. *Political Systems of Highland Burma.* London: Bell.

1961a. *Pul Eliya: A Study of Land Tenure and Kinship.* Cambridge: Cambridge University Press.

1961b. *Rethinking Anthropology.* London School of Economics Monographs on Social Anthropology, No. 22. London: Athlone Press.

LÉVI-STRAUSS, CLAUDE.
    1949. *Les structures élémentaires de la parenté.* Paris: Presses Universitaires de France.
    1956. "The Family," in *Man, Culture, and Society,* ed. H. L. Shapiro. New York: Oxford University Press.
    1958. *Anthropologie structurale.* Paris: Librarie Plon. Translated by Claire Jacobson and Brooke Grundfest Schoepf (1963): *Structural Anthropology.* New York: Basic Books.
    1962a. *Le totemisme aujourd'hui.* Paris: Presses Universitaires de France. Translated by Rodney Needham (1962): *Totemism.* Boston: Beacon Press.
    1962b. *La pensée sauvage.* Paris: Librairie Plon.
    1964. *Mythologiques: le cru et le cuit.* Paris: Librairie Plon.
    1965. "The Future of Kinship Studies," The Huxley Memorial Lecture. *Proceedings of the Royal Anthropological Institute.* London.
LEWIS, I. M.
    1961. *A Pastoral Democracy.* London: Oxford University Press for International African Institute.
    1962. *Marriage and Family in Northern Somaliland,* East African Studies, No. 15. Kampala: E.A.I.S.R.
    1965. "Problems in the Comparative Study of Unilineal Descent," in *The Relevance of Models for Social Anthropology,* A.S.A. Monographs, No. 1. London: Tavistock.
MALINOWSKI, B.
    1929. "Kinship," *Encyclopaedia Britannica* (14th ed.).
Manyoni District Book, District Office, Manyoni, Tanzania.
MEINHOF, C.
    1899. *Grundriss einer Lautlehre der Bantusprachen.* Leipzig: F. A. Brockhaus.
MIDDLETON, J., and TAIT, D. (eds.).
    1958. *Tribes Without Rulers.* London: Routledge and Kegan Paul.
MITCHELL, J. C.
    1956. "The Kalela Dance," *Rhodes-Livingstone Papers,* No. 27, Manchester: Manchester University Press for Rhodes-Livingstone Institute.

MOFFET, J. P.
1958. *Handbook of Tanganyika* (2nd ed.). Dar es Salaam: Government Printer.
MOREAU, R. R.
1944. "Joking Relationships in Africa," *Africa,* XIV, 386–400.
Mpwapwa District Book, District Office, Mpwapwa, Tanzania.
MURDOCK, G. P. (ed.).
1960. *Social Structure in South-east Asia.* Viking Fund Publications in Anthropology 29. New York: Wenner Gren Foundation.
NADEL, S. J.
1951. *The Foundations of Social Anthropology.* London: Cohen and West.
1957. *The Theory of Social Structure.* London: Cohen and West.
NEEDHAM, RODNEY.
1960. "A Structural Analysis of Aimol Society," *Bidjragen tot de Taal-, land-, en Volkenkunde,* CXVII, 81–108.
1962. *Structure and Sentiment: A Test Case in Social Anthropology.* Chicago: University of Chicago Press.
1963. "The Wikmunkan Mother's Brother: Inference and Evidence," *Journal of the Polynesian Society,* 72, pp. 139–151.
OLIVER, R., and MATHEW, G. (eds.).
1963. *History of East Africa,* Vol. I. London: Oxford University Press.
PETERS, C.
1891. *New Light on Dark Africa.* London: Ward.
PETERS, E.
1960. "The Proliferation of Segments in the Lineages of the Bedouin of Cyrenaica," *Journal of the Royal Anthropological Institute,* XC, No. 1, 29–53.
RADCLIFFE-BROWN, A. R.
1935. "Kinship Terminologies in California," *American Anthropologist,* XXXVII, 530–535.
1950. "Introduction," in *African Systems of Kinship and Marriage,* eds. Radcliffe-Brown and Forde. London: Oxford University Press for International African Institute.

1952. *Structure and Function in Primitive Society*. London: Cohen and West.

RADCLIFFE-BROWN, A. R., and FORDE, C. DARYLL (eds.).

150. *African Systems of Kinship and Marriage*. London: Oxford University Press for International African Institute.

REICHARD, P.

1892. *Deutsch Ost-Afrika*. Leipzig: Otto Spamer.

RICHARDS, A. I.

1937. "Reciprocal Clan Relationships among the Bemba of N. E. Rhodesia," *Man,* XXXVII, article no. 222.

1939. *Land, Labour, and Diet in Northern Rhodesia*. London: Oxford University Press.

1950. "Some Types of Family Structure amongst the Central Bantu," in *African Systems of Kinship and Marriage,* eds. Radcliffe-Brown and Forde. London: Oxford University Press for International African Institute.

1960. "Social Mechanisms for the Transfer of Political Rights in Some African Societies," *Journal of the Royal Anthropological Institute,* XC, No. 2, 175–190.

ROUNCE, N. V., *et al.*

1949. *The Agriculture of the Cultivation Steppe*. Dar es Salaam: Department of Agriculture.

SAHLINS, MARSHALL D.

1961. "The Segmentary Lineage: an Organization of Predatory Expansion," *American Anthropologist,* LXIII, 332–345.

SCHAPERA, I. (ed.).

1963. *Studies in Kinship and Marriage*. Royal Anthropological Institute Occasional Papers, No. 16. London.

SCHNEIDER, D. M.

1965. "Some Muddles in the Models: or, How the System Really Works," in *The Relevance of Models for Social Anthropology*. A.S.A. Monographs, No. 1. London: Tavistock.

SCHNEIDER, H. K.

1957. "The Subsistence Role of Cattle among the Pakot and in East Africa," *American Anthropologist,* 59, 278–300.

SMITH, M.G.
1956. "On Segmentary Lineage Systems," *Journal of the Royal Anthropological Institute,* 86, pp. 39–80.

SOUTHALL, A. W.
1952. *Lineage Formation among the Luo.* International African Institute, Memorandum 27. London.
1953. *Alur Society.* Cambridge: Heffer for East African Institute of Social Research.
1961. (Ed.). *Social Change in Modern Africa.* Oxford University Press for International African Institute.

SPEKE, J. H.
1863. *Journal of the Discovery of the Source of the Nile.* London: Blackwood.

STANLEY, H. M.
1872. *How I Found Livingstone.* New York: Scribner, Armstrong and Co.

SWARTZ, M. J., TURNER, V. W., and TUDEN, ARTHUR (eds.).
1966. *Political Anthropology.* Chicago: Aldine.

Tanganyika Census, 1957, Nairobi: East African Statistical Office (rev. ed. 1958).

TUCKER, A. N., and BRYAN, M. A.
1957. *Linguistic Survey of the Northern Bantu Borderland,* vol. IV. London: Oxford University Press for International African Institute.

TUCKER, A. N., and J. TOMPO OLE MPAAYEI.
1955. *A Masai Grammar.* Publications of the African Institute. Leyden and London: Longmans Green.

TURNER, V. W.
1957. *Schism and Continuity in an African Society.* Manchester: Manchester University Press for Rhodes-Livingstone Institute.

VANSINA, J.
1965. *Oral Tradition: a Study in Historical Methodology.* Translated by Wright, H. M. Chicago: Aldine.

VOGT, E. Z.
1960. "On the Concepts of Structure and Process in Cultural Anthropology," *American Anthropologist,* LXII, 18–33.

WALLACE, A. F. C., and ATKINS, J.
1960. "The Meaning of Kinship Terms," *American Anthropologist,* LXII, No. 1, 58–80.

WARD, B. E.
1965. "Varieties of Conscious Model," in *The Relevance of Models for Social Anthropology.* A.S.A. Monographs, No. 1. London: Tavistock.
1966. "Sociological Self-awareness: Some Uses of the Conscious Models," *Man,* N.S., I, No. 2, 201–215.

WILLIS, R. G.
1967. "The Head and the Loins: Lévi-Strauss and Beyond," *Man,* N.S., II, No. 4, 519–534.

WORSLEY, P. M.
1956. "The Kinship Systems of the Tallensi: a Revaluation," *Journal of the Royal Anthropological Institute,* LXXXVI, No. 1, 37–75.

Index

Affines: in cattle trusteeship contracts, 53; and residence patterns, 134, 135, 139, 141, 143, 146–147, 184; conflict between, 192; cooperative relations among, 237–239, 276–283; and marriage stability, 242–245; structural importance of, 246; and descent relationships, 306–308

Age-set (*izika*), 13; influence of Baraguyu on, 177

Agnates: excluded from trusteeship contracts, 53; in neighborhood organization, 143–145, 150; in homestead composition, 153, 195; "conventional" relations between, 269–271

Agricultural subsistence, 24-26, 299

Alarm call, 104, 113

Apthorpe, R. J., 7

Architectural style, 19

Avoidance object, 81–84

Baraguyu, 12, 13; and age-set organization, 13, 103; cultural influences of, 19; and cattle ear marks, 59; cattle songs of, 59; in rain divination and medicines for fertility and protection, 99, 164; and Gogo kinship terminology, 253–254

Beattie, John, 8, 25

Beer (*wujimbi*): and cooperation, 38–39

Beidelman, T. O., 12, 13, 19, 59, 83, 99, 103, 177, 253

Blood: spilling of, and pollution, 100

Blood brothers, 269

Bridewealth: average herd, 50–51; influence on rates of polygyny, 183; negotiations (*kwiguma*), 213–221; transaction, role of mother in, 216; preliminary prestations (*vidodo-*

Bridewealth (*cont.*)
vidodo), 217, 227; and "brideprice" controversy, 225; composition and distribution of, 225–235; size of, 229–230

Buxton, J., 63–64

Calo, see Dispute settlement

Cattle: values, 23–26; tracks, 29, 33; dung used as manure, 43–44; economic role of, 43–47; as wealth, 46, 49–51; exchange of, 47–50; average numbers per capita, 49, 51; trusteeship contracts (*kukoza*), 50–53; complex, 53; as opposed to agricultural values, 53–56; and symbolic distinctions between sexes, 55; culture, classification, and terminology, 56–60; and ritual symbolism, 60; fertility medicines for, 164

Chiwale, J. C., 1, 109

Cibalu (or *cibalwe*), see Circumcision

Cifuta, 80

Cigumo, see Bridewealth

Cilahilo ("clan oath"), 81, 84–85

Circumcision: explained in clan history, 63; age at, 206–207; and kin obligations, 208

Citenjelo ("gravestone"), 148, 155

Clan (*mbeyu*), 7, 15, 19, 76–80, 86; founders of, 13; and social classification, 64, 71; history, functions of, 65–76; in exogamy and marriage, 80–81, 203, 222; oaths (*cilahilo*), 81, 84; sub-divisions of, 86–87; functional and morphological definitions of, 88; significance of, in inheritance ceremonies, 289

Claus, H., 11

Clitoridectomy, 19, 208

Colson, E., 14, 48, 77

Cosmology: in cultivation, 40–43; and right and left hand, 41

Co-wife (*musanji*), and cooperation, 38–39

Cross-cousins (*wahizi*): in inter-clan joking, 89–90; and neighborhood organization, 138, 146; in marriage, 203, 236, 286–287; in inheritance ceremonies, 287–289

Cultivation: cooperation in, 38–43

Culture: homogeneity of, 18; material, 19; structural implications of, 25; and cattle, 56–60

Cunnison, I., 79

Demographic background: population densities, 22

Descent: and corporateness, 3, 6, 9; and neighborhood, 147

Dispute settlement: at neighborhood level, 113; and kinship relationships, 265

Diviner (*muganga*): relation with ritual leader, 106–107; and residential mobility, 136

Divorce: rates of, 141–143; structural implications of, 280

Domestic groups: and ownership of herd, 48; developmental cycle of, 187–201

Dorjahn, V. R., 182

Drought, 13, 20–22; and residential mobility, 34

Dyson-Hudson, N., 1

Economy, 5, 20; marginality of, 1; preconditions in, 3; and social structure, 5, 8

Ehret, C., 69

Evans-Pritchard, E. E., 1, 4, 6, 50, 53, 76, 146, 204, 226, 250

Exogamy: and sub-clan name, 80; and clanship, 80–81; rules of, 202–204

Fallers, L. A., 223, 238, 243

Famine, 13, 20–22; historical chronology and dating, 21, 176; and residential mobility, 117, 135–136

Father-son relationship, 256–266; in residence patterns, 135, 143–145; father's curse, 168–169, 263; in conflict over bridewealth, 183; in witchcraft accusation, 190–192; in holder-heir context, 197

Filiation, 249; structural significance of, 307, 308

Forde, D., 3

Fortes, M., 1, 3, 5, 6, 84, 86, 109, 182, 183, 194, 202, 237, 246, 247, 250, 284, 303, 307

Freeman, J. D., 7

Gluckman, M., 6–7, 243

Goody, J., 8, 109, 182

Gravestone, 148, 155

Gray, R. F., 8, 44, 301, 302

Grazing: rights in neighborhood organization, 111

Gulliver, P. H., 1, 5, 8, 22, 26, 33, 99, 103, 109, 194, 223, 226, 269, 300

Harries–Jones, P., 1, 109

Harris, G., 237

Herding groups, 52

Homestead: groups, 2, 6, mobility of, 7, 8, in property relations, 299; architecture, 156–161; ritual protection of, 161–169; expulsion from, 167–169; population and composition of, 175–187; unit in structure, 200–201

Homestead clusters (*vitumbi*), 131–139; and frequency of kin ties, 141, 147–150

Homestead head, 6; social characteristics of, 175–187; and polygyny, 180–183

Homicide: arbitration of, 101; and collective kin responsibility, 294

House, see *Nyumba*

Husband-wife relationship, 271–276

Identity, 14

Illegitimacy, 257

Incest rules, 204; in *mbuya* relationship, 204

Itumbi (pl. *matumbi*), see Neighborhood

Jacobs, A., 253

Jie, 1, 4, 7, 22, 194, 223, 226, 269

Joking relationships, 88–93; between clans, 63, 72; between sub-clans, 77; in marriage and affinity, 92, 281; and mother's-brother/sister's-son relationship, 284; and cross-cousins, 287, 290

Kaguru, 12, 83
Kaya, see Homestead
Kindred, 7
Kinship terminology, 247–256; reference and address distinctions, 279–280, 284–286; of cross-cousin relationship, 286–288
Kubanya, see Marriage, procedures and phases of
Kuku'ye, see Mother's-brother/sister's-son relationship
Kutowwa macisi, see Spirit possession
Kuwulaga ndugu ("kill the kinship"), 80
Kwetu ("our place"), 117, 128
Kwiguma, see Bridewealth

Labor: division of, 37
La Fontaine, J., 237
Land: rights in, 5, 28–29, 111–112; distribution for cultivation, 26, 29–32; area cultivated per adult, 33
Leach, E. R., 1, 2, 8, 25, 153, 248, 282, 284, 296
Levi-Strauss, C., 3, 84, 182, 203, 248, 250, 252, 265, 292, 296, 305, 307
Lewis, I. M., 4
Lineages, 3–5; "maximal" (*mulango*), 7, 85–86, 203; political functions of, 250
Livestock: exchange, and values attaching to, 2, 3, 54–55; symbolic role of, 9; rights and obligations in, 25, 61; in residential mobility, 123; economic and structural significance of, 301
Locality: factor of, 2, 8, 24; and marriageability, 210; and kinship network, 235–242
Lwanji ("alarm call"), 104, 113

Makumbiko, see Propitiation ceremonies
Malinowski, B., 75, 253
Maloloso, see Dispute settlement
Marriage, 7; proportion among kin, 203; preparation for, 205–211; procedures and phases of, 211–225; gifts to bride, 234–235; spatial range of, 239–242; stability of, 242–245
Masai: relations with, 12, 15; as Gogo cultural category, 15; shared cultural influences with, 19; and herding, 57
Matricentral unit, see *Nyumba*
Mbeho ("wind" or "ritual state"), 158–159, 162
Mbeyu, see Clan
Mbuya ("lover" relationship), 138, 170; and incest rules, 204; and claims on children, 244; and marriage, 275
Mele, see Milk
Menstruation: kin obligations and marriageability, 209–211
Middleton, J., 14
Milk (*mele*): as preferred food, 44; flavored by smoking, 45; distribution among "houses," 45–46
Milungu, see Spirits of the dead
Mnyampala, M., 15
Mobility, residential, 8, 20–22
Models of kinship structure, 307
Moffet, J. P., 11
Mother's-brother/sister's-son relationship: and homicide, 128–130; and residence, 133, 146, 185; in bridewealth transactions, 232–235
Muganga, see Diviner
Muhizi, see Cross-cousins
Mulango, see Lineages, "maximal"
Mulongo, see Sub-clan name
Munyakaya, see Homestead head
Murdock, G. P., 7
Musanji, see Co-wife
Mutemi, see Ritual leader
Muzilo, see Avoidance object

Nadel, S., 8, 306
Naming: system of, 258, 272
Needham, R., 284, 292
Neighborhood, 6, 14, 15, 110–119; founders of, 28, 114; ritual protection of, 115–116; sub-divisions of, 131–139; expansion of, 139–141; and kinship structure, 142–147
Ng'omvia, 68–69
Nuer, 1, 4, 146, 226, 250; social structure compared, 6; numbers of livestock, 50
Nyamwezi: and naming of Gogo, 20
Nyumba ("house"), 28; separation of, in property and production, 32, 169–175, 189, 218–219; ritual and cosmological significance of, 38,

Nyumba (*cont.*)
  157–160, 163, 168, 201, 225; as
  physical unit, 156–159, 169–175;
  and status of married woman, 173–
  175; in marriage contract, 224–225
Nzala, see Famine

Oliver, R., 67, 69

Paternity: rights of, 258–260
Perpetual kinship: explained by clan
  histories, 63, 72; definition of, 79–
  80; compared to joking relationship,
  92; in neighborhood clusters, 132
Peters, E., 4
Political authority: of Gogo ritual
  leaders, 97–98
Political rights: transfer of, 71
Politico-jural domain, 295, 304
Polygyny: value of, and rates, 180–
  183; and problem of bridewealth,
  183
Property relations, 1, 2, 9, 47–50; and
  kinship structure, 25, 297–304
Propitiation ceremonies, 165–167

Radcliffe-Brown, A. R., 84, 204, 243,
  248, 252, 284
Rainfall: average, 13, 33; and seasonal activity, 33–38; and rainmaking ritual, 34, 75
Residence patterns, 6, 9, 125, 128
Residential mobility: and possession
  of livestock, 54; in neighborhood
  structure, 116–128; reasons for,
  117–118, 122–128
Reversal, ritual: in initiation ceremonies, 209
Richards, A. I., 54, 70
Rinderpest epidemic, 49
Ritual area (*yisi*), 6, 14, 15; and protection of crops, 37–38; and clanship, 64; and clan divisions, 86–87;
  populations of, 98–99; boundaries
  and modern relevance of, 105, 106–
  108; and neighborhoods, 116; and
  politico-jural domain, 296
Ritual delegation (*wanyalamali*), 99
Ritual leader (*mutemi*): in protection
  of crops and neighborhood, 37–38;
  115; functions of, 75, 97–105; and
  agnatic groups, 93; position usurped

Ritual leader (*cont.*)
  by "sister's sons," 95–96; relation
  to diviner, 106–107
Rounce, N. V., 33, 50

Sahlins, M., 3
Schaegelen, T., 11, 100
Schneider, D. M., 8
Schneider, H. K., 46
Seasons: and activity, 33–38; and
  lunar months, 35–37
Siblings: and homestead clusters, 147–
  150; relations among, 266–268
Sister's sons (*wehwa*): and usurpa-
  tion of ritual leadership, 95–96;
  ritual role of, in inheritance, 284–
  286
Smith, M. G., 86
Southall, A. W., 5, 12, 18
Space, concepts of, 42
Spirit possession (*kutowwa macisi*):
  and ritual precedence, 189; in au-
  thority among siblings, 194
Spirits of the dead (*milungu*), 72–75,
  78, 164–165; and husband-wife relations, 223; and kinship structure,
  300
Stock trusteeship: and agnates, 53; in
  neighborhood, 137
Sub-clan name (*mulongo*), 7, 15, 67;
  and avoidances, 67; in marriage and
  exogamy, 80, 203; the concept of,
  81–87
Subsistence, the basis of, 26–33
Symbol: black as auspicious, 93

Tait, D., 14
Tallensi, 5, 183, 303
Tanganyika African National Union,
  (TANU), 23
Tenraa, E., 69, 168
Turkana, 1, 5, 7, 195
Turner, V. W., 54

Vidodo-vidodo, see Bridewealth
Vitumbi (sing. *citumbi*), see Home-
  stead clusters
Vogt, E. Z., 1, 8, 305

Wahizi, see Cross-cousins
Wanyalamali (or *wanyakujenda gan-
  dawega*), see Ritual delegation
War, Anglo-German, 22
Ward, B., 307

Water resources: and herding, 57
Wehwa, see Sister's sons
Witchcraft: and death, 84; role of ritual leader in mediating, 101–102; and residential mobility, 119, 123, 128, 135, 136; in father-son relationship, 190–192, 261, 264; in affinal relationships, 192, 193, 274, 275; in inter-house relations, 267; in cross-cousin relationship, 290; and collective kin responsibility, 293

Women: and rights in property, 55–56, 61; in cattle herding, 61
Work party, 28; for manuring fields, 32; for cultivation, 37, 38–43; composition of, 39; and cosmology, 40–42
Worsley, P., 5
Wujimbi, see Beer
Wutani, see Joking relationships

Yisi, see Ritual area